CAMUS

A CRITICAL EXAMINATION

CAMUS

A Critical Examination

DAVID SPRINTZEN

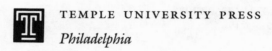

TEMPLE UNIVERSITY PRESS

Philadelphia

Temple University Press, Philadelphia 19122
Copyright © 1988 by Temple University. All rights reserved
Published 1988
Printed in the United States of America

The paper used in this publication meets the minimum requirements of American
National Standard for Information Sciences—Permanence of Paper for Printed
Library Materials, ANSI Z39.48-1984

Library of Congress Cataloging-in-Publication Data
Sprintzen, David.
Camus: a critical examination / David Sprintzen.
p.   cm.
Bibliography: p.
Includes index.
ISBN 0-87722-544-3 (alk. paper)
1. Camus, Albert, 1913–1960—Criticism and interpretation.
I. Title.
PQ2605.A3734Z73627 1988
848'.91409—dc19   87-27808
                                                      CIP

Excerpt on pages 52 and 53 from "The Hollow Men" in COLLECTED POEMS
1909–1962 by T. S. Eliot, copyright 1936 by Harcourt Brace Jovanovich, Inc.,
copyright © 1963, 1964 by T. S. Eliot, reprinted by permission of the publisher.

To Alice and Daniel

If, after all, men cannot always
make history have a meaning,
they can always act so
that their own lives
have one (RRD, 79).

UPON RECEIVING THE DISTINCTION WITH WHICH YOUR FREE ACADEMY has seen fit to honor me, I measured the extent to which that reward exceeded my personal deserts, and this only increased my gratitude. Every man and, even more understandably, every artist, wants recognition. I want it too. But it was not possible for me to learn of your decision without comparing its repercussions with whatever merits I really have. How could a man still almost young, possessed only of his doubts and of a work still in progress, accustomed to living in the isolation of work or the seclusion of friendship—how could he have failed to feel a sort of panic upon learning of a choice that suddenly focused a harsh spotlight on him alone and reduced to himself? And in what spirit could he receive that honor at a moment when other European writers, often the greatest among them, are reduced to silence, and at a time when his native land is experiencing prolonged suffering?

I felt that shock and that perplexity. I could recover my peace of mind, in short, only by adapting myself to an over-generous fate. And inasmuch as I could not measure up to it through my own merits, I could think of no other help than what has always comforted me throughout life, even in the most adverse circumstances: the idea I entertain of my art and of the writer's role. Please allow me to express my gratitude and friendship by telling you, as simply as I can, just what that idea is.

I cannot live as a person without my art. And yet I have never set that art above everything else. It is essential to me, on the contrary, because it excludes no one and allows me to live, just as I am, on a footing with all. To me art is not a solitary delight. It is a means of stirring the greatest number of men by providing them with a privileged image of our common joys and woes. Hence it forces the artist not to isolate himself; it subjects him to the humblest and most universal truth. And the man who, as often happens, chose the path of art because he was aware of his difference soon learns that he can nourish his art, and his difference, solely by admitting his resemblance to all. The artist fashions himself in that ceaseless oscillation from himself to others, midway between the beauty he cannot do without and the community from which he cannot tear himself. This is why true artists scorn nothing. They force themselves to understand instead of judging. And if they are to take sides in this world, they can do so only with a society in which, according to Nietzsche's profound words, the judge will yield to the creator, whether he be a worker or an intellectual.

By the same token, the writer's function is not without arduous duties. By definition, he cannot serve today those who make history; he must serve those who are subject to it. Otherwise he is alone and deprived of his art. All the armies of tyranny and their millions of men cannot people his solitude—even, and especially, if he is willing to fall into step with them. But the silence of an unknown prisoner subjected to humiliations at the other end of the world is enough to tear the writer from exile, at least whenever he manages, amid the privileges of freedom, not to forget that silence but to give it voice by means of art.

No one of us is great enough for such a vocation. Yet in all the circumstances of his life, unknown or momentarily famous, bound by tyranny or temporarily free to express himself, the writer can recapture the feeling of a living community that will justify him. But only if he accepts as completely as possible the two trusts that constitute the nobility of his calling: the service of truth and the service of freedom. Because his vocation is to unite the greatest possible number of men, it cannot countenance falsehood and slavery, which breed solitudes wherever they prevail. Whatever our personal frailties may be, the nobility of our calling will always be rooted in two commitments difficult to observe: refusal to lie about what we know and resistance to oppression.

For more than twenty years of absolutely insane history, lost hopelessly like all those of my age in the convulsions of the epoch, I derived comfort from the vague impression that writing was an honor today because the act itself obligated a man, obligated him to more than just writing. It obligated me in particular, such as I was, with whatever strength I possessed, to bear—along with all the others living the same history—the tribulation and hope we shared. Those men born at the beginning of World War I, who had reached the age of twenty just as Hitler was seizing power and the first revolutionary trials were taking place, who then had to complete their education by facing up to war in Spain, World War II, the regime of concentration camps, a Europe of torture and prisons, must today bring their children and their works to maturity in a world threatened with nuclear destruction. No one, I suppose, can expect them to be optimistic. I even go so far as to feel that, without ceasing to struggle against those who through an excess of despair insisted upon their right to dishonor and hurled themselves into the current nihilisms, we must understand their error. Nonetheless, most of us in my country and in Europe rejected that nihilism and strove to find some form of legitimacy. We had to fashion for ourselves an art of living in times of catastrophe in order to be reborn before fighting openly against the death instinct at work in our history.

Probably every generation sees itself as charged with remaking the world. Mine, however, knows that it will not remake the world. But its task is perhaps even greater, for it consists in keeping the world from destroying itself. As the heir of a corrupt history that blends blighted revolutions, misguided techniques, dead gods, and worn-out ideologies, in which second-rate powers can destroy everything today but are unable to win anyone over and in which intelligence has stooped to becoming the servant of hatred and oppression, that generation, starting from nothing but its own negations, has had to re-establish both within and without itself a little of what constitutes the dignity of life and death. Faced with a world threatened with disintegration, in which our grand inquisitors may set up once and for all the kingdoms of death, that generation knows that, in a sort of mad race against time, it ought to re-establish among nations a peace not based on slavery, to reconcile labor and culture again, and to reconstruct with all men an Ark of the Covenant. Perhaps it can never accomplish that vast undertaking, but most certainly throughout the world it has already accepted the double challenge of truth and liberty and, on occasion, has shown that it can lay down its life without hatred. That generation deserves to be acclaimed and encouraged wherever it happens to be, and especially wherever it is sacrificing itself. And to it, confident of your wholehearted agreement, I should like to transfer the honor you have just done me.

At the same time, after having extolled the nobility of the writer's calling, I should have taken the writer down a peg, showing him as he is, with no other rights than those he shares with his fellow fighters: vulnerable but stubborn, unjust and eager for justice, constructing his work without shame or pride within sight of all, constantly torn between pain and beauty, and devoted to extracting from his dual nature the creations he obstinately strives to raise up in the destructive fluctuation of history. Who, after that, could expect of him ready-made solutions and fine moral codes? Truth is mysterious, elusive, ever to be won anew. Liberty is dangerous, as hard to get along with as it is exciting. We must progress toward those two objectives, painfully but resolutely, sure in advance that we shall weaken and flinch on such a long road. Consequently, what writer would dare, with a clear conscience, to become a preacher of virtue? As for me, I must say once more that I am far from all that. I have never been able to forget the sunlight, the delight in life, the freedom in which I grew up. But although that nostalgia explains many of my mistakes and shortcomings, it doubtless helped me to understand my calling, and it still helps me to stand implicitly beside all those silent men who, throughout the world, endure the life that has been made for them only because they remember or fleetingly re-experience free moments of happiness.

Reduced in this way to what I am in reality, to my limits and to my liabilities, as well as to my difficult faith, I feel freer to show you in conclusion the extent and generosity of the distinction you have just granted me, free likewise to tell you that I should like to receive it as a tribute paid to all those who, sharing the same fight, have received no reward, but on the contrary have known only woe and persecution. It remains for me then to thank you from the bottom of my heart and to make you publicly, as a personal token of gratitude, the same age-old promise of allegiance that every true artist, every day, makes to himself, in silence.

—ALBERT CAMUS
Nobel Prize Address
Stockholm, December 10, 1957

CONTENTS ✺

PREFACE ❧

Nothing authorizes me to pass judgment upon an epoch with which I feel in complete solidarity. I judge it from within, blending myself with it. But I reserve the right, henceforth, to say what I know about myself and about others on the sole condition that by so doing I do not add to the unbearable suffering of the world, but only in order to locate, among the obscure walls against which we are blindly stumbling, the still invisible places where doors may open (A/II, 83).

Few writers have achieved greater public recognition than Albert Camus. Honored with the Nobel Prize for "his important literary production, which with clearsighted earnestness illuminates the problems of the human conscience in our times," his works have fascinated the literate public from the moment of their emergence during the Second World War. Camus has been at the center of the passionate controversies that have rocked the modern world: from existential anxiety in the face of the death of God, and the absurdity of human existence, through practical struggles around capital punishment, social injustice, and national liberation, to growing concerns about torture and systemic violations of human rights.

Numerous and extensive as have been the treatments of his work, whether in the popular press or in academic periodicals, few have adequately appreciated its cultural significance. Small wonder that academics often treat his work as if it were simply the product of a previous era. I believe that judgment is deeply flawed, and that Camus's work remains of vital interest to a civilization now struggling to come to terms with a scientific and technological vision deeply at odds with the religious perspective from which its cultural meanings have historically derived. What is more, I intend to show that his analyses offer constructive suggestions for the dilemmas of our age and that we neglect them at our peril.

Such reflection gains increased urgency in an era in which world wars and mass genocide threaten to be surpassed by nuclear annihilation—a capacity that few now doubt is within our collective power. Addressing our civilization at its metaphysical and mythic roots, Camus seeks to diagnose those interior forces seemingly propelling us toward destruction: to explore their inner logic in order to suggest the preconditions of, and the practical steps required for, a cultural rebirth. In a world without transcendent significance, in which we are all condemned to death, what, he asks, are the possibilities for an honest and clear-sighted coming to terms with our condition? Can we not find a way to celebrate our life on this earth in dignity and self-respect? And what are the paths that lead in that direction?

It is therefore as a thinker at grips with the drama of Western civilization, which was the conceptual horizon of his world, that his work is considered here: to listen carefully to its contemporary resonances, while exploring its Greco-Roman and Judeo-Christian roots. Why have so many been drawn to him, both ennobled and perplexed by his writings? And why does his work continue to receive a respectful reading by the literate public, despite its being all but out of fashion among the intelligentsia? In part, I suggest, this is because he addresses the deepest mythic level of our being. And not by inadvertence.

Of his plays he wrote, "There is no theater without language and style, nor any dramatic work which does not, like our classic drama and the Greek tragedians, involve human fate in all its simplicity and grandeur" (CTOP, x). The simplicity and grandeur of human existence as experienced in the twentieth century is the context of all he lived and wrote. Settings cut to the bone: the essentials grasped; the central dramatic myths explored in whose terms we confront our destiny. Such is the core of Camus's work. Small wonder then that his titles have such a mythic resonance: *The Stranger*, *The Plague*, "The Misunderstanding," *The Fall*, "The State of Siege," *Two Sides of the Coin*, *Exile and the Kingdom*, *The Rebel*, "The Just," *Summer*, *Nuptials*, and (uncompleted) *The First Man*.

Focusing upon the central drama of the West—its root metaphors or metaphysic, its agony and its future, its exile and its kingdom—his work speaks to us at a level below that of conscious awareness. Precisely because it touches the deepest sources of our being, it engages us even when we are not aware of its force. It subtly confronts us with a mirror and seeks to mark out a tortuous and risky path toward our natural salvation. By accepting the invitation it offers and the challenge it demands, we can learn about ourselves through direct encounter with this mythological mirror.

Why then have most academics dismissed him as dated, a product of the immediate post-war period, and not very profound? While his craftsmanship is invariably admired, his positions are not carefully studied. Thus his work appears in considerations of modern, especially European, literature, as well as in analyses of the cultural scene in postwar Europe. But little serious attention is paid to its content. Certainly not by philosophers or political theorists. Ironically, given the antireligious thrust of his writings, an exception might have to be made for sectors of the theological community.

In a sense, Camus has fallen through the cracks in our intellectual subcul-

ture. While his concerns were cultural and philosophical, and his sensitivity
and practical orientation were moral and political, his media and artistic focus
were literature and theater, interspersed with journalism. Philosophical treatment of his work has been sparse and episodic at best: an occasional glimpse
at an essay, novel, or play, taken in isolation from its place in his writing and
from its historical context, and thus almost always misread.

On the other hand, Camus's writings have received extensive and careful treatment at the hands of literary critics such as Germaine Brée, Philip
Thody, Henri Peyre, Justin O'Brien, and Carl Viggiani. Many of these have
been thoughtful, sensitive, and provocative. But few have done justice to the
philosophical and political significance of his work.

An interesting third category is provided by analysts with a prior ideological commitment. In the English-speaking world, that bias has usually
been anticommunist or antirevolutionary, often liberal. Here Camus is portrayed as an opponent of Marxism and revolution and is often praised for his
pacifism and his liberal humanism—a portrait generally concurred in by the
radical left, especially in Europe. Once having served their purpose, however,
he is often dismissed without a second thought. Serious reflection on the
nature of his political thought is perhaps not to have been expected from
them, nor has it generally been forthcoming.

Nevertheless, many volumes have been devoted to Camus, some with
notable success. Far be it from me, who has benefited so deeply from them,
to deny their contribution. But another task remains to be done. That task
is to show how Camus's writings provide significant insight into our cultural
self-understanding. Even more, that we are poorly served if his explorations
on the nature of revolt, dialogue, and community are not taken seriously;
that the traditional reading of his positions on revolution and violence, as
well as on the values to which revolt gives a promise, are in error; and that
his analyses of political action offer a radical and nondogmatic perspective
from which contemporary struggles can gain significant illumination.

Not only is his thought worthy of more serious consideration than it has
usually received, but, of particular interest to American audiences, it draws its
strength in large part from a manner of thinking far closer to the American
pragmatists, especially John Dewey, than has been generally noticed. Like
Dewey, for example, Camus treats theories as hypotheses and treats goals as
guides to action, while requiring that values be grounded in and tested by
experience. And, like Dewey, he sees experience threatened both by the dead
weight of sanctified habit and by the rigidity of absolutist thought, what
Dewey called the quest for certainty. The failure to appreciate adequately
what might be called Camus's ethical pragmatism contributes to much of the
misreading to which he has fallen victim.

Careful attention will thus reveal that his thought could hardly be more relevant to the present. Not only does it address our need to learn how to live in a world in which religious belief encounters increasingly serious and pervasive doubt, but it offers a novel way of confronting the ideologies of both right and left, thus shedding new light on the nature of dialogue, friendship, and community. At a time in which such outstanding contemporary thinkers as Jorgen Habermas, Hans Georg Gadamer, Richard Bernstein, and Anthony Giddens have evidenced a renewed concern for language, communication, and the needs of community (replacing prior academic preoccupations with foundations and structures), Camus's exploration of the preconditions for the creation of dialogic communities—his *civilisation du dialogue*—makes a significant contribution to the consideration of these issues.

Jean-Paul Sartre, his one-time friend and then polemical adversary—who was himself often guilty of the grossest misinterpretation of Camus, as the body of this work will show—offered a moving eulogy to Camus, which may serve as an appropriate initial summation. He wrote that Camus's

obstinate humanism, narrow and pure, austere and sensual, waged an uncertain war against the massive and formless events of the time. But on the other hand through his dogged rejections he reaffirmed, at the heart of our epoch, against the Machiavellians and against the idol of realism, the existence of the moral issue.

In a way, he *was* that resolute affirmation. Anyone who read or reflected encountered the human values he held in his fist; he questioned the political act (Brée 2, 173–4).[1]

It is to this effort to grasp the philosophical resonance of Camus's thought, as it echoes forth in strength and weakness the sounds and turmoil of our world, that my work is committed. I take him at his word when he writes: "I do not believe . . . in isolated books. With certain writers . . . their works form a whole in which each is clarified by the others, and reflect each other" (A/II, 63–4).

In treating his work as a whole, I seek to elucidate the vision that many among us have found so compelling. Why has it touched us? To what extent does it offer answers to the profound challenges with which we are confronted? Toward what future does it point? And what limitations does it reveal, for him and for us? I engage his work in dialogue, treating it as an invitation to reflect upon the essentials of that cultural drama in which all of us are implicated. I am confident he would have welcomed such an undertaking.

Before turning to the body of the text, it may be helpful to focus briefly upon the scope and direction of Camus's work as it suggests the structure of this project.

Camus's standpoint is naturalistic. He shared Friedrich Nietzsche's view that "when one speaks of humanity, the idea is fundamental that this is something which separates and distinguishes man from nature. In reality, however, there is no such separation: 'Natural' qualities and those called 'human' are inseparably grown together" (PN, 32).

This metaphysical naturalism feeds a tragic vision, deeply marked by the sense of God's absence. For ours is an age in which absolutes have been found wanting and satisfactory alternatives lacking. Human beings, torn from a world they can no longer believe in, long for another whose outlines are not yet clear.[2] No wonder Camus preferred classical drama and the Greek tragedians. But, though his vision of our world is tragic, it is certainly not marked by resignation or despair.[3]

His literary and theoretical work begins with varied attempts to articulate the essential parameters of his original experience, from within the frame of that tragic naturalism. In *Two Sides of the Coin*,[4] and later in *Nuptials*, we have the sensitive physical being reflecting upon the extent of meaningfulness in a world stripped of the conventions of civilization. The first of these works expresses a sensitivity to human dignity, to silent suffering and the passionate will to live, qualities that permeate and pervade Camus's entire outlook. In this book, he was later to write, lie the roots of his thought, however awkwardly expressed. "It is in this life of poverty, among these humble or vain people that I most surely reached what seemed to me the real meaning of life."

In the second work it is the pagan Algerian who speaks—of the beauties of nature, of his rejection of any illusions as to human destiny, and of the desiccation of time. While *Nuptials* and *Two Sides* are sometimes overlooked in considering Camus's thought, the sensitivity and perspective they articulate are crucial.

The unity of Camus's thought may be traced from these two early works through *Summer* (a collection of essays spanning the years 1939 to 1953) to a tentative and suggestive completion in *Exile and the Kingdom* (1957). This line of development provides the framework for Camus's artistic and theoretical output. It is in that artistic output, however, what he called his "real work," that the philosophical tale resides.

Within the framework of his carefully conceived artistic production lie four *récits, nouvelles*, or *romans: The Stranger, The Plague, The Fall*, and *Exile and the Kingdom*; four plays: "Caligula," "The Misunderstanding," "The State of Siege," and "The Just"; and two philosophical essays: *The Myth of Sisyphus* and *The Rebel*. His editorials, reviews, speeches, interviews, and dramatic adaptations complement and nuance that more precisely articulated corpus without modifying its basic themes.

In that work one can see the exploration and development of a few fairly well-defined stages. In each stage a play, a novel, and an essay were the media for exploration of a basic problem. In his completed work two stages have been developed; a third, lacking such clear outlines, may be discerned; a fourth and fifth are but hinted at.[5]

The first stage concerns the individual's encounter with the absurd. It achieves its theoretical articulation in *The Myth of Sisyphus*, as a philosophical consideration of problems initially posed in *The Stranger* and "Caligula," and implied in *Two Sides of the Coin* and *Nuptials*, then a little later in "The Misunderstanding."

The second stage, a development from but in no sense a denial of the insights achieved in the previous works, directly treats the individual's encounter with others, and with himself as among others. Here *The Plague* performs the experiential spadework, reaping the harvest of what was most tragically sown in "The Misunderstanding." "The State of Siege" then focuses the problem onto the plane of the social; while "The Just" serves as the dramatic prologue to the detailed consideration of these issues in *The Rebel*.

At this point, the clarity of the artistic outline slackens. With *The Fall* we encounter a species of oppression significantly different from that found in "Caligula," *The Plague*, or "The State of Siege"; an oppression by duplicitous monologue in the service of self-promotion, offered as the existential ground of the ideological oppression studied in Stage 2. This monologue contrasts sharply with the silent innocence of Meursault, or the silent yet tragic dignity so prominent in *Two Sides*.

With *Exile and the Kingdom*—so similar in title and structure to *Two Sides of the Coin*—a more positive orientation begins to find expression, reaching a tentative symbolic fulfillment with the action of D'Arrast in "The Growing Stone." This development—the encounter with the absurd; the attempts at resolution; the stoic acceptance-in-revolt; the experience of the absurd on the social level in oppression; the explicit revolt; the encounter with ideology; the search for community through dialogue; then the self-reflective and critical exploration of Western competitive individualism—finds a temporary resting point *entre oui et non* in these stories of exile, "The Renegade" excluded. The transition from this philosophico-literary perspective to the artistic and sociopolitical problems involved in the practical construction of a dialogic community, with which my work concludes, is only a development of the inner logic of Camus's life and thought.[6]

One final word on language. Camus's experience was male-oriented, and so is his language. While I have of course kept his formulations in all quotations, I have sought to avoid sexist language in my own writing. Gender-related expressions have been used only when justified by the context. The issue of Camus's position on sex is itself discussed in the text.

ACKNOWLEDGMENTS ❧

In a work that has required as much time and effort as this one, the result must needs be in large part a product of collective effort. It is not possible even to list, not to say express my appreciation to, the many people without whose assistance this project would never have been completed, but certain individuals deserve special mention.

My friends Jeffrey Isaac and James Edwards carefully read extensive portions of the manuscript at different stages of its development. Without their comments and suggestions, the final product would be far less satisfactory than it is. John McDermott was the inspiration not only for my study of Camus but for my philosophical career. He has encouraged, nurtured, and sustained my work throughout. My debt to all three of them is enormous.

In addition, I benefited greatly from extensive, stimulating, and sustained discussions with Terry Hillman, Arthur Lothstein, Peter Manicas, John Pavlidis, Jeffrey Reiman, and Ronald Santoni, as well as from my colleagues in the Department of Philosophy at C. W. Post College of Long Island University.

Support came at a crucial time from my thesis adviser at Penn State University, Henry Johnstone, for which I will always be grateful. Valuable assistance in transcription came from Joy Sanderson. Financial assistance was provided by the Research Committee of C. W. Post College. Finally, the enthusiastic support and encouragement of my editor at Temple University Press, Jane Cullen, was crucial in bringing this work to fruition.

PART ONE ❧

Introduction

To create a language and to bring myths to life (LCE, 16).

1 ✦

Experiential Sources

From the shores of Africa where I was born, with the help of distance, the face of Europe can be seen better (A/II, 63).

FRAMING A VISION

As children our immersion in the present is both total and transcendent. It is total in that our horizon is consumed by the immediacy of the sounds, shapes, colors, odors, natural qualities, and above all, by the affective tonality of a world that is both mood and temperament. It is transcendent in that we recapitulate the universal confrontation of sensual consciousness with the natural world, which is the inevitable experience of our species. From birth we are thus bathed in the historical waters that are the dramatic unfolding of our culture, and constrained by the ontological structure of the human condition. While the latter confronts us with inescapable challenges to growth, to the mastery of skills, and to the development of intelligent sensibility, the former structures the horizon of individual consciousness, shaping the mental frame in whose terms such challenges will be experienced.

Between the experience and the articulation falls the shadow, to paraphrase T. S. Eliot. As awareness emerges from within the inchoate present, it tends to shape itself in accordance with the dramatic contours of its culture. At first we see the world through the eyes of others. The cultural drama becomes the horizon of our awareness, shaping the prereflective quality of experience. Soon childhood exploration becomes adult problem solving: technical problems calling for practical solution absorb our attention, while our personal version of the cultural mindscape sets the horizon of understanding that conditions our action. The structures of the drama itself are taken for granted as necessary, self-evident, unquestioned, even unquestionable.

But it occurs to some of us, occasionally, to wonder at the structure of the world in which we live, to determine its limits, to understand its necessity, to appreciate its contingency, and to explore its hidden possibilities. With this "weariness tinged with amazement" that places in question the very dramatic horizon itself, philosophy begins. It is a matter of merely academic interest whether such reflection dresses itself in the majestic garb of abstract treatises on metaphysics and epistemology, of logic and ethics, or whether it wears the more modest garments of concrete and sensual imagery embodied in essays, plays, or novels. Such reflection either invites us to share in the exploration of the problems of existence, or it does not. Only in the former case does it call for serious reflection, seeking to initiate a dialogue on the essentials of our shared experience—perhaps even opening up for us the horizon of our "ownmost" possibilities.

Camus's writing was clearly of such dimensions. Marked personally, culturally, and theoretically by the historicity of its emergence, it aspires to a perspective from which the dramatic structure of our world can obtain coherent articulation, and constructive reformulation.

Since this work is both deeply personal and profoundly cosmic, it is appropriate and necessary to explore briefly its personal roots in order to appreciate adequately its cosmic significance. Those roots are in that Mediterranean land of stark beauty and precise definition wherein a pagan body came to consciousness in a Christian world.

I was born poor, under a happy sky, in accord with nature, and without hostility. My life did not begin therefore with inner turmoil, but with plenitude. . . . I feel that I have a Greek heart. . . . The Greeks do not deny the gods, but *they keep them within bounds*. Christianity [on the other hand] . . . is a *total* religion (A/I, 225–6).

A French-Algerian, born and raised in the sunbathed and impoverished working-class districts of North Africa, Camus's relation to European civilization was deeply ambivalent. His thinking was profoundly European, tormented by problems inherited through several thousand years of Judeo-Christian history, but his physical sensibilities were pagan—that is, Greco-Roman—rooted in the sensual vitality of a body immersed in the sun, sand, and sea of the Mediterranean shore. Half in and half out of European civilization, he experienced "both sides of the coin." He knew the strengths and weaknesses, the possibilities and disasters, the grandeur and vulgarities of the European civilization with which he felt total solidarity. He was at one with it in its struggle for survival against the forces of nihilism, emerging with powerful destructive force in the fascist movements of the 1930s and 1940s. And he experienced the vitality, the force for renewal, that was the offering of a guilt-free body at grips with the beauties of nature, which he felt was emerging on the shores of North Africa, on the margins of European civilization. As his exile was double—forced both by natural and social events out of a union with the North African world, and by the movement of European history out of the ultimate meaningfulness that had been its Judeo-Christian promise, so his need for the resurrection of the kingdom was more poignant and deeply felt. The challenge of his life was to find a path out of this desert of alienation, desiccation, and dehumanization toward a renaissance in human living—and to give preliminary form to such a renaissance.

Writing of *The Rebel*, his major work devoted to the search for those positive values he felt "we can no longer do without," he observes:

All those for whom the problems discussed in this book are not simply rhetorical have understood that I was analyzing a contradiction which initially had been my own. The[se] thoughts . . . have nourished me; and I wanted to further them by removing those elements which I felt impeded them from developing. In fact, I am not a philosopher, and I only know how to speak about what I have experienced. I have experienced nihilism, contradiction, violence, and the vertigo of destruction. But . . . I have welcomed the power of creating and the honor of living. Nothing authorizes me to pass judgment upon an epoch with which I feel in total solidarity. I judge it from within, blending myself with it. But I reserve the right, henceforth, to say what I know about myself and about others on the sole condition that by so doing I do not add to the unbearable suffering of the world, but only in order to locate, among the obscure walls against which we are blindly stumbling, the still invisible places where doors may open. . . . I am only interested in the renaissance (A/II, 82–3).

NATURE AND HISTORY

Situated as he was on the margin, half in and half out of Europe, completely involved and profoundly agonized, deeply sensitive and passionately inquiring, he sought to grasp the essentials of the drama, to lay bare the mythic structures of that agonized experience—of those interior forces working for self-destruction—in order to awaken the Western mind to a grasp of its possibilities for cultural renewal.

In his "Diplôme d'Etudes Supérieures" on "Métaphysique Chrétienne et Néoplatonisme" Camus sought to come to terms with the conflict between Hellenism and Christianity with which his experience resonated. Making a point of methodological significance for the entire body of his work, he insisted that, in contrast to the pagan world, "the novelty of Christianity is to be sought on the affective level from which the problems arise rather than in the system which tries to respond to them" (E, 1224). His manner of framing these contrasting metaphysics is so significant for an understanding of his perspective that it deserves to be quoted at length:

Hellenism . . . implied that man was self-sufficient and had within himself the capacity to explain destiny and the universe. His temples were built to his measure. In a certain sense the Greeks accepted an aesthetic and sportive justification of existence.

The design of their hills and the running of a young man on the beach would reveal the secret of the world to them. Their gospel said: our Kingdom is of this world. It is the "Everything which satisfies you, Cosmos, satisfies me," of Marcus Aurelius.

This purely rational conception of life—that the world can be completely understood—leads to a moral intellectualism: virtue is something which is learned. . . . All Greek philosophy makes the wise man an equal of God. . . . The entire universe is centered around man and his works. If moral evil is simply ignorance or error therefore, what place can there be for the notions of Sin and Redemption? . . .

The Greeks still believed in a cyclical world, eternal and necessary, which was not compatible with a creation "ex nihilo" leading toward an end of the world. . . .

What constitutes the irreducible originality of Christianity is the theme of the Incarnation. Problems are made flesh, and they immediately assume that tragic and necessary character which is so often lacking in certain Greek mind games. . . .

The problems [of the world] themselves are incarnated and the philosophy of history is born. . . . It is no longer a question of knowing and understanding, but of loving. And Christianity will only give body to this idea, so foreign to the Greeks, that man's problem is not to perfect his nature, but to escape from it (E, 1225–6, 1229, 1228).

Whatever the historical accuracy of this analysis, two points ought to be noted. First, Camus underlines a difference of temperament distinguishing the sensitivity of the pagan Greek from that of the Christian. These contrasting sensitivities account for the distinctiveness of their metaphysical perspectives, according to Camus. Second, the dynamic tension between these two perspectives sets the context for much of his subsequent intellectual reflections. Throughout his work these contrasting themes find expression, from the early concern with death, hope, and salvation in *Two Sides of the Coin* and *Nuptials*, through the struggles with natural evil in *The Plague* and the concern with totalitarianism in *The Rebel*, to the problem of self-consciousness, guilt, innocence, and bad conscience in *The Fall*, and ultimately, throughout, with the pervasive concern for working our way out of our exile to an earthly kingdom.

What affective tonality does Camus find at the root of these contrasting metaphysical formulations, leading him to identify more closely with the Greeks? It is the centrality of bodily experience: the sensual, pulsating organism in innocent union with a natural world. The body, a creature of time and place, ever renewed by the cycles of nature, desiring, feeling, moving, growing, aging, and ultimately dying; the body, animated by activity, exhausted by effort, and cleansed by the sea; the body, exalted by beauty and ravaged by time, continually consecrating our sensual union with the earth in a present devoid of any transcendent future. The innocent harmony of this transient body with the cycles of nature is the locus of the pagan sensitivity with which Camus feels that profound accord he wishes to celebrate. No sense of original sin here; no dichotomy between sensual wants and spiritual needs; no guilt or shame about nudity; and no mystified hope for another life. No mystification of reason, only the demand for a lucid perception of the body's place in nature. Time is the matrix of action, marking the passage of days by which life exhausts itself, not a transcendent symbol of a redemptive suffering. Time is cyclical, not linear: It takes us nowhere but to death while taking nature to eternal renewal. This nature of seasonal cycles is not a place for progress as far as human destiny is concerned. Our fate is sealed, our destiny circumscribed. The injunction from Pindar that Camus offers as the epigram to *The Myth* sets the frame: "Oh my soul, do not aspire to immortal heights, but exhaust the field of the possible" (MS, 2; E, 93).[1] Actually, *The Myth of Sisyphus* can be understood as an attempt to resurrect this pagan sensibility from within the heart of—and in opposition to—the decaying bourgeois Christian world.[2]

Camus is not, of course, a pagan Greek. He could no more be one than could a modern Greek. Too much Christian history stands between him and them. But he shares with them a sensibility, however transfigured, that adds an original dimension to his reflection upon our epoch.

The root of that vision is the body's passion for living, grounded in an unreflective sense of natural innocence. Sharing the Greeks' sense for human dignity, he felt no need to apologize for his belief that happiness is a legitimate human aspiration. It is simply the articulation of this dignified sense of natural innocence. He once said that sin was a concept he could never understand, meaning that *he* had no experience of sin. He did not feel that he had to justify his existence or that existence needed any justification. Nevertheless, he did experience quite profoundly the problem of evil. He rejects the Christian conception that evil is a necessary part of a salvific process in which all will be set right in the fullness of time, as well as the Greek notion that it is only the result of ignorance or error. Evil always remained for him an unjustifiable rupture, an inexpiable injustice. Suffering and injustice lacerated him. He shared with Ivan Karamazov the torment occasioned by the suffering and death of the innocent, as he shared Ivan's refusal to deify a creation or to love a creator that could permit such events. He was at one with Doctor Rieux in rejecting Father Paneloux's claim that "either the suffering of innocence was a necessary element in a divine justice or we must believe in God and accept all on faith." For him, "Christianity in its essence . . . is a doctrine of injustice. It is founded on the sacrifice of the innocent and the acceptance of this sacrifice. Justice on the contrary does not proceed without revolt" (A/I, 46).

Yes, there is evil and unjust suffering, but they call not for acceptance and resignation, but for revolt. Revolt against a condition in which "men die and they are not happy"; revolt against a world in which some people use others for their personal satisfaction or in the service of an ideology proclaiming that all wrongs will be righted in the future or the hereafter. Rather, what alone is given to us is the moving present, and it is here that we must root our being if we are to be nourished and to grow in happiness. The Greeks knew this. They had a vision of life appropriate to their climate: a clear, lucid view of our possibilities for happiness and of the inevitability of death. All was of this world, with the afterlife but a pale replica of this life.

No doubt there were mysteries; but they were not transcendent or super-natural, and they did not cloud one's thinking. Camus could not accept the Greek notion that unaided reason can penetrate the secrets of nature any more than he could accept the notion that the world was made to the measure of human beings. Yet he remained committed to a reason without shadows. He rejected Greek anthropomorphism, but shared their overriding concern for human destiny. No place here for the spirit of totality to take root: that will to deny the evidence of the body, of the senses, of nature; the unlimited desire to make the world over again, to reject this life for the future or the hereafter. The needs of the body and the cycles of nature placed limits on human endeavor and offered commensurate rewards. Despite the sacredness of life, there is no messianism in this world of light and death, of which Camus could say, "All my Gods have feet of clay" (*Nuptials*, in LCE, 105).

At the center of Christianity, on the other hand, stands the mystery of the Incarnation—of the transcendent becoming finite, of innocent suffering offering redeeming grace, which in "the fullness of time" will remake the world and humans. Innocence crucified, accepted, and believed in is the core of the Christian solution to the problems of evil and death. And to this solu-tion Camus's rejection resounds, viscerally at first, and then with increasing clarity and persistence. Yet he shared the Christian sense of the tragedy of the human condition. He felt passionately the need to give coherence, order, and meaning to the human drama. "Greek by his need for coherence," as he wrote of Augustine, "Christian by the uneasiness of his sensibility" (E, 1295); Camus located himself at the crossroads of these conflicting sentiments. If he rejected the often naïve Greek rationalism, he similarly rejected a Christian mysterious irrationalism. Reason, however limited and circumscribed, is all we have to light our way, and it must be held responsive to the demands of the poor creature enamored of the natural light that leads only to death. Of Christianity he writes:

Providentialism, creationism, philosophy of history, concern for humility, all
of these themes we have noted confront the attitude of the Greeks. That Greek naïveté
of which Schiller speaks was too pervaded by innocence and light to abdicate
without resistance. The effort of the conciliators [of the first few centuries of
the Christian era] was to transform the very instrument of this attitude—Reason ruled
by the principle of contradiction—into a notion shaped by the idea of participation
(E, 1307).

Ultimately, Christianity sacrifices not the individual, but rationality—our sole resource for working out our natural destiny—on the altar of messianism, thus bathing the suffering of innocence in the waters of a transcendent and mysterious grace. Greek light is overwhelmed by Christian shadows. Totality replaces moderation. And the body, rooted in the present and demanding dignity and happiness while lucidly facing death, is reduced to a humiliated supplicant bowing down in prayer and hoping to see "as through a glass darkly" an infinite and unknowable God upon whose will our salvation depends.

THE ALGERIAN MAN

Within the geography of Camus's mind, the "Algerian Man" has a unique place. Here is the "natural home" of the human spirit, both ground and limit. Playing a logico-biographical role, it refers to the actual experiential conditions out of which Camus emerged, while taking its contours and meanings from the reflective appreciation that he brought to bear upon their description. It is a mythologized portrait of a collective type, suffused with the unique perspective and sensitivities of the author.

In speaking of the Algerian Man, I am formalizing a type that emerges from Camus's earliest writings—especially *Two Sides of the Coin*, *Nuptials*, and *The Stranger*—remaining in the background of his thought throughout. In *Nuptials* he writes of Algeria,

Intelligence does not occupy the place here that it does in Italy. This race is indifferent to the mind. It worships and admires the body. From this comes its strength, its naive cynicism, and a puerile vanity that leads it to be severely criticized. . . . It is true that a certain intensity of living involves some injustice. Yet here are a people with no past, with no traditions, though not without poetry. . . . These people, wholly engaged in the present, live with neither myths nor consolation. Investing all their assets on this earth, they are left defenseless against death. The gifts of physical beauty have been heaped upon them. And, also the strange greediness that always goes along with the wealth that has no future. Everything people do in Algiers reveals a distaste for stability and a lack of regard for the future. People are in a hurry to live . . . and still, . . . one can find a certain moderation as well as a constant excess in the strained and violent faces of these people, in this summer sky emptied of tenderness, beneath which all truths can be told and on which no deceitful divinity has traced the signs of hope or of redemption. Between this sky and the faces turned toward it there is nothing on which to hang a mythology, a literature, an ethic, or a religion—only stones, flesh, stars, and those truths the hand can touch ("Summer in Algiers," LCE, 89–90).

Here is the human animal practically at one with nature. "I certainly have no illusions," writes Camus. "There is not much love in the lives I am describing. I should say rather that there is no longer very much. But at least they have eluded nothing" (LCE, 91). Their life is of the present; it can only end in death. "They wagered on the flesh, knowing they would lose" (LCE, 81). They seek no consolation; they accept without question the physical conditions of their lives, and seek simply to drain its possibilities to the utmost. "There is nothing here for people seeking knowledge, education, or self-improvement. The land contains no lessons. It neither promises nor reveals anything. It is content to give, but does so profusely" (LCE, 81).

Doubtless such a life has its limits. It also has its advantages. The pristine quality, the freshness and virility, with which the Algerian Man encounters and exhausts his physical condition stands in quite vivid and powerful contrast to the insipid and sterile life of a somewhat decadent Western civilization. In discussing the Algerians' attitude toward swimming, Camus notes:

These are healthy pleasures. They certainly seem ideal to the young men, since most of them continue this life during the winter, stripping down for a frugal lunch in the sun at noontime every day. Not that they have read the boring sermons of our nudists, those protestants of the body (there is a way of systematizing the body that is as exasperating as systems for the soul). They just "like being in the sun." It would be hard to exaggerate the significance of this custom in our day (LCE, 82).

Camus's comrade Vincent exemplifies this direct and unself-conscious union of the physical being with his natural environment. In an illuminating footnote, his "naturalistic morality" is compared with a certain variety of that "systématique du corps" just mentioned:

May I be foolish enough to say that I don't like the way Gide exalts the body? He asks it to hold back desire in order to make it more intense. This brings him close to those who, in the slang of brothels, are termed "weirdies" and "oddballs." Christianity also seeks to suspend desire. But, more naturally, sees in this a mortification. My friend Vincent, who is a cooper and junior breast-stroke champion, has an even clearer view of things. He drinks when he is thirsty, if he wants a woman tries to sleep with her, and would marry her if he loved her (this hasn't happened yet). Then he always says: "That feels better!"—an energetic summary of the apology one could write for satiety (LCE, 83).

Innocent with respect to social codes or "original sins," Vincent fulfills his desires as he experiences them and does not think twice about them. He bears no guilt and harbors no regret. He is what he is, and that's all. His is a portrait of a being totally at one with an essentially ahistorical society, in relatively direct contact with an encompassing natural environment. He does have a "morality,"

which is very well defined. You "don't let your mother down." You see to it that your wife is respected in the street. You show consideration to pregnant women. You don't attack an enemy two to one, because "that's dirty." If anyone fails to observe these elementary rules "he's not a man," and that's all there is to it (LCE, 87).

Vincent may well be a stranger to "polite society"; but he is clearly a man, with his own qualities and limitations, upon whom Camus is somewhat reluctant, if not unwilling, to pass judgment. His is a portrait that we would do well to keep in mind if we seek to understand "the stranger." While, no doubt, involving a certain barbarism, this natural vitality expresses, for Camus, an aspect of human existence without a respect for which it must wither and die. The importance of this "pagan" experience becomes even clearer as Camus contrasts civilization with culture:

At a time when doctrinaire attitudes would separate us from the world, it is well for young men in a young land to proclaim their attachment to those few essential and perishable possessions that give meaning to our lives: the sun, the sea and women in the sunlight. They are the riches of the living culture, everything else being the dead civilization that we repudiate. If it is true that true culture is inseparable from a certain barbarism, nothing that is barbaric can be alien to us (Preface to *Rivages*, quoted in Parker, 40–1).[3]

Sensitive individuals—from the simplicity of a Vincent to the sophistication of a Gide—may encounter, in many ways, "manifestations of the absurd," of which the recognition of eventual death may be only the most common and most definitive. Some perhaps never do. There is certainly no necessity, either factual or ethical, for this encounter, which tends to occasion a break in our habitual patterns of activity and assumed meaningfulness, forcing us to stop, reflect, and struggle to come to terms with the awareness of no longer being at one with our world. We are thus propelled forth in the search for an intellectual reconstruction of meaning that will return some peace to our conscious life. Those to whom such a project is alien may continue to live their lives on essentially the same qualitative level of felt experience with which they began—though occasionally they kill people unintentionally. With others, it is different. And so with Camus's Algerian Man. No doubt he has a distinctive sensibility and awareness, which makes its distinctive contribution to the illumination of consciousness. But his special significance emerges from reflection upon the ahistorical nature of his encounter with Western civilization.

With Camus this awareness of a break between the individual and his habitually accepted and instinctively unified natural environment seems to have been triggered by three crucial types of destructive experience: a sensitivity to the overwhelming power of nature (cf. esp. "The Wind at Djémila"); a poignant awareness of the tragedy of solitude and eventual death (cf. esp. "Irony" and "The Desert"), including a life-threatening encounter with illness at the age of seventeen; and the experience of travel, which effectively cuts one off from familiar scenes and places one face to face with the potential strangeness of existence (cf. esp. "Death in the Soul").

The melancholy that is likely to follow such a realization is well embodied in Camus's first work, *Two Sides of the Coin*:

And what other advantage does one seek to draw from travel? Here I am without adornment. A city in which I cannot read the signs, strange features with nothing familiar to cling to, without friends to whom to speak, without entertainment. . . . Strange faces will appear. Churches, gold and incense, everything rejects me in a daily life in which my anguish gives to each thing its price. And it is here that the curtain of habits, the comfortable weaving of gestures and words in which the heart becomes drowsy, slowly raises itself again and finally unveils the pale face of apprehension. Man is face-to-face with himself: I defy him to be happy. . . . It is thus . . . that travel enlightens. . . . That which gives to travel its worth is fear. It breaks a sort of internal decor in us. It is no longer possible to cheat—to hide oneself behind the hours at the office and at the shipyard (these hours against which we protest so strongly and which protect us as surely from the suffering of being alone) (*L'Envers*, LCE, 87–9, 108–9).

The restrained irony that pervades this work constitutes Camus's first published attempt to confront the experience of absurdity into which he had been precipitated. But the solution remains essentially artistic—a matter of style—while the felt dilemmas lose none of their experiential force. Germaine Brée beautifully summarizes the results of this attempt when she writes:

Poverty, old age, the solitary travels of a young man without money, the silent, helpless night of vigil beside a mother loved but inaccessible, all these forms of life strip the individual bare of illusion, habit, diversion, and bring him face to face with the incomprehensibility of his life and of his death. And in those moments of nakedness, when all rationalization and all protective ideas and beliefs disappear, the beauty of the earth secretly suffuses the soul, reducing to nought the "absurd" human being, tempting man away from a wounded humanity into its own indifferent perfection and immortality. "But these are the eyes and voices which I must love. I belong to the world through all my gestures, to men through all my pity and gratitude. Between these two facets of the world I do not wish to choose. . . . If I listen to the irony slinking behind all things, it slowly emerges, blinking its small clear eye: live as if . . ." (Brée, 75–6).

The world of the human and the world of the nonhuman—*Two Sides of the Coin*—bound together by an "as if," and at the end a certain death. In *Nuptials* further meditation on the meaning of the eventuality of death seems to take us a step beyond this "stylistic" solution toward a suggestion of the positive role that consciousness can play in replacing the "as if" with lucidity. Camus observes:

The true, *the only, progress of civilization* . . . lies in creating conscious deaths. . . . As for me, here in the presence of this world, I have no wish to lie nor to be lied to. I want to keep my lucidity to the last, and gaze upon my death with all the fullness of my jealousy and horror. It is to the extent I cut myself off from the world that I fear death most, to the degree I attach myself to the fate of living men instead of contemplating the unchanging sky. Creating conscious deaths is to diminish the distance that separates us from the world and to accept a consummation without joy, alert to rapturous images of a world forever lost (LCE, 77–8, my italics).

An almost solipsistic, lucid partial reintegration into the cosmos is suggested here as the way to heal the rupture of the recognition of death—but at the expense of the world of the human.[4] A dichotomous antagonism, a rejection, and an acceptance—such seems to be the stage of development to which Camus has arrived.[5]

2

The Death of God

We can no longer do without positive values. Where will we find them? We have to look within ourselves, in the heart of our experience, namely in the interior of rebellious thought, for the values we need (A/II, 80).

ALONE IN THE WORLD

"God is dead," proclaims Nietzsche's madman, and we have killed Him. The Christian God is no longer believable. Yet this cosmic deed remains light years away from being understood. It is a frightful, portentous event. For when the belief in God evaporates, the entire structure of Western beliefs must come tumbling down. Is this not a cataclysmic event? Does it not threaten to wrench from the West the root structure of the meaningful drama by which we live? But we do not yet know that we no longer believe. We still go through the rituals, say the right words on the right occasions, and act as if our life had cosmic significance. But our belief lacks coherence and substance, its shell is cracking, and our civilization totters on the brink of the cataclysm.

Such was Nietzsche's vision in the 1880s when, "philosophizing with a hammer," he touched his tuning fork to the most elusive and yet profound resonances of the experience of the West. Nietzsche did not kill God, writes Camus; he found Him dead in the hearts of his contemporaries and proclaimed this fact aloud. But he came too soon. The civilized, who were amused and amazed, viewed him only as a madman, remaining secure in their sense of cosmic importance.

But the deed had been done, and its reality was beginning to gnaw at the vitals of our civilization like a cancer in the body politic. Nihilism was the emerging legacy of this deed: the systematized belief in nothing, the sense that without God our lives are devoid of significance. Morality loses its foundation; everything is permitted but nothing makes any difference. We are adrift in a Newtonian world of matter in motion following purposeless natural laws, which during the course of Darwinian evolution has given birth

14

to sensitive and reflective animals who differ from the rest of creation solely in the knowledge of their impending death. It's only a matter of time.

Nothing—no God, no purpose, no morality, no conscience—hinders such animals from grasping for whatever they can get, as soon as they can get it. "Everything is permitted" means the law of force, power, and efficiency. From nihilism to Nazism the path is direct. And the defeat of Nazism is only a temporary setback, generated by a vitalized conservative reflex, in the seemingly inevitable "progress" of the West toward realizing the full significance of the death of God. Now "beyond freedom and dignity," we are rapidly approaching "1984."

What is absurd about life, writes Camus, is neither the universe nor people, but the confrontation of the two. Energized by the demand for an ordered, dignified, meaningful existence, suffused with the memory of several thousand years of Judeo-Christian providence, confronting a world eternally indifferent to that need and unresponsive to that memory, such is the source of our experience of the absurd.

The experience of absurdity, however, is not universal, not inevitable, not necessary, not even necessarily true. But it is rooted in historical reality, it is legated to us by the failure of the Judeo-Christian drama that has been at the center of our experience.

As this dramatic setting collapses, sometimes slowly and surreptitiously creeping behind the curtain of ordinary events, sometimes violently ripping off the masks of habit and belief with which we dress our appearances, the experience of meaninglessness moves to center stage. The absurd, says Camus, is but "one perception among many." Yet, once it appears, it casts a pall across our world, coloring our activities, values, and purposes with its hue. We see ourselves in a new light. No dimension of experience can long remain immune from its influence, try as we may to go on with our habits and our "daily round." Even those who are able to submerge their attendant anxiety with a nervous and often obsessive reaffirmation of normality find themselves in a transformed social world. The conservative reflex, try as it may, cannot hold back the effects of the cataclysmic event. It is a matter of taking stock of our experience—and that of our epoch—and seeking to develop a response that will preserve the values that are worth saving.

To demonstrate the absurdity of life, however, cannot be an end, writes Camus. To encounter absurdity is only the beginning. The beginning of awareness; the beginning of reflection; the beginning of the long and arduous effort to find our way out of the dead end which is the nihilistic conclusion to the death of transcendent values.

If the death of God is the central given for Camus, and the perception of life's ultimate absurdity the seemingly obvious consequence, the nihilistic conclusion is no more logically necessary than is the leap of faith. Suicide, whether philosophical or natural, involves an abdication of the struggle to give meaning to our life on its own terms. For Camus, the central challenge of our times, and of his life, was to confront nihilism head on: to accept life as given, pervaded as it is by an absurd sensibility and lacking transcendent values, while remaining committed to the possibility of meaningful living. The significance of this challenge cannot be understood, and the intensity of the struggle to combat it cannot be grasped, unless the profound passion for life that underlies the entire effort is appreciated. For the reflective person who is not deeply moved by the pulsating rhythms of bodily existence, no articulation of the meanings of life will suffice to render life worth living. Starting from the experience of life's vitalizing energy in need of an integral ordering, and confronted with the memory of a cosmic setting that has collapsed, Camus commits his being and his thought to the struggle to find an alternative to nihilism. He writes from within "a world where everything has lost its meaning" in order to "throw some light on the blind battle we [are] waging and thereby to make our battle more effective" (RRD, 3, ix).

PERSONAL REVOLT

If the Christian God is dead, it might be asked, why discuss Christian doctrine? An answer to this query is called for at two levels: cultural and personal. But first, the problem of method. Camus always insisted that there is a profound difference between the quality of an experience as it is lived and the nature of the reflection to which it gives rise. The same experience, of the death of God for example, can generate profoundly different intellectual attitudes. Not only must we evaluate the theories by which life's sufferings and hopes find expression, but we must locate them within the experiences from which they arise and to which they lead. It is because Camus rejects the notion of the independent reality of thought that he rejected the career of the philosopher, as he understood it, for that of the artist.

The artist is wedded to the concrete; and the life of ideas for Camus is always the life of actual human beings struggling to give meaning and dignity to their lives. The essential value of thinking lies not in a succession of logical thoughts, but in their concrete "truthfulness," the manner in which they remain truthful to an experience. What is called for are responses to experiential exigencies, which point the way toward the enhancement of concrete possibilities.

No wonder Camus could assert that the sole purpose of *The Rebel* was to point the way toward a renaissance in human living. I will return to this problem later. Here I simply wish to underline the methodological point in order to understand Camus's belief that the psychic dynamic sustaining Christian belief has not disappeared. Far from it: Christian experience underlies the thinking of the West. It is our psychocultural ontology. Culturally speaking, Christianity may be suffering an eclipse, despite the many who still desperately cling to the remnants of traditional faith. Yet our need for such values remains. It is Camus's belief that we suffer deeply from their loss— even if we lack reflective appreciation of that fact. He seeks simply to give expression to that appreciation, while trying to chart a pathway out of the desert of meaninglessness and desolation that is its cultural legacy.

This is civilization's problem. We must know if man, solely by himself, can create his own values, without the help of rationalist thought or of the eternal. I don't much like the already too popular existential philosophy, and, to be truthful, I believe its conclusions to be false. But it draws its truthfulness from a malaise which pervades an entire epoch from which we do not wish to separate ourselves. We want to think and live in our history. We believe that the truth of this century can only be realized by bringing its drama to completion. If the epoch has suffered from nihilism, we will not obtain the ethic which we need by ignoring nihilism. No, everything is not summed up with negation or absurdity. We know that. But we must first present negation and absurdity because our generation has encountered them and we must come to terms with them (A/I, 110–2).

In short, the absurd is a point of departure, not a conclusion. It is the rock to which we must hold firm if we are to find our way out of our desert of doubts; if we are to avoid deluding ourselves while we develop a reflection that points to a sustaining rebirth. The often unarticulated and yet *deeply* felt root of this absurd is the experience of the sensual and self-conscious animal demanding order and dignity, rooted in the spontaneous vitality of natural existence. For one who is not excited by the sensual, aesthetic, interpersonal, and sportive qualities of living, no search for the meaning of life will fill the void. Such at least was Camus's conviction.

The absurd is born of the confrontation of such a sensibility—matured by several thousand years of Judeo-Christian history—with the post-Newtonian, post-Darwinian, post-Freudian, urban-bourgeois world. The challenge of the absurd concerns the meaning of this life. As psychologists know, the root of depression may lie in object-loss—or perhaps, even more deeply, in the loss of the social and personal setting from which our life draws dramatic sustenance. In the words of Ernest Becker, a human being must feel like "a locus of value in a world of meaning" or suffer the most profound despair. "Neither the confrontation with an obstinate adversity nor the exhaustion arising out of an unequal struggle gives birth to true despair. That comes rather when we no longer know our reasons for fighting, or even if we should fight at all" (A/II, 14–15). The experience of the absurd is precisely such a cosmic object-loss, threatening us with cultural depression.

Here Camus's response is rejection—almost visceral at first, then slowly gaining in clarity and articulation. Initially, rejection of the meaninglessness that the absurd threatens; then of the intellectual responses that seek to deny or repudiate an experience that so pervades him that he cannot conceive of himself apart from it. The absurd reasoning of *The Myth of Sisyphus* is not primarily an abstract philosophical analysis. It is a deeply personal attempt to come to terms with his experience while remaining truthful to its givens. This reasoning claims interpersonal, even universal, significance only for those who share the experience. Those who look to *The Myth of Sisyphus* to prove that life has meaning and that suicide is not a legitimate response to the absurd are rightly disappointed. Camus does not accomplish that goal. He could not. He did not even try. Rather his essay is a reflection upon his own experience and that of an epoch and a civilization whose drama he shared.[1] It is not a demonstration. It is an exploration and an experiment. It is simply a question of honesty and persistence.

Thus the personal origins of revolt for Camus are to be found in his refusal to accept either the nihilistic conclusion that life is valueless or the religio-philosophic conclusion that one must abandon reason and experience for the leap of faith. Camus will reject any value attributed to human life that seems to be imposed on it from without. Of the evidence offered by our senses we can be sure. He will hold to this to the end. What is offered to us that transcends the bounds of experience is at best a hope and a promise, which threatens to make of our experience a desert. On the other hand, can we find in our experience alone the source of a value that can sustain our efforts?

It is here that the pagan joys of Camus's youth assume an almost mythic dimension, offering the promise of a cultural rebirth:

For the first time in two thousand years the body has been shown naked on the beaches. For twenty centuries, man has strived to impose decency on the insolence and simplicity of the Greeks. . . . Today, reaching back over this history, young men sprinting on Mediterranean beaches are rediscovering the magnificent motion of the athletes of Delos (LCE, 82).

They are thus recapturing a dignified innocence and natural vitality, free of Christian guilt. What need here for a transcendent grace to expiate an original sin?

The threat to this revitalized living does not come so much from the experience of cosmic nothingness as from the routine of daily living that sanctifies habit and deadens the senses, often submerging the vital present in an unarticulated hope for a salvific future. Aspirations, Advancement, Progress, Vocation, Morality, Salvation, all our "Later-ons" seek in their insidious way to steal from us our only wealth: the magnificent present. Yes, the enemy is hope for the future or the after-life—and the life of routine, of normality, that is consecrated to it—grounded in an abstract thinking cut off from the living present. It is the insidious form by which nihilism seeps into ordinary lives.

Habit robs us of the meaning of our lives. The beauty of nature and the community of friendship are subordinated to the judgments of the "spirit of seriousness." The terrain is prepared for the invasion of alien and destructive forces: for nihilism, in short. It is out of the habitual failure of lucid perception that Meursault, who had instinctively rejected but not yet freed himself from the grasp of such absolutes, enters into complicity with the natural world in the death of another human being, thus destroying the implicit community of human beings confronting their fate. It is out of habitualized boredom that Oran offers itself as the appropriate locus for the invasion of the plague—as prewar France, doing political business as usual in the face of mounting danger, left itself vulnerable to Nazi devastation through an inability to appreciate clearly and grasp in dignity the fraternal human community.

Camus identified bourgeois society, certain of its virtues and their divine sanction, the self-confident and self-centered spirit of seriousness itself, as the very seed-bed of contemporary nihilism—contrary to the views of those commentators who saw Camus as a liberal critic of revolutionary politics.[2] By submerging Christian values in market hypocrisy, parroting a formalism of virtue without concrete substance, it has robbed our lives of transcendent significance while offering as replacement the mercantile aspirations of material accumulation. It has deadened sensitivity with crass commercialism, using controlled market allocations to sustain a routinized work ethic with the threat of material scarcity. Increasingly, humans find themselves cut off from nature and set at odds with their fellows by a competitive scheme that destroys their dignity in a world not of their own making. The degradation of work and of comradeship thus joins hands with the mystification of time casting a deadening pall over everyday life.

While more needs to be said about the contribution of bourgeois society to our contemporary ills, it must be clear that the precondition of any renaissance for Camus involves the transformation of bourgeois sensibilities. The inability to grasp even the possibilities of such a transformation dooms us to the ravages of nihilism. To this preliminary effort *The Myth of Sisyphus* was dedicated.

We must not fail to appreciate the profound sense in which *The Myth* is a continuation of the stranger's systematic attack on the values of Bourgeois-Christian civilization: of what Nietzsche called the spirit of seriousness. This is the hidden meaning of Camus's ethics of quantity, namely that hierarchic values rooted in a divine transcendence are denied by the realities of the absurd. There is only one source of value for the human being suffused with the absurd perception: lucid consciousness. The natural world is without value; it simply is, in all its impersonal grandeur and destructiveness. The supernatural seems at best an unsubstantiated hope, at worst a vain delusion. In either case it is a distraction that threatens to rob us of the weight, the beauty, the intensity of the present, until death takes it from us forever. Value is to be found for contemporary humanity, if at all, only in the sentient animal's conscious confrontation with life. And this confrontation can be sustaining only if it is freed from the hope for a transcendent salvation, for which experience offers no evidence and which an inevitable death seems to deny. To replace the spiritually transcendent with the materially efficient or consumable in the not-too-distant future is hardly an ennobling prospect that speaks adequately to the existential problem.

Yes, the encounter with death is the ultimate "absurd wall," which seals the empirical meaninglessness of a life devoted to transcendent values. But a lucid perception of that reality and of the absurd, by cutting to the core of a ritualized life, can be the occasion for a liberating transformation of consciousness. Liberation from habitual enslavement to unobtained and un-believable abstract values can become the condition for the discovery of those sensual values offered in the spontaneity of innocent involvement with nature and others. An ethics of quantity is meaningless, or worse an invitation to the rule of force, without a preliminary transformation of awareness. "The suc-cession of presents before a lucid consciousness in the face of death is the ideal of the Absurd Man." For a life devoted to hope and embedded in routine, an eternity of presents would not suffice. The multiplication of meaninglessness by infinite time would simply leave us with an infinite meaninglessness.

Lucid perception of the absurd, then, is not an end but a beginning, for a consciousness committed to integrity, to honesty, and to seeking from life its utmost significance. "The only progress in history," wrote Camus early in his life, "was the creation of conscious deaths." It matters not what one's place in life, whether conqueror or post office clerk. For a transformed consciousness, freed from bondage to alien absolutes, whether spiritual or material, death is the only limit; beyond that all else is possibility.

It thus becomes clear that not only can a life be lived without transcendent appeal but that it will be lived better and more fully on such terms. Lucid reason, noting its limits, becomes the occasion for the human animal, while locating itself firmly in its epoch to regain contact with its trans-historical destiny. Freeing itself from the grasp of history, it may return to the eternal source of its being in union with the natural world and with others in an experience that is fated to pass away. "All my idols," wrote Camus, "have feet of clay."

PART TWO

Dramatic Contours

Having started from an anguished awareness of the inhuman, the meditation on the absurd returns at the end of its itinerary to the very heart of the passionate flames of human revolt (MS, 47).

3 ❧

The Stranger

A man devoid of hope and conscious of being so has ceased to belong to the future, and no gospel keeps its meaning for him (MS, 31; E, 121, 1436).

WHO IS THIS STRANGER?

"Mother died today. Or maybe it was yesterday, I don't know. I received a telegram from the rest home: MOTHER DECEASED. BURIAL TOMORROW. VERY TRULY YOURS. It doesn't say anything. Maybe it was yesterday" (STR, 1).[1] Not exactly the normal reaction of a son to the news of his mother's death. What kind of person responds in this matter-of-fact way? Are we not at first put off by such casualness? Perhaps even scandalized by our initial encounter with Patrice Meursault?

Is not this Meursault a stranger to our normal feelings and expectations? We sense a distance. Not that he seeks to scandalize or offend. Far from it. He is rather quite unassuming, almost shy. He wants neither to offend nor to be hated. Expressing an air of naïveté, he often experiences an undercurrent of uneasiness as to what is expected of him. Occasionally he is moved to apologize without quite knowing what he is guilty of. When asking his boss for two days off to attend his mother's funeral, for example, he feels that he "ought not to have said that to him." Or, when sensing the reproach of the director of the rest home, he begins to explain himself.

A subtle tension thus pervades our relation with Meursault from the first. Between the complete unassuming naturalness of his actions and observations, on the one hand, and his insensitivity to normal feelings and expectations, on the other, a gulf emerges that makes it quite difficult for us to coordinate our emotional response to him. We are drawn to identify, even sympathize, with him. And yet how can we not feel a condemnation begin to arise within us to which we are not yet able to give expression?

In short, we are disoriented, perhaps even slightly offended, by our encounter with a being who shows no sign of sharing normal human feelings. Nor does he attest to any normal aspirations. Slowly we are familiarized with his world, even led to see our own world through his eyes. Stripped of our normal "conceptual lenses," we see that world increasingly as arbitrary, capricious, pretentious, even hypocritical. By the time of the trial we may even find ourselves tempted, if not actually inclined, to side with Meursault against the prosecutor and jurists who inhabit the world that was ours at the beginning of the novel. However short-lived that experiential voyage may prove to be, the stylistic accomplishment is remarkable.

Perhaps Meursault is Camus's portrait of the being he might have become had not M. Germain, to whom he dedicated his Nobel Prize address, rescued him from the life of physical plenitude and spiritual exhaustion that was the lot of lower-class French Algerian youth. Recall Camus's friend Vincent, mentioned in "Summer in Algiers," whose direct and uncomplicated lifestyle and morals, though lacking in love, suggest a closeness to the vital and sensuous qualities of existence.[2] Meursault resides in that shrunken present rich with sensations that lead nowhere. But that must not be misunderstood. He is not without feelings or morals. He feels for Salamano, is moved by the testimony of Celeste, and feels concern for several individuals, including the magistrate. Throughout his ordeal, he treats everyone with consideration and is even able to see the point of view of the prosecutor. He simply refuses to interpret his experience or to give it a significance beyond what is immediately present to the senses.

A lively sensitivity to the play of light and shadow colors his day. The weather, qualitative changes in experience and in the modulations of nature practically enrapture him. He takes them as they are, asking and expecting nothing more. At the same time he remains practically blind to the socially established meanings with which others embellish events.

Nowhere is this more evident than in his relation with Marie. Like Vincent, he knows nothing of love and cares nothing for the institution of marriage. But when Marie smiles in a certain way he is attracted to her and wants her. His desires are not without warmth, but they lack premeditation or foresight. They are spontaneous responses to sensuous qualities and reflect little if any conceptual interpretation or social propriety.

The fascination of Meursault and the young journalist with one another may also be seen in this light. Camus became a journalist as a result of having by chance had Louis Germain as his teacher. And so with the novel. Had Meursault not been compelled by familial poverty to give up his education and abandon his career aspirations, he might have found himself in the audience covering a murder trial. Thus their fascination with each other suggests the chance nature of their destinies and their reciprocal being for one another. In the journalist Meursault sees the person he might have become, fascinated with the person the journalist Camus might have been.

And similarly with the problems of poverty with which Camus's early sensibilities were clearly marked. For it is poverty that keeps Patrice Meursault from pursuing his education and would have done likewise for young Albert. The testimony of his friends about never being invited into his home bears witness to an anguished sensitivity, as does his evocative discussion of the novel *La Douleur*, which had such a profound impact upon him. Camus's first effort at a full-length novel, *A Happy Death*, is quite explicit on the destiny of those condemned to poverty, whatever the natural gifts of their environment. Without money with which to buy the time to be happy, *that* Mersault would have been condemned to the exhausting rigors and spiritual depletion of the 9-to-5 job, which, however necessary to make ends meet, leads only to a wasted life and meaningless "natural death."

Who then is this Patrice Meursault who so innocently disconcerts us? A clerk without ambition, who rejects his boss's offer of advancement and a position in Paris. A man who will marry Marie if she wishes, but who considers marriage no big deal. Obviously intelligent, but having been compelled by poverty to give up schooling, he concluded that ambition was a waste of time and effort. All that mattered was living one day at a time, accepting the pleasures offered, and expecting no more.

Having given up the future, his life follows the trajectory of the moment: job, acquaintances, social routines, climate. Even his language, with its simple factual statements, its lack of connectives, its concentration on sensations and images, bears witness to the pervasiveness of the present. Events happen and Patrice responds. Camus observes: "He limits himself to *responding to questions*. At first, these are the questions which the world asks us every day —[at the end] they are the chaplain's questions. Thus, I define my character negatively" (TRN, 1923).

Such is the person we encounter at the outset. It is not clear what effect the death of his mother had on him. Judging by his explicit response, it would seem to have had no effect, other than to mildly annoy his employer and thus cause some discomfort for Patrice. Yet it is here that the narrative begins. The opening lines suggest that Meursault began writing the chronicle shortly after receiving the note from the rest home—perhaps as a diary or a random collection of notes. The exact status of the narrative is not clear or consistent. Pursuing internal clues would lead one to conclude either that he kept a running account of his life from then on, making somewhat regular entries after the day's or week's events, or that everything was essentially written from the perspective of a post-sentence reevaluation of his life. Or perhaps it is simply an oral report of his life given at sporadic moments to an impartial observer. In any case, the entries in the first part of the narrative tend to be more direct, more in the style of an immediate, noninterpretative reporting of events in temporal sequence, whereas those of the second part involve greater editorial selectivity. If we take seriously this change in perspective as the narrative proceeds, we would probably be led to a conclusion emphasizing its temporal elaboration. In any case, the world we see is the world Patrice is conscious of seeing *as he sees it*. The meaning of these events is, in the first instance, the meaning of these events *to him*. And it is to that meaning that I now turn.

MEURSAULT'S WORLD

What then is the world that is revealed to us through this stranger's eyes? One in which events just happen. Of course, a habitual pattern carries us from day to day. But there does not seem to be any logic to the pattern. "Rising, streetcar, four hours in the office or the factory, meal, streetcar, four hours of work, meal, sleep, and Monday Tuesday Wednesday Thursday Friday and Saturday according to the same rhythm" (MS, 12–13). Expressions, movements, modes of dressing and of carrying oneself strike the observer as do colors, lights, sounds, and temperature. Social and natural events merge and interpenetrate, without priority or distinction between them. The social is rather but an aspect of the natural. There is but one unitary present, with the world of habit being altogether natural and inevitable for Meursault.

It is from this perspective that the world is revealed to us in the first part of the narrative. Nothing significant seems to happen. Each event takes place on the same metaphysical plane. If one thing is singled out for attention rather than another, that is only because it momentarily grabbed Patrice's attention. No hierarchies of value are recognized. Occasional lyrical passages relieve the emotional tedium like shafts of radiant sunlight bursting through the skies of an otherwise overcast day. But that is their only significance. Each of the first five chapters concludes essentially with the observation "that, after all, nothing had changed" (STR, 19).

With the killing of the Arab, however, "it all began." Meursault understood that with that shot he "had broken the harmony of the day, the marvellous silence of a beach where [he] had been happy" (STR, 50). The natural order is shattered. The cyclical time of a habitual life immersed in nature is transfigured by a single event. All later events now take on the meaning of either leading up to or following from it. If the metaphysical ground of the first part is cyclical nature, that of the second is historicized nature, nature subjected to the organization and interpretation of society. Rather than eternal repetition, events now become the children of the past and the parents of the future, in a linear history that leads either to death or to transfiguration. Each life becomes a unique journey, each event a transition. This metaphysical transformation demands an appropriate existential one. Patrice can no longer act as if his life will be eternal repetition. The unity of nature and history is sundered, and historically socialized reason emerges to insist on a different kind of accounting.

Under the pressure of events, this realization begins to dawn on Patrice. First, in jail, he is called upon to recount the events at the beach. He is questioned about his past and initially draws a blank, noting that he has lost the habit of self-interrogation. Thinking about his past is the beginning of an experiential transformation by which he comes to locate himself in a linear historical world, which location is the precondition of his being able to take personal responsibility for his life.

With this dawning recollection of his past, a sense of perspective emerges. The flatness of the experiential landscape undergoes seismic transformation. Preferences are recognized and valued. An emerging selectivity stylistically transforms the narrative. Criteria of value are suggested. The sensually given is subject to reflective appraisal, and the previously implicit ethics of quantity begins to acquire an appreciation of experiential qualities that only conscious attention can bring. This qualitative self-appropriation of life comes to consummation in the encounter with the chaplain, when the values by which Meursault had lived are reflectively articulated and defended. Thus completes the reconstruction of his experience. From the reconstitution of his memory to the reaffirmation of his life, Meursault has achieved a reflective grasp of the life he has lived, and has found that it was good. He has also realized that to have so lived was to have rejected the expectations of the established social order. Thus a de facto rebel becomes a de jure one. An explicit articulation of these emerging values confronts a chaplain who embodies the rejected order. But I am jumping ahead of my story.

The world was initially composed of natural and social habits—habits of things and of people. Each had its regularity and its unique sensuousness. Patrice observes and responds. He never asks why, what ought to be done, although he does comment upon connections between events—why, for example, the people in the streets on Sunday behave as they do. He thus reveals an ability to analyze facts for their connections, but no interest in exploring purposes or goals. Occasionally he notes the purposes of others—as with Raymond's desire to get even—but for him, and for us through his eyes, this is but another fact that he observes and to which he responds.

Social conventions also lose their privileged status and appear not to differ from natural occurrences. Like voyagers from another planet, we are often left to wonder at the natives' strange behavior, their dance of social etiquette and the mirage of their personal beliefs. A feeling of purposelessness textures the narrative, pervading Part 1. A feeling of strangeness is subliminally generated in the reader by the contrast between the pure contingency of the events recounted and our subterranean sense of their familiarity and ordinary meaningfulness. This contrast is brought explicitly to the fore in Part 2 by the establishment's insistence on the purposefulness of its world. "The meaning of the book consists precisely in the parallelism of the two parts," affirmed Camus (TRN, 1924).

The use of the disconnected compound past (*passé composé*)—of which so much has been made in critical studies since Sartre's "Explication de l'Etranger"—tends to reduce each fact to an irreducible and unconnected given, thus strengthening this emerging sense of the absurdity of the human situation when it lacks any aspiration to order. Clearly this is Camus's intention. That our world is governed by chance is brought home so much more forcefully when presented by and realized in the life of one who is so unassumingly natural and unself-conscious. A simple individual, without depth or contrivance, presents our world to us in a way that reveals it as being without deeper significance. Confronting such a world tends to make people uncomfortable. "Do you want my life to have no meaning?" the magistrate cries. Whatever his intentions, Patrice's way of living is felt as threatening to society's institutions, beliefs, and aspirations.

ESTRANGEMENT

The social order from which Meursault is so estranged is the world of ambition and the desire for advancement that his employer expects, as well as the decorum and grief to which all at the burial bear witness. It is the wearing of black as a show of mourning, and the sustained sadness that forbids the beginning of a liaison on the day following the burial of one's mother, not to say the sacrilege of viewing a Fernandel film. It is also the expectation that one ought to cry at the funeral of one's grandmother, about which Camus personally felt such conflict and hypocrisy. And it is certainly viewing love as a serious matter and treating marriage as an important social institution. Here we glimpse the deeper social meaning to which normal people cling with ferocious tenacity. The rituals and ceremonies, the institutions and practices, by which society daily reenacts the drama of its cosmic significance are grounded in a system of values and beliefs that give shape to a living that might otherwise hover precariously close to the abyss of nothingness. Not to speak of the offices, hierarchies, and prerogatives by which the power and self-esteem of the few may be protected from the desires of the many.

The personal appropriation of that ritualized belief system defines and valorizes an individual's place, giving us our sense of what it is important to do, to strive after, to avoid, and to become. People act in the belief that some things matter more than others, and because they feel that it is worth the effort. This is quite normal. Precisely so.

Meursault had in fact given up on these beliefs when he gave up his ambition. We can take him to have been an intelligent working-class French

Algerian whose social development was short-circuited by the need to leave school and get a job. We may even conjecture that this necessity followed upon an upbringing in which circumstances—perhaps including his more than average intelligence—had conspired to keep him somewhat apart from others, not fully integrated into social norms and practices. All this might of course have described Camus himself to some extent.

In any case, giving up ambition and, by implication, the belief system by which it is sustained, Meursault settles into a style of life in which inarticulate personal needs and satisfactions dictate spontaneous responses to the demands of nature and others. He goes along with the flow of habits and events. Such is the path of least resistance, except when his inclination moves him otherwise. And why act differently when "it's all the same to him"?

But then the beach, where "the trigger gave way [and Meursault] . . . understood that [he] had broken the harmony of the day, the marvellous silence of a beach where [he] had been happy. Then [he] pulled the trigger four more times on the motionless corpse where the bullets buried themselves effortlessly. And it was as if, with these four brief shots, [he] was knocking on the door of misfortune" (STR, 50). What could have been simpler or more natural? Heat, exhaustion, the beating of the sun, the shaft of light, the threatening confrontation—and the body tightens up to defend itself: The hand clenches the revolver, and the trigger gives way. With perhaps a touch of exasperation, even annoyance, at the intrusion of the threatening other into this already oppressive situation, the tension previously held coiled within his body bursts forth with those four fatal shots, as if it had been waiting for that moment of release.

All of which is, in one sense, no great deal. Oppressive conditions give rise to tension. The tension is released, and life goes on. Yet a person was killed. Surprisingly perhaps, the authorities initially show little interest in Meursault. As they become aware of his strangeness, their attitude changes. He does not "live by the rules." He does not think like ordinary people. He does not pay his respects, but seems indifferent to everything that is usually taken seriously. Is not such an attitude offensive? Who is this person, to treat cavalierly what we hold so dear? How can he act this way? There must be something the matter with him. Otherwise there would have to be something the matter with us for taking so seriously that which is not worthy of such respect. If we can't get him to see the error of his ways, thus acknowledging the Truth of ours, we must treat him as a traitor to the human community, and make him pay for his transgression.

Thus a transformed portrait of Meursault emerges. Initially he had simply appeared to be a bit odd, certainly not offensive or brutish. But he didn't want to see his mother's body, he smoked at her funeral, he rejected a chance to move to Paris, and he didn't take marriage seriously. He even seemed inordinately sensitive to trivial matters but awkward, even dense about the norms of social behavior. Now that queerness becomes perversity, indifference metamorphoses into insensitivity, and passivity into calculated criminality. No longer will Meursault's life be allowed to follow the trajectory of inclination and habit. The socialized demand for coherence and purposefulness now takes control. What may well have been lurking in the background now takes center stage, insisting that events conform to its terms. The portrait of a cold-blooded, ruthless murderer takes shape. And why *did* Meursault fire those four extra shots into the body of a corpse, asks the prosecutor, if not to make sure that the job was well done?

Returning to the beach and Meursault's description of what took place, the *why* seems about as relevant as asking a plant why it grows toward the light. Genetics, habit, and inclination seem sufficient. The *why* presupposes a world of purposeful beings who act for more or less premeditated reasons. But is that what took place on the beach?

I walked slowly toward the rocks and it felt like my forehead was swelling and pulsating under the sun. All this heat pressed down on me. . . . I gritted my teeth, clenched my fists in my pants pockets. . . . My jaws would contract with every sword-like reflexion that darted up from the sand, from a bleached shell, or from a piece of broken glass. . . .
As soon as [the Arab] saw me, he raised up a little and put one hand in his pocket. Naturally my hand closed around Raymond's revolver which I hadn't removed from my jacket. . . . A whole beach vibrating with the sun was surging behind me. I took a few steps toward the source. . . . The scorching sun attacked my cheeks and I felt drops of sweat forming in my eyebrows. It was the same sun as on the day I had buried Mother and, as then, my forehead hurt and all my veins were pulsating underneath my skin. Because of this heat which I could no longer stand, I took a step forward. . . . The Arab took out his knife and pointed it at me in the sun. The light flashed on the steel and it was like a long blade attacking me on the forehead. At the same instant, the sweat that had been forming in my eyebrows ran down all at once over my pupils, covering them with a warm, thick veil. . . . I felt nothing more then but the cymbals of sun on my forehead, and, indistinctly, the bursting blade of light from the sword continually in front of me. This burning sword was eating away at my eyelids and digging into my aching eyes. It was then that everything reeled. . . . It seemed to me that the heavens had opened to their full extent in order to let it rain fire. My entire being became tight and I closed my grip on the revolver. The trigger gave way (STR, 48–50, modified).

No interpretation, no motive, no conscious revolt is apparent. Only the quasi-instinctive, perhaps physiological, response of a natural animal to an oppressive situation. Under the pressure of the sun, he tenses up and the trigger yields. The Arab, the sun's rays striking off the blade of the knife, the taut grasp of the revolver—all are part of one natural environment whose elements are in tension with one another. Whom can one ask for a motive? The environment is returned to equilibrium by the removal of a nexus of tension. That is all.

But Meursault is a human being and a member of society, and its officials soon see that much more is at stake than simply the killing of an Arab by a French Algerian—about which, it should be noted, little official concern was likely to have been expressed at that time. "For the magistrate," writes Barrier, in his perceptive study of *The Stranger*, "a consciousness which is so non-human represents the grave threat of dismantling the entire edifice of values upon which the very order of society is based" (Barrier, 69).

Two points should be noted here. Meursault is portrayed as a brute, a person so cold and calculating as to smoke at his mother's funeral, begin a liaison on the following day, and commit pre-meditated murder without the least feeling of remorse. Such a "moral monster" would of course be a threat to any order. But Meursault is still more threatening, for he does not even recognize, not to say acknowledge, the values and norms by which the fabric of society is woven together. If he would repent and admit guilt, he would at least implicitly legitimize the claim of those values. Even a murderer can be pardoned—far more easily, Camus suggests, than one who not only refuses to acknowledge social norms, but fails even to perceive their existence. His refusal thus constitutes a sort of inarticulate metaphysical rejection by which he places himself beyond the horizon of the normal social world. As a spiritual alien upon whom accepted social absolutes make no claim, his being can only appear to the "good people" as a threat to the values and beliefs that are dear to them.

But why, one might ask, must the officials insist upon portraying Meursault as a ruthless killer, one who is morally guilty of matricide? Why must such evil motives be imputed to him in the first place? Why must society—in the persons of the magistrate, defense attorney, and prosecutor—refuse in principle to see him as he is?

We might reflect here upon the problem faced by the early Christians who had to come to terms with the Jews' rejection of Christ as the Messiah. With unbelieving pagans a more energetic propagation of the faith would have sufficed. But the challenge posed by the Jews was of another order. To them the revelation had been given. How can one account for the rejection of a faith that seems both self-evident and salvific? If Christians were not to doubt their faith's evidence, truth, or significance, what were they to make of the Jews' rejection? Either the Jews were ignorant innocents—like children or, perhaps, brutes—or they were willful, insensitive, and possibly downright evil.

Similarly, Meursault is too intelligent to be dismissed as a fool, but his attitude directly challenges the certainty with which the established order confronts the cosmic abyss. By imputing an evil nature to him, the prosecutor can both bring him within the normal cosmic drama and explain the specific reason for his behavior. Let's look at this logic. "To understand is, above all, to unify. The mind's deepest desire, even in its most elaborate operations, parallels man's unconscious feeling in the face of his universe; it is an insistence upon familiarity, an appetite for clarity. Understanding the world for a man is reducing it to the human, stamping it with his seal" (MS, 13).

A motive, no matter how malevolent, bespeaks an intelligible individual. A motivated act is an intelligible act; its world, a familiar world. To insist upon there being a motive—to insist so unself-consciously that the possibility that there might not be one does not *even* arise—while, at the same time, characterizing that motive as the willful rejection of humane sensibilities, here truly is the "best of all possible worlds." Presented with a criminal who is metaphysically comprehensible but morally reprehensible, society may, at one and the same time, reaffirm its cosmic drama and purge itself momentarily of any repressed and taboo inclinations that threaten to shatter it.

What would it mean to accept Meursault as he presents himself? How would we make sense of a world in which chance was pervasive, and in which natural processes predominated to no purpose? Would not a recognition of the essential arbitrariness of the social order and its hierarchies circumscribe the domain of meaning, rendering it contingent and without direction? And what of the "justice" system? And the organization of power and social prerogatives? Is it any wonder that an "evil" Meursault is more intelligible and less threatening than a impulsive one?

A world that can be explained even with bad reasons is a familiar world. . . . On the other hand, in a universe suddenly divested of illusions and lights, man feels an alien, a stranger. His exile is without remedy since he is deprived of the memory of a lost home or the hope of a promised land. This divorce between man and his life, the actor and his setting, is properly the feeling of absurdity (MS, 5).

Meursault is thus inadvertently the most dangerous of rebels, for he rejects the metaphysical foundation of normal social order.[3] As a de facto rebel who becomes conscious of his rebellion only at the end, he must be "put in his place." Society must either obtain his complicity or his destruction. That is the way with absolutes. They brook no opposition.[4]

Barrier correctly observes that for Camus "Meursault is innocent of the *moral* crime of which he is accused and the society guilty for condemning him for such a crime" (Barrier, 74). Rather, Meursault's revolt, involving as it does a reaffirmation of the manner in which he lived his life, contains for Camus elements essential to the establishment and maintenance of human dignity.

CONSCIOUSNESS AND DEATH

Having been indicted for "not playing the game," Meursault will no longer be allowed to freely follow the flow of his feelings. Viewed as a criminal, he will learn deprivation. At first, quite naturally his attention turns toward his immediate surroundings. But that is not long sustaining. Cut off from the world, he is forced back upon himself. Robbed of access to space, and confronted with the fact that he can no longer take the future for granted, he begins to think about his past life—and especially Marie.

With the slow awakening of his memory, a new depth of being emerges. He begins to appear as a being "for himself." Rather than just being there, his life appears as something to be lived, valued, retained, reconstituted, re-affirmed, and, perhaps, redirected. It is to be reflectively taken in hand, to be consciously molded in accord with his personal evaluation of what matters. Memory fuels self-consciousness, as habituated passivity gives way to lucid affirmation. This subterranean transition develops throughout Part 2, reaching its culmination in the encounter with the chaplain. At first, he is called upon to recount his life. Repeatedly he must retell the story of the beach confrontation. Then, as days turn into weeks and months, the rhythm of the days fades into the monotony of an unchanging present. With the turn inward, the being that he is "for himself" begins to emerge, fascinating him. He finds a reflected image of himself in a mirror. He is drawn to the journalist who suggests the being he might have been. The automaton woman reappears—that being who is completely other than himself—and there seems to be a mutual fascination with each other: she, for whom every action is rationally precalculated and purposeful; he, for whom none had been. It is as if the journalist and the automaton woman are the mirrors wherein Meursault may see the range of beings he might have been.

As Meursault comes to self-awareness, the narrative undergoes stylistic transformation. In place of the seemingly unedited description of chance events in temporal order, we now have the selective reporting of particular events. Long periods are now condensed into a few paragraphs, while a single significant day requires its own chapter. Important encounters are presented in detail, while others drift into obscurity. And judgments emerge, almost unintentionally. But it is the encounter with the chaplain following the condemnation to death that is required to make this existential transformation explicit.[5]

Without doubt the thought of death can remarkably concentrate one's attention. Today and tomorrow can be taken as they come only so long as one expects them to keep coming. Once the death sentence is handed down, the image of the guillotine looms over our horizon, threatening decisively to sever our relation with our future possibilities. And so with Patrice.

No matter how hard I tried to persuade myself, I could not accept that insolent certitude. Because, in the final analysis, it came to a disproportion between the judgment on which the certitude was based and its imperturbable course, from the moment when this judgment had been pronounced. The fact that the sentence had been read at eight o'clock rather than at five, that it might have been something entirely different . . . it seemed to me that all of this took away from the seriousness of such a verdict (STR, 89–91).

And yet, however chancy the process leading up to the judgment, "from the second it had been given, its effects became as sure, as serious" as the most palpable and inescapable of facts.

Doubtless, there is something absurd in the disproportion between the haphazard and contingent nature of daily existence and the certainty of the punishment's execution. Confronted with this absurdity, Meursault's initial response is typical.

What interests me just now is if I can avoid the machine, if there can be a way to escape the unavoidable. . . . I don't know how many times I've asked myself if there are any cases of condemned men who were able to fool the machine, who were able to disappear before the execution. . . . I scolded myself for not having paid enough attention to the accounts of executions. . . . There, perhaps, I might have found accounts of escape. I would have learned that in at least one case, the wheel had stopped, that in its never-ceasing momentum, hazard and chance, one time only, had caused a change in the normal order of things. One time! In a way, I believe that would have sufficed for me (STR, 89).

Patrice is struggling here to find grounds for the "leap of faith." Faced directly with death, his passionate will to live becomes explicit in his search for a way out. "What mattered was the possibility of escape, of being able to jump out of the path of inevitability, a crazy course which offered all chances of hope." Here, through his struggle, we encounter the fundamentals of the human condition that constitute the problematic of *The Myth*.

Only after having confronted the facts of his impending execution will he allow himself the luxury of hoping that his appeal might be granted. That thought let loose a "surge of blood that ran through my body, causing tears to come to my eyes. I needed to work at moderating my cries of ecstasy, to reason with them so to speak" (STR, 94).

It is precisely at such a moment that the chaplain entered, after having thrice been rejected by Meursault. This missionary for Jesus, who exudes the self-satisfaction of those who "know" themselves to be "in the Truth," incarnates a religious hope built upon acquiescence in the sacrifice of inno-cence. For the nonbeliever, however, who feels the full weight of finitude bearing down upon him, the chaplain's complacent acquiescence in, and even

complicity with, this capricious and unjust order of things is ultimately unbearable. Having struggled vainly to reconcile two contradictory visions of
his future, Meursault's outrage finally coalesces in an explosive rejection of
rationalized injustice. As the chaplain literally pins Patrice to the wall, chas-
tising him for his attachment to this life, and challenging him to deny that
he had come to hope for another, de facto rebellion finds articulate expression, retrospectively justifying his previous life. Having made explicit the link
between the leap of faith and the rejection of life, Meursault can no longer
contain the rage welling up within him. The only after-life for which he could
hope would be "a life where I could remember this one" (STR, 98). No, the
chaplain was not his "father: he was with the others." And what is this "truth"
he is offering but a path of illusions built upon renunciation? Meursault will
not acquiesce in this life-denying myth. His truth had been of this earth, and
it will remain so.

He had lived by the impassioned and transitory values of this life. "I had
been right. I was still right" (STR, 98). So what if they were finite? He
had not been wrong. He may have failed to reflectively appreciate the life
he had lived. He may have let that life slide along, rather than consciously
giving shape to it. But he had not betrayed it. If he had lived in a way
that involved de facto alienation from social norms, *that* had not been a
mistake. "Far from his being deprived of all sensitivity, a profound, because
tenacious, passion animate[d] him" (TRN, 1920). He had glimpsed a truth
that involved rejection of normalized hypocrisy. "It was but a negative truth
—the truth of being and feeling—but one without which no conquest over
self or world will ever be possible."

It thus becomes clear what Camus meant when he referred to Meursault
as the sole Christ we deserve today. For this sacrificial figure's innocence is
born out of social and even metaphysical naïveté, upon which altar he will
be crucified. Unlike Jesus, however, who can accept his death in resignation,
asking his father to "forgive them for they know not what they do," Meursault
rejects such resignation. Acceptance of the unjust suffering of innocents—for
Camus, the rock upon which Peter's church is built—can be counterposed to
the revolt that bursts forth like a mighty stream, drowning the chaplain in its
righteous indignation and passionate reaffirmation. Perhaps it makes sense for
one who believes in a salvific afterlife to be so forgiving, but that makes only
more poignant the loss of this life for which Meursault can find no redeeming
features. Resignation and forgiveness only add insult to injury, compounding
injustice with complicity. No, rather than forgiving them, Patrice wants his
revolt confirmed in the cries of hatred with which he hopes to be greeted by
a crowd of spectators on the day of his execution.

From the death of his mother to his impending execution, passing through
his killing of the Arab and society's condemnation of him, *The Stranger*

reveals a more sophisticated development of that transition from natural to conscious death that had been the basic structure of *A Happy Death*. What could be more natural for Meursault than the dying of an elderly woman who had lived out her life? Thus his response. But such nonchalance with respect to natural processes leaves us totally prey to chance and to the dissolution of human meanings. Thus the death of the Arab, but one more natural event for Meursault. And yet, it was by his hand that the trigger was pulled, a point of which the authorities make much. Consciousness was a participant in and contributor to this death, even if only by inadvertence. Such will *not* be the case for society. It intends consciously and quite deliberately to kill Meursault for transgressing the moral bounds of its world. For these bounds constitute society's response to the existential challenge of finitude. However unjust this sentence, the chaplain intercedes on behalf of accepting it as the price that must be paid if belief in the transcendent significance of human life is to be sustained. Patrice rebels so vehemently because death is not an entree into another life but the end of this one, and we should not so easily acquiesce in its realization. Death will come, inevitably, but we need not—must not— assist it. Not by inadvertence and certainly not by conscious decision. As for rational justification of such complicity, that is an evil of another order. We must rather draw forth from this dawning recognition of human finitude a renewed appreciation for what life has to offer. A passionate will "to exhaust the field of the possible" must replace our "longing for immortal heights."

A CRYPTOMYTHIC TALE

If Meursault is not guilty of murder, nevertheless a human being *is* dead and Meursault *did* pull the trigger. Although not guilty of having *willed* the slaying, he *is* guilty of permitting himself to become an accessory in the destruction of a human life. Actually, his guilt seems to lie precisely in his *not* having willed anything.[6] Lacking lucidity, Camus seems to be suggesting, we are ever in danger of entering into complicity with the forces of destruction. Consider the drama of "The Misunderstanding" or the citizens of Oran at the onset of *The Plague*. Human revolt at this stage of Camus's development primarily consists in the struggle to maintain a lucid awareness of our condition. Meursault at the crucial moment fails to take control of himself, to maintain the necessary human distance from the forces of nature. He succumbs passively to union with nature—at the expense of the human.

This failure is similar in source to the temptation that Camus speaks of in his contemporaneous essay "The Minotaur, or the Stop at Oran."

The Minotaur is boredom. . . . These are the lands of innocence. But innocence needs sand and stones. And man has forgotten how to live among them. At least it seems so, for he has taken refuge in this extraordinary city where boredom sleeps. Nevertheless, that very confrontation constitutes the value of Oran. The capital of boredom . . . is surrounded by an army in which every stone is a soldier. In the city, and at certain hours . . . what a temptation to identify oneself with those stones, to melt into that burning and impassive universe that defies history and its ferments! That is doubtless futile. But there is in every man a profound instinct which is neither that of destruction nor that of creation. It is merely a matter of resembling nothing (LCE, 130).

The stranger, it might be thought, bespeaks an inner call of our being, a countercultural invitation to return to a precivilized innocence, free of the burdens of individuality and conscience. One might think here of Freud's death instinct, the purported desire to return to our inorganic origins that constituted for Freud such a profound threat to the requirements of civilized living. Freud is, of course, not alone in speculating upon such presocial needs, desires, or longings. Whatever their scientific warrant, the pervasiveness of attention to them suggests that these reflections are giving expression, however inadequate the form, to very significant human concerns. At an archetypal level, Meursault might remind us of Rousseau's noble savage, whose innocence has not yet been sullied by sophistication and social pretention. There is, however, a price to be paid for such natural innocence, of which both the killing and society's response give us a sense.

Two further points about the dramatic significance of this cryptomythic tale need to be noted. First, there seems to be some ambiguity in the novel concerning the positive aspects of Meursault's character. Many have taken him to be bored with, and generally indifferent to, living. Certainly he shows no enthusiasm for all those futures we hold so dear. Similarly for matters of social etiquette. At the same time, he is fascinated by the behavior of the automaton woman—to the extent of trying to follow her when she leaves the restaurant—while he carefully attends to events at the home, at the trial, or, on Sundays, in the street in front of his balcony. Further, he evinces an enthusiasm for swimming, for hopping on the truck to take off for the port with Emmanuel, and, of course, for Marie Cardona. The "normal" reading of his character as indifferent to life may tell us more about the readers than about the person being interpreted. Such a reading of Meursault may be further confirmation of the extent to which we readers predicate the significance of *our* lives on the meaningfulness of belief systems that are being placed in question by him. Thus we would be finding him guilty in a manner similar to that of the jurors.

Whether or not Camus is successful in making this point, however, his intent should not be in doubt. "Meursault is not . . . a derelict for me, but a poor and naked man, in love with the sun which leaves no shadows. Far from his being deprived of all sensitivity, a profound, because tenacious, passion animates him, the passion for the absolute and for truth. *It concerns a truth which remains negative, the truth of being and feeling, but one without which no conquest of self and world will ever be possible*" (TRN, 1920, my italics).

The second point concerns the mythic significance of Oran. Given the previous description of the quality of Oranian life, the selection of Oran as the location for the outbreak of plague should not come as a surprise. The citizens of Oran, in their passive innocence, their boredom, their lack of lucidity, succumb to the temptations of habit. They are a sort of collective Meursault without the inarticulate passion, captives of the forces of nature and habit, waiting for whatever may befall them. The plague, a symbol of the unreasonable in nature that constitutes a permanent threat to the realm of the human, gains supremacy in proportion to the degree to which the inhabitants have abandoned the spirit, with its vigilant lucidity. A failure not unlike that of which Meursault is guilty.[7]

FROM REBELLION TO CONDUCT

With Meursault confronting death and opening up, "for the first time, to the tender indifference of the world" (STR, 100), Camus has completed his dramatization of the development of the human spirit from complete immersion in the natural/social world to the emergence of the self-conscious and self-possessing individual.[8] What remains is for such an emergent being to find a way to live. What meaning can a Meursault thus come unto himself find in his life? And what positive relations can he establish with his fellows? In this context we can appreciate the evocative explorations of the human condition encountered in *Nuptials*, and then the more argumentative theoretical exposition set forth in *The Myth of Sisyphus*. We would not be misled in viewing these works as the developing expressions of the being that Meursault has become.

I have already delineated the essential parameters of the Camusian vision. As natural animals we are extensions of the natural world with which we instinctively feel at one. But as conscious beings who can reflectively grasp the structure of that world, and of our distinctive place in it, we must recognize that our humanity is built upon the partial separation from nature of the realm of the human. We must, without imperiling our ties to nature, distance ourselves from its random course. And we must to some extent take upon ourselves the responsibility for the life we live. We must come to terms with our past and our future, incorporating into our lives the meaning that emerges from reflective appreciation of our finitude. We do not have unlimited time! Our potentially joyful union with nature will eventually be shattered by death. The "must" here is of course an ethical one. Meursault's rejection of the chaplain's consolations is not essentially negative. "There is a refusal which has nothing in common with renunciation. . . . If I obstinately refuse all the "later-ons" of the world, it is as much a matter of not renouncing my present riches. . . . Everything that is proposed to me is an effort to discharge man of the weight of his own life. . . . Between the horror and the silence, the certitude of a death without hope . . . I understand that all my horror of dying comes from my jealousy for living" (*Noces*, LCE, 76).

At this point, Camus explicitly refuses to view the absurd as a justification of resignation—as it had been for Sartre in "The Wall," of which Camus was quite aware at this time.[9] In response to the chaplain's invitation to resignation, Meursault recapitulates Camus's response before the religious inscriptions in Florence: "'One must,' said the inscription. But no, and my revolt was right. This joy which was in process, indifferent and absorbed like a pilgrim on the earth, I had to follow it step by step. And, for the rest, I said no. I said no with all my strength. . . . I did not see what uselessness took away from my revolt and I know well that it added to it" (*Noces*, LCE, 99). The revolt here articulated still lacks clarity as to what is being rejected —death, or the nihilistic resignation drawn therefrom—as well as a positive direction. Yet it has given forceful expression to the decision to affirm life in its present richness.

The conclusion of *The Stranger* is thus a beginning. Meursault now understands "why [his mother] had pretended to start over." We have come full circle. "Freed of the illusions of another life," our world has been returned to us fresh, inviting, uncertain, awaiting the significances we can give to it. The burdensome metaphysical and social rationalizations that fogged our vision and clogged our senses have been lifted. No wonder that sense of liberating release to which Meursault gives expression in opening up "for the first time, to the tender indifference of the world" (STR, 100).

There can be little doubt that Camus personally felt the oppressive weight of social expectations and conventions, even to the extent of exhibiting traits of which he was not at all proud. The normal and expected, even the admired and rewarded, can often be quite violative of our self-respect and personal integrity. We can both play up to those expectations and at the same time be disgusted by so doing. The struggle to find acceptance, along with the distaste for such a need, can play havoc with a desire to be true to oneself. This tension plays like a basso continuo to the explicit themes of Camus's life and work. Thus Meursault's revolt is not only the metaphysical rejection of social hypocrisy, but also the personal purgation of the temptation to play by the rules—even to be the dandy—and the reaffirmation of the individual's right, experienced by Camus almost as a characterological duty, to bear witness in one's actions to the truth of one's experience.

Meursault's revolt thus consummates a series of rejections:

- Of resignation in the face of death's inevitability.
- Of acceptance of the meaninglessness of a life without transcendence.
- Of any "leap of faith" in an afterlife *at the expense of* the only life we are given with certainty.
- Of the rituals of habit through which one's life is reduced to a meaningless routine—often rationalized in terms of a hoped-for life hereafter.
- Of the oppression of normal social order in which we are expected to be, feel, and behave in accordance with the "rules of the game."

The Stranger thus charts a pathway toward self-conscious affirmation, providing the metaphysical ground from which the positions first struggled with in *Two Sides of the Coin* and *Nuptials* and then reflectively articulated in *The Myth of Sisyphus* could emerge.[10] It has cleared away the theoretical terrain, while existentially instantiating the necessary personal perspective. "*The Stranger* is the zero point," comments Camus (TRN, 1924). But it is to *The Myth* that I must now turn to begin to harvest the fruits of this perspective.

4

The Myth of Sisyphus

The important thing . . . is not to be cured, but to live with one's ailments (MS, 38).

MEURSAULT AND THE MYTH

"A man devoid of hope and conscious of being so has ceased to belong to the future, *and no gospel keeps its meaning for him*" (MS, 31–2, E, 121, 1436).[1] Meursault, who had been "devoid of hope" since long before we met him, finally became conscious of that fact in his encounter with the chaplain. He realizes that the chaplain has nothing to offer him, except the illusion of another world that would turn his attention away from the few precious moments that still remain for him. The "good news" is a lie. Confronting his own death, he struggles for a response that can sustain him. But he cannot —or, at least, those of us who are still just emerging from a no-longer-believable system of ultimate Truths, and that includes Camus, cannot—so easily dispense with the often inarticulate need for absolutes. The All or Nothing has profound attraction.

He is offered a solution in which all the past contradictions have become merely polemical games. But that is not the way he experienced them. Their truth must be preserved. . . .

My reasoning [Meursault might have said] wants to be faithful to the evidence that aroused it. That evidence is the absurd. It is that divorce between the mind that desires and the world that disappoints, my nostalgia for unity, this fragmented universe, and the contradiction that binds them together. . . .

He is asked to leap. All he can reply is that he doesn't fully understand, that it is not obvious. Indeed, he does not want to do anything but what he fully understands. He is assured that this is the sin of pride, but he does not understand the notion of sin; that perhaps hell is in store, but he has not enough imagination to visualize that strange future; that he is losing immortal life, but that seems to him an idle consideration. An attempt is made to get him to admit his guilt. He feels innocent. To tell the truth, that is all he feels—his irreparable innocence. . . . Hence, what he demands of himself is to live *solely* with what he knows, to accommodate himself to what is, and to bring in nothing that is not certain. . . .

41

Living an experience, a particular fate, is accepting it fully. . . . To abolish conscious revolt is to elude the problem. The theme of permanent revolution is thus carried into individual experience. . . . Revolt . . . is a constant confrontation between man and his own obscurity. . . . [It] is the certainty of a crushing fate, without the resignation which ought to accompany it. . . . It may be thought that suicide follows revolt—but wrongly. . . . [The absurd] escapes suicide to the extent that it is simultaneously awareness and rejection of death. . . . The contrary of suicide, in fact, is the man condemned to death.

That revolt gives life its value. Spread out over the whole length of a life, it restores its majesty to that life. To a man devoid of blinders, there is no finer sight than that of the intelligence at grips with a reality that transcends it. The sight of human pride is unequaled. . . . I understand then why the doctrines that explain everything to me also debilitate me at the same time. They relieve me of the weight of my own life, and yet I must carry on alone.

Consciousness and revolt . . . are the contrary of renunciation. . . . It is essential to die unreconciled and not of one's own free will. Suicide is a repudiation. The absurd man can only drain everything to the bitter end, and deplete himself . . . for he knows that in that consciousness and in that day-to-day revolt he gives proof of his only truth, which is defiance (MS, 49–50, 54–5).

It is at precisely this point that we left Meursault—or, rather, we turn, with him, to reflect upon the meaning of our common situation and the earthly possibilities that are the legate of our absurd fate. Such is the significance of *The Myth of Sisyphus*.

PERSONAL ROOTS

The Break from Religion

If it is a consciousness such as Meursault's that gives rise to the meditation on the possibility of living "without transcendent appeal" that is *The Myth*, it is not at all surprising that Camus should locate the triggering event in a confrontation between a man condemned to death and a Catholic chaplain holding out the promise of immortal life. For *The Myth* is pervaded by traces of an agonized break with Christianity and may actually make complete sense only to one who has shared similar roots. Absent a consciousness once steeped in the eternal, the struggle to face life on its own terms—"without the aid of eternal values, which, temporarily perhaps, are absent or distorted in contemporary Europe" (MS, Preface)—without falling into the abyss of nihilism, hardly makes sense. *The Myth* is thus a testament to a personal struggle that echoes the trauma of a civilization.

While Camus has gone to significant lengths to objectify the content and deemphasize the importance of personal religious struggles, early manuscripts leave clear traces of their imprint.[2] Rather than speaking impersonally of what is demanded by the absurd, Camus had written, "What *I* demand of *myself* is to live *solely* with what *I* know. . . . *I* want to find out if it is possible to live without appeal" (E, 1440).[3] The personal effort of will is underscored by assertions such as claiming to "hold certain facts from which I do not *want* to separate myself," in which passage the *want* is ultimately replaced by the more impersonal *cannot* (E, 1439; MS, 51).

This effort at depersonalization needs to be seen in the light of a culture breaking away from Christianity—and, for the Frenchman Camus, that meant primarily from Catholicism. It should therefore not be surprising that Camus refers to the absurd as a "trinity." "What other trinity can I recognize," he had asked, before changing *trinité* to *verité*, "without giving rise to a hope which I don't have and which, within the limits of my condition, signifies nothing" (MS, 51; E, 1439). He goes on to observe, in a passage also dropped from the final version, "The road which leads to these facts . . . requires a great deal of effort, a very great tension, and a concerted act of will to keep one's eyes focused on that which, for so long, had blinded me" (E, 1439–40). Is it any wonder then that he can speak of this "transfigured" consciousness as offering to man "the wine of the absurd and the bread of indifference on which his greatness feeds" (MS, 52; E, 137) or that he can later counterpose both the actor (cf. MS, 82ff) and the conqueror (cf. MS, 89) to the Church? Or that he can observe that the wisdom that Sisyphus teaches "drives out of this world a god who had come into it with dissatisfaction and a preference for futile sufferings"? (MS, 122).

The Existential Connection

If, however, the origins of this essay in a sensibility in rebellion against Christian absolutism are beyond question, that existential negation, with which Camus is all too often uncritically associated, hardly provided the answer for him. Quite the contrary! He finds in existentialism the same unquenchable thirst for the Absolute and an impassioned inability to come to terms with nonbelief. This connection between Christian and existentialist belief is nicely suggested by the manner in which Camus exchanges one for the other in his study of Franz Kafka. Where, for example, the published version identifies *The Castle* with the "leap of faith" that is the "secret" of "the existentialist revolution" (MS, 131), an earlier manuscript had spoken instead of the secret of "Christian religion" (E, 1454). And his introduction to the belated publication of the essay on Kafka had clearly stated its aim as "defining an absurd way of thinking, that is, one delivered of metaphysical hope, by way of a criticism of several themes of existential philosophy" (E, 1415).

Initial signs of this distancing from existentialism may be gleaned from a consideration of Camus's 1938 critique of Sartre—at a time, it should be noted, when the initial ideas for both *The Stranger* and *The Myth* were taking shape. Camus notes Sartre's "taste for impotence . . . which leads him to choose characters who have arrived at the limits of their selves, stumbling over an absurdity they cannot overcome." They do so, he suggests, "through an excess of liberty," which emerges out of a fundamental rootlessness. "These beings, with no attachments, no principles . . . are so free they disintegrate, deaf to the call of action or creation." Sartre's "characters are, in fact, free. But their freedom is of no use to them." Speculating on Sartre's version of our absurd condition, Camus senses a twofold problem. First, these characters have absolutized their freedom to compensate for a transcendent absolute by whose loss they are haunted. Second, but less clearly, this liberty in which they are "enclosed" bears witness to a deeper isolation from the world around them and, most particularly, from nature. Freed "from [their] own nature, and reduced to self-contemplation, [Sartre's characters] become . . . aware of [their] profound indifference to everything that is not [themselves]. [They] are alone." But, so cutoff, they cannot be called to significant action and are left to contemplate the futility of their situation. "Life can be magnificent and overwhelming," comments Camus, "that is its whole tragedy." Sartre's hero in *Nausea* can only dwell upon "those aspects of man he finds repugnant" because, haunted by life's ultimate insignificance, he has no sense for "man's signs of greatness." Not tragic but pathetic and futile is the Sartrean vision of humanity from which Camus wishes to distance himself (LCE, 204, 205, 201).

Yet the tendency to lump Camus and Sartre together under the aegis of existentialism is not completely inappropriate. They do share basic concerns, nurtured by a common historical situation. If we were to seek that commonality, it most probably would lie in their effort to help us face a world in which transcendent absolutes can no longer be appealed to or relied upon. From within this shared historical and existential situation, both Sartre and Camus speak to the possibilities by which we can reconstitute a meaningful life. Demystification in the service of a liberation in which people take that control which is possible over their own lives may be said to be their shared goal. With their common emphasis on "the return to consciousness, the escape from everyday sleep," which, according to Camus, "represents the first steps of absurd freedom," "the initial themes of existentialism keep their entire value" (MS, 59).

Despite obvious similarities of theme and mood, however, important differences remain that bear directly upon my investigation. For the early Sartre of *Being and Nothingness* and before, which is all that would be relevant at this point, the For-Itself is the absurd passion to be God. It is thus haunted by an Absolute which it needs but cannot be. "Solid as a rock," this In-Itself is characterized by unchanging self-identity and persistence in being—at least from the point of view of the For-Itself. The For-Itself wishes "freely" to be the In-Itself that it is not. Being an "absurd" and contradictory passion, the problem of the Absolute is concretized in innumerable strategies of "bad faith" in which the For-Itself seeks to found itself as a being not subject to the vagaries of that temporalizing freedom that it is. Bad faith is flight from freedom by which the For-Itself seeks to hide from itself recognition of its finite and contingent being.

For Camus, on the other hand, not "bad faith" but metaphysical "hope" is the continual temptation that ever draws the human being from the possibilities of "authentic" living. Of course, Camus does not talk of "authenticity" as does Sartre, and explicitly seeks to avoid preaching. From his own experience he speaks to those who have shared his sensibility and his concerns. But his passionate commitment cannot fail to make its mark; so much so, in fact, that many have taken him as arguing for an advocacy position, which he disavows. Of course, he does not use such a morally charged term as "authenticity" in contrasting his suggested lifestyles with their opposites. But is this not the feeling he conveys? To call "the leap of faith" "philosophical suicide" is not exactly being nonevaluative and purely descriptive.

Our Experiential Location

"What distinguishes modern sensibility from classical sensibility," observes Camus, "is that the latter thrives on moral problems and the former on metaphysical problems" (MS, 104). Rooting intellectual problems in the soil of sensibility as he invariably does, Camus focuses upon the existential sources of our contemporary metaphysical concerns. And where better to observe the human effort to make sense of, and come to terms with, our shattered world than in its dramatic rendering by some of its most sensitive souls? "It would be impossible," he claims, "to insist too much on the arbitrary nature of the former opposition between art and philosophy" (MS, 96).[4]

"To think is first of all to create a world (or to limit one's own world, which comes to the same thing). . . . The philosopher, even if he is Kant, is a creator. He has his characters, his symbols, and his secret action. He has his plot endings" (MS, 99–100). Similarly, "the novel has its logic, its reasonings, its intuition, and its postulates. It also has its requirements of clarity." The best novels "carry with them their universe" (MS, 100). How better to give expression to a world that has lost its depth? "For the absurd man it is not a matter of explaining and solving, but of experiencing and describing" (MS, 94). "Incapable of refining the real, [absurd] thought pauses to mimic it" (MS, 101).

It might be suggested that the novel is the appropriate philosophical expression of the experience of life's absurdity (along, perhaps, with the epigram). How better to express the felt pervasiveness of the absurd? "Great feelings take with them their own universe, splendid or abject. They light up with their passion an exclusive world in which they recognize their climate. There is a universe of jealousy, of ambition, of selfishness, or of generosity. [Or with Caligula, of the demand for salvation.] A universe—in other words, a metaphysic and an attitude of mind" (MS, 10).

It is within the universe lighted up by the experience of absurdity that Camus's effort at clarification begins. He accepts the truths of science as legitimate expressions of reason's effort to make sense of existence. He recognizes their tentative and hypothetical nature. However legitimate they may be within their sphere—and he does not in any way disparage them—they do not speak to his personal quest. Out of this experience of disproportion between the facts of experience as reason reveals them, and the *exigence onto-logique* for some fundamental meaning to life as we deeply feel it, emerges the sentiment of life's absurdity. At the present moment, reason does not offer any answer to the metaphysical demand generated by that *exigence onto-logique*. Yet the demand remains. What he asks for is a rule of life for that condition which he recognizes as his. He does not want someone to tell him how to deny what seem to him palpable givens. He wants to know whether, starting from within the existential confines defined by the absurd, life can still be shown to be worth living—and, if so, what the rule of conduct is for that condition.

Limitations of Intent

If *The Myth* treats of a culturally important idea, however, it is not the only, nor necessarily the most pervasive, one. In fact, Camus's essay "leaves out altogether the most widespread spiritual attitude of our enlightened age: the one, based on the principle that all is reason, which aims to explain the world" (MS, 42). (It is, of course, that attitude with which he will be primarily concerned in *The Rebel*, although I have already suggested some of its possible roots in the disabused sensibility here studied.) Rather, his aim is "to shed light upon the step taken by the mind when, starting from a philosophy of the world's lack of meaning, it ends up by finding a meaning and depth in it" (MS, 42).

But I must not jump too far ahead, lest I go astray. If there is a logic that Camus is pursuing here, it does not follow that he is arguing for a philosophy. He is seeking to diagnose a malady, albeit an intellectual one, from which he and many of his contemporaries suffer in order to point the way toward a cure. He is not claiming that those who do not suffer from that malady are wrong, any more than he suggests that his cure is proof of the illegitimacy of other remedies. He is simply seeking to determine the logic of those alternative prescriptions.

Could he have been clearer about the personal roots or the conceptual limitations of his essay? "Let us not miss this opportunity to point out the relative character of this essay," he wrote in an early footnote (MS, 5), commenting on the many possible reasons for suicide. The self-imposed limits of the essay are repeated on numerous occasions, as when he contrasts the Western "acceptance of the world" with Oriental thought's choice "*against* the world.*" Such a choice, he notes, "is just as legitimate and gives this essay its perspectives and its limits" (MS, 64).

More to the point, after criticizing the "leap," he asserts that it is "just as legitimate as any attitude of mind" (MS, 33). It is "not the affirmation of God that is questioned here," he says further on, "but rather the logic leading to that affirmation" (MS, 42n). "I am taking the liberty . . . of calling the existential attitude philosophical suicide. But this does not imply a judgement. It is a convenient way of indicating the movement by which a thought negates itself and tends to transcend itself in its very negation" (MS, 41). To the charge that he is not doing justice to the richness of existentialist thought he responds that he is "simply borrowing a theme from them and examining whether its consequences can fit the already established rules. It is merely a matter of persistence" (MS, 37–8).

But if proof is not the issue, what then is? What are those "established rules"? And what is being herein "essayed"? "What have I done however other than to reflect upon an idea that I have found in the streets of my time? That I have nourished this idea (and that a part of me may always nourish it) with my entire generation, that goes without saying. I have simply taken the necessary distance from it in order to treat it and to decide its logic" (*L'Eté* LCE, 159).

Wanting to purge his thought of the purely personal, and to explore its implicit logic, Camus continually refined his essay, as we have seen, in the direction of greater objectivity and universality of expression. Thus many readers were led to read more into his argument than he intended. And yet, repeatedly, throughout the essay, he sought to underscore its limits. Not a philosophy of the absurd, nor an effort to prove that suicide is unjustifiable, nor even a critique of religion and the "leap of faith," *The Myth* expresses Camus's determination to work out a rule of life consonant with the absurd. "To prove the absurdity of life cannot be an end, but only a beginning" observed Camus, when reviewing Sartre's *Nausea* in 1939. "It is not this discovery which is interesting, but the consequences and the rules of action that can be drawn from it" (LCE, 201–2).

It is perhaps impossible to insist too greatly upon the personal roots and the continuing personal significance of the meditation that is *The Myth*. Beginning with a sense of what the world holds and of the truths of science,

Camus comes to reflective consciousness within the conceptual confines of a world that hasn't any rational grounds for transcendent belief nor any obvious and self-evident factual bases. These are the "facts" with which he begins. He does not assert that new facts might not arise that would change this situation or that new insights or transformed belief systems might not lead to other rational conclusions as to the meaning of life. He asserts only that these views are not currently available to him and that he does not see them as being on the horizon. In short, it is presently impossible for him rationally to ground such beliefs.

At the same time, he brings to his quest a deep-seated need for transcendent significance to give depth to the activities of ordinary life. He is sure that he shares this need with many of his generation and perhaps with most reflective westerners.

What is the upshot of this deeply felt experiential bind? Must life be judged meaningless because we cannot rationally satisfy our need for transcendent significance? Is suicide not a rational response? Or must one make the "leap of faith," believing that since life cannot flourish without transcendent significance, there must be such a "truth"?

These questions focus Camus's inquiry. He holds, as he says, certain truths from which he cannot separate himself. These truths are not a priori or axiomatic. They are simply experiential givens that provide the context for the emergence of an absurd sensibility. They inscribe themselves within the experience of one who is also committed to living only with what he knows. To respect intelligence for Camus is equivalent to refusing to "play fast and loose with the order realities take" in his experience. Can one live meaningfully while remaining within the bounds of the experientially given?

Camus is not denying the right of an individual to "take the leap" but merely contesting the claim to a logic that leads there. Nothing in experience rationally justifies such a faith. Reason, of course, does not rule it out. In fact, reason has nothing to say about it. That is his point. Neither are individuals obliged to remain committed to, or limited by, reason. They may, like St. Thomas, say that where reason ends faith begins. For Camus, that attitude is as legitimate as any other. He simply wants to point out that no rational justification or any empirical evidence sustains it (MS, 40). And he rejects "the leap" simply because it does not answer to the demands that he has placed upon his inquiry. These demands begin with a commitment to the facts as the senses reveal them, and to the inferences that reason can draw from those facts, and nothing more. "My reasoning wants to be faithful to the evidence which aroused it" (MS, 49–50).

Is this enough? In the Western world, metaphysically sculpted by Greco-Roman and Judeo-Christian perspectives, that *exigence ontologique* has taken the shape of transcendence, usually contoured by belief in divine purposeful-ness and an afterlife. Within an experience so contoured, to encounter the nonexistence of the transcendent is to confront a world pervaded by the sense of Divine Absence. In such a world we may feel uprooted, cut adrift, torn between the inner need for a ground of being and the outer reality of a life that is purposeless and no longer worth the effort. The temptation is no doubt profound to insist that the need *must* be met: to believe even though, or, out of spite perhaps, because, it is absurd. Or to conclude, like Bazarov, that life is not worth living because it lacks ultimate significance, and that it is therefore legitimate "to smash everything." Or, like Camus's imaginary Ger-man friend, that the only "values" are those of the "purported" animal world, namely force and violence.

Here is the nub of the problem to which *The Myth* is addressed. Torn between the nihilistic abyss of metaphysical despair and the illusory summit of metaphysical hope, Camus searches for a middle way—"I only wish to remain on this middle path where the intelligence can remain clear"—a path that, while remaining true both to the experiential givens and to reason as our only but limited guide, leads us into a life that, though without ultimate significance, is found to be worth the effort.

THE SEDUCTION OF HOPE

Kafka's Nostalgia

The "intellectual ailment" that, phoenix-like, continually gives rise to metaphysical hope seems rooted in the quasi-ontological need to believe life has a transcendent purpose. In this soil, which has so long nurtured reli-gion, Camus strives to clear away the brush of logical confusions, and then to uproot that hope by which "man is delivered from the weight of his own life" (MS, 136) and led to submit to a nonexistent future. The full destruc-tive implications of that seemingly ineradicable hope do not become clear until *The Rebel*. But *The Myth* traces the failed logic by which humans seek to restore a faith when all seems lost. An undercurrent of this work is the powerful undertow that, regardless of the facts, would drag even the most sophisticated thinkers into the maelstrom of a transcendent belief that they do not seem quite able to give up.

It is this undertow by which Sartre is pulled along, according to Camus. Here lies the root of that ontological "desire to be God," which Sartre saw at the base of human effort, and later admitted to have been the constitutive structure of his own "project to be." Even later, it is Sartre's commitment to what Camus believes to be a messianic vision of the role of the Communist party that dynamizes his attack on *The Rebel*. Camus has this in mind when he criticizes "existential *preaching* . . . with its spiritual leap which basically escapes consciousness."

Nowhere, perhaps, is this struggle to draw hope out of the depths of despair more poignantly expressed than in the writings of Franz Kafka. In *The Castle*,

the absurd is recognized, accepted, and man is resigned to it, but from then on we know that it has ceased to be the absurd. Within the limits of the human condition, what greater hope than the hope that allows an escape from that condition? As I see once more, existential thought in this regard . . . is steeped in a vast hope. The very hope which . . . inflamed the ancient world. But in that leap that characterizes *all* existential thought . . . in that surveying of a divinity devoid of surface, how can one fail to see the mark of a lucidity that repudiates itself? (MS, 135, my italics).

In *The Trial* Kafka described the human condition from the perspective of the absurd, but found that terrain too barren and desolate. He could neither live there nor find a way out. He remains haunted by the absent absolute, which becomes the central theme of *The Castle*. "*The Trial* poses a problem which *The Castle*, to a certain degree, resolves. The first describes, following a quasi-scientific method, and doesn't conclude. The second, to a certain degree, explains. *The Trial* diagnoses and *The Castle* imagines a treatment" (E, 205; MS, 130).

In the movement from the one to the other Camus sees Kafka making explicit the experiential path by which existentialist thinkers have sought to resolve their personal struggles.

The more truly absurd *The Trial* is, the more moving and illegitimate the impassioned "leap" of *The Castle* seems. But we find here again in a pure state the paradox of existential thought as it is expressed, for instance, by Kierkegaard: "Earthly hope must be killed; only then can one be saved by true hope," which can be translated: "One has to have written *The Trial* to undertake *The Castle*" (MS, 134).

Camus finds in Kafka both the evocation of the absurdity of contemporary existence and the inability to give up hope in a salvific future.[5] In spite of failure, discouragement, and lack of support or evidence, "nostalgia for a lost paradise" draws him on. "Here is found the secret of the melancholy peculiar to Kafka . . . that probably futile trip, that probably wasted day, that probably empty hope. 'Probably'—on this implication Kafka gambles his entire work" (MS, 131).

"If nostalgia is the mark of the human, perhaps no one has given such flesh and volume to these phantoms of regret" (MS, 137) as has Kafka. But have I not here drawn forth the threadbare strands by which we struggle to sustain a transcendent faith by which we can no longer live, but have not yet learned how to live without? Are these not the existential roots that tear apart the modern soul? Are not here the Christian themes of existential thought? It may sound strange to suggest that even such an avowedly atheistic existentialist as Sartre is deeply marked by Christian themes, and yet, at the ontological level here being excavated, that is what Camus is suggesting. The metaphysics of Christianity is the historical ground of that ever renascent hope that must be laid to rest.

Kirlov's Gift

The burden of that liberation is freely undertaken by Kirlov, who will finally "bring forth into the light of day this subterfuge" (E, 1455; cf. E, 211 & MS, 138) that is Christ's message. Christ died so that we might be saved, but from what? From the responsibility and anguish, from the burden and ultimate failure, that are the lot of natural existence. Christ brings the message of resignation in this life and of subordination of concrete meanings to otherworldly perspectives. Salvation is promised to those who turn their backs on the incarnate present. Metaphysical hope is born out of historical humiliation. Resignation to the suffering of innocents will be rewarded by eternal life.

Kirlov in fact fancies for a moment that Jesus at his death *did not find himself in Paradise*. He found out then that his torture had been useless. "The laws of nature," says the engineer [Kirlov], "made Christ live in the midst of falsehood and die for a falsehood." Solely in this sense Jesus indeed personifies the whole human drama. He is the complete man, being the one who realized the most absurd condition. He is not the God-man but the man-god. And, like him, each of us can be crucified and victimized—and is to a certain degree (MS, 107).

It is this subterfuge that Kirlov will lay bare. The illusions of another life rob humans of the possibility of recapturing their capacity to make something of this life. These illusions must be torn away. By killing himself he will reveal that there are no limits other than mortality to what humans can be.[6]

Freed of the illusions of another life, we can now face the challenge of what to make of this one. "If God exists, all depends upon him and we can do nothing against his will. If he does not exist, everything depends on us." Only by realizing that we cannot look elsewhere for salvation, will we be able to turn our attention to the truly herculean task of assuming responsibility for the direction of our own lives. Enthralled and seduced by the exemplary sacrifice of Jesus, we remain prisoners of illusion. Kirlov, "out of love for humanity," must kill himself in order to "show his brothers a royal and difficult path" to their own liberation. "Once he is dead and men are at last enlightened, this earth will be peopled with tsars and lighted up with human glory" (MS, 108–9).

In dramatic form, Kirlov offers the sacrifice that Meursault is forced to make. But his decision to kill himself expresses a still lurking messianic sensibility, by which he dreams of being the man-god. His attitude remains framed by the metaphysical "all or nothing." "'Do you believe in eternal life in the other world?'" Stavrogin had asked. To which Kirlov responded: "'No, but in eternal life in this world'" (MS, 108).

Camus describes Kirlov's thinking as follows: "If God does not exist, Kirlov is god. If God does not exist, Kirlov must kill himself. Kirlov must therefore kill himself to become god." For Camus, it is no wonder that the followers of Kirlov are led to such destructive extremes of behavior. Such is the snare of Absolute Truth.[7]

Meursault's revolt, on the other hand, bespeaks a quite different sensibility that has dispensed with such messianic aspirations. It is the aim of *The Myth* to make this alternative believable.

THE ABSURD

The Emergence of the Absurd

In a now classic statement, Camus observes that the absurd emerges in "that odd state of soul in which the void becomes eloquent, in which the chain of daily gestures is broken, in which the heart vainly seeks the link that will connect it again" (MS, 10). To be sure, his description of the collapse of the stage setting is in no way exhaustive of the situations in which the absurd may arise. But it is suggestive. In "The Hollow Men," T. S. Eliot brilliantly evokes this contemporary sense of dislocation:

> Between the idea
> And the reality
> Between the motion
> And the act
> Falls the Shadow . . .

> Between the conception
> And the creation
> Between the emotion
> And the response
> Falls the Shadow . . .

Between the desire
And the spasm
Between the potency
And the existence
Between the essence
And the descent
Falls the Shadow . . .

Camus explores five sources of existential dislocation: society, time, nature, others, and death. At any moment, in ways often quite unexpected though seemingly endemic to the modern world, the natural flow of events may be cut short. We may feel life slipping away from us, or lose our sense of purpose, or be struck by the inevitability of our own death. Nature may be brusquely encountered as a powerful and alien force; or we may suddenly recognize the ceremony that is social routine.

"But one day the 'why' arises and everything begins in that weariness tinged with amazement" (MS, 13). From dislocation to articulation and response, a new world emerges, frightening and uncertain. There is no unique experience of the absurd, rather an innumerable series of fundamentally dichotomous experiences. Intellectual problems arise as soon as one tries to make sense of the experience. "Between the certainty I have of my existence and the content I try to give to that assurance, the gap will never be filled" (MS, 19).

If there is an initial common response to the encounter with absurdity, it is probably a mixture of outrage and despair. While the despair invites passivity, the outrage demands satisfaction, thus instituting the original movement of revolt. Outrage, it should be noted, is the root experience that's seen in *The Rebel* as giving rise to rebellion (MS, 47).

Expressions of outrage vary as to direction, scope, and intensity. At one extreme might be Caligula's metaphysical rebellion against the order of things when he realized that "men die, and they are not happy." Alternatively, despair might turn inward as resignation, resentment, indifference, or the more definitive judgment that it's not worth the effort to which suicide testifies.

In any case, we must take care to avoid excessive pathos. Whatever the importance of this sensibility of life's fundamental dislocation and its attendant quest, Camus takes pains to remind us that the perception of the absurd is "but one perception among many," and its standpoint is provisional. For example, the absurd plays a quite limited role in *The Rebel*.

"The feeling of the absurd is not, for all that, the notion of the absurd," writes Camus. "It lays the foundation for it, and that is all. It is not limited to that notion, except in the brief moment when it passes judgment on the universe. Subsequently it has a chance of going further. It is alive; in other words, it must die or reverberate." " 'Begins,' that is important," says Camus of the collapse of the stage setting. "Weariness comes at the end of the acts of a mechanical life, but at the same time it inaugurates the impulse of consciousness" (MS, 10).[8] It is consciousness that inaugurates and maintains the break, and there alone a response is to be made. "If I were a tree among trees, a cat among animals, this life would have a meaning, or rather this problem would not arise, for I should belong to this world. I should *be* this world to which I am now opposed by my whole consciousness and my whole insistence upon familiarity" (MS, 38). Without that ontological "insistence upon familiarity" there would still be no absurd.

Camus is thus speaking from within a certain sensibility in which "the stage setting has collapsed." It is as if we had been unceremoniously thrust out of our cosmic home. We have lost our place. Our world no longer seems to have been prepared for us. Our destiny is not overseen by a providential deity. Even worse, it seems not to be overseen by any deity whatsoever. We have become metaphysical refugees, aliens in a world not of our choosing. Each of us is now alone, to confront our individual destiny with, at best, a highly uncertain sense of the human collectivity.

The Meaning of the Absurd

And what exactly is this absurd?

If I accuse an innocent man of a monstrous crime, if I tell a virtuous man that he has coveted his own sister, he will reply that this is absurd. . . . The virtuous man illustrates by that reply the definitive *antinomy* existing between the deed . . . and his lifelong principles. "It's absurd" means "It's impossible" but also "It's contradictory." If I see a man armed only with a sword attack a group of machine guns, I shall consider his act to be absurd. But it is so solely by virtue of the *disproportion* between his intention and the reality he will encounter, of the contradiction I notice between his true strength and the aim he has in view (MS, 22, my italics).

The (implicit) unity of experience has been shattered. The intention and the reality meet across a now unbridgeable abyss, united only by nostalgia. Consciousness struggles to maintain its grasp of a world that eludes it. "My reasoning wants to be faithful to the evidence that aroused it," observes Camus.

That evidence is the absurd. It is that divorce between the mind that desires and the world that disappoints, my nostalgia for unity, this fragmented universe and the contradiction that binds them together. . . . It [is] a matter of living and thinking with those dislocations. . . . There can be no question of masking the evidence, of suppressing the absurd by denying one of the terms of the equation. It is essential to know whether one can live with it or whether, on the other hand, logic commands one to die of it. I am not interested in philosophical suicide, but rather in plain suicide. I merely wish to purge it of its emotional content and know its logic and its integrity (MS, 37).

THE SEDUCTION

The Myth of Sisyphus thus has a very limited and well-defined objective: from *within* the existential space defined by the experience of a generation, to explore the possibilities for meaning that life offers *on its own terms*. Can one remain true to the experience of the absurd, yet go beyond the nihilism that has seemed to be its unavoidable companion? "I want to know whether I can live with what I know and with that alone" (MS, 40).

Camus, like so many others, felt the appeal of the transcendent. Such belief, however poignantly desired, seems rationally unjustified. On what grounds can one defend that belief without denying the experience that had initially given birth to the inquiry? Is there not something dishonest in such a procedure? Unable to shake the feeling of dishonesty, Camus explores the possibility of living with what experience alone reveals. Hence his rule of method: "If I attempt to solve a problem, at least I must not by that very solution conjure away one of the terms of the problem" (MS, 31).

As for the Christian appeal to a faith in that which transcends understanding, Camus cannot see the logic.

Even if fellow-feeling inclines one toward [salvific hope], still it must be said that excess justifies nothing. That transcends, as the saying goes, the human scale; therefore it must be superhuman. But this "therefore" is superfluous. There is no logical certainty [there]. There is no experimental probability either. All I can say is that, in fact, that transcends my scale. If I do not draw a negation from it, at least I do not want to found anything on the incomprehensible (MS, 40).

"To Chestov," Camus observes, "reason is useless but there is something beyond reason. To an absurd mind reason is useless and there is nothing beyond reason" (MS, 35). "It is a matter of living in that state of the absurd. I know on what it is founded, this mind and this world straining against each other without being able to embrace. I ask for the rule of life of that state. . . . I ask what is involved in the condition I recognize as mine" (E, 128; MS, 40–1). As for those who invite "the leap," "they do not respond to my intention" (E, 128; MS, 41).

If, rather than offering an answer, hope may be seen as a seductive subterfuge, it is educative nonetheless. "We recognize our course by discovering the paths which stray from it" (MS, 113). Most particularly when, as with

Kafka or Dostoevsky, they are fertilized by the soil of the absurd. What is in the nature of the terrain that continually calls forth such metaphysical fruit?

Salvific faith answers existential despair. Hope and suicide are one to the precise extent that both are grounded in the inarticulate sense of life's intrinsic meaninglessness. Hope—and Camus uses the word here *only* in the metaphysical sense—means that life is worth the effort only to the extent that it has transcendent significance. On its own terms it is a loss. A mind so imbued must look beyond. But, as we have seen, there is no logic to that transition. The "because" is emotional, not rational. It is to this "golgotha" of the intellect that Camus refers when he speaks of philosophical suicide. It is the consequence of the conclusion that only a leap of faith in the existence of transcendent meaning can rescue life from the hopelessness and futility that otherwise would be its fate.

But what generates such a conclusion? Is it self-evident? An unalterable and eternal verity? Or, perhaps, just a Western imposition that contains poised within the destructive seeds of nihilism?

One kills oneself because life is not worth living, that is . . . a truism. But does that insult to existence, that flat denial in which it is plunged come from the fact that it has no meaning? Does its absurdity require one to escape it through hope or suicide —that is what must be clarified, hunted down, and elucidated while brushing aside all the rest. Does the Absurd dictate death? (MS, 8–9).

Joining with Nietzsche's effort to contribute to a transvaluation of values by unmasking everything by which the nihilism of our age was being hidden from itself, Camus has sought to describe that lived but inarticulate nihilism that is at the root of contemporary transcendent faiths. In *The Myth* the problem is first posed by Christianity, and then by the philosophical suicides of existentialism. In *The Rebel*, picking up the untapped strain of rationalism, which is "the most widespread spiritual attitude of our enlightened age," Camus explores the nihilistic roots of historical messianisms—of which more later.

Responding, in 1950, to a reporter's question, Camus observed, according to Emmett Parker:

The world . . . was governed by the nihilists and it was up to those who believed in the existence of certain values to affirm them and to give them form. . . . The struggle against nihilism was a battle against time. Crying that time was short was a waste of time. "But if we succeed during this time in defining what is opposed to nihilism, illustrate it, make others share it, then our chances of success will increase and we will gain time." The true task of the artist, Camus insisted, was to maintain, amid outcries and violence, our lucidity, our generosity and our will to live (Parker, 117–8).

THE *EXIGENCE ONTOLOGIQUE*

Some Conceptual Ambiguities

Whatever may be the plays on words and the acrobatics of logic, to understand is, above all, to unify. The mind's deepest desire, even in its most elaborate operations, parallels man's unconscious feeling in the face of his universe: it is an insistence upon familiarity, an appetite for clarity. Understanding the world . . . is reducing it to the human. . . . That nostalgia for unity, that appetite for the absolute, illustrates the essential impulse of the human drama (MS, 17; E, 110).

Clearly the demand for unity is answering to a felt, though inarticulate, need to belong. Remember our starting point: the dawning realization, for Camus personally and for the West more generally, that our existence is without transcendent significance. Having been put on this earth for no apparent reason, we find, according to contemporary science, that we evolved in a more or less haphazard way from other species on an earth whose origin is uncertain, whose place in a practically infinite universe is negligible, and whose future is insignificant. The struggle to come to terms with these emerging scientific truths—especially in the face of a several-thousand-year history that has embedded in our collective psyche the sense that, devoid of transcendent purpose, life is not worth living—has left us facing a metaphysical void. It is as if some of us were thrashing around in search of a myth to replace Judeo-Christianity, while others, disillusioned by that loss, have been drawn to nihilistic beliefs and actions.

I said that this world is absurd, but I was too hasty. This world in itself is not reasonable, that is all that can be said. But what is absurd is the confrontation of this irrationality and the wild longing for clarity whose call echoes in the human heart. The absurd depends as much on man as on the world (MS, 21; E, 113).

Thus Camus presents his sense of what we may call the *exigence ontologique* by which the human being's most fundamental needs are to be understood. Here is the source of that metaphysical demand for rationality or coherence. Here also is the companion existential demand for familiarity, for a feeling of being "at one with" or "at home in" the world around us. It is these twin and coordinate demands for coherence and familiarity that Camus has in mind whenever he refers to the hunger for unity, for a truth that will at least momentarily assuage our sense of estrangement, of alienation.

It is of course important to recognize the common root of the need to unify as well as to underscore the distinct though companion aspects of its expression. The existential sense must be seen and appreciated as distinct from the metaphysical demand. The former is often inarticulate, more a matter of mood, or feeling tone, that pervades our individual experience, qualifying, behind our back as it were, our encounter with others, with nature, and with our sense of life and its possibilities. Of course, this existential sense relates to the lived meaning of our world; it is not simply a matter of biology or physiology, hence it implicates the metaphysical concern with the articulate structure of meanings by which we live. Thus this distinction has something arbitrary in it. But it is, nonetheless, not without significance, as it highlights distinct strands of this basic "exigence."

By metaphysical demand for coherence is meant, then, the conceptual and often reflective concern to make coherent sense of the human condition. To develop a theoretical frame within which particular human actions—even one's entire life—may be seen as part of a more comprehensive frame of reference. This is what Camus means when he suggests that if at least one thing could be explained this thirst for unity would be assuaged, and we would not feel that the world is so alien.

But there is an important confusion that seems to operate in Camus's conception of coherence. Instead of distinguishing between rational coherence and purposefulness, he often speaks as if they were interchangeable. But this is certainly in error. It is entirely possible for us to conceive of a universe —many scientists, in fact, believe this to be the case—which is essentially coherent, operating entirely in accord with known or knowable natural laws. Given that we have not yet established the truth of such a perspective, many scientists may be said to have a faith about the nature of our universe. It might even be said that science presupposes such a faith, though that claim is more dubious. In any case, it is perfectly conceivable that the universe is so ordered. But that in no way assures its purposefulness, nor does it providentially guarantee our future. In fact, our fate may be no less absurd, at least as far as our needs and aspirations are concerned.

The point to be underscored here is that the universe may be rationally coherent yet not purposeful. There may still be a quite poignant divorce between our desire for familiarity and a world in which we are but the intelligible products of natural forces operating in accord with impartial physical laws. The question of purpose, on the other hand, would seem to require the existence of some being—a god of sorts—whose purpose this world is. It is this notion that seems required by the more profound sense of need that has become so pervasive in the West. Certainly this need is the hidden source of the derailments that Camus explores in *The Rebel* as well as of the longings for oppression that feed the hero of *The Fall*.

Nevertheless, the absurd registers the distance between what we need in order to be at one with ourselves and our destiny and the objective scene in which we find ourselves called upon to make our way. In Heideggerian terms, we find ourselves thrown into a world, not of our choosing, that cares not for our concerns. We try to humanize our surroundings and to build a world in which we feel we belong. But otherness pervades our efforts, insuring the ultimate personal defeat that is death and, as Djémila proved, wearing away our collective efforts through time. "From the point of view of Sirius," reflects Camus, what can be the ultimate significance of anything we do? "That idea has always contained a lesson" (MS, 78).

But precisely what lesson? we might ask. And what bearing does it have on the *exigence ontologique* that finds expression in our desire to unify the world? Under what conditions can life still be found to be meaningful? That last question suggests a prior one: What is it that threatens to rob life of its meaning? The fact that we are finite and fated to die? Or that life has no overall purpose or direction? Or that it lacks intrinsic coherence? Or that we cannot understand how we got here and what makes the world function as it does? Do we really need to understand existence in order to feel that it makes sense? Does making sense equal being worth the effort?

Sometimes Camus writes as if the ultimate absurdity consists in our being fated to die. At other times, he suggests that understanding the nature of existence would reconcile us to our condition. At still other times, the absurd seems to emerge out of the arbitrary and random nature of our lives—perhaps as an expression of its lack of purpose or direction.

But these are clearly not equivalent expressions of one common problem, however related they may be. Would Camus, for example, mean to suggest that obtaining an adequate and comprehensive theory of existence would assuage our *exigence ontologique*? I doubt it.

On the other hand, if we were given an indubitable assurance of personal immortality (even without understanding how and why) or of divine purposefulness, I suspect that would be felt to be more satisfactory. Of course, these distinct possibilities are themselves melded into one for Camus, though in principle they need not be.[9]

For *The Stranger*, for example, the absurdity of existence is expressed both by the randomness of events and by society's need to impose rational coherence. From the counterposition of these two factors the absurd trinity dramatically emerges. What then can we say of Meursault's personal struggle to face his imminent death? Here, at least, Camus seems to come down on the side of living on, rather than of comprehension or coherence.

In short, although Camus occasionally confuses the issue, he is primarily concerned with the loss of belief in any extrinsic or transcendent meaning to existence. References to unity suggest the need to feel that life is the expression of an overriding purpose that gives direction to daily activity, thus saving it and releasing us from the insignificance that would otherwise follow from the inevitability of our death. Unity thus means overarching purposefulness, within which our finitude is framed by transcendent meaningfulness. To feel that we are not alone, but rather have a place in an all-encompassing and eternally significant cosmic drama, would dramatically transform the meaning of our situation.

Such a sense of belonging would answer the fear of death with a promise that would make it all worthwhile. Here is the root need upon which Camus focuses his attention. It is the gnawing, and potentially debilitating, sense that the need cannot be met—or at least, the growing doubt that there is any adequate way of addressing it—that brings contemporary humanity to the brink of a metaphysical abyss.

The Search for Totality

The gnawing emptiness occasioned by the metaphysical abyss demands consolation. Even more, it wants hope. It yearns for a total solution to human contingency. The *exigence ontologique* that demands satisfaction is potential prey to the offering of totality. Here, according to Camus, among individuals suffering anomie and longing for a place to belong, is where the deranged temptations of the modern world have taken root. The exploration of this pathology of the intellect, rooted in the psychic soil of a decimated sensibility, is the concern of *The Rebel*. But if false alternatives are the concern in that work, a historically cluttered terrain overgrown with encrusted but failed religious beliefs hides the game being hunted here. "I don't know whether this world has a meaning that transcends it. But I know that I do not know that meaning and that it is impossible for me just now to know it" (MS, 51).

Do we really need such transcendent props in order to go about our finite business? Can we not satisfy our need to belong on a more modest scale? Can we not develop an experiential and felt unity that, while not answering ultimate demands, "is enough to fill a man's heart"? "I have nothing to do with ideas or with the eternal," observes Camus's conqueror. "The truths that are within my range are those that the hand can touch. I cannot separate myself from them" (E, 167; MS, 89). "Knowing whether or not one can live without appeal is all that interests me" (MS, 60).

The desperation of our metaphysical predicament has tempted many toward extravagant solutions—even to the extent of seeming to flirt with, if not actually welcome, nuclear annihilation as the fulfillment of divine prophecy, thus putting an end to our historical misery. None of these most recent threats to humanity's survival would have surprised Camus or his mentor on this issue, Nietzsche—both of whom thought that the death of God threatened to bring crashing down the entire edifice of a civilization built on its foundation.

But if these are our times, we must try to find a way to live in them.

If I hold as true that absurdity which determines my relation to life, if I am thoroughly imbued with this sentiment by which the spectacle of the world seizes me—with this clarity of insight which scientific research imposes upon me—I must sacrifice everything to these certainties and I must face them squarely in order to be able to sustain them. Above all, I must determine my conduct in relation to them and pursue them in all their consequences. I am speaking here of honesty. But I want to know beforehand if thought can live in these deserts (E, 113; MS, 21–2).

Before considering his "relative utopias" (A/I, 159), I should clear up any lingering confusions concerning the apparently opposed emphasis placed on diversity in *The Myth* and on unity in *The Rebel*. The context is crucial. Unity, in *The Rebel*, is counterposed to totality, an ideological claim that purports to offer a definitive interpretation of, and solution for, life's struggles. Since daily living does not seem to generate such meanings on its own, Camus believes that they can only be imposed upon it. Any such imposition would seem to require belief in a special insight or revelation available to a select group. Whatever the legitimacy of such a claimed truth, from the perspective of those to whom it is not given but upon whom it is imposed it can only be experienced as oppressive. Such claims not only delegitimate alternative experiences, justifying subordination, but constitute methodologically closed circles that are self-justifying. Personal expression and individual dignity can obtain no independent status within the metaphysical horizons of such an empirically closed universe. But of these issues, more later.

By unity, on the other hand, is meant the integral experiential coherence that organically emerges from the free exercise of individual or collective choice. There is nothing here antagonistic to the experienced diversity of qualities, activities, beliefs, and lifestyles described in *The Myth*. Quite the contrary, such unities presuppose and value it. This is the meaning of giving style to one's life, which constitutes the existential core of Camus's vision in both art and politics.

And that is precisely what Camus praises in *The Myth*. By unity he there means what totality means in *The Rebel*. The transformation of expression registers an altered problematic. Where *The Rebel* sought to demystify ideology, the central concern of *The Myth* was to combat nihilism (and the illusory hope often built upon it). The emphasis on diversity is directed at freeing experience from the constraints of preexistent hierarchies of meaning so that lucid consciousness may be able to confront anew the practically infinite variety of qualities and values that experience concretely offers. "How could the Church"—that classic repository of transcendent hope—"have failed to condemn" the actor for his "emotional debauchery, [and] the scandalous pretention of a spirit which refuses to live only one destiny and gives itself over to all forms of excess?" asks Camus (MS, 82; E, 161). Here diversity clearly means liberation from transcendent illusion. But it does not mean randomness and total incoherence. That was the Achilles' heel of Meursault's life.

Between the "all or nothing" there remains a world "of which man is the sole master" (MS, 117). Form must be given to that world for it truly to be ours. Suggestive of his later emphasis upon style, Camus invites us, like his absurd heroes, to gather together the strands of our life: "To create is also to give a form to one's destiny" (MS, 117; E, 192).

AN UNCERTAIN PATH

Thus the absurd, teaching us that "there is no tomorrow" (E, 141; MS, 58), transforms our moral perspective. "Deprived of the eternal," says the conqueror, "I want to ally myself with time" (MS, 86). "Before encountering the absurd, the average man lives with purposes. . . . To the extent to which he imagined a purpose to his life, he adapted himself to the demands of a goal to be achieved and became the slave of his freedom" (E, 140, 141; MS, 57, 58). Once the illusions of another life are gone, along with the attendant psychic and moral constrictions of our thinking, feeling, and behaving, a new world opens up for us.

All that remains is a fate whose outcome alone is fatal. Outside of that single fatality of death, everything, joy or happiness,[10] is liberty. A world remains of which man is the sole master. What bound him was the illusion of another world. The outcome of his thought, ceasing to be renunciatory, flowers in images. . . .
Not the divine fable that amuses and blinds, but the terrestrial face, gesture, and drama in which are summed up a difficult wisdom and an ephemeral passion (MS, 117–8).[11]

No longer aspiring to immortal life, we are free at last to seek to "exhaust the field of the possible." Unleashing the once chained passion for living, however, requires the will to maintain lucid consciousness of concrete details freed both from the potential seduction of transcendent meanings and from resignation attendant upon the realization of the absence of absolute significance. This is the original *personal* meaning of revolt for Camus. Revolt is initially the upsurge of outrage upon the realization of the fact of death, and the impassioned refusal to allow that fact to rob life of its significance. His confrontation with death at an early age when he contracted tuberculosis was the initial crucible for the forging of this consciousness of revolt. Consequently, Camus focuses upon the way that daily living to which his social condition condemned him tended to fritter away his newly found precious and irreplaceable existence. Revolt then becomes the rejection of the daily routines of habit with their attendant moral injunctions. Thus, *A Happy Death*. Refusal "to play the game" demands that revolt generate a new morality. These two strands of revolt, therefore, merge into the rejection of efforts to compensate for the emptiness that finitude threatens by having recourse to hope, to a transcendent ground for meaning. That was the experience Camus describes before the inscriptions in Florence, recapitulated by Meursault in his cell. With that rejection of a transcendent ground comes the rejection of its attendant moral injunctions.

Revolt thus rooted in the consciousness of one's irreplaceable finitude demands a passionate and lucid commitment to the possibilities of animal existence no longer hemmed in by the illusory moralism of the transcendent. No wonder Camus can conclude that the absurd offers the possibility for the first time of truly living. "It was previously a question of finding out whether or not life had to have a meaning to be lived. It now becomes clear, on the contrary, that it will be lived all the better if it has no meaning" (MS, 53). From a rule of despair Camus draws an invitation to live.

Living is keeping the absurd alive. . . . Revolt . . . is a constant confrontation between man and his own obscurity. . . . It challenges the world anew every second. . . . Metaphysical revolt extends awareness to the whole of experience. It is . . . the certainty of a crushing fate, without the resignation that ought to accompany it (MS, 53–4).

Revolt, freedom, and passion thus become the rules of conduct of this newly discovered life.

An adequate response to the absurd, should such be possible, will clearly require a detailed consideration of the "social question."[12] That is clearly the position that begins to emerge with his *Letters to a German Friend*. But it is the metaphysical condition of the single individual that initially poses the question. And it is probably the experiential problem of a culture that increasingly throws one forth to struggle on one's own—increasingly cut off from traditionally sustaining communities—which undergirds the contemporary experience. "The important thing . . . is not to be cured," Camus observed, "but to live with one's ailments" (MS, 38).

"For anyone who pursues the quantity of pleasures, only efficacy matters," Camus had written (MS, 71; E, 153). "The absurd teaches that all experiences are unimportant, and . . . it urges toward the greatest quantity of experiences" (MS, 62). "The present and the succession of presents before a constantly conscious soul is the ideal of the absurd man" (MS, 63–4). "No depth, no emotion, no passion, *and no sacrifice* could render equal . . . a conscious life of forty years and a lucidity spread over sixty years" (MS, 63). "Being aware of one's life, one's revolt, one's freedom, and to the maximum, is living, and to the maximum. Where lucidity rules, the scale of values becomes useless" (MS, 63–4; E, 144).

Having thus "lost the sense of hierarchy" (MS, 56), values can only be rooted in the experiential soil fertilized by a lucid consciousness. Lacking such transcendent standards, however, how is one to choose among actions?

On what grounds? By what criteria or standards? For what goals? Ultimately, there are no justifications. An ethic of quantity thus replaces one of quality: "What counts is not living the best, but living the most" (MS, 61; E, 143). No wonder that Ivan Karamazov was so tormented by the absurd; or that Camus's "German friend" confronted him with such a profound ethico-metaphysical challenge.

It would seem that we have been freed of the illusion of hope only to be plunged into a maelstrom in which everything is permitted and moral standards no longer have a leg to stand on. Experiences are equivalent so long as consciousness is present. Consciousness is, of course, the presupposition, because it is from consciousness alone that human experience comes to be and that the quality of finitude gives the moment its irreplaceable urgency. Beyond that, however, who is to judge? Are we not reduced to the multiplication of experiences and their reflective description? What other rule of conduct can one draw from the absurd?

Is this not the import of Camus's descriptions of his heroes of the absurd? Clearly not models to emulate—for that would imply a principle of selection among lifestyles. Camus simply offers descriptions of modes of living that draw forth and illustrate the lessons of the absurd. Their common presupposition is the lucid consciousness that refuses transcendent consolation and devotes itself to "obeying the flame" (MS, 62).

But then, so does Caligula, not to speak of his German friend. And there's the rub. Camus seeks a rule of conduct by which life can be found to be worth living, and he must confront the fact that a reason for living can also be a reason for dying—or for having others die. This poses the problem central to the rest of his work. But its roots are clearly here in the struggle to legitimate a revolt against the gods that justifies individual and collective efforts to take control over our lives without having recourse to those eternal values that are absent or distorted in contemporary Europe.

5 ❧

Caligula

For the dramatist the passion for the impossible is just as valid a subject for study as avarice or adultery (CTOP, vi).

LOCATING THE WORK

Caligula's place within the developing corpus of Camus's work is unique. Begun with the fiery exuberance of youth, it underwent periodic revision almost to the year of his death, testifying to the subtle transformations of sensitivity and perspective that his work reveals.

Four stages are worthy of note. The initial inspiration to dramatize the life of the Roman emperor flowered in the climate that gave birth to *Nuptials* and *A Happy Death*. The latter work certainly seems to be *Caligula*'s twin. Both express a passionate will to live and a contempt for the hypocrisy of the everyday, torn as they are between celebrating life and coming to terms with death. Struggling to emerge from the habitual, the daily routine and social ritual, the individual stands forth in hard-won uniqueness, only to come face-to-face with a reality of death made more poignant by that singular achievement. The intrinsic tension seems almost to invite repose. Its ambiguous legacy haunts all three works—as it does *The Minotaur* of 1939. This legacy invites the emergent individual to merge with nature, to become one with it and to resemble nothing. Much here is reminiscent of Nietzsche's brilliant study of the Dionysian, which impressed Camus in those years.[1]

This initial period is submerged and somewhat hidden by Camus's increasing preoccupation with the absurd, which surfaces in 1938 and 1939. As *A Happy Death* gives way to *The Stranger*, so *Caligula* is put aside, only to be taken up again after *The Stranger* is completed and *The Myth of Sisyphus* nears final form. The version that first appeared in public resulted from this radical rethinking. Here we begin with the emperor's realization that "men die and they are not happy." No attention is paid to Caligula's life before the death of his sister and mistress, Drusilla. Rather, the focus is upon his rebellion against what he feels to be a metaphysical injustice. "Really, this world of ours, this scheme of things as they call it, is quite intolerable. That's why I want the moon, or happiness, or eternal life—something, in fact, that may sound crazy, but which isn't of this world" (CTOP, 8).

As this initial version achieves published form, the related problems posed by the absurd and by rebellion intermingle, thus placing *Caligula* at a transition point in the development of Camus's writing. More explicitly than in *The Stranger* or *The Myth*, and conjointly with "The Misunderstanding," with which its publication was at first joined, this version directs us toward the emerging problems posed by revolt. Yet we are still dealing with a work primarily focused upon individual attempts to come to terms with the dawning sense that this world may have no transcendent significance. In short, it remains essentially a study in the problems of the absurd.

The last two major revisions, those of 1947 and 1958, do not radically alter the structure and dynamics of the play. Insofar as they bear upon its content—as opposed to Camus's effort to polish the work stylistically—these modifications seek to sharpen the conceptual focus concerning possible alternative responses to the absurd. Most particularly, the revisions of 1947 develop in detail the rationales for the divergent paths taken by the protagonists, while those of 1958 essentially humanize and contextualize, thus making more credible, the character of the cynical bureaucrat Helicon. But of this, more later.

Clearly, therefore, this work was essentially completed in the early 1940s, contemporaneously with *The Myth* and *The Stranger*, and properly forms an integral part of Camus's "first series" on the absurd. The previous dionysian themes constitute its prehistory, feeding that underground source that, like the stream drawing Meursault toward his confrontation with the Arab, offers the possibly illusory promise of refreshment, serving both as a potentially fertilizing resource and as a dangerous temptation, but that nevertheless, continually recedes into the background of Camus's explicit preoccupations. Rather the axis of the published work revolves around the struggles, on the one hand, of the 29-year-old emperor to come to terms with the twin problems of the inevitability of death and the hypocrisy of social conventions, and, on the other, those confronting "the others" who must come to terms with the reality with which he confronts them. These were also the central preoccupations of the 29-year-old Camus during the war years.

A METAPHYSICAL REBEL

Caligula's Project

"Men weep because . . . the world's all wrong," complains Caligula (CTOP, 15). The spiritual twin of Scipio, possessed of a profound sensitivity and passion for life, he realized upon Drusilla's death that life unfolds in time, is of limited duration, and is without guarantees or transcendent significance.

To love someone means to be willing to age with that person. I am not capable of such love. Drusilla old would have been far worse than Drusilla dead. People believe that a man suffers because the being he loves one day dies. But his true suffering is less futile; it comes from realizing that not even grief lasts. Even sadness is deprived of meaning (TRN, 105; CTOP, 71).

Sobering indeed is the realization of time's inexorable flow, which, like the winds of Djémila, erodes even the objects of our most precious cares. That, of course, is the source of "the absurd," the encounter with which literally sets the stage for the drama.

Caligula finds this state of affairs intolerable. He is a rebel against an absurd world. Either the world must be changed *fundamentally,* or people must stop acting as if it had a meaning that it does not have. In a sense, he is an idealistic youth who has been disabused of his ideals. Having been brought up to believe this world has a transcendent meaning that can justify life, he feels cheated and disgusted. If life has no ultimate meaning, how can people continue to live as if it did? Either they are fools or hypocrites, conditions that, as emperor, he can and will rectify. "Of what use to me is this amazing power which is mine if I cannot change the order of things, if I cannot make the sun set in the east, decrease suffering, and put an end to death?" (TRN, 27; CTOP, 16).[2]

Of course, it is not the realization of the absurd that is central here. It had center stage in the initial drafts of the play, which date from 1936–1937. That experience, to which *Two Sides of the Coin* bears witness, transformed and transfigured Camus's orientation from the sportive concerns of youth through the encounter with tuberculosis to the confrontation with finitude. But what sense to make of finitude when all of our culturally embedded meanings point beyond? Here are the existential termites gnawing at the metaphysical foundations of the Western world. As Camus has noted on several occasions, metaphysical problems plague the modern world as never before—precisely because our once taken-for-granted foundations are no longer secure. Since this is the situation confronting contemporary experience, Camus's attention has focused on alternative responses—to explore their logic and dissect their consequences.

One possible response is to go on as if nothing has changed. What is more normal than that, to which the patricians attest? Another is to focus upon immediate satisfactions, as do so many of Camus's women, including Caesonia. While Scipio turns toward Nature as a quasi-salvific divinity, and

Cherea seeks to preserve the space for art and human relations in the face of a totalizing logic, Caligula finds these efforts derisive and self-deluding.

A twofold theme is being orchestrated here, and it is somewhat contradictory. On the one hand, the metaphysical order of things is unsatisfactory and must be changed. On the other hand, since things don't make any ultimate sense, it is dishonest to act as if they do. Thus decency requires that we reorder our experience to coincide with the revised conception of the order of things. Here the focus is transformation not of the metaphysical structure of things, but rather of the existential quality of our lives. Caligula is a metaphysical rebel who embarks upon both courses of action at the same time— but not with the same energy.

In fact, although he sends Helicon off to find the moon, little attention is devoted to that project.[3] Even more, by saying his need is for the impossible, he attests from the outset to the fact that he places little or no hope in the projected transformation of the metaphysical order of things. It is his own form of self-delusion. He thus embodies Camus's sense that the absurd currently defines the limits of our experience, thus existentially constituting the situation with which we must come to terms.

The Psychic Subsoil

If there is no serious question about the actual possibility of a metaphysical revolution, the same is not true of the existential significance of the ontological need. Camus refers to this play, along with "The Misunderstanding," as constituting "a theater of the impossible." If a metaphysical revolution is clearly impossible, the passion motivating it may nonetheless express significant human needs that must be addressed and worked through. These two plays, he says, "try to give life to the apparently insoluble conflicts which must be traversed by all active thought before arriving at the only solutions which are worthwhile" (TRN, 1742). And he defends his attempt by noting, "For the dramatist the passion for the impossible is just as valid a subject for study as avarice or adultery. Showing it in all its frenzy, illustrating the havoc it wreaks, bringing out its failure—such was my intention" (CTOP, vi).

That this passion for the impossible has, for Camus, deep roots in the human psyche should not be in doubt. One of the first indications of his focus upon Caligula appears in a January 1937 *Notebook* entry. Concluding an outline for *Caligula or the Meaning of Death*, Caligula observes that he "is not dead. . . . He is in each of us. If power were given to you, if you had enough heart, if you loved life, you would see unchained, this monster or this angel which you carry within you" (TRN, 1733). How can Camus claim that Caligula is a universal temptation or suggest that there is something angelic about such a monster? What is fermenting in this psychic subsoil?

It must be noted that this concern never leaves the play, even though it does undergo significant alterations. In the 1947 version it is an embarrassed Cherea, not Caligula, who suggests that all of us harbor Caligula within us when he observes that "one cannot like an aspect of oneself which one always tries to keep concealed." But there is no longer any suggestion of positive approbation of these traits. Three years earlier Cherea had been able to say, "I do not hate you. I understand and I approve of you" (TRN, 1765), only to have these phrases removed by 1947.

Clearly Camus is walking a fine line. There is something essentially human yet quite macabre about Caligula. To explore these depths was not nearly so touchy a matter in the pre–World War II years. But with the onset of Nazism, of which Caligula can be seen as an unconscious premonition, it becomes clear that Camus has hit upon something both significant and quite dangerous.

AN ABSURD GOD

Condemned to Death

"Your pleading comes too late, the verdict's given," Caligula tells Cherea. "This world has no importance; once a man realizes that, he wins his freedom" (CTOP, 14). If there is no transcendent purpose to life, then there is no compelling reason to subject one's actions to moral constraints. In ordinary circumstances we are prisoners of our fears of divine retribution or our hopes of divine salvation. Alone "among a nation of slaves" (TRN, 1759), Caligula is freed of such illusory scruples: freed to act upon whim, desire, or calculation. And so are we all, if we but realize it. That was the truth for which Kirlov died.

Of course, prudential concerns drawn from the realities of social intercourse and the practical demands of group living might limit the behavior of ordinary mortals. But these need not inhibit an emperor. Caligula thus concludes that "everything is permitted." He will exercise the liberty of action that his insight, logic, and social position combine to make possible.

But there are other motives that move the emperor, as they do his artistic creator. Caligula is committed to the Truth—which functions as a reflective expression of that "passion for living" (TRN, 1727) that he shares with Scipio, Mersault, and the idealized youth of Camus's Algeria. Life is too precious to be wasted through habit, or squandered in superficial social ritual. And yet it is ultimately meaningless. Caligula lives this ambiguity as he levels all values, thus bringing the truth of the absurd home to his subjects, while teaching them the value of that present which they took for granted.

I can see, too, what you're thinking. What a fuss over a woman's death! But that's not it. . . . Love, what is it? Nothing much. Her death is . . . only the sign of a truth which makes the moon essential to me. . . . [But] I am completely surrounded by lies, and I want people to live in the truth. And I've the power to make them do it. Because I know what they lack. . . . They are deprived of understanding, and need a professor who knows what he is talking about (TRN, 16; CTOP, 8–9).

An Absurd Teacher

"Once more the gods have come to earth. They have assumed the human form of our heaven-born emperor, known to men as Caligula" (CTOP, 39). This new divinity is not, of course, the god of Judeo-Christian mythology. Caligula incarnates a rather different perspective. He comes to: "teach us the indifference that kindles love anew"; "inform us of the truth of this world which is that it has none"; and "grant us the strength to live up to this incomparable truth" (TRN, 63; CTOP, 40–1).

Such a god is not constrained by rationality or moral scruples, though he does act in accord with the logic of an absurd world. Being subject to no higher law, why would he not do "whatever he felt like?" And being emperor, who is to stop him? "Intendant, you are to close the public granaries. I have signed a decree to that effect . . . famine begins tomorrow. We all know what famine means, it's a plague. Tomorrow there will be a plague, and when it pleases me I will put an end to it. After all, I don't have so many ways of proving that I am free. One is always free at the expense of others. It's boring, but normal" (TRN, 46; CTOP, 28–9).[4]

How instructive it is to be subject to a god who does whatever pleases him at the moment. "I see that you . . . have finally understood that it is not necessary to have done something in order to die" (TRN, 39–40; CTOP, 24). Letting his desires (or fantasies) become the springs of actions dramatically confronts us with the truth of our world, demystifying our faith in its intelligibility and purposefulness. And since when have we failed at least subconsciously to appreciate the absolute contingency of our finite existence? Is this not the reason for our passionate insistence upon the absoluteness of our religious beliefs as they ground our "eternal" social norms? Is it not precisely this sense of their unquestioned place in a divinely ordained social order that the Patricians exude?

Do we not find here the root of the scandal that is Caligula's behavior? For is he not right, when he admonishes Scipio for complaining about the human cost of his actions, that "if you knew how to count, you would know that the smallest war undertaken by a reasonable tyrant would be a thousand times more costly than the caprices of my fantasies"? (TRN, 69; CTOP, 44). No, he is not a tyrant in the usual sense, for he does not believe in any realizable ideal for which he is willing to sacrifice human lives. Rather, he chooses to "play the part of fate," having "adopted the foolish and incomprehensible appearance of the gods" (CTOP, 44). By so doing, he threatens, even more than death, the meaning of our lives. "At least," says Scipio, the actions of a normal tyrant "would be reasonable, and the important thing is to comprehend" (TRN, 69; CTOP, 44).[5]

Not only is his behavior not constrained by rational or moral principles, nor by practical political realities, but, even more, no values or goals hold any sway over his felt preferences. On what grounds can one challenge an assertion of value in an absurd world? Do not all such claims reduce to matters of felt preference and actual political power? It is to address these very questions that Camus, struggling with the horrors of the Second World War and seeking to shed light on the "blind battle" that he and his comrades of the Resistance were then waging, wrote his poignant "Letters to a German Friend."

"I wish men to live by the light of truth" (CTOP, 9), he says. But that light when emitted by an absolutistic sun reveals everything to be "on an equal footing: the grandeur of Rome and your attacks of arthritis" (CTOP, 11). From the perspective of the all or nothing, the relative values of daily life are insignificant. Even worse, they are a cruel delusion. "What I most admire," Caligula likes to observe after an execution, "is my indifference" (TRN, 86; CTOP, 58).

While Caligula is thus free to express his whims, the rest are subject to them. A momentary disposition, a chance encounter, a slip of the tongue may suffice for him to put an end to a life. Even more, he may have no reason at all, or simply think it would be amusing.

Because of our needs, we will have these people put to death in accordance with an arbitrarily established list. On occasion we will modify that order, entirely arbitrarily. . . . In reality, the order of executions has no importance. Or rather, these executions have an equal importance, from which it follows that none has any. Moreover, each of these people is as guilty as the other (TRN, 22; CTOP, 12).

There need be no reason for being put to death, nor any right time. "Judges, witnesses, accused—[we are] all sentenced to death in advance" (TRN, 28; CTOP, 17). And there is no appeal. Life is a death sentence; the truth of which it is the aim of Caligula's divinity to bring home to his subjects. "Kill him slowly, so that he may experience dying" (TRN, 86; CTOP, 58).

Execution relieves and liberates. It is universal, fortifying, and fair in both precept and practice. One dies because one is guilty. One is guilty because one is Caligula's subject. Now everyone is a subject of Caligula. Therefore, everyone is guilty. From which it follows that everyone dies. It's only a matter of time and patience (TRN, 46–7; CTOP, 29).

In an absurd world, life is a gift ever on loan. We should not take it for granted nor act as if our success or our future is assured. Such is the sublime wisdom that Caligula teaches. As for Caligula himself, "who would dare to condemn [him], in this world without a judge in which no one is innocent!" (TRN, 107; CTOP, 72).[6]

THE OTHERS

To be one of Caligula's subjects is to have your world undermined, to have your values and beliefs mocked and discarded, and to face the possibility that at any moment whatever you hold dear may be taken from you—your life included.[7] For the subjects of Caligula, the reality of their situation confronts them at every turn.

The existential parameters of an absurd world are dramatized by Cherea, Scipio, and Caesonia, those alter egos of Caligula, who carry the burden of the dramatic action precisely because they so deeply share aspects of Caligula's experience. Helicon, the Patricians, and the servants, on the other hand, like the chorus in a Greek tragedy, represent ordinary humanity. Their fate is no less affected by Caligula's metaphysical revolution, but their preoccupations and deliberations are more sketched than developed.

Caesonia speaks for the body and for love. She has "never had any other god than her body" (TRN, 19; CTOP, 10). She is of the moment, the immediate. She expresses the joys and sufferings of life without reflective overlay or grand design. Reminiscent of Meursault, she is prototypical of Camus's feminine literary characters, having appeared as Marie Cardona in *The Stranger* and as Martha and Lucianne in *A Happy Death*, and reappearing as Maria in "The Misunderstanding," Victoria in "The State of Siege," and perhaps even Rieux's mother in *The Plague*.[8] Like these characters, her attitudes and values are simple and direct. "There is good and bad, high and low, justice and injustice." "At my age one knows that life is not good. But if suffering is on the earth, why wish to add to it?" (TRN, 27, 26; CTOP, 15, 14). Similarly, with her advice. What Caligula needs in order to come to terms with Drusilla's death, she tells him, "is a good, long sleep. Let yourself relax and, above all, stop thinking. I'll stay by you while you sleep. And when you wake, you'll find the world's got back its savor" (CTOP, 16). No great adventures or flights of the spirit; but a naturalness and simplicity, pervaded by a maternal care that nurtures and an acceptance of aging that consoles.

Scipio too embodies a commitment to nature, but it is a poet's nature, not a woman's. It is the natural world, whose expression is embodied in literature. With Wordsworth, he seems to believe that "One impulse from a vernal wood / May teach you more of man, / Of moral evil and of good / Than all the sages can." He writes of "a certain harmony . . . between one's feet and the earth," and observes that "everything . . . takes on the appearance of love." But, unlike Caesonia, this is an emotion to be dreamed of and written about, speaking more to the imagination than to the body.

In wandering and reverie, Scipio believes that nature soothes the spirit, revives the body, and frees the mind from concern for recognition and advancement. He advises Caligula to trust in nature, which "has cured wounds more serious" than those from which the emperor suffers (TRN, 55; CTOP, 35). But, though "the same fire burns in both our hearts" (CTOP, 56), Caligula has been forever cast out of the edenic relation to nature that he had once shared with Scipio, by his encounter with the absurd. He has left Scipio, "following him as usual," but incapable of sharing that insight by which he has been sundered in two. Caligula had "wanted to be a just man." He had told Scipio "that life is not easy, but that there was religion, art, love to carry us along" (TRN 19; CTOP 10). And Scipio continues to embody the vision they once shared—so much so that, in the latest editions of the play (where Camus has Scipio's character assume a more mature aspect), Scipio finds that he "cannot be against him" (TRN, 83), even though Caligula had had Scipio's father put to death. Scipio thus refuses to participate in the assassination of one "who so greatly ressembles" him, and whom he now believes he understands (TRN, 101).[9] All he can do is absent himself from the collective decision whose necessity he recognizes, while retreating to a restorative nature that is unable to counter Caligula's passion.[10]

Cherea is less poetic, more practical. His focus is on how people can live together. He shares some of the metaphysical concerns of Caligula, but tempers them with a feel for others, and for the conditions that make social relations possible. Having wished, perhaps like Camus himself, to have been "left to [his] books" (CTOP, 6)[11] he was forced by the emperor's actions to become involved with politics. "I desire and need security," he tells Caligula. "Most men are like me. They are incapable of living in a universe in which the most bizarre thought can become a reality at any moment. . . . I feel like living and being happy, [and] I believe that by pushing the absurd to its logical conclusions one can be neither of them" (TRN, 77, 78; CTOP, 51).

Cherea thus focuses the metaphysical and moral challenge posed by Caligula.

[Caligula] is putting his power in the service of a higher and more deadly passion [than that of murder]. He threatens everything which is most important to us. Doubtless, this is not the first time that one among us was possessed of unlimited power; but it is the first time that such a one made use of it without limits. . . . That is what frightens me about him, and what I wish to combat. To lose one's life is a small matter, and when the time comes I will have the necessary courage. But what's intolerable is to see one's life being drained of meaning, to be told there's no reason for existing. A man can't live without a reason for living (TRN, 34; CTOP, 21).

Without a reason for living there obviously cannot be any reason for doing one thing rather than another. Thus at a lower level the metaphysical challenge robs ethics of its rationale. "I believe," says Cherea, "that there are actions which are more beautiful than others." To which Caligula counters that "all are equivalent." "In order to be logical," observes Cherea, "I should then kill or subjugate" those for whom I have at times such a desire. But "if everyone concerned themselves with fulfilling [such desires], we would not be able to live or be happy" (TRN, 78–9; CTOP, 52–3).

But what kind of rejoinder is that to the metaphysical challenge posed by Caligula? Cherea seems to recognize the theoretical inadequacy of his position when he earlier asserts that "one must strike when one cannot refute" (TRN, 35; CTOP, 21). But are we not then simply reduced to a struggle over power?

Caligula's logic is coherent but neglects, Camus seems to suggest, the competing logics generated by perspectives rooted in nature, the body, and others. By failing to recognize these competing claims—thus operating with a truncated set of existential premises—Caligula presents the spectacle of a mind gone mad with reason. Cherea senses as much when he observes that "life is not possible if one pushes the absurd to its logical conclusions." But he is not able to counter with an equally persuasive logic. At this stage in the development of his thought, Camus is himself struggling to find a rationale to counter the implicit nihilism of the absurd without abdicating to the proponents of philosophical suicide and the leap of faith. Poignant expression of the seriousness and difficulty of this struggle is given in his "Letters to a German Friend," where the passionate logic of Nazism is countered by an equally passionate but not very convincing assertion of the value of human dignity. Cherea's willingness to stake his life in defense of human dignity will have to await *The Rebel* for a more articulate exposition.[12]

While Caligula's three alter egos share aspects of his passion, they do not follow him in his logic—a logic that leads to the subordination and eventual rupture of human relations. Faithful to the destructive potential of that logic—a potential he seems ever more aware of and committed to —Caligula destroys his relation to the body (symbolized by the murder of Caesonia), cuts himself off from the healing and restorative powers of nature to which he had once been drawn (symbolized by the rejection and departure of Scipio), and alienates himself from the world of others, thus motivating the distinctive rebellions of Cherea and the Patricians, culminating in his own death.[13]

Caligula may be said to embody the absolutistic impulse essential to Western philosophical and religious traditions. When the mind demands totality and coherence at all costs, it is implicitly committed to the path of spiritual imperialism. Inevitably, it ruptures concrete relations with nature, the body, and others, leveling human values and wreaking havoc everywhere, ultimately engulfing itself.

As people who have made it, the Patricians express the self-confidence and righteousness of the ruling classes. No doubt the world has been made for them, and they deserve their place. Their superiority has been ordained, it is as it should be, and it will not change. Of course, youth will have their dreams and should be humored, but not taken too seriously. Suffering comes and goes, but who is "able to suffer for more than a year"? They will have nothing of such youthful romantic sentiments. "Happily, grief is not eternal" (TRN, 9; CTOP, 4) while life reasserts its normal routines.

The Patricians thus embody what Nietzsche called the spirit of seriousness, so well expressed by Meursault's prosecutor. Their place at the apex of the social order is assured. But heaven help those who tamper with the order of things, especially if they have the temerity to "insult . . . our dignity" (TRN, 31; CTOP, 19).[14]

Helicon, on the other hand, is the one character in the play who expresses no opposition to Caligula's action. The only time he seems upset with his boss is when the latter refuses to resist his own assassination. Helicon rejects this passive submission to a destiny which Caligula himself has brought about (cf. TRN, 108). He cares nothing for metaphysical concerns. Far more practical, as befits a former slave, he is loyal to the emperor for the kindness he has been shown, and he knows that his position and power depend directly upon that of Caligula. If Caligula is overthrown or killed, Helicon's fate will be similar.

In so describing Helicon, however, it must be clear that I am speaking of the person who appears in the final edition of the play. For no other character received as extensive a development following the original publication as did Helicon. He first appears in 1944 as little more than an unthinking lackey. He is ordered around by Caligula, without thinking does as he is told, and gives no thought to the meaning of anything. "As you know well, I never think"; to which the 1947 edition adds, "I am too intelligent for that" (TRN, 15; CTOP, 8). He thus expresses Camus's simple, and perhaps stereotypical, distaste for official bureaucrats.

From 1947 through 1958, however, Helicon becomes a more articulate nihilist. It remains true that few things interest him, and that he agrees to help Caligula, as he says, quite reminiscent of Meursault, because he has no reason not to (CTOP, 9). Yet he now can distance himself from Caligula sufficiently to justify not concerning himself with anything because Caligula, as an idealist, "has not yet understood" (TRN, 18).

Even more, Camus has come to appreciate somewhat more sensitively the needs that might motivate one loyally to perform some of the more distasteful though routine bureaucratic indecencies. In addition, Camus has developed a more refined distaste for the "guardians" of culture, for the intellectual and financial elites with whom he had had close and increasingly unpleasant relations in postwar Paris. Most particularly, he has developed a heightened sense of the hypocrisy of the liberal intelligentsia, who were quite willing to defend freedom with the lives of others, but were often quite unwilling to expend their personal privileges on behalf of the "lower" classes (cf. TRN, 89–90).[15] Thus Helicon emerges as Caligula's loyal functionary precisely out of appreciation for the latter's generosity. His behavior offers a more sympathetic gloss on the subservience of the servants who, like the bureaucrats in Hitler's Germany, carry out Caligula's demonic orders, often against their will.

FROM ABSURDITY TO REVOLT

While the drama plays itself out on the ideological plane and in the confrontation of alternative psycho-logics, an almost inarticulate existential undertow seems to pull Caligula toward his own destruction. The demand for the moon but gives articulate expression to the basic need for an ultimate and transcending purpose. Only in the context of that root metaphysical demand does the action of the play make any sense. That metaphysical demand, expressing a deeply felt need, is what makes the character of Caligula so peculiarly modern.

"He is in each of us" (TRN, 1733), Camus had written. (Or at least in most Western males, but we will return to that later.) This is the ground of Caligula's universality. Here lies the existential root of the demand for a metaphysical revolution that has for centuries plagued the West. "Each person carries within himself a part filled with illusions and misunderstandings which is destined to be killed" (TRN, 1742), observed Camus. This reiterates Cherea's comment that Caligula is an aspect of himself that he tries to keep concealed (CTOP, 51).

No doubt here is the source, for Camus, of the appeal of religions and totalizing ideologies. But if we all share with Caligula the secret demand for a metaphysical revolution "which is destined to be killed," and if, even more, we may harbor the wish that life be brought into conformity with our deepest desires, we must find a way to live through and purge those desires before they wreak havoc upon the world, our self included. Caligula does not. In seeking to bring into the world that "new man" (TRN, 1733–4) which his insight required,[16] "he challenges friendship and love, simple human solidarity, good and evil. He takes those about him at their word and forces them to be logical; he levels everything around him by the strength of his refusal and by the destructive rage to which his passion for life leads him" (TRN, 1727; CTOP, v–vi).

If Caligula embodies a pathology, it lies, no doubt, in his insistence upon the all or nothing of metaphysical rebellion: either life has eternal significance or it is meaningless.

If his truth is to rebel against destiny, his error is to deny men. One cannot destroy everything without destroying oneself. That is why Caligula destroys the people around him and, faithful to his logic, does what he has to to mobilize against him those who will finally kill him (TRN, 1727–8).

If the metaphysical rebel is right to rebel against that which in the order of things threatens to reduce the human to insignificance, he is wrong to cut himself off from that human community from within which alone a meaningful response is possible. The world must be refashioned from within. It is the task of the rebel to "correct creation," but not to seek to replace it. There is no outside from which to leverage actions, while resentment only sustains the urge to destroy. " 'Caligula' is the story of a superior suicide. . . . Unfaithful to mankind through fidelity to himself, Caligula accepts death because he has understood that no one can save himself all alone and that one cannot be free at the expense of others" (CTOP, vi). Caligula realizes that he "has not chosen the path that was required. . . . [His] liberty . . . leads to nothing" (TRN, 108; CTOP, 73).

What then is to be done in an absurd world? What is the required path? Cherea joins with the Patricians to eliminate Caligula because he realizes that life is not possible if Caligula is permitted to pursue his logic to its culmination. What coherent alternative perspective, however, is being offered in its place? And how does Cherea propose to address the ontological need to which Caligula gave such demonic expression? "I can deny something without feeling obliged to besmirch it or to deny to others the right to believe in it" (TRN, 66; CTOP, 42–3), Scipio observes. But neither he—who leaves the scene without taking up arms against Caligula—nor Cherea, nor the play itself, has any coherent response to the gauntlet laid down by Caligula. Life may not be possible without our confronting and purging the Caligula within us, but the therapeutic path remains elusive. No wonder Caligula insists to the last that he "is still living" (TRN, 108; CTOP, 74).

PART THREE 🖎

Confrontation and Struggle

Better than [Prometheus's] revolt against the gods, it is his sustained persistence which makes sense to us. Along with his admirable determination to neither separate nor exclude anything which has always reconciled . . . the suffering hearts of men and the springtime of the world (LCE, 142; *L'Eté*, 87).

6

Social Dislocations

All of us ate the same sour bread of exile, unconsciously waiting for the same reunion (P, 167).

MISUNDERSTANDINGS

Seeking Reconciliation

"The Misunderstanding" appears to be a transitional work. Written during the bleakest days of the occupation when, in the words of Germaine Brée, "Europe had, like Camus's inhospitable inn, become a charnel house, a mother wearily slaughtering her sons, hallucinated by dreams of a future felicity" (Brée, 183), its tragedy arises from an inability of individuals to speak with, rather than to, one another. Preoccupied with their personal projects, each has formulated a life trajectory deaf to the speech of the other. But these monads function in a context of social relations; in fact, their projects presuppose the being of those very others from whom they have cut themselves off. Blind to the commonality of their situation, they seek to shape the world in the frame set by their essentially solipsistic projects. In their effort to impose their own world on the others, each encounters the other's similar and counter effort. Interwoven monologue has replaced dialogue, and tragic misunderstandings are inevitable.[1]

In the language of Camus's later writings, we have here the encounter of opposing total views upon a common situation—without either the shared recognition of that commonality or the granting of legitimacy to the perspectives of the other.

Cut off by their projects both from the other and from the natural world, which is itself reduced to being only the setting for their efforts, each lives in a world of abstractions—always excepting Jan's wife, Maria. While she comes from the land of the South, speaking the direct language of concrete feelings, and serves as a constant reminder of the lost worlds of natural beauty and human interaction, Martha is wrapped up and lost in her longing for a mythical South, as is Jan with the gift of salvation he is going to bring home.

But it is not so much the abstractions that are at fault, as it is their exclusive and all-consuming nature. Treated as salvific, they don't admit of modification. Jan will not listen to his wife's plea; Martha cannot respond to her mother's weariness. Each project excludes the others. Lacking the preconditions of dialogue, without realizing it, we are at a dead end.

The place of "The Misunderstanding" in Camus's thought is suggested when he says of Jan's motivation for returning that "one cannot always remain a stranger [outsider]; a man needs happiness, it is true, but he also needs to find his place in the world" (quoted in Thody, 63). Jan thus stands halfway between Meursault and Rambert. Meursault is a stranger in the human world who finds his happiness in union with a natural world in which all human projects are alien. And Rambert longs for happiness above all, but realizes that one cannot be happy alone, and joins the work teams in the collective fight against the plague.

Halfway between the solitude of Meursault and the solidarity of Rambert, Jan seeks in vain "for the word which will reconcile everything"; but that word eludes him. His project is fundamentally flawed. Having returned home out of pity and duty, rather than love or affection, in order to bestow upon his family a gift of grace, he sees himself as their savior. His gift is conditional upon their recognition. But his project lacks mutuality. He does not listen to their speech. It is as if they were but the occasions for the fulfillment of his project.

They, of course, are no more open to hearing his words. Long drained of any sensitivity to the concerns of others by the trying nature of their day-to-day existence, each encountered individual is but one more occasion for pursuing their project of salvation—a project that devours their own lives as much as those of their victims. The inability to find the word that will reconcile everything is therefore meant to be structural, not occasional: their incompatible definitions of their situation exclude the possibility of meaningful communication. That, at least, is Camus's intention, which invites him to recreate in modern dress the contours of classical tragedy.

If we reflect upon the underlying metaphysic, we can glimpse the movement from the concerns of the absurd to those of revolt. For "The Misunderstanding" seeks to dramatize the tragedy resident in the effort to achieve individual salvation in the context of an essentially common condition. With no perception of the limits intrinsic to individual endeavor, or the mutuality of human relations, or the necessity of opening up to the world of the other, or the commonality of human destiny, the self-absorbed project of the single individual whose perspective is fundamentally inadequate to the social context can only generate a tragic outcome.

The suggestion of the play is thus clear. The absurdity of our individual situation can only be constructively addressed by nourishing the dimension of human existence that is fed by dialogue. As Jan's mother sobs, upon realizing what has happened, "Oh, why did he keep silent? Silence is fatal" (CTOP, 123).

"The Misunderstanding" is thus a cry from the depths of historically generated despair that has given birth to oppression and torture in the name of salvation. It is a cry for "relativized utopias"; for a commitment to a community rooted in the dialogic opening up to the fallible world of the other. "It amounts to saying," wrote Camus, "that in an unjust or indifferent world man can save himself, and save others, by practicing the most basic sincerity and pronouncing the most appropriate word" (CTOP, vii).

Born in "this narrow world in which we are reduced to gazing up at God," cheated of her generous sentiments by a condition for which she is at best only partly responsible, reduced to the barrenness of a life without significance, Martha, perhaps the most pitiful of Camus's characters, is finally disabused of her dreams of salvation and draws the nihilistic conclusion in her advice to Maria.

Pray your God to harden you to stone. It's the happiness He has assigned to Himself, and the one true happiness. Do as He does, be deaf to all appeals, and turn your heart to stone while there is still time. . . . You have a choice between the mindless happiness of stones and the slimy bed in which we are awaiting you (CTOP, 133).

Countering Martha's despair, her mother offers a muted expression of a lost hope. "It only proves that in a world where everything can be denied, there are undeniable forces; and on this earth where nothing's sure we have our certainties. And a mother's love for her son is now *my* certainty" (CTOP, 120, my italics).

Martha's despair suggests the depths to which humans can be reduced by an unjust fate—an emptiness of which nihilism is but a pale theoretical reflection, and from which no theory can provide salvation—while the mother's belated affirmation suggests the possibility of an existential alternative to nihilism. Yet it falls to Maria, the play's embodiment of outraged innocence, to intimate the direction of a possibly more constructive response to our absurd condition. Her revolt emerges as a simple and direct expression of the agony of her despair: "Oh, God, I cannot live in this desert! . . . Have pity on those who love each other and are parted" (CTOP, 133). The Old Manservant, misinterpreting her plea to God as a call to him, responds in the negative. Merely one more misunderstanding, perhaps, but the ambiguous suggestion is clear. In our present dead end, wherein reconciliation has failed miserably, the recourse to God is a nonstarter. The necessity for a more openly collective manner of addressing the problem of salvation is evident.

Taking Stock

In the effort to elaborate a constructive frame within which life might have meaning without transcendent justification, the works so far considered have proved singularly unsatisfactory. *Two Sides of the Coin* had suggested the importance of the realm of the interpersonal, which had remained more or less muted in *Nuptials*, *The Stranger*, and *The Myth of Sisyphus*, exacting its claim in ritualistic fashion in *The Stranger*, and being forced to reassert itself against its better judgment in "Caligula."

With "The Misunderstanding" the demands of the interpersonal now emerge tragically onto center stage. As I have sought to show, the tragedy results from the insistence of individuals that they work out their destiny in terms of their own projects, deaf to the demands of that interpersonal situation that their projects presuppose and from which alone, it is implied, life can obtain whatever fulfillment may be possible. This tragedy of situation demands the recognition of the commonality of our condition. Perceptions need to be explicitly shared if together we are to construct a viable alternative to our lost paradise, in a universe without absolute answers in which, at best, our misapprehended deity only answers, "No." The inadequacy of solely individual strategies is thus clearly suggested by "The Misunderstanding." It will be for *The Plague* to begin to explore the possibilities of a more collective response.

THE BREAD OF EXILE

"With the experience of the absurd, suffering is individual. Beginning with the movement of revolt, it becomes conscious of being collective. . . . The first advance, therefore, of a mind seized by the strangeness of things is to recognize that it shares this strangeness with all men, and that human reality . . . suffers from this distance from itself and from the world. The pain [*mal*] which was experienced by a single man becomes a collective plague" (L'HR, 36; R, 22). Could Camus have been more explicit about his intention? The transition from *The Stranger* to *The Plague* turns upon the emerging perception "that all . . . were, so to speak, in the same boat" (P, 61). The imprisonment of Meursault has become the shared experience of the citizens of Oran, who are often referred to as "prisoners of the plague." In fact, at an early stage in the development of the manuscript, Camus had considered calling it "The Prisoners."

A concern with imprisonment runs through his writings, and with good reason. With *The Plague*, the metaphor of prison helps to transcribe the traumatic experience that was the German occupation of France during World War II. At a deeper level, however, the continuity with the stage of the absurd is maintained by the recognition that in prison our life is finite, time and space are circumscribed, and our liberty of action is constrained by forces beyond our control. Thus the metaphor of prison can be used to depict those aspects of finitude—especially when linked to a death sentence whose date is uncertain—from which the absurd seeks to draw its lesson.[2] This image of imprisonment helps to dramatize the tragic vision that pervades Camus's work. It articulates a metaphysic within which his practical and personal concerns take shape.

Before considering that metaphysic as it finds expression in *The Plague*, thus locating this novel within the theoretical development of Camus's work, it is important to note four complementary perspectives from which the novel can be viewed: the personal, the historical, the cultural, and the metaphysical. By considering these dramatically interwoven thematic strands, the sensuously textured tapestry that gives experiential richness to the sparse contours of the chronicle of the plague can be more adequately appreciated.

At its most obvious, *"The Plague . . .* has as its evident content the struggle of the European resistance against Nazism" (TRN, 1965; LCE, 339). It also had its quite personal accent, for Camus was quite literally trapped in occupied France. Rambert essentially transcribes the qualitative feel of this experience, in which Camus found himself cut off from his wife, his family, and his native Algeria when the Allies invaded North Africa. Camus's feelings during his recuperation in the mountains of central France from an attack of tuberculosis must certainly have been echoed by Rambert when the latter exclaimed that "his presence in Oran was purely accidental, he had no connection with the town and no reasons for staying in it; that being so, he surely was entitled to leave" (P, 77). As Rambert so poignantly exclaimed, "I don't belong here!" If most people in occupied France felt deprived of their right to live in accordance with their normal habits and expectations,

those . . . like Rambert . . . had to endure an aggravated deprivation, since, being travellers caught by the plague and forced to stay where they were, they were cut off both from the person with whom they wanted to be and from their homes as well. In the general exile they were the most exiled; since while time gave rise for them, as for us all, to the suffering appropriate to it, there was also for them the space factor; they were obsessed by it and at every moment knocked their heads against the walls which separated their infected refuge from their lost homes (P, 67; TRN, 1236).

Still more, there is "the case of parted lovers," which includes Rieux and, in another sense, Grand. There was "the trouble they experienced in summoning up any clear picture of what the absent one was doing," and of reproaching themselves for having paid too little attention to the "way in which that person used to spend his or her days" (P, 68). "Thus, each of us had to be content," writes the narrator, "to live only for the day, alone under the vast indifference of the sky. This sense of being abandoned, which might in time have given characters a finer temper, began . . . by sapping them to the point of futility" (P, 68). The year or so immediately following the Allied landing in North Africa, it might be noted, was certainly not a particularly happy or productive one for Camus.

Camus had resented the war from the outset. It did not make sense to him that such extraneous events, with no direct or perceptible relation to his life and his personal and philosophical concerns, could so wrench him out of his orbit. World historical events, to borrow Hegel's fine phrase, might be the focus of his theoretical and dramatic activities—even to the extent of his preparing to devote the second stage of his "work" to the theme of revolt— but such events were not really the substance of his personal life. Even his journalistic and political involvements bore witness to a sensibility more in tune with the demands of immediate experience than with those of historical analysis. What was this *drôle de guerre* and by what right did it rob his life of its personal trajectory?

The initial dialogue between Rambert and Rieux concerning Rambert's desire to get out of Oran might have taken place within the soul of Camus. Rambert comes to this discussion with "the sulky, stubborn look of a young man who feels himself deeply injured." Rieux "wished nothing better than that Rambert should be allowed to return to his wife and that all who loved one another and were parted should come together again." He recognized that Rambert didn't belong here, but said, "That's not a sufficient reason. Oh, I know it's an absurd situation, but we're all involved in it, and we've got to accept it as it is."

Rambert is bitter. " 'You're using the language of reason, not of the heart; you live in a world of abstractions.' " To which Rieux responds that he "was using the language of the facts as everybody could see them—which wasn't necessarily the same thing." Rambert "was right in refusing to be balked of happiness. But was he right in reproaching him, Rieux, with living in a world of abstractions? . . . Yes, an element of abstraction, of a divorce from reality, entered into such calamities. Still, when abstraction sets to killing you, you've got to get busy with it" (P, 78–81). The concern with happiness has clashed with the hard facts of life as well as with the role of abstract forces in structuring that "force of evidence" with which one must come to terms. We thus see dramatically transcribed a deeply personal conversion from the individualism of the Absurd to the emerging theoretical concern with solidarity that is so central to the stage of Revolt.

Only slowly did Camus come to terms with his own situation, resume his writing, and make contact with resistance forces, most particularly the Combat network. Ultimately he became the chief editor of the underground network's newspaper, *Combat*. This position, when made public upon the liberation of Paris, contributed significantly to his becoming a major public figure in postwar France. In much of this, the resemblance to Rambert is close—though far more as a transcription of feeling than of action.

Camus did, however, deepen his appreciation of the efforts of ordinary people to make sense of their life, faced with a daily routine that leaves little place for imagination and hope. No doubt his own origins among the poorest of French North Africans left him with a profound respect for the quiet dignity of those whose condition does not let them aspire beyond the simple pleasures eked out from, and the silent sufferings endured within, the daily struggle for subsistence. In such circumstances, simply doing one's job may embody nobility. Certainly the young Camus knew such poverty, as is borne witness to by much of his early work, especially *Two Sides of the Coin* and *A Happy Death*. The central theme of the latter, for example, concerns the need to have money in order to free oneself from the habitualized routine of a subsistence job, buy the time to be happy, and thus escape from the inevitability of a natural death to the passionate lucidity of a conscious one.

"'Oh, doctor,'" exclaimed Joseph Grand, that nondescript clerk in the municipal office who "had suffered for a long time from a constriction of the aorta" (P, 17), "'how I'd like to learn to express myself!'" (P, 43). If only he could "find his words" he would be able to tell his lost love, Jeanne, what he feels. It would be "hat's off," and he could achieve that minimal acknowledgment that would reconcile him to his life. Throughout the turmoil of the plague, Grand sticks to his work in the municipal office, while working with the sanitation teams in off-hours, and in the evenings continues his project of writing the perfect novel.

"'There lies certainty,'" observes Rieux, "'there, in the daily round. . . . The thing was to do your job as it should be done'" (P, 38). Yet the routine of such a life tends to wear one down. "'Oh, doctor,'" Grand exclaims somewhat later, "'I know I look a quiet sort, just like anybody else. But it's always been a terrible effort only to be—just normal'" (P, 237).

In his ability to continue at his work with care and concern for others, in the shadows of anonymity, Grand incarnates Camus's sense of the nobility of the ordinary. "In short, he had all the attributes of insignificance" (P, 41). No doubt, it is this that Camus wishes to celebrate by having Rieux observe that "Grand was the true embodiment of the quiet courage that inspired the sanitary groups," and, thus, "if it is a fact that people like to have examples given them, men of the type they call heroic, and if it is absolutely necessary that this narrative should include a 'hero,' the narrator commends to his readers . . . this insignificant and obscure hero who had to his credit only a little goodness of heart and a seemingly absurd ideal" (P, 123, 126).

It was in order to bear witness to the intrinsic nobility of the efforts of the average person that Rieux (and Camus) "resolved to compile this chronicle . . . so that some memorial of the injustice and outrage done to them might endure; and to state quite simply what we learn in a time of pestilence: that there are more things to admire in men than to despise" (P, 278). In this, Camus uses Rieux to express one of the more profound sources of his art: the felt obligation to give voice to those whose quiet dignity speaks loudly in action and in suffering, but who cannot find their own words with which to do it justice. From this source, Camus feels, artists can draw creative and vitalizing energy, as well as a justification of their work.

BUSINESS AS USUAL

But if, through the person of Grand, Camus wishes to pay tribute to the quiet courage displayed by his compatriots during the occupation and in The Resistance, and by most of the world's poor and working people in their daily effort "just to be normal," his attitude toward the behavior of his fellow Frenchmen is more complex. They certainly did not deserve what befell them, but they were not without responsibility for it. In fact, on this nuanced perception of their complicity in the pestilence-occupation hangs the deeper meaning of this tale and its place in Camus's work. What was it about Oran or about the Third Republic that made it the appropriate host?

Why Oran? Why this "treeless, glamourless, soulless" town that seems restful but puts you to sleep? (P, 5). In 1939 Camus had called it a spiritual desert, "without soul or resources" (LCE, 111). "Compelled to live facing a glorious landscape," he wrote then, "the people of Oran have overcome this formidable handicap by surrounding themselves with extremely ugly buildings" (LCE, 116). Their "statues are both insignificant and solid. The mind has made no contribution to them, matter a very large one" (LCE, 125), "while the streets of Oran reveal the two main pleasures of the local young people: having their shoes shined, and promenading in these same shoes along the boulevard" (LCE, 113). Little wonder that "the Oranais are devoured by the Minotaur of boredom" (LCE, 116). "'To be nothing!' . . . Without knowing it, everyone in this country follows this precept" (LCE, 131). With the forces of nature in possession of the spirit of the town, one is at times tempted "to defect to the enemy! . . . to merge oneself with these stones, to mingle with this burning, impassive universe that challenges history and its agitations" (LCE, 130).

Clearly, here is the spiritual meaning of Oran for Camus. Beyond a certain subliminal metaphysical ambivalence in which that negative temptation to merge with nature reverberates with the echoes of a more positive temptation to transcend the limits of one's individual destiny, to which Camus had given expression in *A Happy Death* and in *Nuptials*, there is a positive critique embedded in the spiritual failure that is Oran. That critique reappropriates, at the level of community, the theme of the failure of lucidity that is Meursault's root error in *The Stranger*. To this issue, and its metaphysical significance, I will turn shortly. But there is a more mundane source of "dehumanization" to which we must attend if we are to appreciate the historical, cultural, and sociopolitical resonances that reverberate throughout *The Plague*, and help it assume its place within the work of Camus.

"The truth is that everyone is bored," notes the narrator, "and devotes himself to cultivating habits. Our citizens work hard, but solely with the object of getting rich. Their chief interest is in commerce, and their chief aim in life is, as they call it, 'doing business'" (P, 4). It is not that the citizenry of this mythologized version of the Third Republic are evil or malicious; they don't aspire so high. "What they lack is imagination. They take their place in the epoque as if at a picnic. They do not think on the scale of pestilences. And the remedies which they imagine are hardly adequate for a head cold" (TRN, 1948). "Really, all that was to be conveyed was the banality of the town's appearance and of the life in it. But you can get through the days there without trouble, once you have formed habits. And since habits are precisely what our town encourages, all is for the best" (P, 5).

And what was the pervasive character of the experience through which they lived? Preoccupied with their practical concerns and their personal satisfactions, they took life for granted.

In this respect, our townsfolk were like everybody else, wrapped up in themselves: in other words they were humanists: they disbelieved in pestilences. A pestilence isn't made to man's measure; therefore we tell ourselves that pestilence is a mere bogey of the mind, a bad dream that will pass away. But it doesn't pass away, and from one bad dream to another, it is men who pass away, and the humanists first of all, because they haven't taken their precautions. Our townsfolk . . . went on doing business, arranged for journeys, and formed views. How should they have given a thought to anything like plague, which rules out any future, cancels journeys, silences the exchange of views. They fancied themselves free, and no one will ever be free so long as there are pestilences (P, 35).

"It will be said, no doubt, that these habits are not peculiar to our town; really all our contemporaries are much the same. Certainly nothing is commoner nowadays than to see people working from morn till night and then proceeding to fritter away at card-tables in cafes and in small-talk what time is left for living. . . . In other words [Oran is] completely modern" (P, 4). The Oranais have lost contact with passion, love, nature, and art. Habit rules the day, under cover of propriety, in the service of business. No wonder that the primary concern of the officials is to hide the reality of plague: to deny the evidence, to reject the possibility, and above all to avoid taking any extraordinary measures—even precautions to preserve the public's health—that might interfere with doing business. "'Take prompt action if you like,'" says the prefect, "'but don't attract attention'" (P, 44). Nor is it any wonder that into this world of the everyday, plague entered with such devastating force: destroying routine, undermining habit, separating people, and rendering vain their normal hopes and expectations.

All this had, of course, its educational side. Being cut off from the future, the people of Oran found themselves thrown back upon their personal resources. They were forced to attend to the present with a heightened sensibility to the most minute details. No longer able to take tradition as a self-evident guide to action, they had to reconstitute their sense of the meaningful. The poignant transformation of the relation between Dr. Castel and his wife suggests these revitalizing possibilities. They were aging, time was now so palpably finite that they had better not let it any longer slip away through the interstices of their daily life. A new love was thus able to take hold, by which they were able to celebrate their day-to-day existence together.

At a more general level, the social order was put, as it were, to the metaphysical rack. Values had to be forged, and personal relations too, into the teeth of a much constricted sense of time. This need for a "transvaluation of values," to borrow a phrase from Nietzsche, was lived by each and every citizen in the crucible of a very personal suffering. Thus emerged the sanitary squads—at first, simply to aid the citizens in combatting the plague. Slowly, almost imperceptibly, they began to resonate communal values, like the resistance movement itself, pointing toward the need for a social and political transformation whose outlines remain unclear. Before attending to these constructive possibilities, let us explore more fully the cultural ramifications of the life of the Oranais.

Oran is a thoroughly bourgeois town. And it is the quality of its social life that constitutes the dramatic setting for the invasion of the pestilence.

Having cut themselves off from nature and from one another, the citizens of Oran have succeeded in reducing passion and spirit to the habitualized pursuit of material success and physical satisfaction. Care and concern for others, for the quality of public life, or for the possibilities of human excellence, have simply been lost in the shuffle. There is no sense of the deeper significance, the "sacredness," of the everyday. Rather than seeking to "exhaust the field of the possible," habit and routine have become the order of the day; propriety its rules and regulations; diversion and leisure its sustaining satisfaction; and material success its aim and crowning achievement.

The forces of dehumanization may thus be said to have crept into the hollowed core of bourgeois society long before the arrival of plague. With its public life so pervaded by the concern with doing business, personal relations inevitably suffer. Concern for others and for the collective well-being cannot compete for attention with business or pleasure. Naïve faith in material progress—guided perhaps by the unseen hand of the market—

that has so marked modern bourgeois society, leaves little place for collective efforts to shape our destiny. The human community is thus desensitized to human values and lacks direction and purpose. It is thus that plague might be said to have already crept into the life of this mythologized Third Republic, its presence so pervasive and "natural" that the people could not recognize it. In a sense, they were already the unwitting and even innocent carriers of the germ. With their resistance to the forces of dehumanization so weakened, their personal relations so desensitized, and their sense of the human collectivity so attenuated, they were well-prepared to receive in full force the invasion of this most virulent and destructive pestilence.

PRELIMINARY RESPONSES

The response of the citizens to the pestilence is itself highly instructive. Initially they withdrew even more into their private lives. It was as if they viewed the plague as an intrusion for which they had no responsibility. The threat simply came from others. They resented it, and rejected it. But it did not lead them, at least initially, to take stock of their own lives, habits, routines, or values. They saw it as an imposition from which they would protect themselves by cutting off all but the most practically necessary ties. This initial privatization led to a further disintegration of civic life—reducing Oran to the basic necessities of daily life and commerce. Ironically, this made the citizenry collectively more vulnerable to the onset and sweeping occupation of the city by the plague. Taking stock collectively and developing a communal response were impossible. There is an infernal dialectic at work here. As collective action becomes impossible and public deterioration inevitable, it becomes increasingly rational for individuals to look to their own resources for their immediate preservation. But this "rational" response only makes each in his or her own solitude more vulnerable to the pestilence in the long run—hence, at each stage, rationally reinforcing the individualist imperative.

Meanwhile, the task of public safety fell even more upon the shoulders of a bureaucracy suited only, at best, to maintaining business as usual. Anything threatening the normal flow of business is anathema to such public officials. They do not routinely address human concerns. They have their regulations, their standardized ways of processing information and of making decisions. Facts that do not fit the prescribed molds cannot be processed. If they cannot be processed, for the bureaucracy they do not exist. So it is at first with the plague. They deny the evidence.

While the administrators, and Dr. Richard in particular, well express the officialdom of mercantile society, Judge Othon embodies both its self-righteous posture and Camus's sense of its hidden humane potential. Echoing themes that recur throughout his work, Camus invites us to consider what it means to be a judge. Is not a judge one who claims the right to pass judgment upon others? Is it by chance that society places its judges on perches high above the rest of us? Do not those who comfortably occupy that role tend to assume they are better than those upon whom they so freely pass judgment?

Judge Othon seems literally to clothe himself in respectability, to be above reproach, to be bourgeois respectability and propriety incarnate. Feelings of tenderness and affection, tolerance of personal idiosyncrasies, enjoyment of the spontaneity of children, all seem alien to him. The executor of eternal values, he speaks only of *them*, not of *us*, as though he were of another race. No wonder Tarrou calls Othon "'Enemy Number One'" (P, 134) and later wonders, "How can you help a judge?" (P, 219).

Implicated, however, in his wife's quarantine after she cared for her mother, Othon is no longer above suspicion. Even a clerk is now free to challenge a judge. Turning the tables, the clerk suggests that Othon is infected and should be excluded from the community of humans. That even a judge cannot avoid infection reveals our natural vulnerability. The pretentious cloak of bourgeois respectability is stripped off, laying bare its eternal values as but an ideological cover for privilege and a rejection of the commonality of our condition. With the death of his son, this fact is brought crashing down upon Othon.

Commenting upon the significance that Nietzsche saw in the death of God, Camus will later write in *The Rebel* that with this insight "the time of exile begins, the endless search for justification, the aimless nostalgia, 'the most painful, the most heart-breaking question, that of the heart which asks itself: where can I feel at home?'" (R, 70). How continuous this is with the narrator's description of the Oranais, "who drifted through life rather than lived, the prey of aimless days and sterile memories." Othon is forced to live like all the others who are under suspicion, in the decontamination camps. When he is released, the judge rises to unexpected heights, returning voluntarily to the camp to work with and to serve those whom he now considers his equals. He now makes common cause with his fellows. The transformation of Othon may be taken as pointing the way toward our "relative salvation," a path Camus will develop elsewhere. As the narrator observes, and as Othon's life after infection corroborates, the Oranais behaved "like wandering shadows that could have acquired substance only by consenting to root themselves in the solid earth of their distress" (P, 66). With this interweaving of dramatic scenario and philosophical vision we reach the metaphysical significance of this chronicle: Solidarity is born out of metaphysical solitude.

THE ACHE OF SEPARATION

The significance of finding ourselves in a post-Christian world is felt in the ache of separation that dramatizes the experience of exile. Here again, Rambert carries the burden of the metaphysical theme, thus facilitating the transition from Camus's personal experience to its theoretical expression. Echoing existentialist philosophy—as expressed, for example, in Martin Heidegger's notion of thrownness—Rambert "explained that his presence in Oran was purely accidental, he had no connection with the town" (P, 78). But is this not the condition of all of us on spaceship earth, in a seemingly infinite universe, subject to the impartial laws of nature in which human beings are but random products of natural selection?

If Rambert's situation starkly reveals the nonrationality of our condition, as his efforts to escape its limits suggest a possibly universal urge to transcend finitude, his explicit values and practical strategies are but one of the ways in which we may respond. While persevering in his futile effort to escape quarantine and be reunited with his love, he challenges Rieux whom he accuses of "being capable of dying for an ideal. . . . I've seen enough of people who die for an idea. I don't believe in heroism. . . . What interests me is living and dying for what one loves'" (P, 149). "There's no question of heroism in all this," responds Rieux. "It's a matter of common decency. That's an idea which may make some people smile, but the only means of fighting the plague is—common decency" (P, 150).

Two conceptions of what matters in life are at odds here, entailing differing attitudes toward our involvement with others. Rambert's conception of love is immediate and personal. Like stage settings, extensive personal relations often interfere with satisfaction. There is something very real and tangible in his commitment that is not easily denied. Only such romantic love can yield the happiness that makes life worthwhile, he feels. And yet ultimately he concludes that he cannot turn away from Oran's fight against the plague. After deciding to join the volunteer work teams, he responds to Rieux's observation that "there was nothing shameful in preferring happiness" with the powerful: "Certainly. But it may be shameful to be happy by oneself."

The moral quandary in which each finds himself is summed up by Rieux: "For nothing in the world is it worth turning one's back on what one loves. Yet that is what I'm doing, though why I don't know. That's how it is, and there's nothing to be done about it. So let's recognize the fact and draw the conclusions" (P, 188–9). The most immediate and precious human values are often put to the rack by our condition, calling for a collective response. But there are no assurances of success, nor any clear sense of what success may consist in. There are, however, some immediate and tangible costs but no viable alternatives. Here, in this metaphysical blind alley, is the suggestion of a direction, the sense of a deeper value. The ache of separation bears witness to the longing for union that is the metaphysical root of love: to be one with another. Our existence, for which ultimately there are facts but no reasons, bears witness to the pervasive demand to alleviate the ache that is the experience of our finitude. The separation of lovers occasioned by the plague may have only brought more clearly into focus the already existing fact that love had been allowed to be reduced simply to the habitual satiation of physical needs apart from the vitalized and sensitive sharing of common experiences and perceptions that alone can seriously address our metaphysical hunger. Thus the recognition of the common tragedy that is the plague can make our collective predicament evident to all, thus establishing the minimal conditions for bringing human beings together in a collective effort.

A CHRISTIAN WITNESS

If the plague dramatizes our finitude, it does so as a force of nature, thus avoiding the question of radical evil. We may through negligence participate in evil, but we do not positively will it. "The evil that is in the world always comes from ignorance," observes Rieux, expressing a modified humanist faith, "and good intentions may do as much harm as malevolence, if they lack understanding. On the whole men are more good than bad. . . . But they are more or less ignorant . . . the most incorrigible vice being that of an ignorance that fancies it knows everything and therefore claims for itself the right to kill" (P, 120–1). Belief in the possession of a truth that justifies murder —what may be called the problem of historical evil—was the problem faced by Tarrou, to which I will shortly turn. In *The Plague*, Tarrou sets forth the problem of logical murder, which Camus will take up in detail in *The Rebel*. But it is with Father Paneloux that we directly encounter the effort to make sense of natural evil.

We first meet Paneloux, perhaps the most sympathetically drawn Christian in all of Camus's fiction, as "a stalwart champion of Christian doctrine." In an early draft of his manuscript the narrator remarks that Paneloux "had published . . . commentaries on St. Augustine which showed him entirely in accord with the doctrine of his master" (TRN, 1979). His initial response to the plague is thus not surprising.

Calamity has come upon you, my brethren, and, my brethren, you deserved it. . . .
　　If today the plague is in your midst, that is because the hour has struck for taking thought. The just man need have no fear, but the evil doer has good cause to tremble. For plague is the flail [*fléaux*] of God and the world His threshing floor, and implacably He will thresh out His harvest until the wheat is separated from the chaff. There will be more chaff than wheat, few chosen of the many called. Yet this calamity was not willed by God. Too long this world of ours has connived at evil, too long it has counted on the divine mercy, on God's forgiveness. . . . For a long while God gazed down on this town with eyes of compassion; but He grew weary of waiting . . . and now He has turned His face away from us. And so, God's light withdrawn, we walk in darkness, in the thick darkness of the plague (P, 86–8).

Here we witness an unquestioning faith in the purposefulness of divine creation, along with the Augustinian solution to the problem of evil: that it is but a privation of good. If God does not sustain us in the good, we fall prey to the evil inherent in our sinful nature. As creatures ever turning away from God, we are responsible for our torments. We are not innocent, though God is blameless. Even more, this pestilence is both just divine retribution and an occasion for individual enlightenment. "The first time this scourge appears in history, it was wielded to strike down the enemies of God. . . . Thus from the dawn of recorded history the scourge of God has humbled the proud of heart and laid low those who hardened themselves against Him. Ponder this well, my friends, and fall on your knees" (P, 87).

Not revolt but guilt, self-condemnation, and passive acceptance are the message of the Christian Paneloux. "No man should seek to force God's hand or to hurry on the appointed hour, and from a practice that aims at speeding up the order of events which God has ordained unalterably from all time, it is but a step to heresy" (P, 90). We must accept our suffering with a renewed faith in divine justice. Punishment is our just reward for turning away from God. Only if we humble ourselves before the plague in contrition for our sins can we be reconciled to God and the divine order of things.

In short, Christianity justifies suffering in the name of guilt—original sin —and absolves God and his Creation of responsibility. It is the message, as Camus had noted as early as his dissertation, that builds our salvation upon our acceptance of guilt for the death of the innocent Christ. Its message is that God's grace is available only to the contrite—while rebellion is a prideful challenge to God's divinely ordered world.

But then Judge Othon's son dies, "racked on the tumbled bed, in a grotesque parody of crucifixion" (P, 193). Surely *he* could not have been guilty. "In the small face, rigid as a mask of greyish clay, slowly the lips parted and from them rose a long, incessant scream, hardly varying with his respiration, and filling the ward with a fierce, indignant protest, so little childish that it seemed like a collective voice issuing from all the sufferers there" (P, 194). This moves Paneloux to fall on his knees and ask God to spare the child, but to no avail.

In the face of the palpable purposelessness of this crushing fate, there can be no more self-satisfied and rational faith. Outraged by the "death-throes of an innocent child," a "mad revolt" bursts from Rieux. To Paneloux's searching "perhaps we should love what we cannot understand," Rieux angrily retorts: "No, Father, I've a very different idea of love. And until my dying day I shall refuse to love a scheme of things in which children are put to torture." This metaphysical rebel echoes Ivan Karamazov, whom Camus quotes in *The Rebel*: "If the suffering of children . . . serves to complete the sum of suffering necessary for the acquisition of truth, I affirm . . . that truth is not worth such a price" (R, 56). Rieux rejects a grace he cannot understand for the practical efforts to ameliorate human suffering. "Salvation is too big a word for me," he says to Paneloux. "I don't aim so high. I'm concerned with man's health; and for me his health comes first" (P, 197).

The metaphysical dimension of this confrontation was underlined earlier when Rieux comments upon Paneloux's first sermon. "Paneloux . . . hasn't come in contact with death; that's why he can speak with such assurance of the truth—with a capital 'T'. But [if he] . . . heard a man gasping for breath on his deathbed . . . he'd try to relieve human suffering before trying to point out its excellence" (P, 116). No, truth with a capital "T" is an abstraction —in a sense, just like the plague, and just as deadly. In its Christian form it justifies submission and the acceptance of the death of innocence; in its revolutionary form it justifies radical intervention and the putting to death of innocence. Both in their own way join with those plaguelike forces that destroy the natural community of people in the face of death.

But there is a path beneath the absolute, and apart from it, that offers the possibility of a common ground where divergent commitments to the transcendent can still meet. "What I hate is death and disease," observes Rieux. "And whether you wish it or not, we're allies, facing them and fighting them together." "We're working side by side for something that unites us— beyond blasphemy and prayers. And it's the only thing that matters" (P, 197).

However much Paneloux is moved by the suffering of the judge's son, and however much he commits himself to the day-to-day struggle to ameliorate the plague victims' suffering, these are not answers, but only challenges posed to his faith in divine providence. Dedicated Christian that he is, he recognizes that there can be no more temporizing with faith. He addresses the predicament of the modern Christian in his second sermon. "My brothers, a time of testing has come for us all. We must believe everything or deny everything. And who among you, I ask, would dare to deny everything?" (P, 202).

In the crucible of such events, either one must be willing to place total trust in the goodness of a transcendent and somewhat inscrutable God, or, like Ivan, one must question that God in the name of a value one comprehends. The father was reported as admonishing:

There was no question of not taking precautions or failing to comply with the orders wisely promulgated for the public weal. . . . We should go forward, groping our way through the darkness, stumbling perhaps at times, and try to do what good lay in our power. As for the rest, we must hold fast, trusting in the divine goodness, *even as to the deaths of little children,* and not seeking personal respite. . . .

The love of God is a hard love. It demands *total self-surrender, disdain of our human personality. And yet it alone can reconcile us to the suffering and the deaths of children,* it alone can justify them, *since we cannot understand them, and we can only make God's will ours.* That is the faith, cruel in men's eyes, and crucial in God's, which we must ever strive to compass. We must aspire beyond ourselves toward that high and fearful vision. And on *that* lofty plane all will fall into place, all discords be resolved, and truth flash forth from the dark cloud of seeming injustice (P, 205–6, my italics).

Father Paneloux[3] has drawn the conclusion of the Kierkegaardian leap of faith; we must accept all and make God's will ours; for that "alone can reconcile us to the suffering and the deaths of children."

Paneloux councils an "active fatalism," a "humiliation to which the person humiliated [gives] full assent. True, the agony of a child was humiliating to the heart and to the mind. But that was why we had to come to terms with it. And that, too, was why . . . since it was God's will, we, too, should will it" (P, 203). Any other path would be dishonest, seeking the comforts of belief, without bearing its burdens.[4]

However active Paneloux's practice, it is ultimately constrained and probably vitiated by its metaphysical resignation. Here, in Camus's view, is the root moral failure of Christianity. It is built upon the acceptance of the death of innocence and is thus the ultimate negation of revolt.

A MORE MODEST FAITH

Rieux "is the only one who might still be able to play the role of confessor. He has been the priest of a religion without certainty and without hope —entirely relative and entirely human" (TRN, 1988). Thus Camus, in his *Carnets*, counterposes the doctor to the priest. No doubt Camus's experiences and beliefs find expression in most of his central characters, especially Tarrou and Rambert, but it is probably Rieux who comes closest to the views of the author at this time in his life. In some working notes for the rewriting of the novel he had written: "One of the possible themes: conflict of medicine and religion; the powers of the relative (and how relative) against those of the absolute. It is the relative which triumphs or more exactly which does not lose" (TRN, 1949). While explicitly rejected by Camus in *The Myth*, Paneloux's leap of faith dramatizes the only authentic religious position in the contemporary world. In his speech to the Dominican monks in 1946, Camus had voiced Rieux's faith first expressed to Rambert, "that there was some common ground on which they could meet," (P, 80) by observing, "I share with you [Christians] the same revulsion from evil. But I do not share your hope, and I continue to struggle against this universe in which children suffer and die" (RRD, 53).

Thus for Rieux life is finite, suffering is all around us and to some extent inevitable, but we can strive to reduce its scope and amount. We must balance Tarrou with Rambert and Grand. The absurd as metaphysical solitude is our collective situation, and our minimum responsibility is to do whatever is possible, within the limits of "our station and its duties," to limit the damages. This sense of the morally self-evident is rooted in a metaphysical vision generated by the experience of absurdity. Echoing the theme of *The Myth*, expressed in its opening epigram, Rieux observed that "for those . . . who aspired beyond and above the human individual toward something they could not even imagine, there had been no answer. . . . If others, however, . . . had got what they wanted, this was because they had asked for the one thing that depended on them solely. . . . It was only right that those whose desires are limited to man and his humble yet formidable love should enter, if only now and then, into their reward" (P, 271).

Yet Rieux "realized the bleak sterility of a life without illusion" about its ultimate absurdity. For those of us who feel the gut need for a transcendent faith, "how hard it must be to live only with what one knows and what one remembers, cut off from what one hopes for" (P, 262, 263). With needs similar to those of Paneloux, but incapable of believing, "Tarrou had lived a life riddled with contradictions and had never known hope's solace." The struggles of this post-Christian saint living in an era of the death of God sheds light upon the struggles of Rieux and Paneloux, helping to place them in their appropriate historical context.

SAINT WITHOUT GOD

"I had plague . . . long before I . . . encountered it here," comments Tarrou. "Which is tantamount to saying I'm like everybody else. Only there are some people who don't know it, or feel at ease in that condition; others know and want to get out of it" (P, 222). After having witnessed a trial and an execution, Tarrou's "real interest in life" became the death penalty.

So I became an agitator. . . . To my mind the social order around me was based on the death sentence, and by fighting the established order I'd be fighting against murder. . . .

Needless to say, I knew that we, too, on occasion, passed sentences of death. But I was told that these few deaths were inevitable for the building up of a new world in which murder would cease to be. . . . Whatever the explanation, I hesitated. But then I remembered that miserable owl in the dock and it enabled me to keep on. *Until that day when I was present at an execution* . . . and exactly the same dazed horror that I'd experienced as a youngster made everything reel before my eyes.

Have you ever seen a man shot by a firing squad?

And thus I came to understand that I, anyhow, had had plague through all those long years in which, paradoxically enough, I'd believed with all my soul that I was fighting it. I learned that I had had an indirect hand in the deaths of thousands of people; that I'd even brought about their deaths by approving of acts and principles which could only end in that way. . . . When I spoke of these matters they told me not to be so squeamish; I should remember what great issues were at stake. And they advanced arguments, often quite impressive ones, to make me swallow what nonetheless I could not bring myself to stomach. . . .

In any case, my concern was not with arguments. It was with . . . that foul procedure whereby dirty mouths stinking of plague told a fettered man that he was going to die, and scientifically arranged all things so that he should die, after nights and nights of mental torture while he waited to be murdered in cold blood. My concern was with that hole in a man's chest. And I told myself that . . . nothing in the world would induce me to accept any argument that justified such butcheries. . . .

I'm still of the same mind. . . . As time went on I merely learned that even those who were better than the rest could not keep themselves nowadays from killing or letting others kill, *because such is the logic by which they live;* and that we can't stir a finger in this world without the risk of bringing death to somebody (P, 226–8, my italics).

This, however, simply formulates the rebel's essential "no." But what can be done about it? "'It comes to this,' Tarrou said . . . 'what interests me is learning how to become a saint. . . . Can one be a saint without God?— that's . . . the only problem I'm up against today.'" The encounter with the plague makes clear the difficulty of this endeavour. To become *engagé* is almost certainly to be guilty of increasing someone's suffering; but to remain apart, free from involvement, pure, is to be equally guilty of standing idly by while others suffer and die. Tarrou suggests sanitary squads be formed to combat the plague.

I only know that one must do what one can to cease being plague-stricken, and that's the only way in which we can hope for some peace or, failing that, a decent death. . . . Only this can bring relief to men, and if not save them, at least do them the least harm possible and even, sometimes, a little good. So that is why I resolved to have no truck with anything which, directly or indirectly, for good reason or for bad, brings death to anyone or justifies others' putting him to death (P, 228–9).

With his response to the plague, an essential theme of the novel finds expression: the metaphysical need for collective security.

What's natural is the microbe. All the rest—health, integrity, purity (if you like)—is a product of the human will, of a vigilance that must never falter. The good man, the man who infects hardly anyone, is the man who has the fewest lapses of attention. And it needs tremendous will-power, a never-ending tension of the mind, to avoid such lapses (P, 229).

If a collective commitment is essential to combat plague, however, the desire to remain pure and not infect anyone makes such a commitment practically impossible. Tarrou feels this deeply. He must always remain something of an enigma, an outsider to the human community, an exile.

Each of us has the plague within him. . . . We must keep endless watch on ourselves lest in a careless moment we breathe in somebody's face and fasten infection on him. . . . That is why some of us, those who want to get the plague out of their systems, feel such a desperate weariness . . . from which nothing remains to set us free except death.

Pending that release, I know I have no place in the world of today; once I'd definitely refused to kill, I doomed myself to an exile that can never end. . . . I leave it to others to make history. I know, too, that I'm not qualified to pass judgment on those others. There's something lacking in my mental make-up, and its lack prevents me from being a rational murderer. . . . All I maintain is that on this earth there are pestilences and there are victims, and it's up to us, so far as possible, not to join forces with the pestilences (P, 229).

But that is not enough; to purity must be added a program of not only assisting the victims, but freeing them from their status as victims.

The ground for such a program—only hinted at by the sanitary squads —is suggested by the friendship between Rieux and Tarrou, born of the common struggle with the plague, and sealed by their swim in the ocean. As Tarrou insisted, "It's too damn silly living in and for the plague. Of course, a man should fight for the victims, but if he ceases caring for anything outside that, what's the use of his fighting?" (P, 231). As "they swam side by side, with the same zest, in the same rhythm, isolated from the world, at last free of the town and the plague . . . neither said a word, but they were conscious of being perfectly at one" (P, 233).

Fascinated by the simple details of ordinary life, to which his journal bears eloquent witness, Tarrou nevertheless remains torn between his capacity to celebrate the ordinary and his demand for purity. Riddled with contradictions, he can sense the possibility of a "third category: that of the true healers" but cannot instantiate such a strategy in his life. Programmatically he is at a dead end. He is at one with Paneloux in suggesting that evil is just a privation of good, resulting from inattention, or a failure of lucidity, when he asserts "that all our troubles spring from our failure to use plain, clean-cut language" (P, 230). That implies that the world is acceptable as it is, and thus in no need of a practical and constructive program for collective amelioration. But this is a position he cannot accept. Thus Tarrou incarnates demands for sanctity with an inability to "correct creation" in the relative, which is the perfect complement from a post-Christian perspective of Paneloux's leap of faith. Striving to be a saint without God, free of complicity in the suffering and death of innocence, he too chooses a path of purity which is not of this world. His death, along with that of Paneloux, dramatically comments upon Camus's sense of the concrete future of such transcendent aspirations.

His struggle to remain innocent in a society that exacts complicity in murder suggests, however, a new dimension of revolt that anticipates the struggles of Kaliayev and les justes. What Tarrou faces, and revolt must come to terms with, is the problem of social action. In order to be effective, such action must move out into an external world where the results are no longer controllable. What is more, the very structure of the social situation will involve one in opposition to, and perhaps lead to the destruction of, other human beings. In short, whatever the limitations of Tarrou's response, Camus has for the first time in his work directly faced the challenge posed by an evil that is internal to the human world.[5]

AN ADVOCATE FOR PLAGUE

Cottard is the only one of Camus's characters who welcomes the plague and anguishes at the prospect of its coming to an end. Yet there is sympathy in Camus's portrayal of him, for he too suffers the yoke of separation and yearns to belong.

Wanted by the authorities, who are closing in on him at the onset of the plague, Cottard suffers from his isolation from the community and fears incarceration above all. In desperation he attempts suicide, only to be rescued by Grand, out of simple compassion. "I can't say I really know him, but one's got to help a neighbor, hasn't one?" (P, 19).

As plague occupies Oran, the authorities' attention is diverted, freeing Cottard from the daily pressures of being under suspicion. He relaxes, becomes humorous and friendly, and begins to feel at home with others. "Say what you like, Tarrou, but . . . the one way of making people hang together is to give 'em a spell of plague" (P, 175).

None of this impedes his ability to traffic in the plague's underground, making money through the black market and off the suffering of others. But without maliciousness. He is merely doing what he knows best. He lives well, but is not without concern for the well-being of others. Perhaps he simply lacks the imagination to conceive of the consequences of his actions. Here he would not differ greatly from most of what could now be called his fellow citizens. The same is true for the authorities—a feeling that well represents Camus's sense that most collaborators in wartime France were primarily guilty, not so much of evil as of a failure of imagination. It may even be said more generally of Camus—as we have noted with Rieux and Tarrou —that he does not see as much evil in mankind as narrowness of vision, self-preoccupation, venality, self-interest, and above all an inability to appreciate the meaning and consequences of one's actions.[6]

Cottard thrives along with the plague. Of course, *that* is his condemnation: to feel at home in a situation that is wreaking havoc on the community. He is thus in league, albeit not viciously, with the forces of inhumanity. He even profits from their occupation of Oran. It is not surprising, therefore, that a growing sense of anxiety and ultimately panic grips him as the plague recedes. As the state of siege is lifted, the authorities will be free to turn their attention to hunting criminals. This "man who hated loneliness" is once again overwhelmed by the fear of being cut off from the community, not realizing that his fate is an inevitable result of a lifestyle that exists at the expense of others. Nor does he seem able to do otherwise. Camus does not explore how Cottard became the way he is. His actions during the plague seem natural; criminality seems to be his nature, redemption beyond his ken. The significance of this portrayal of criminality is not completely clear.

DRAMATIC LIMITATIONS

It is noteworthy that we do not get any comprehensive presentation of the forces that collaborated with the plague. It is difficult to envisage active support for the plague—however much Cottard may be taken as one who welcomed it and benefited from it—because it is difficult to defend the plague's reign. This is a key limitation of Camus's mythic transformation of occupied France.

What, it might be asked, is the material base that facilitated the plague's entry into Oran, so abrupt and pervasive? It is almost as if a fifth column were already at work within the city, perhaps in the form of authorities who unduly delayed taking the appropriate measures. Where are the representatives of the business establishment who, during the Popular Front, proclaimed, "Better Hitler than Blum"? Where are the internal forces of fascism? The members of Action Française? The supporters of a renascent French patriotism and anti-Semitism? Those who made it impossible for France to come to the aid of the embattled forces of Republican Spain? In short, where is the class struggle? What was the social and class base of the opponents of fascism? From what segments of society did the resistance draw most of its strength? And where was the grand bourgeoisie while the underground network was being developed? Unfortunately, Camus does not address these questions.

By mythologizing the resistance as a drama of the human condition, Camus's work gained in metaphysical scope and in internal development. But he pays a serious price at the level of historical and theoretical applicability. That is partly the result of his choice of metaphysical symbol. The plague is a microbe, a force of nature that strikes at the human community. But it is not a human force, not even primarily carried by humans. How could human beings identify with and justify its rule as a social strategy? How could anyone offer it as a solution to the drama of the absurd, as a response to the need for moral regeneration, renewed patriotism, and social reconstruction, or as a legitimate way of keeping social order and peace?

Even more, as a transcription of the struggles of his generation, where in *The Plague* is the conflict of competing visions of human destiny that Camus so agonizingly transcribed in his *Letters to a German Friend*? Where are those Nazis who, believing as Camus himself did, "that this world had no ultimate meaning," "deduced the idea that everything was equivalent" and that "those who, like us young Germans, are lucky enough to find a meaning in the destiny of our nation must sacrifice everything else"? (RRD, 3). That this was Camus's position can be gleaned from his own assessment of the novel in 1942:

The Stranger describes the nudity of man in the face of the absurd; *The Plague*, the profound equivalence of all points of view in face of the same absurd. It is a progress which will become more precise in other works. But in addition, *The Plague* demonstrates that the absurd teaches nothing (TRN, 1928).

In fact, this early evaluation of the novel's significance may suggest the source of the mythic symbol.

In sum, this mythic frame does not adequately allow Camus to pose the problem of human evil any more than it does justice to questions of social policy, political opposition and dissent, class conflict, and social antagonisms in general. That Camus sensed this may be seen from the further development of his work. Nevertheless, it is important to underline the extent to which revolt and resistance are shortchanged in *The Plague* if we are to be able to appreciate both the nature of Camus's development and the kind of critical scrutiny he was increasingly to face. In this work we are left with only Tarrou's reminiscences, without any clear sense of the political issues that so fiercely divide equally sincere human beings, leading some to see murder as not only acceptable but often necessary and justifiable.

In his response to Roland Barthes, and earlier to Sartre and Jeanson, Camus failed to pick up the deepest sense of the criticism. He is certainly right when he insists upon the explicit thematic development of his work. "Compared to *The Stranger*, *The Plague* does, beyond any possible discussion, represent the transition from an attitude of solitary revolt to the recognition of a community whose struggles must be shared. If there is an evolution from *The Stranger* to *The Plague*, it has moved in the direction of solidarity and participation" (LCE, 339). There is, however, another more subtle message that operates at the level of what might be called stylistic metaphysics. Here the commitment at the core of the emerging response to the plague has been so devoid of specific historical and political content—in the service, perhaps, of the mythologized enactment of the human condition—that its message goes little beyond eternal vigilance and mutual respect and solidarity in the face of recurring threats to human living. But where should we look for these threats? Are there no important differences between the dangers of human evil and natural disaster? Can we not organize our society in such a way as to minimize the disasters? Are all things eternally equal and equivalent? What is the morality thus suggested, if not that we should cultivate—not our private garden, as with Voltaire—but our collective garden, devoid of the clamors of political action, class conflict, national enmities, and struggles for historical and economic progress? Are we being urged, at least by implication, to accept stoically the limited possibilities for satisfaction in human life—with a small community of friends, ever vigilant against external dangers, but with no sense of the political and economic dangers coming from our fellows, and no suggestion for forestalling these threats? Is this not precisely Rieux's position? In short, have not the cyclical and eternally recurrent features of the human condition taken hold of this dramatized Camusian universe to such an extent that we are deprived of constructive possibilities for political action? Are we not reduced to a kind of defensive psychosis, with perhaps some commitment to giving money or verbal support to the likes of Amnesty International and the Red Cross, but no more? This may not have been Camus's intent—he may not have even been aware of this sense of his work —but does this not seem to be the central thrust of the novel?

Nevertheless, *The Plague* has made clear the need for the establishment of a shared consciousness of our common condition as the precondition for the development of a human community. The entire movement of Camus's thought leading up to and including the novel has revealed the importance, nay, from a social standpoint, the necessity, of such a development. From this perspective, *The Plague* clearly represents a development that finally brings to the fore our collective condition and, by so doing, suggests the framework for a solution to the tragedy of "The Misunderstanding" and *The Myth*. Yet the question of revolt still lacks satisfactory articulation. Revolt has achieved the social dimension hinted at in "Caligula," the recognition that individuals insist upon a certain dignity; that we must establish a communal framework of shared perceptions and meanings if we are to live a meaningful and fulfilling life in the face of a condition that denies humanity; and that there is an essentially communal base to living that must be reflectively grasped as the precondition of constructive human action. This transition stage *The Plague* has clearly established.

But if the social dimension is so essential, what happens to revolt when that dimension itself becomes oppressive? The universe of *The Plague* is Manichean: the good of communal revolt against the evil of the plague. The meaning of the struggle is grounded in the human values that emerge in, and are attested to by, the struggle. But what happens when the oppressive element is similarly human? When, as Tarrou claimed, it is the human being who carries the germ within him? Or when, further, it is humans that deny humans? How does revolt emerge there? And, more difficult still, on what does it seek to base its claims? Construct its community? Where then are the meanings and limits of the endeavor to be found? On these questions *The Plague* offers little assistance. It will be the task of the works that follow to address them.

With "The State of Siege" the problem of oppression and the destruction of felt human meaning will be posed by human beings. The logic of tyranny and the rupture of dialogue are once again encountered, but in a new setting. Here social revolt comes to the fore for the first time, tackling—in the person of Diego—but not resolving the dilemma that Tarrou embodied. It is "The Just" that seeks to study the limits that such revolt must set for itself in terms of its own rationale: It poses the problem. *The Rebel* then undertakes to analyze the logic of revolt through a study of the dialectic of its betrayal. These two plays articulate an essential dimension of Camus's thought: the emergence of social revolt in "The State of Siege" and the problem of its limits in "The Just." My discussion of them will also serve as a preface to the consideration of *The Rebel*.

7

Society and Rebellion

It is simply a matter of not adding to the profound miseries of our condition an entirely human injustice (E, 1528).

SLAVERY AND FREEDOM

A Medieval Morality Play

Camus writes of "The State of Siege" that his avowed aim "was to divest the stage of psychological speculations in muffled voices so that it might ring with the loud shouts that today enslave or liberate masses of men. . . . I focused my play on what seems to me the only living religion in the century of tyrants and slaves—I mean liberty" (CTOP, ix).

"The State of Siege" is a medieval morality play in modern dress. Offering a perspective on the contemporary world, its characters are dramatized attitudes and intellectual positions. They are people only so far as people may take up and embody such attitudes. The developing confrontation of these embodied perspectives reveals the logic of revolt for Camus. The spectacle may be viewed as a dramatic commentary on his statement to the Dominican monks in 1946: "Between the forces of dialogue and the forces of tyranny a great unequal battle has begun" (RRD, 53).

The Plague Strikes

The action begins with the appearance of a dreaded and frightful omen, a comet, over the city of Cadiz. Like the rats in Oran, the appearance of the comet disturbs the normal routine. The citizens are at loose ends. The resident nihilist, Nada, is engaged in argument with The Judge "for taking liberties . . . with the Creator" (CTOP, 140).[1] The metaphysical rebel is accused of blasphemy by the spokesman for the creator. The omen, says The Judge, reminiscent of the "first" Father Paneloux, was meant for those whose hearts are evil, "and who of you can say his heart is pure? . . . Fear and kneel!" The Judge stands as the creator's self-appointed representative on earth. Guilt and self-flagellation are probably the best ways to keep the people in line, the herd docile.

106

Diego, a medical student, perhaps a young Dr. Rieux, refuses to join in with Nada's negativism. At one with the status quo, on the side of right-eousness, his initial attitude is simple and unreflective. (Diego never loses his attachment to the concrete present, even in his revolt. This attachment prescribes the limits to his revolt and makes his death so much more tragic.) Meanwhile the Herald appears with orders from The Governor (reminiscent of the official response to the appearance of the rats in Oran): "Good Govern-ments are governments under which nothing happens. . . . And accordingly each of you is ordered to deny that any comet has ever risen on the horizon of our city" (CTOP, 141–2).

Comets are to be referred to as natural phenomena, no more. To this posi-tion of The Governor and Nada, Diego counterposes his defense of honor. But his position remains immediate, naïve: events have yet to challenge it. His first rejection of that which would destroy the human occurs in his encounter with Nada, but only as an impulsive, still inarticulate and unself-conscious reaction. The Governor and Nada suggest the union Camus sees, and later studies in *The Rebel*, between the passion for total order and that for total destruction: one attitude is built on a lie, the other on scorn. Both lack a positive intersubjective base. In Nada's encounter with The Plague, this will become clearer. Actually The Governor has no passion for total order, just for things as they are, for habit: he doesn't aim so high.

The chorus provides the social context, witnessing to the vitality and poetry of daily life. "So now [man's produce] throng[s] the cities of men in testimony that the fathering sky has kept its tryst with fertile mother earth" (CTOP, 144).

With the engagement of Diego and Victoria, we celebrate rebirth, remi-niscent of *Nuptials,* to which the chorus subscribes: "Yes, thank heaven, all is as it should be; the world has kept its balance. . . . Summer is here, happiness is ours. Nothing else counts, for we stake all on happiness." These affirma-tions are contrasted with Nada's nihilism. As for The Governor: "I like my habits, and change is the one thing I detest. . . . Nothing new is good. . . . I stand for immobility."

Then the plague strikes.

The response of the authorities to the epidemic is characteristic: The Judge will not sully his hands with involvement in the collective calamity. He is above it all, as was Judge Othon in *The Plague*. He speaks of guilt, evinces recrimination, insists upon isolation—and will not make common cause with others. The Priest, meanwhile, revels in sin. Preying upon guilt, he seeks to turn the people into a helpless, supplicating mass, while The Governor maintains the façade: business as usual. The effect of these official responses upon the populace is clearly demoralizing: "Thou hast signed in the sand, / Thou hast written in the sea; / Nothing endures but misery."

Thematically continuous with Dr. Rieux in *The Plague*, Diego, "wearing the plague-doctor's mask," is "busy with the sick." In times of plague, life cannot continue as before. The naïve immediacy of his previous attitude is shattered. "Has something changed between us?" asks Victoria. "I've been hunting for you everywhere. . . . And now I've found you, you are wearing that mask, that ghastly reminder of the disease. Do please take it off and hold me in your arms" (CTOP, 157).

As it must, plague has come between single individuals and their love. In the play as in the novel, individual life can remain isolated and self-contained only at the expense of the collectivity. The assured world is cracking. Our normal life supports are threatened. "Even honor is no help." The initial reaction, however, tends toward avoidance, denial, even of the most courageous and moral. Inevitably, love is attenuated, and suffers.

Plague has shaken beliefs. The common people bear the brunt, "Who is wrong and who is right: / Truth is but surmise. / Death and death alone is sure, / All the rest is lies!"

Nothing, of course, that has happened to this point could not have been accounted for within the framework of the novel. But when The Plague and The Secretary appear, the situation is transformed.

Regulations Are Promulgated

The human plague displaces the natural authorities without much struggle, but with an appropriate air of legality. In the process of convincing The Governor, he is about to eliminate Nada when The Secretary observes "that this fellow is the sort that doesn't believe in anything, in other words the sort of man who can be very useful to us" (CTOP, 163). With The Governor agreeing "of his own free will," and the First Alcade maintaining the appearance of continuity and normality, The Plague takes over.

In this encounter between Plague and Governor, the play's structural weaknesses—which contributed to its popular failure—first become apparent. The Governor emerges as nothing but a stick figure, not a person but a symbol without depth or resonance. He strikes no responsive chord, being but a caricature of the uncaring bureaucrat. Since he stands for nothing, no struggle takes place, and the action lacks drama. It is as if, in the manner of medieval morality plays, the author is imposing the action upon the audience in order to illustrate a predetermined thesis. The force of the play can thus only reside in the espoused ideas—however caricatured their expression—and the orchestrated spectacle. Hardly an appealing scenario for a modern audience.

With The Plague now in control, regulations are promulgated in bureaucratese. "It is intended to get them used to that touch of obscurity which gives all government regulations their peculiar charm and efficacy. The less these people understand, the better they'll behave" (CTOP, 165). The principle of tyranny is clearly the destruction of sense, the impossibility of dialogue: Shared meanings are replaced by commands sustained by collective intimidation. Total order will now be obtained, though Nada questions the difference. "What can that matter to you [people of Cadiz]? Plague or Governor, the government goes on." A series of five orders is promulgated.

1. Contamination is marked and isolated. The destruction of person-to-person relations is begun under the slogan of brotherhood.
2. The staff of life is subjected to detailed regulations—*and the human being is assumed guilty until proven "innocent."*
3. The restriction of movement and denial of all forms of liberty bring to light by negative means the constituents of human liberty.

With the last two regulations, this atomization of individuals from that community which alone can support them is made total.

4. "It is strictly forbidden to give help to any person stricken with disease. . . . A favorable view is taken of reports made by any member of a family as regards any other member or members of the said family, and such reports will entitle their makers to the double food ration, known as the Good Citizenship Ration" (CTOP, 167).

As the regulations take effect—and The Plague seeks to destroy the bonds that might tie citizens together, thus forming a potentially significant resistance factor—the citizens fall to fighting among themselves while the authorities abdicate their responsibility to unite the community. A voice cries out: "Do not leave me, Priest; I am one of the poor men of your flock. (The Priest begins to walk away.) Look! He's going. . . . No, stand by me, it's your duty to look after me, and if I lose you, then I've lost all. (The Priest quickens his steps. The poor man falls to the ground with a great cry.) Christians of Spain, you are forsaken!"[2]

5. "Lastly . . . so as to avoid contagion . . . each of you is ordered to keep permanently in his mouth a pad soaked in vinegar. This will not only protect you from the disease but teach you the art of silence."

Each statement sets into relief the life being suppressed and the new order being established. Not merely a social order but a transformed conception of rights and values is at stake. As The Plague observes: "I am the ruler here; this is a fact, therefore it is a right. A right that admits of no discussion; a fact you must accept."

The problem of total justice has thus been posed—in such terms as to make humans be seen as guilty. "Certificates of existence" must be drawn up: "The whole point of our government is that you always need a permit to do anything whatever" (CTOP, 175). Bureaucracy is but the organizational expression of the individualist application of the demand for totality. If total justice is insisted upon, and if the state takes the responsibility for achieving it, then no private life is possible. "What interests us is your public life and that as a matter of fact is the only one you are allowed by us to have." Further, there can be no standard of value beyond the public, the existent.

The entire movement of thought implied in this totalization and rationalization of existence comes to a head in the encounter with The Fisherman, who is asked for his "reasons for existing." "Make a note," responds The Secretary, "that the undersigned admits that his existence is unjustifiable. That will simplify matters when the time comes to deal with him. Also, that will bring it home to you, the undersigned, that the certificate of existence granted you is temporary and of short duration" (CTOP, 177).

No wonder that nihilism and total rationality, seemingly opposed phenomena, can join forces and work so well together. Camus suggests that they complement one another, representing the same negation of the meaning of daily life and its spontaneous offerings. "Nada: . . . the more one suppresses, the better things are. . . . So let's annihilate everything, I say. . . . God denies the world, and I deny God. Long live nothing, for it's the only thing that exists." This he will achieve by drinking, to which The Secretary responds: "A clumsy way of going about it. We have a better one. . . . We'll find you a job in our administration" (CTOP, 179). And what is that better way? "We start with the premises that you are guilty. But that's not enough; you must learn to feel yourselves, that you are guilty. And you won't feel guilty until you feel tired. So we wear you out, that's all. Once you are really tired, tired to death in fact, everything will run smoothly" (CTOP, 180).

Revolt Emerges

A basic theme of Camus's thought has thus been brought into relief, clearing the path that leads from the demand for total rationality to the denial of life. Ultimately, human existence is unjustifiable, and humans are ontologically guilty. Further, the attempt to establish a new pattern for existence based upon total justice seems inevitably to lead to mutilation and destruction—whether in the logical ecstasy of Caligula, in the bureaucratic depersonalization of our human plagues, or later in the duplicitous dialogue of our "judge-penitents." All start with the assumption of total culpability, based upon different forms of metaphysical revolutions, and end in the legitimation of enslavement and terror. They begin from a fundamental inability to come to terms with life as it is offered—to find *within it* areas of innocence, of direct value, and the grounds for what Camus calls in *The Rebel* a "reasonable culpability." None is capable of loving, whatever the effort to force a relation. Oppression is only the testament they pay to the human need for dialogue!

"Execution," says The Plague, "that puts it in a nutshell. And the man who is to die is expected to collaborate in his own execution" (CTOP, 18). Since all are guilty, the only acknowledged rights are those granted by the authorities. The transformation thus effected is succinctly summarized in Nada's remarks to The Woman: "You will not be given accommodation because your children are homeless. You will be given it if you supply a certificate. Which is not the same thing" (CTOP, 185).

It is only "natural" that such oppression stir revolt in Diego and muted whispers from the chorus. Diego challenges The Plague with an assertion of innocence. But fear breaks the back of his naïve rejoinder and he flees. The Chorus, forlorn, seeks to adapt to a stifling and degrading condition.

Diego takes refuge in The Judge's house, only to find the disintegration inevitably spawned by self-righteousness and self-sufficiency. Unable to make common cause with another human on the level of equality, The Judge brings forth the disintegration implicit in a household built on appearance and hypocrisy. Diego enters as The Judge is about to kick out the servant, who has "loyally . . . served you all your life." She is infected. And so is Diego. He must leave. The Judge will submit to any order, accept any fact, to protect himself. He will not jeopardize his position to preserve a common value. This judicial posture, with its consequent abdication of responsibility, is nothing but pure positivism.

Ironically, The Judge's position turns against him: The house is quarantined owing to Diego's presence, and the collective force of our common condition strikes home. As Diego notes, "The law's infallible as you pointed out just now . . . so here we are, all on the same boat—judge, accused, and witnesses. Brothers all!" (CTOP, 190). One cannot remain above the battle. We are all implicated. Either we acknowledge this, and make common cause with the hope of constructive achievement, or we condemn ourselves to atomization and an increasingly self-destructive self-seeking. When The Judge, rejecting solidarity, chooses recrimination and blame, his family disintegrates. His marriage is revealed to be built upon hypocrisy and self-righteousness. "I spit on your law," says The Judge's wife. "I have on my side the right of lovers not to be parted, the right of the criminal to be forgiven, the right of every penitent to recover his good name. . . . Justice . . . is on the side of the sufferers, the afflicted, those who live by hope alone" (CTOP, 192).

Diego and Victoria have left. They struggle to come to grips with the collective disaster that threatens to drive them apart as their love draws them together. It would be so simple to forget all, to limit the universe to themselves. But Diego feels a wider bond: "I'm too proud to love you if I can no longer respect myself" (CTOP, 195). He is infected and the thought that he will die and she will survive torments him. He loves life; nothing beyond has any meaning for either of them. Yet there are conditions under which he cannot continue to live. The conflict between private happiness and collective responsibility threatens to tear Diego and Victoria apart. "What do I care for your love," he cries, "if it doesn't rot along with me?" (CTOP, 196). Victoria speaks of the demands and fulfillments of love. Diego sways between opposed commitments, then says, "Let me go my own way. I cannot stand aloof with all this suffering around me" (CTOP, 197). The transition from a sense of pity to the realization of solidarity emerges in agony.

But Victoria's rejoinder challenges revolt's legitimacy from another angle:

When it's the utmost I can do to bear the weight of my love, how can you ask me to take on my shoulders the burden of the sorrows of the world as well? No, that's . . . one of those futile, preposterous crusades you men engage in as a pretext for evading the one struggle that is truly arduous, the one victory of which you could be rightly proud (CTOP, 198).

Once again, Rambert's question: Can one love and be happy alone?

Honor Triumphs

The problems involved with the emergence of rebellion have thus been set forth, and the limits that make it worth the effort have been suggested by Victoria. Diego states the other side: "To die is nothing. But to die degraded . . ." (CTOP, 202). The ground of his solidarity, upon which his revolt is based, as well as the limits it imposes on action are becoming clearer: "The men of my blood belong to the earth and to the earth alone" (CTOP, 202). Camus's faith in revolt finally achieves full articulation in Diego's encounter with The Secretary.

You have imposed on men the pangs of hunger and bereavement to keep their minds off any stirrings of revolt. You wear them down, you waste their time and strength so that they've neither the leisure nor the energy to vent their anger. So they just mark time. . . . Each of us is alone because of the cowardice of the others. . . . [But] there is in man . . . an innate power that you will never vanquish, a gay madness born of mingled fear and courage, unreasoning yet victorious through all time. One day this power will surge up and you will learn that all your glory is but dust before the wind (CTOP, 206).

This excessively optimistic statement of the emergence of rebellion no doubt suggests a simplified conception of human nature requiring further development. This initial articulation of political rebellion, emerging out of an insistence on collective dignity, hardly offers a political strategy.

By standing forth in rebellion, insisting on solidarity in dignity, Diego, however, in ungagging his compatriots, offers the promise of that living community that challenges dictators. The play then pursues, in schematized fashion, the emergence and ultimate success of a revolt rooted in communal solidarity.

The human plague tries to break the back of the revolt by turning the citizens against one another, to destroy the emerging solidarity before which it would stand helpless. The Secretary lets the people have the notebook so that private vengeances and recriminations may take over. The Judge's Daughter brings the spirit of The Judge's household into the rebellion and thus threatens to dissipate its strength. The citizens fall upon each other.

Rebellion does not come easy. Victoria is stricken and Diego must ask himself how far he will go in revolt. How far is it worth going? How far has he a right to go? Can he sacrifice his own life for such a cause? Has he a right to sacrifice another's? In a sense, the tables are turned between Diego and Victoria. The Chorus of Women berates Diego in a manner reminiscent of *The Myth* for having previously left Victoria: "A man cries for the impossible, a woman endures all that is possible. . . . Deserter! That body was your homeland; without it you are nothing any more; do not count on your remembrance to save you" (CTOP, 219).

The Plague is power. He makes his last attempt to break the revolt by hitting where it hurts most—to tempt and threaten Diego into submission. Diego offers an exchange: his life for Victoria's. "My life is nothing. What counts for me are my reasons for living." But in this situation they will prove reasons for dying. The Plague offers his own exchange: both their lives in return for ending the revolt. He berates Diego: "Don't you realize that ten years of this girl's love are worth far more than a century of freedom for those men?" Here is the Grand Inquisitor's challenge all over again. But Diego refuses, and The Plague is vanquished, but not without exacting a further toll: Diego's death.

With The Plague's departure, civil authority returns in the person of The Governor. Cynically, The Plague observes that he is

sodden with inertia and forgetfulness of the lessons of the past. And when you see stupidity getting the upper hand again without a struggle, you will lose heart; cruelty provokes, but stupidity disheartens. All honor, then, to the stupid, who prepare my way. . . . Perhaps there will come a day when self-sacrifice will seem quite futile, and the never-ending clamor of your rebels will at last fall silent. Then I shall reign supreme, in the dead silence of men's servitude (CTOP, 227–8).

With The Plague gone, Nada, like Cottard in *The Plague*, is reduced to isolation and despair. "One day you'll find out for yourselves that man is nothing and God's face is hideous!" Before their reborn faith in living, suicide seems alone bearable, but not without challenging the basis of their new-found hope: "As you see, fishermen and governments may come and go, the police are always with us. So after all, justice does exist" (CTOP, 231). To which The Chorus answers: "There is no justice—but there are limits. And those who stand for no rules at all, no less than those who want to impose a rule for everything, overstep the limit" (CTOP, 231).

Heroism Is Not Enough

With "The State of Siege" I have reviewed the logic of social revolt. In its most complete expression it requires incorporating into consciousness all those dimensions that our previous encounter with the absurd has brought forth. Such a realization is enough to dim any simple appeal to heroism. It is rather a question of dignity, of that minimal honor and liberty, without which life cannot be called human. Victoria and the chorus of women insist upon this point. They serve to restrain Diego's often impetuous desire to revenge the insult. For what is at stake is not simply honor, but the right to live, freely and fully. Although honor must be preserved, of itself it is no more than an abstraction to which life will be sacrificed. No, honor must rest on precisely that quality of concrete living that preserves it from the distortions of justifications. It must be that practical rebellion against the attempts of ideology to question the meaning of life from the perspective of totality. It must also find its justification in a sustaining human community, rather than in the lonely flight of solitudes.

In the last analysis a metaphysics of totality may be justified, but it is not given to us, as finite beings, to see this. The encounter with the absurd has revealed that at present all we can know about the meaning of our life with any degree of certainty is our desire for meaning, the certainty of suffering and death, and the limits that existence places on whatever partial meanings and unities we may be able to achieve. This framework provides the natural conditions of our life and of any endeavor to find a comprehensive rationale for it. What can justify the sacrifice of this limited amount of which we are certain for that eternity of which we can concretely know nothing? Camus's suggestion is that the willingness to sacrifice this present to that "future" stands in inverse proportion to the degree of fulfillment we are able to achieve in this present. With the characters of Nada, The Plague, and The Judge, Camus suggests that at the core of total revolt is an almost constitutional incapacity to find fulfillment in daily life, and that their rationalism or nihilism are equally forms of negation of the possibility of concrete intersubjective meaning. In Camus's adaptation of Dostoevsky's "The Possessed," Stavroguine explicitly reveals what is here only suggested, that the destruction of life, which their inability to love seems only accidentally to occasion, is really the inevitable outcome of their position. Later, with the judge-penitent after the fall, the destruction of human relations implicit in this sickness of the soul turns into a quite subtle program of enslavement through universal guilt.

Revolt can only obtain justification, therefore, to the extent that it originates from—and remains true to—a diametrically opposed conception of meaning that finds its justification in the collective living of sensual and free beings. Thus Diego's revolt must, in principle, be limited, not total. Its poignancy is made the clearer when it is realized that he must risk everything he finds worthwhile in order to preserve the relative values that are being threatened. Bravado is no alternative to a lucid consciousness. In a world where order is not given, but in which the passion for order can bring forth a new dimension of disorder, revolt can find its strength and its direction only by making common cause against that which will deny the human. This provides both the grounds of its justification and the limit within which it must be confined if it is to remain true to its origins.

With "The State of Siege" the problem of the generation of social revolt is set forth. No practical program is offered. "The Just" poses more subtle questions: Within the framework of revolt, what rights do we have? What limits does revolt itself prescribe? To what extent, and with what consequences, can one justify the sacrifice of another, or of the present for the future? In short, can revolt justify murder?

THE LIMITS OF REVOLT

Staging The Rebel

"The only revolution on a human scale would have to involve a conversion to the relative which would precisely signify fidelity to the human condition" (E, 1692). "The Just" may be taken as a dramatic staging of *The Rebel*. The essay even devotes one chapter to a discussion of the play's characters and their moral dilemma. Is there a logic to the point of murder? Camus asks. Can one kill in the name of justice? Given the personal constraints revealed in the encounter with the absurd, and the social ramifications explored in *The Plague* and "The State of Siege," what, if any, are the limits intrinsic to social action? In Camus's terms, what is the justification and scope of revolt?

In the name of justice and the future of humanity, "Les Justes" propose to murder the Archduke. Seeking "to achieve dramatic tension through classical means; that is, the opposition of characters who were equal in strength and reason" (CTOP, ix), Camus portrays the moral struggle within this insurrectional group. Stepan embodies Camus's image of the revolutionary: complete dedication to the cause of justice. Confronting Stepan is Kaliayev, that most scrupulous assassin. His need for innocence is insatiable, while his joy for life is torn apart by a deep sensitivity to the suffering occasioned by an unjust world. He can neither live in complicity with injustice nor justify murder. It is Dora, speaking for the concrete (as is so often the case with Camus's women), who forces the just to remember that their love of life alone justifies their rebellion. Skouratov, on the other hand, is a Dostoevskian police chief who presents the case for the status quo with cunning and modulated force. He seeks to isolate Kaliayev, using the power of the concrete to break the almost religious tie that binds him to his comrades, thus constituting the community of his revolt. It is this quasi-mystical tie to them that alone allows him to support the weight of his own injustice—an injustice that, though shattering, he feels to be unavoidable in this world. Finally, the Grand Duchess, driven to distraction by the irredeemably unjust character of the world, finds the only hope for abject creatures to lie in prayer and forgiveness. Five key encounters frame the problem: between Stepan and Kaliayev before the first attempt; among the entire group after Kaliayev fails to throw the bomb upon seeing the children in the carriage; between Dora and Kaliayev before the second attempt; after the assassination, between Kaliayev and Skouratov in jail; and then between Kaliayev and the Duchess.

On Killing Children

The depth of Kaliayev's moral commitment is made evident in his initial encounter with Stepan. If he fails in his mission, he says, he will kill himself. To this Stepan responds, "To commit suicide a man must have a great love for himself. A true revolutionary cannot love himself. . . . For me hatred is not just a game. . . . We have joined together to get something done" (CTOP, 243).

Revolution in the name of justice is evaluated by the efficacy with which it is carried out, Stepan believes. The cause alone has meaning. Hatred toward those who oppose it is justifiable, and nothing must be allowed to deflect the revolutionary from pursuit of the cause.

"I joined the revolution," answers Kaliayev, "because I love life." To Kaliayev's search for an immanent meaning Stepan responds with a transcendent justification: "I do not love life; I love something higher, and that is justice." "We consent to being criminals," he concludes, "so that at last the innocent, and only they, will inherit the earth" (CTOP, 245). But can an idealized future justify the loss of the present? To what extent? Are there no limits?

Finding children in the carriage alongside the Grand Duke, Kaliayev fails to throw the bomb. Distraught, he returns to the group because "you were the only people who could judge me, could say if I was wrong or right, and I'd abide by your decision" (CTOP, 255).

Les Justes confront the problem of the limits of terrorism, but Stepan is not placated: "Not until the day comes when we stop sentimentalizing about children will the revolution triumph, and we be masters of the world. . . . Nothing that can serve our cause should be ruled out. . . . Just because Yanek couldn't bring himself to kill, children will go on dying of starvation for years to come. . . . Don't meddle with the revolution, for it's task is to cure all sufferings present and to come." To which Kaliayev responds, "I shall not strike my brothers on the face for the sake of some far-off city, which for all I know, may not exist. *I refuse to add to the living injustice all around me for the sake of a dead justice.* . . . I have chosen death so as to prevent murder from triumphing in the world. I've chosen to be innocent" (CTOP, 256–60, my italics).

Kaliayev's position has been profoundly transformed. Confronted by Stepan's justification of revolutionary activity, he realizes the force of Dora's remarks: The future is not certain, and it can serve as the ground of justification only at the expense of a present whose felt meaning and denial have been the source of rebellion's outrage. Yet is Kaliayev's love for the unknown multitude who now walk the earth less abstract than Stepan's others who are yet to come?

For Kaliayev, innocence is the demand to live in a world that insistently exacts guilt. For Rieux, Tarrou, Diego, Meursault, even Caligula, revolt is the reaction of innocence to such a world. In demanding the right to live in a world obstinate in its opposition to innocence, however, such men are in danger of entering into complicity with evil in their very attempt to cleanse their life. Certainly that was the case with Caligula, as Tarrou had found out; and so it becomes with Les Justes. Tarrou had sought purity through withdrawal from such a world. Until, that is, The Plague had drawn him back from his solitude. Kaliayev, however, feeling his solidarity with others, yet recognizing that the world's injustice exacts complicity, concludes that he must murder to purify the world and can be cleansed for complicity with evil only by sacrificing his life. The logic of such complicity is destruction. Meursault and Tarrou pose the problem differently: They both remain utterly pure, innocent, and, Camus asks, do they—can one—thus remain human?

In a sense, they are inhuman figures. This is crucial for an understanding of the nature and force of revolt—and the limits it poses to itself. (The converse, the denial of innocence and its significance for revolt, will be met explicitly in *The Fall*.) This tragedy of lost innocence becomes clear in Kaliayev's final dialogue with Dora, as does the price they must pay for their purity.

With Stepan insisting that "there is no alternative between total justice and utter despair," Yanek resumes his mission to execute the Grand Duke, carrying "the bomb as if it were a cross" (CTOP, 274).

And the Deed Shall Be Paid For

And the deed shall be paid for. In jail Kaliayev encounters Foka, a murderer with no sense of guilt or demand for innocence, who has entered into complicity with the police, becoming the hangman, in order to shorten his sentence. And then there's the chief of police. Skouratov has thought out the problem and come to terms with the status quo. He is the opposite of the rebel in Camus's sense. "One begins by wanting justice—and one ends by setting up a police force" (CTOP, 281). If his failure resides in his having given up the struggle and allied himself with the evil of the status quo, his arguments nonetheless carry weight and pose serious questions, which Kaliayev must meet. In the end he feels he can do so only with his own death.

Skouratov is a Stepan who has come to power, except that he shows a greater sensitivity to concrete living. "I won't even say that your ideas are wrong. Except when they lead to murder" (CTOP, 281). Whether he is sincere or simply playing games—and it may well be the latter—he seeks to play upon Kaliayev's need for innocence, emphasizing the concrete character of his act in order to bring him to break from his comrades. Certainly an idealized meaning, this cause of justice, but what of the actual human being?

"If you persist in talking about a 'verdict,'" comments the police chief, "and asserting that it was the party . . . that tried and executed the victim— that, in short, the Grand Duke was killed not by a bomb but by an idea—well, in that case, you don't need a pardon. Suppose, however, we say that it was you, Ivan Kaliayev, who blew the Grand Duke's head to pieces—that puts a rather different complexion on the matter, doesn't it? . . . I'm not interested in ideas, I'm interested in human beings. . . . Murder isn't just an idea; it is something that takes place. And, obviously, so do its consequences. Which are repentance for the crime, and punishment. . . . You should not forget, or profess to forget, the Grand Duke's head. If you took it into account, you would find that mere ideas lead nowhere" (CTOP, 282–3).

Enter the Grand Duchess—a woman who cannot bear the face of an unjust and suffering world, now robbed of her only "tranquilizer," and who can only come to terms with her shattered life by appeal to a transcendent faith. But her faith needs the reassurance of Kaliayev's admitted guilt—of his acceptance of complicity with a guilty world and acknowledgment of the consequent need for salvation. "In the old days when I was sad, he used to share my sorrow—and I did not mind suffering . . . then. But now . . . I cannot bear being alone and keeping silent any longer. But to whom am I to speak?" (CTOP, 286). More forcefully still, she suggests Kaliayev's links with the man he murdered.

Their common humanity—or perhaps, through the exigency of the demand for justice, their common inhumanity; either way, their common humanness, is made manifest.

The Grand Duchess demands repentance and salvation—in a word, faith. The world is too much for her. She seeks to shore up her belief by exacting complicity, reducing Kaliayev to that abject condition that alone can support her life. But his sense of innocence is too strong. His honesty, and his comrades, are enough to sustain him.

The complicity of the Grand Duchess's faith—and by implication Skouratov's justice—is made passionately clear by Kaliayev. At least, they both share his guilt.

Like Rieux and Paneloux, Kaliayev and the Grand Duchess cannot communicate; their revolts are on different planes. For her, "God reunites"; for him, by "dying, I shall keep the agreement I made with those I love . . . and it would be betraying them to pray" (CTOP, 289–90).

As he mounted the gallows Kaliayev is reported to have said: "Death will be my supreme protest against a world of tears and blood. . . . If I have proved equal to the task assigned, of protesting with all the manhood in me against violence, may death consummate my task with the surety of the ideal that inspired it!" "Yes," utters Dora, "it was the purity he longed for. But oh the cruelty of that consummation" (CTOP, 294).

Commenting on his intent in his preface, Camus observes: "My admiration for my heroes, Kaliayev and Dora, is complete, I merely wanted to show that action itself had limits, there is no good and just action but what recognizes those limits and, if it must go beyond them, at least accepts death" (CTOP, x). To which Dora may be heard to respond: "Sometimes when I hear what Stepan says, I fear for the future. Others, perhaps, will come who'll quote our authority for killing; and will *not* pay with their lives" (CTOP, 296).

The problem of *The Rebel* has been posed.

8 ᕚ

Revolt and History

I realize that it is not my role to transform either the world or man: I have neither sufficient virtue nor insight for that. But it may be to serve, in my place, those few values without which even a transformed world would not be worth living in, and man, even if "new," would not deserve to be respected (A/I, 206).

FROM THE ABSURD TO REVOLT

"The important thing now . . . is not to go to the root of things, but, the world being what it is, to know how to live in it. In the age of negation, it might have been useful to reflect upon the problem of suicide. In the age of ideologies, it is necessary to come to terms with murder" (R, 4; L'HR, 14). Theoretically, *The Rebel* picks up where *The Myth* left off. "The absurd, considered as a rule of life, is . . . contradictory" (R, 9). "When we first claim to deduce a rule of behavior from it, [awareness of the absurd] makes murder seem a matter of indifference. . . . If we believe in nothing, if nothing has any meaning and if we can affirm no values whatsoever, then everything is possible and nothing has any importance" (R, 5). However, "after having rendered the act of killing at least a matter of indifference, absurdist analysis . . . finally condemns it." With its repudiation of suicide, absurdist thought, in affirming "the desperate encounter between human inquiry and the silence of the world," "admits that life is the only necessary good since it is precisely life that makes the encounter possible" (R, 6; L'HR, 16–7).

"This basic contradiction, however, cannot fail to be accompanied by a host of others from the moment that we claim to remain firmly in the absurdist position and ignore the real nature of the absurd, which is that it is an experience to be lived through, a point of departure, the equivalent in existence of Descartes's methodical doubt" (R, 8). "It is obviously impossible to formulate an attitude on the basis of a specially selected emotion" (R, 9). "If it was legitimate to take absurdist sensibility into account, to make a diagnosis of a malady to be found in ourselves and in others, it is nevertheless impossible to see in this sensibility, and in the nihilism it presupposes, anything but a point of departure, a criticism brought to life. . . . Absurdism, like methodical doubt, has wiped the slate clean. It leaves us in a blind alley" (R, 10).

"The first and only evidence that is supplied to me, within the terms of the absurdist experience, is rebellion." But rebellion confronts a world without preestablished order. It says no to the outrage, but how and to what does it say yes? "Its pre-occupation is to transform. But to transform is to act, and to act will be, tomorrow, to kill, and it still does not know whether murder is legitimate. Rebellion engenders exactly the actions it is asked to legitimate. Therefore it is absolutely necessary that rebellion find its reasons within itself, since it cannot find them elsewhere" (R, 10).

Thus is situated the problem of *The Rebel* as legated to it by *The Myth*'s analysis of our contemporary condition.[1] Echoing the *Letters*, he observes, "Man is the only creature who refuses to be what he is. The problem is to know whether this refusal can only lead to the destruction of himself and of others, whether all rebellion must end in the justification of universal murder, or whether, on the contrary, without laying claim to an innocence that is impossible, it can discover the principle of reasonable culpability" (R, 11). With *The Rebel* Camus seeks "once again to face the reality of the present, which is logical crime, and to examine meticulously the arguments by which it is justified; it is an attempt to understand the times in which we live" (R, 3).[2]

FRAMING THE ANALYSIS

Before proceeding to a detailed analysis of this work, however, it is important to underscore both its very personal origins and its precise and limited objectives. Whatever may have been the misunderstandings occasioned by its style of expression or the historical context of its publication, *The Rebel* is not offered as a comprehensive or universal theory of human nature, or of politics and social theory, nor does it attempt to present any precise program of action. Rather its aim is diagnostic, attending to what Camus feels to be a pathology of the Western mind prevalent for the last 150 years. Of course, references had to be made to prior times, to other places, as well as to events that were not solely influenced by the way people think. But that must not mislead the reader. Camus believes that the way people think affects the way they act. Even more, he believes that there are certain very fundamental concerns that tend to condition a wide range of thought and action. These concerns, metaphysical in nature, bear upon human destiny as cultural and historical forces have contoured the terms in which such issues find expression. He writes that, having "lived for a long time without morality, like many men of my generation, having in effect given expression to nihilism without always having been aware of it, I finally understood that ideas were more than pleasing or emotionally moving games, and that, in certain circumstances, to accept certain thoughts is equivalent to accepting murder without limits" (E, 704).

In Camus's view this pathology of the intellect pervades the thought and hence the experience of the modern world. This "partly explains the direction in which our times are heading and almost entirely explains the excesses of our age" (R, 11). One might well pause before the scope of the latter claim—and I will have something to say about it further on—but the former seems reasonable enough. At issue here is the view that thought has at least a relative autonomy with respect to the myriad forces that influence events, and that it is of some consequence to the direction of events to understand the way people think. While one may certainly question both his "working hypothesis" and the significance he attaches to it, he certainly seems on solid ground when he suggests that, if true, that hypothesis contributes to understanding the flow of contemporary events.

And what is that "working hypothesis" that admittedly "is not the only one possible" and "is far from explaining everything"? It is "the astonishing history . . . of European pride" (R, 11) by which human beings have turned toward historical revolution to compensate for the loss of trans-historical salvation. "Twentieth century marxists (and they are not the only ones) find themselves at the extremity of this long tragedy of contemporary intelligence which could be summed up by writing the history of European pride. . . . What is at issue is a prodigious myth of the divinization of man, of domination, of the unification of the universe by the power of human reason alone. What is at issue is the conquest of totality" (A/I, 194–5).

Camus's thesis can initially be set forth briefly. In the post-enlightenment Western world, people no longer believe in God. Having lost faith in the vertical transcendence of the divine, they have turned toward history for salvation. Since they seem unable to do without an absolute, horizontal transcendence emerges as compensation, holding out the promise of the "end of history," by which the sufferings of this life will be overcome. From the perspective of this historicized absolute, values become gauges of efficacy. The end justifies the means—any means.

In this context the noble aspirations of humanity, which have so often given rise to rebellion in the name of justice, have become caricatured, and often reduced to the justification of murder in the name of the historicized absolute that Camus intends when he speaks of the divinization of man. The history of European pride is precisely the belief that collective effort can end the suffering and injustice that have characterized human history. This enterprise he calls the quest for totality; that is, the attempt to refashion the totality of human history in accord with a supposed total understanding of the human condition and a rationalized praxis that follows from that conception.

Thought thus becomes an instrument in the collective effort to overcome historical injustice and the limitations of our natural condition. "It is not logic that I refute, but ideology which substitutes a logical succession of reasonings for living reality. Traditionally, philosophers tried to explain the world, not to impose a law on it. That is the task of religions and ideologies" (A/I, 60–1). The reduction of philosophy to ideology in the service of a totalizing praxis is the contemporary response to a metaphysical imperative legated to us by the collapse of traditional religion. It is also the source of the degeneration of twentieth-century revolutions, as they seek to serve, often unwittingly, as religious surrogates. The task of *The Rebel* is to diagnose this pathology of the intellect that underlies and undermines revolutionary experience in order to contribute to the rebirth of creative rebellion.

Before turning to a detailed exploration of this "working hypothesis," a few words on the style of presentation are in order, followed by a brief consideration of the relation of metaphysical analysis to practical experience.

METHODOLOGICAL CONSIDERATIONS

The Rebel is not a popular work, in the traditional sense. It is a crafted literary effort, whose dramatic imagery and balanced cadences have garnered literary acclaim and sarcastic comment. Too sovereign, too perfect, too noble in sentiments, some said. In a work concerned with the "blood-stained face" of contemporary events, the anguished speech of the oppressed and the exploited, of the degraded and the humiliated, is given short shrift. Little reference is made to the writings or speech of workers, union organizers, journalists, or men of affairs. Primary attention is paid rather to literary figures, to writers, and to theorists of revolution, with some notable exceptions. This suggests not only the audience to whom Camus was speaking, but his conception of the place of this work within the corpus of his writings, as well as within the frame of French literature and culture. I think we would be correct to say that he saw this as his mature philosophical statement. *The Rebel* was meant not only to complete the "second series" of his work, but to take its place—and establish his place—within the grand tradition of French letters. Such was his primary audience and his unspoken aim. This is not to say that his intent was solely literary. Far from it! But the implicit view of the relation of literature to the broad movements of culture and society requires more detailed consideration.

Everyday action takes place within a conceptual frame by which the experienced world is defined. Whatever may be the natural contours of our environment, different cultures at different times and places have understood and lived their situation in unique ways. It is for this reason that thought and experience must be historically contextualized. Even where such universal themes as death are concerned, cultures face them within the meaning-frame of their uniquely structured experiential world. That world as lived is what I mean when I speak of a cultural drama.[3]

Thus the actions, thoughts, feelings, values, and beliefs of individuals are constituted by the cultural drama whose roles and institutions provide the script within which minor improvisations are permitted. Personal problems are simply variations on the metaphysical themes at the root of cultural dramas. It is the more insightful participants in the culture—philosophers, artists, scientists—who are able to reflect on the taken-for-granted script, thus raising it, at least in part, to the level of explicit text. It is thus not by chance or artistic preference that Camus focuses on the writings of Nietzsche or Dostoevsky, of Hegel or Marx or Sade, when he seeks to make explicit the root structure of thought at stake in the Western world. Rather, it is to such thinkers that one ought to turn to find the structure of Western metaphysics within which meaning-frame the problem of revolt gains that articulated coherence that has given direction to the insurrectional movements that have sculpted the modern world. Let us look briefly at this methodological point from another angle.

Having insisted that thinking is always rooted in feeling, Camus has located the origins of rebellion in the experience of outrage. That initial experience inevitably seeks to give itself expression in thought and deed, in reflection and action. For most reflective beings, and certainly for those who have had a major influence upon recent European history, organized action generally follows reflection. Admittedly, what is done reacts back upon what is thought, thus modifying it. But even then how we evaluate the results is essentially framed by the preestablished structure of meaning that is the world as we live it, that world itself having emerged in the process of our coming to consciousness within the historical contours of our cultural drama. In short, our personal incorporation of the metaphysical frame of our cultural drama tends to prestructure our thinking. This is true both of the initial articulation given to the rebellious outrage, and of subsequent developments and reevaluations. What must be emphasized is that we come to consciousness *within* and *in terms of* our history.

This is not said to deny the possibility of obtaining a perspective *on* that history. Quite the contrary, otherwise the entire effort of *The Rebel* would be a methodological anomaly from the outset. Rather, it is meant to underscore the historically relative nature of all inquiry, that of *The Rebel* included, as Camus sought to make quite explicit. It is also noted in order to focus our attention on the importance of the metaphysical dimension of all thinking, including that of political movements that present themselves as being concerned only with matters of practice. In Camus's view, practical and historical movements are significantly influenced by the often inarticulate metaphysical structure of thinking that frames their problematic and programmatic focus.

And further, it is to the works of theorists and artists that one should turn in order to get the best possible grasp on that hidden but pervasive metaphysical dimension.

Never is this more important than when reaching down to the deepest existential sources of action: our need to find and sustain meaning in our lives. Existentially, the lived world is the pervading quality underlying practical concerns. The root conceptual structure of that world determines the meaning of particular events. It thus frames the interpretation we give to encountered resistances, as well as the strategies and programs we consider appropriate. Practical thinking takes place within the metaphysical contours of this lived world. It is because action can be seen as essentially following the lines and remaining within the conceptual frame thus formed by our taken-for-granted metaphysics, that Camus can claim that the excesses of the age are "almost entirely" explained by the hypothesis he is offering.

The historical circumstances—political, economic, national—to which action must respond invariably occasion reflective revisions of strategies and tactics, of policies and programs. Yet they rarely impinge fundamentally on the metaphysical frame that establishes the *a priori* conditions within which action is seen to take place. It is this world as real that constitutes the horizon for our lived encounters and projected futures. Further, it is our sense of ourselves thus situated that sets forth the conditions to which we demand that events conform. In the long run, of course, both existential project and metaphysical frame are continually undergoing modifications. We demand that action conform to those prereflective conditions of meaning without which it would be lacking in coherence and value for us. Those existential demands for coherence and value find their place within the metaphysical contours of our world, thus framing the possibilities of our thought and action.

It is therefore to this metaphysical level that Camus feels we must turn if we are to understand the excesses of the modern age. It is here that he seeks to locate the degeneration of rebellion. At stake is a diagnosis of that pathology of the intellect that reveals, behind the appearances, a structure of thought that has led historical rebellions from their initial generous impulses down the twisted path of totalizing revolutions to the justification of murder, often in spite of themselves.

And why this concern with rebellion? Because rebellion bears witness to a refusal to give up. Amid the decaying ruins of a civilization that seems to be tumbling down in a cacophony of nihilistic resonances, rebellion testifies to our refusal to submit, to accept our own or another's degradation. At a deeper level, the rebel rejects the notion that life is meaningless, not worth the effort, and that nothing matters. "Rebellion is born of the spectacle of irrationality, confronting an unjust and incomprehensible condition. But its blind impulse is to demand order in the midst of chaos and unity in the very heart of the ephemeral. It cries out, it demands, it insists that the scandal cease and that what has, up to now, been built upon shifting sands should henceforth be founded upon rock" (R, 10; L'HR, 21–2).

Rebellion is thus a living answer to the temptations of nihilism. In a world without transcendent values, rebellion attests to our willingness to put our lives on the line for what matters to us. The French resistance bore witness to that. "Insurrection is certainly not the sum total of human experience. But history today, with all its storm and strife, compels us to say that rebellion is one of the essential dimensions of man." It bears witness to an often inarticulate demand for meaning, thus offering the promise of an articulate value by which we may still be able to give meaning and direction to our lives. "Not knowing more or being better aided, I had to try to draw a rule of conduct and perhaps a first value from the only experience with which I was in accord, which was our revolt" (E, 1705). For revolt "is our historic reality. Unless we choose to ignore reality, we must find our values in it. Is it possible to find a rule of conduct outside of the realm of religion and its absolute values? That is the question raised by rebellion" (R, 21). And also its promise.

THE SOURCES OF REVOLT

"What is a rebel?" asks Camus. "A man who says no, but whose refusal does not imply a renunciation. He is also a man who says yes. . . . In other words, his no affirms the existence of a borderline. . . . Rebellion cannot exist without the feeling that, somewhere and somehow, one is right" (R, 13). Rebellion is thus grounded in, and seeks to make explicit, the experience of a value.

At the same time that there is a rejection of the intrusion, there is in all rebellion a complete and instantaneous identification of man with a certain part of himself. He thus implicitly brings into play a value judgment which is so little gratuitous that he defends it in the midst of danger. . . . This value which preexists all action contradicts purely historical philosophies. . . . The analysis of revolt leads at least to the suspicion that there is a human nature, as the Greeks thought, and in contradiction to the postulates of contemporary thought. Why rebel if there is nothing permanent in oneself to preserve? (R, 13–4, 16; L'HR, 26, 28).

This analysis of rebellion should first be placed within its appropriate theoretical frame. We are social as well as natural animals. We live in groups. We may be tempted on occasion by the lure of solitude, as was Camus in *A Happy Death*, for example. Cut-off from others, however, we are anguished and spiritually impoverished. If the movement from the absurd to revolt means anything, it refers to our need for others in the face of the metaphysical solitude that is our natural condition. Both by origins and by need, there-fore, we live among others and, even more, need to live *with* others. We need others to be there for us, when and as we need them. And we often want to be there for others. "Being-with" another seems so necessary to our experiential fulfillment that Camus's thought was drawn toward it as if by magnetic attraction. Whether in friendship, comradeship, community, or love, being-with stands out as the envisioned consummation of myriad prac-tical struggles. At the deepest level, this need seems to constitute who we are.[4] How we envision our most intimate relations speaks volumes as to our character and the structure of our world. To be human is to be a part of a collectivity. Human groups are organized patterns of action and expectation. They are governed by norms, both explicit and implicit. Norms exist. They control the operation of institutions. We assume our place within the insti-tutions, living more or less in accord with their norms, even if we have never thought *about* them. And we know others do likewise—and they know that we know.

Often, nay inevitably, such *normal* situations are less than fulfilling. Sometimes they are downright degrading and oppressive. There are many ways of responding to dehumanization, oppression, or humiliation: internal withdrawal, such as schizophrenia; external withdrawal, such as migration; subsurface resentment, such as bitchiness; abstract activity, such as pure mathematics; location of a substitute enemy, such as displacement; or con-frontation, the no of the rebel: so far but no farther.[5]

Rebellion says no to the continuation of an intolerable situation, asserting the rebel's right to a limited social space and personal integrity. At the core of the rebellion that asserts a limit to humiliation lies a passionate commitment to life and to the dignity and self-respect without which that life would be felt to be without meaning.

The immediate occasion may be trivial or traumatic. It may be a demand for a fair share in distribution or a refusal to submit to an insult. It may be phrased in very personal terms, or it may invoke the language of rights. At its root, however, the rebel's outrage gives expression to the sense that one's integrity has been violated. This does not mean that all outraged sensibility is justified. Each act of rebellion must be examined with respect to the world it assumes, the ontology of need it expresses, and the future it envisions. Nevertheless, beneath the specifics lies a common root. We feel that our integrity has been violated in such a way that it is all but impossible to bear the affront. Our integrity holds us together, making us able to survive as an individual, at the biological as well as the psychic level. The rebel's no to the intrusion upon his or her living space would seem to be but an expression—however historically specific in form and occasion—of the organism's need to preserve its vital integrity. This seemingly pervasive or universal need may well be continuous with the organism's defense against alien intrusions, so well expressed by the immunological system's way of repelling foreign bodies. Here, too, at this root biological level, the organism seems to be saying: so far, but no farther; my survival is threatened by the intrusion into my personal (biological) space of this alien body.

To ground rebellion in the rejection of a violation of the individual's integrity, however continuous that may be with the universal biological basis of the species, is not, it must be repeated, to claim any universality in the articulation of the rebellious outrage. Nor is it to give approval to all acts of rebellion, however much it suggests an initial sympathy with the individual who feels the need to rebel. But it is to claim that rebellion attests to a fundamental human demand that is always worthy of respect. This demand suggests the existence of a human nature to be defended. And this nature roots the sense of value that finds expression in the demand for justice, whatever the historical and cultural determinations of its formulation might be.

The demand for justice is the usual form in which the initial outrage gives itself expression. In fact, the demand may be so passionate, the commitment to the struggle so intense, that rebels often feel there is no dignity in a life without redress. Thus they are often willing to risk their prior status or position, perhaps even their lives, within *normal* society, for this value of which they feel the need.

In short, rebellion attests to the demand for the preservation of one's integrity, often expressed in terms of the demand for justice or the maintenance of dignity. It is *implicitly* a claim, as yet inarticulate, that the human being must have, and has a *right* to have, sufficient space for action. Whatever the *explicit* justification of the act of rebellion, implicitly it attests to this need and to the feeling that "one has a right" to its being respected. By saying that this situation or act is unjust, it implicates a universal value. Not, of course, asserting that all hold to this value, but rather that the scope of this claim is universal. Camus's claim amounts to the assertion that at the core of the act of revolt is this claimed universal right.

To rebel is to put oneself at risk. Each revolt is a break from the normal, challenging the status quo with demands for a new order. The nature and scope of the risk is defined by, and defines, the significance of the value to the rebel and the degree of his or her commitment to it. Rebellion thus attests to the existence of a value that transcends the immediate situation—and, at the risk of death, transcends the individual's life. It asserts, at least in degrees, that life itself is not the only or exclusive end, but that *meaningful* life, a life worth living, is demanded. "The rebel does not ask for life, but for reasons for living" (R, 108). By insisting that the outrage be stopped, the movement of rebellion effects the transition from the realm of facts and norms to that of values. "Not every value entails rebellion, but every act of rebellion tacitly invokes a value" (R, 14). Thus, rebellion, in which "the transition to rights is manifest" (R, 15, L'HR, 27), offers us the experiential location from within the world revealed by the absurd for a source of values to which we may appeal, and from which we may hope to develop an ethic relevant to the dilemmas of our age. The challenge facing rebellion is to develop that ethic in a manner consistent with the values that gave it birth.

ETHICAL REFLECTIONS

If we stop for a minute and think about the problem of conduct, it becomes clear that simple personal preference is not a sufficient guide. To assert complete meaninglessness is as justified at this level as to assert definitive Truth. Saying everything is permitted is logically equivalent to saying all is obligated. Here is the dead end of absurdist thought and the edge of the abyss of nihilism, to which the Second World War and its aftermath gave palpable testimony. With these alternatives we are dealing with the simple positing of a perspective—a personal, even collective, assertion, to which others may or may not give assent. And from which deductions about conduct may or may not follow.

Inevitably, one assertion encounters an opposed assertion, constituting the paradigm situation of interpersonal conflict. How can such conflict be mediated? Are there no values that can transcend these conflicting perspectives, holding out the possibility of a common ground on which the combatants can meet? Can we not find values to sustain our lives and give direction to our efforts beyond the level of ideological warfare? "Caligula," "The Misunderstanding," and *The Plague* were Camus's efforts to show the pervasively social character of our situation and the disasters following upon our failure to do justice to the social. *The Rebel* thus focuses upon the limitations intrinsic to the effort to establish an intersubjective frame for value claims. Such claims constitute a demand upon the other for acknowledgment. They must be justified and defended. What is to be their ground? Ultimately I shall maintain—along with Camus—that a claim becomes intersubjectively justifiable only as a proposal. It is an invitation to a dialogue. And democracy is essentially the development of such proposals—it is collective inquiry. But of that, more later.

Initially, the rebel says no. But this is not so much a deduction as an impulsive rejection, almost an instinctive act of self-defense. "The movement of rebellion is founded simultaneously on the categorical rejection of an intrusion that is considered intolerable and on the confused conviction of a firm right, more precisely the impression on the rebel's part that he "has the right" (R, 13; L'HR, 25).

Neither values nor rebellion is deduced. The values are lived prereflectively until their denial is felt to be unbearable. Only then, through the act of rebellion, does the value get existentially recognized—in reaction to the experience of its denial. Before that it is simply lived as valued, without being consciously appreciated. Revolt thus struggles to gain articulation in the face of a threat to the heretofore inarticulate value that sustains it. But the specific context of its emergence cannot but mark the manner and content of the claim. We need not disparage the initial more or less brute response that initiates the movement of rebellion. Yet it is with the effort to articulate the rationale for the revolt and its strategic rules of conduct that the problem studied in *The Rebel* primarily lies. The invocation of the implicit human community becomes the frame for evaluating the coherence of the rebellious activity. But the implicit universality of the claim to justice is almost invariably in tension with the more precise and limited content that the historical context of its emergence circumscribes. Within the dialectic of this tension resides the conflict whose logicopolitical development *The Rebel* sets out to analyze and diagnose.

The implicit universality of the claims of rebellion is viewed by Camus as suggesting the boundary conditions by which all subsequent action ought to be constrained. Since it is the "we are" affirmed by the rebel that sets forth the essential ground of justification, the rebel would violate the legitimating rationale by engaging in action that undercut the implicit human community. Thus we find boundary conditions to rebellious action implicit in the initial affirmation. No precise guides to conduct follow from this framework. Rather, a context is suggested that would delimit the range of the ethically permissible.

The matter might be put as follows. Starting with an implicit sense of the communality of the human condition—our metaphysical isolation as dramatized, for example, in *The Plague*—Camus seeks a frame of reference that can serve as a common ground for human combatants. This frame is to provide nonrestrictive and nonideological boundary conditions for humane conduct. In a sense the search is for an ethical equivalent of the Cartesian certitude, but its function is not the same. Rather than serving as the base for a deductive proof, what is sought is the establishment of an agreed upon standpoint within which individuals may be able to explore acceptable alternatives as guides to moral action. Camus thus suggests a way to go beyond the positing of preference—as legated to us by the absurdist analysis, for example—to the establishment of a jointly experienced and at least originally indubitable common frame of reference that our condition as human beings can provide. Such a naturalistic frame for morality was originally staked out in Camus's earliest writings. But he does not seek to "establish" this naturalistic frame of reference. He offers it as an "at least originally indubitable" truth within whose frame dialogue may begin. Here in our common human domain may be found an original matrix of meanings—itself implicitly appealed to by almost all acts of rebellion—which, by becoming the explicitly acknowledged context of our efforts, may offer us the possibility of developing an ethic in this absurd world without transcendent justification.

It is noteworthy—and in opposition to Cartesianism—that the question of theoretical Truth takes second place in this endeavor. The clarity and distinctness with which Cartesian philosophy grounds its Truth is ultimately a purely individual matter. The social question is that of an intersubjective grounding of policy decisions. Here the appeal to facts is not as arbiters of policy, but as instruments to call forth potentially common responses. Facts can guide; they cannot demonstrate. Truth considered concretely becomes the continually revisable question of the adequacy of one's policies with respect to the movement of collective experience.

The fundamental concern of ethical inquiry, therefore, is not primarily the passing of judgment on particular actions or the deduction of values from first principles. Its focus ought rather to be on establishing values through an open and experimental inquiry—ideally, through dialogue: an open inquiry between persons. Values emerge from human experience, and intellectual formulations should be taken as claims whose justification must be sought by appeal to such intersubjectively grounded experiences. Justifications are not so much proved as established; only the inner self-contradiction of claims may be proven.

The task of ethical thought then is to spell out the boundary conditions of any ethical inquiry, to establish the essential constants in human action and conjoint living with which conduct must come to terms. Within this framework we do not deduce rules of action; ethics is not mathematics or even law. Rather, we grasp limits to humane action and recognize that certain commitments cannot go together with others. This approach reveals limitations intrinsic to the realm of values, establishing binding hypotheticals, constants of action within particular frameworks.

Thus value claims should take an *if–then* form: *if* that is wished, *then* this must be taken into view. But the need to act in accordance with any specific ethical or human framework—with the if-clause of the hypothetical —can never be deduced. That is the force of freedom to which all deductive ethical theories seek in vain to give the lie.

This point can be made quite briefly. A deductive theory seeks grounds in first principles. The establishment of first principles requires assent. Once given, the rules of action are said to follow necessarily, given appropriate circumstances. But the problem of ethics is always that of specific action. Therefore we can either deny the applicability of the value in this situation, or deny the adequacy or truth of the first principle. For the former there can be no deductive rule (hence the failure of Kantianism); for the latter, ultimately, no argument. Where, logically, could we turn to support an ethical first principle? Thus if the other to whom the principle is offered as an ultimate reason denies its force or relevance, the only remaining dialogue is confrontation. Ethical systems then become totalizing ideologies seeking to extract commitment, in whose terms opposition must be purged, or at least responded to in nondialogic terms. Here the encounter between persons reduces to conflict over issues with acceptable answers predetermined by an unalterable adherence, on the basis of prior attachment, to first principles that are but arbitrary posits.

The problem posed here is of the essence of any deductive ethical standpoint. The ethical question is to establish in specific situations the good in action. But a deductive standpoint seeks to deduce such action from principles that always stand in need of elaboration and justification. If all is implicit in them but not yet known, how can we assent to the first principles until we know the full consequences of that assent? And, if we could know the full consequences, why would we need the first principle and its deductive elaboration? It is just the novelty and unpredictability of the ethical situation that is in question. And the deductive model cannot be a guide here. (To this issue I will turn in greater detail in Chapter 13.)

What then is an alternative? To attempt to establish preferable ways of acting in the concrete.

This requires carefully questioning the historically and culturally sedimented values at stake in particular situations. If ethical conflicts arise, deductive proofs are of no consequence. What is required is a procedure for solving the problems and for maintaining the values from both the long- and the short-run point of view—and this cannot be predetermined: that is of the essence of human freedom.

What, then, can be the function of an ethical inquiry? For Camus the concern is primarily with those natural and historical conditions that must be taken into consideration if the ethical resolution is to be consistent with humane values: to reveal those constants of the human condition a consideration of which seems essential to the resolution of human conflict. It is further to reveal the values to which human living bears witness, values that provide the framework and guidelines for the further expansion of human action. And it is finally to attempt to reveal how totalizing definitions of the value to which revolt bears witness can distort that value and thus be self-defeating. All this, of course, calls into question the metaphysical assumptions of that world in which the notion of humane takes on its normative force.

THE GROUNDS OF REVOLT

Since the framework of this inquiry is provided by human nature and its interactions, Camus focuses upon the conditions that this starting point presupposes. Since the ethical objective involves the establishment of human community, he explores the possibility of grounding and limiting this potential community in the factual commonness of the human being's natural and social situation. His search is for ethical boundary conditions imposed upon conduct by the conditions of existence. There can be no question of the so-called naturalistic fallacy here since he does not seek to deduce anything from this fact.

He begins with the fact that as natural beings we have much in common, including certain biological needs and limits as well as the finality of death—in short, a common finitude. From these facts, nothing logically can be deduced about action. But that is not the concern. Rather, it is the establishment of grounds for the reflective evaluation of modes of conduct.

If human beings do in fact share certain traits and face a common destiny, is it not possible that making this communality explicit and raising it to the level of common perception could establish at least a minimal framework for the appreciation of shared values? And can this not provide a metaphysical base for the elaboration, construction, and development of an ethical frame for human community? If dialogue is to be possible and concrete unity established—if, in short, people are to be able to come together communally in any sense—they require a shared conceptual frame for such interaction. The awareness of our common condition and the minimal evaluative standpoint this may establish—or at least that it would be quite difficult to deny—would seem to offer the possibility of providing such a foundation.

In order to exist, man must rebel, but rebellion must respect the limit it discovers in itself—*a limit where minds meet and, in meeting, begin to exist.* . . . [Rebellion] is a perpetual state of tension. . . . *It is the first piece of evidence (which attests to a value beyond the individual).* . . . This evidence lures the individual from his solitude. It founds its first value on the whole human race. I rebel—therefore we exist (R, 22, my italics).

From the point of view of an understanding of the inner logic of Camus's thought, the role of the absurd consciousness is crucial. While on one level it represents the individual's developing awareness—as with the stranger, for instance—of an unbridgeable gulf between people and their destiny, from the perspective of *The Rebel* the encounter with the plague has forced recognition of the implicit communality of our condition. "We see that the affirmation implicit in every act of rebellion is extended to something that transcends the individual insofar as it withdraws him from his supposed solitude and provides him with a reason to act" (R, 16).

Thus the absurd consciousness mediates the transition from the natural awareness of the first part of *The Stranger*, through the trial, *Nuptials*, and "The Misunderstanding," to the communal consciousness that first appears in limited form in *The Plague*.

The establishment of this standpoint does not solve the problem of values, but constitutes an essential first step. It establishes a recognition of the human framework in terms of which a resolution may be envisaged. As Camus had said of the absurd: "To prove the absurdity of life cannot be an end, but only a beginning" (E, 1419). "If men cannot refer to a common value, recognized by all as existing in each one, then man is incomprehensible to man. The rebel demands that this value should be clearly recognized in himself" (R, 23).

But in demanding this value for themselves in the name of their humanity, rebels are, at least implicitly, though far more often than not explicitly also, demanding it for humans in general. This is the force of Camus's contention that the rebel's act is implicitly universal. It is the assertion of a limit not simply in their own name, but in the name of a conception of human nature that is being transgressed. And the transgression is seen as implicitly self-destructive as well as destructive of the humanity of the rebel, whether or not directly affected. Ultimately we have a demand for simple justice. The act of self-definition is here crucial. Rebels are distinguished from those who simply oppose by the fact that they define their opposition at least implicitly in terms of a definition of themselves that is essentially universal in extent and ultimately grounded in the recognition of a common human destiny. The mere assertion is not enough, however. Its formal universality must ideally be transformed into a universality of content. This universality of content can be progressively approached, Camus suggests, only with and through the particular life of dialogic communities (to a consideration of which I will turn later).

THE MEANING OF REVOLT

Born out of a clear refusal to accept that which denies the human, and a passionate but vague affirmation of the individual's right to justice and freedom, rebellion emerges in practical struggles to give itself historical form.

It invariably claims that its cause is just, that a universal value is being defended in the name of humanity, and, implicitly at least, that *all* people have a right to that value—or at least have a right not to have their chances of realizing it infringed upon. The demand is for justice, and in defense of human integrity, or for the reestablishment of a transgressed prior unity. But the position of the rebel is circumscribed, the perspective limited, the formulation of the requirements of unity incomplete. Desired is a concrete unity experienced by the living being. As such, it is essentially open. Any attempt to define this unity definitively before its realization results in ideology. Such an attempt must ultimately deny the value that gave birth to this movement in the name of the intellectual reconstruction that explains it. Rebellion originates in a particular condition and out of a particular experience. Instead of justifying the claim by the experience, the experience tends to be justified by the claim. But what will then justify the claim? As soon as the claim is absolutized, it is removed from the level of an appeal grounded in experience and is placed on the level of a posited doctrine. By the necessities of the dialectic of interpersonal relations, and its theoretical counterpart in the movement of lived ideas, its opposite is bound to be called forth. Thus the possibility of experimental development and reasoned criticism is excluded. This rejection, implicit or explicit, of the fallibilities of a finite position, which is the claim of totality, inevitably condemns those who see differently. The experiential ground or open framework in terms of which the parties might come together and engage in constructive dialogue is implicitly denied by the totalizing theory. This denial soon makes its explicit appearance on the level of ideological conflict and war.

The history and pathology of revolt that Camus presents is thus the history of a movement in which a living, qualitative experience gives rise to claims of limits and rights the articulation of which transforms that reality into fodder for thought. Ideology, used here in the sense of a conceptual search for totality, can be summed up as fidelity to thought products at the expense of fidelity to the experience in which thinking takes place. It is ultimately the demand for a metaphysical revolution in which the world of experience is to be transformed in accordance with the demands of a totalizing theory.

In point of fact, ideology is implicit as soon as thought is viewed from the perspective of experience conceived simply as a matrix in which theoretical distinctions may arise and be meaningfully employed. From this perspective *The Rebel*—and in fact Camus's thought in general—can be seen as a study of the pathology of thought's infidelity to its origins.[6]

By being cut off from its existential origins, thought is being deprived of its vitalizing source as well as of the natural community that could serve as the framework for its elaboration. The only possibility for communication then rests upon prior acceptance of thought's first principles, the natural ground of such acceptance having been denied. And since thought cannot ground itself, the first principles must stand as posits in the dialogic situation, requiring force to assure their social preeminence.

The appeal to indubitable evidence, intuition, or any such evidential grounds may be seen as essentially just such a procedure. By seeking to resolve a dispute by means of such an appeal, the standpoint of concrete experience is transcended, thus effectively cutting discussion off from its origins, and the further development that that would permit, and rendering itself unsolvable. From the point of view of dialogue and communication, such a claim—and one makes a claim only insofar as the situation is social—can result only in spiritual imperialism and ideological warfare. In fact, the claim is an implicit declaration of war, for it is made in order to be recognized. Yet a claim that has cut itself off from its origins or seeks to ground itself in its origins deductively, which comes to the same thing, involves a transformation of the dialogic situation into a power relation.

Ideological warfare is the inevitable result of a totalizing approach, which suggests why Camus did not wish to consider himself a philosopher. For he considers ideological warfare to be at the center of the Hegelian enterprise, perhaps the crowning modern philosophical achievement.[7] In his words: "The entire history of mankind is [according to Hegel] . . . nothing but a prolonged fight to the death for the conquest of universal prestige and absolute power. It is, in its essence, imperialist" (R, 139).

In this light, the pathology of the development being considered was stated a bit earlier in *The Rebel*: "In principle the rebel only wanted to conquer his own existence. . . . But he forgets his origins and by the law of spiritual imperialism, he sets out in search of world conquest by way of an infinitely multiplied series of murders" (R, 103).

Ideology is therefore spiritual imperialism. Initiated by the yearning for unity, the rebel forgets the sources of his movement and attaches himself to a definitive theoretical standpoint from which he may easily produce an explanation and a justification of acts that will prove the existence of the unity he insists upon having. In terms of this position, opposition ultimately can have no legitimate standing, since by definition it is not on the same plane of being as the ideologue, who, by his grasp of the truth, claims a unique and indisputable position.

Revolt can be seen as the formulation of a commitment and the suggestion of a solution, which is to be worked out and progressively realized, if possible, through dialogue. Ideology, on the other hand, perverts the commitment by hypostatizing its ongoing meaning. Ideology turns the axis of involvement from the human centers that meet in terms of a common experience to the articulation of that experience in terms of which those centers are essentially ancillary. In the first context, meaning is experienced and lived in the present, with the future being only "present-ed" as a possibility for consideration and guidance. With ideology, on the other hand, the existential relation of past–present–future is transformed from moments of a unitary moving present to distinct dimensions of being, which live only as objects for, and in the context of, their theoretical formulation.

The problem is essentially the same as that of the relation between means and ends, of which more later. *The Rebel* is concerned with justifications, with reasons—and with efficacy only to the extent that reasons are objectively efficacious (an empirical and scientific question always). It is not primarily concerned with history or causality.[8] The problem of ideology concerns giving objective reality to the logical independence of thought. An ideology may well be called a hypostatized and logicized reason that has lost its grip on the moving present (its origin) in terms of which alone it might have been valid. It is, in short, a reason gone mad.

The philosophical enterprise arises in, and may find justification as the articulation and direction of, the movement toward unity and lived meaning. Now, however, it becomes the totalizing grasp of the fixed structure of Being or History. From the point of view of dialogue and community, as soon as this philosophical imperialism insists upon colonization, it gives birth to the ideological conflict of equally unjustifiable posited presuppositions, articulated as the search for grounds rather than consequents. Yet it is consequents, thoughts opening out to new experiences and leading to practical resolutions, that seem to be both the initial impetus and encompassing purpose as well as the experimental justification of inquiry. Finally, inquiry itself is but one of the most rigorous forms of intellectual revolt.

At the root of the excesses of our age Camus thus finds the metaphysical demand for totality.[9] An intellectual movement that, in responding to the legitimate human need for dignity and self-respect, ends by betraying its own rebellious origins through an infernal dialectic in which it denies freedom in the search for perfect justice. But perfect justice, should it ever be approachable, would have to be rooted in respect for freedom, without which there can be no dignity and self-respect.

Responding to the demands of revolt requires the integral union of freedom of expression and action with the establishment of a social order in which individuals can achieve the dignity and self-respect without which they cannot live. Justice as the equitable distribution of benefits and burdens provides the necessary conditions for the achievement of human dignity in accord with spontaneous free expression. Rebellion must cleave to the mutually implicated claims of freedom and justice if it is not to become the disease of its own cure. Unity, which Camus systematically counterposes to the demands of totality, is precisely this ontological need for an integral ordering of human living that balances freedom and justice, while subordinating the imperious metaphysical claims of the intellect to the practical exigencies of daily living. In this way alone will it be possible to restore to human experience the values of which it is capable and to open the way to a celebration of the ordinary, of daily labor, of friendship—to the life of a Joseph Grand. This must be the content of any renaissance in human living toward the achievement of which Camus's effort was so totally committed.

I will refrain finally from saying that the conclusions of this experience, whose personal character I wish again to underline, have universal value. *The Rebel* proposes neither a formal morality nor a dogma. It affirms only that a morality is possible and that it costs dearly. . . .

When the labor [*travail*] of the worker like that of the artist will have an opportunity for creativity [*fécondité*], then only will nihilism be definitively outlived and the renaissance make sense. Each in our place, by our works and our acts, must serve this creativity and this renaissance. It is not certain that we will succeed in this endeavor, but, after all, it is the only task which is worth undertaking and persevering in (E, 1713–5).

The actual preconditions and metaphysical roots of this effort for the construction of unity are still to be studied. Before that, however, it will be necessary to study in detail the logic that finds expression in the demand for a metaphysical revolution, and then to explore the psychic subsoil that existentially roots this pathology in an oppressive demand for totality. Only then can we consider Camus's positive program for constructive revolt through art and politics.

9

Metaphysical Rebellion

The era of tragedy seems to coincide . . . with an evolution in which man, whether or not consciously, separates himself from a traditional form of civilization with which he finds himself in opposition, without yet having found a new form which will satisfy him (TRN, 1701).

METAPHYSICAL REBELLION

"Metaphysical rebellion is the movement by which man protests against his condition and against the whole of creation. It is metaphysical because it contests the ends of man and of creation. . . . The metaphysical rebel protests against the condition in which he finds himself as a man" (R, 23).

No minor problem this. Like Hamlet, the rebel feels that something is rotten in the world around him. But unlike Hamlet, he sees the problem not primarily as a failure of individuals or even of a social system. Rather, the essentials of existence are in question. "Metaphysical rebellion is a claim, motivated by the concept of a complete unity, against the suffering of life and death and a protest against the human condition both for its incompleteness, thanks to death, and its wastefulness, thanks to evil" (R, 24). It is the scope of the revolt that makes it metaphysical. Why is Being thus, rather than other? And why is the *thus* so inconsiderate of our deepest desires and values? This rebel is offended by an order of things that is experienced as a violation of personal integrity and as essentially unjust.

All this, no doubt, invokes the perspective of the rebel. In a sense, this is the old problem of the absurd reborn. The problem with the world emerges because it fails to live up to the rebel's demands. The rebel makes a claim. Give up that claim, reject those demands, and the world no longer appears unjust. Rebellion would be pointless and would not even arise. One path to the resolution of the rebel's outrage is thus suggested.

On the other side, a vision of the world is invoked. The rebel sees the world as inadequate, pervaded by evil and death. But he may be mistaken. Evil may be only an illusion of inadequate or partial perception. Death may be but a seeming affair whose eternal compensation requires different senses to perceive. Thus a very different strategy is possible in response to the rebel.

Metaphysical rebellion therefore clearly has its theoretical premises. The world must be seen as less than it might have been, and the individual or group must feel it has the right to something better. Camus addresses the first issue by noting that "it would be possible to demonstrate . . . that only two possible worlds can exist for the human mind: the sacred (or, to speak in Christian terms, the world of grace) and the world of rebellion" (R, 20–1). In the sacred world our place is ordained by divine dispensation; to question it is prideful or demonic. As folk wisdom would have it, if God had wanted us to fly, He would have given us wings. Thus statuses and roles are eternally fixed. Our place, our obligations and responsibilities, our means and ends are not open to question. The purpose of life is given and determining; the place of politics is ethically prescribed and circumscribed. And it is usually assumed —certainly in the West—that there is a goodness to this cosmic order, which assures that justice will be done, on earth as it is in heaven.

But before man accepts the sacred world and in order that he should be able to accept it—or before he escapes from it and in order that he should be able to escape from it —there is always a period of soul-searching and rebellion. The rebel is a man who is on the point of accepting or rejecting the sacred and determined on laying claim to a human situation in which all the answers are human—in other words, formulated in reasonable terms (R, 21).

This is our reality, feels Camus, which 150 years of Western history have written in blood: our collective struggle out of, and perhaps back into, a sacred world.[1]

But were there no revolts prior to the last 150 years? Surely Camus cannot mean that revolt and revolution are recent historical phenomena? Of course not. He suggests so much with his references to the Reformation, to the revolt of Prometheus, to Lucifer and Cain, and most explicitly in his discussion of the slave rebellion led by Spartacus. "When a slave rebels against his master," asserts Camus, "the situation presented is of one man pitted against another, under a cruel sky, far from the exalted realms of principles" (R, 108). Such rebellions may "advance the concept of a principle of equality," thus expressing "the transition from fact to right . . . analyzed in the first stage of rebellion" (R, 108, 109). But they go no further. They contest the right of one individual to rule, or challenge the practical morality of a group. They demand better, fairer, more equitable treatment for themselves or others. But they do not question the structure of the world. Rather, they often invoke that structure as justification of their right to challenge the present rulers as usurpers. Such was the nature of the Reformation— a "rebellion inside Christianity" (R, 111). In fact, most prior revolutions refused to call themselves such. They claimed to be *the* legitimate upholders of the eternal verities, which the present rulers were violating, having usurped the levers of office, or misused the functions they had a right to exercise. In the case of Spartacus, Camus suggests that this inability even to conceive of an alternative order of things was the cause of his humiliating defeat. "At the decisive moment . . . within sight of the sacred walls [of eternal Rome], the army halts and wavers, as if retreating before the principles, the institutions, the city of the gods" (R, 109).

Thus what Camus means to suggest is that prior to the last 150 years in the West a sense of a cosmic order was taken as given. It was sacred. It defined the place of humans. No doubt, it evolved over time. But its changes were less the result of rational and explicit interrogation than of unarticulated accommodations to changing conditions. At any specific moment, the order was lived as unquestionable. In fact the issue did not even arise. Revolts took place *within* the metaphysical contours laid out by this *cosmic order*. They were rarely directed at the order itself. This did not make them less violent or destructive, simply less metaphysical. They were not challenging one unity with another. When this did happen, it was usually the case of two groups, such as distinct tribes, each with its own gods and its unquestioning belief in its own sacred world, confronting one another. Quite a different matter indeed from the internal disintegration of the sense of the cosmic order that has been the pervasive metaphysical reality of our times, the implications of which Camus wishes to bring to our attention.

Before turning to our specific historical reality, a word about the second of these previously noted theoretical premises. "The spirit of rebellion can exist only in a society where a theoretical equality conceals great factual inequalities" (R, 70). Thus when Camus speaks of rebellion as "the act of an educated man who is aware of his own rights" (R, 20), he is not emphasizing education so much as he is stressing the importance of an explicit sense of having a right to better than one is receiving. It is not simply suffering that generates metaphysical rebellion, but suffering joined to a conscious appreciation of rights. "Poverty and degeneration have never ceased to be what they were before Marx's time," observes Camus, criticizing Marx's concept of the "mission of the proletariat," "factors contributing to servitude not to revolution" (R, 214). Further, the rights in question are not primarily individual rights, in the bourgeois sense, as Camus makes clear by his insistence upon the sense of solidarity that often generates revolt and sometimes sustains it. Such is clearly the case when the being of the rebel is not directly threatened by the injustice that generates outrage.

In short, "not every value entails rebellion," but "every act of rebellion tacitly invokes a value" (R, 14). The value in question is justice, rooted in the demand for the preservation of human integrity. At issue is the metaphysical base of the rebel's sense that he has a right. This is the soil that nurtures the sense of dignity. That is why Camus can call rebellion "the movement that enlists the individual in the defense of a dignity common to all men" (R, 18). "It would therefore be impossible to overemphasize the passionate affirmation that underlies the act of rebellion . . . [revealing] the part of man which must always be defended" (R, 19).

THE JUDEO-CHRISTIAN LEGACY

However universal the demand for integrity, the Western sense of the individual's uniqueness and rights to relatively fair and equal treatment has given a special poignancy to our emerging sense of justice. With the development of the Judaic view of God's concern for His people into the Christian universalization of the dignity of the person, mediated by the Greco-Roman sense of reason and the individual, a philosophical vision of "the rights of man" has emerged that gives particular force to the claims of rebellion. "The problem of rebellion seems to assume a precise meaning only within the confines of Western thought" (R, 20), because of the confrontation of a "theoretical equality" with "great factual inequalities." In the context of the rights of man, what must one feel about an order of things that plays havoc with individual destiny?

Thus the problem of revolt that Camus is studying is historically specific in two senses. Metaphysical revolt presupposes certain views of the nature of human beings and of the world to which they feel rightfully accustomed. These views have developed primarily in the West. On the other hand, the emergence and development of metaphysical rebellion cannot be adequately understood without grasping the culturally specific ontology that emerges in a Judeo-Christian world. Here the depth structure of psychic needs must be emphasized as must the patterns of belief and institutionalized practices. At the center of Camus's concern is the meeting place of metaphysical views about the nature of the world and the place of human beings therein with the pattern of conceptual needs to which they have become accustomed, and without which they might not be able to make sense of, or be comfortable with, their life.

A pattern of thinking and feeling has developed that is particular to Western civilization. It thus marks the mind and heart of those who grow up within it. The structure's metaphysical frame pervades the personal concerns of individuals. It thus tends to condition the explicit conflicts upon which practice and theory concentrate. That frame has been shaken by the failure of its explicit formulations over the past 200 or more years. But the explicit struggle to deal with the loss of belief in the Christian cosmic drama has, nevertheless, played itself out within the preset contours of the Judeo-Christian meaning-frame.[2] For Camus the historical specificity of metaphysical rebellion, not to say its logical presupposition, is given by the root structure of the Judeo-Christian vision of the world.

"It is a Christian way of thinking to consider that the history of man is strictly unique" (R, 189). For the first time in the West, and perhaps uniquely on earth, people have come to see their lot as strung out on a temporal scale. Previously the cycle of the seasons marked the progression of events. Now birth and death are no longer part of an unending cycle; they are singular moments in an unrepeatable and irreplaceable linear drama. Thus origins and ends assume transformed significance, while death fundamentally challenges the meaning of an individual life. Here the birth of the messiah is no longer a cyclical event, repeated in festivals and rituals.[3] It now marks a unique historical moment that once and for all transfigures what went before and will go after. And so with The End. The day of judgment will put an end to this historical process, ushering in a definitive reconciliation. Perhaps only such a messianic apocalypse could respond to the desperate cravings for salvation of individuals facing the prospect of a certain death without the assurance of a cyclical resurrection.

Of course, the Christian drama was a sacred one, at its outset easily merging experientially with the rituals and festivals of a cyclical world. Thus Easter merges with pagan festivals of rebirth, symbolically expressed in the ritual use of Easter eggs. But that may be seen as simply a preemptive compromise. The deeper metaphysical burden would have its day. It is not appropriate here to pursue the historical intricacies.

Sacred history slowly becomes profane history. The future replaces the past as the reference point. Death and evil are seen as unmitigated threats to the meaning of life and the trust that can be placed in the world around us. No longer is nature our home. Rather, it increasingly becomes the setting in which this cosmic drama of individual salvation is played out. Even later, it becomes a resource to be used for individual or collective purposes. Ultimately, nature becomes "natural resources," even "raw materials." As human events become pervasively historicized, sacred beliefs are first rationalized, then merged with the practical concerns of public life. They become subject to the struggle for power and to the test of material success. Justification might be by faith alone, according to Luther and Calvin, but "good works will not be wanting in those who believe."

"Christians were the first to consider human life and the course of events as a history that is unfolding from a fixed beginning toward a definitive end, in the course of which man achieves his salvation or earns his punishment" (R, 189). Here is a mindscape that dramatizes to the point of unbearable singularity the life passage of each individual. This life is our only one. It has a quite specific date of birth and an equally specific, though yet unknown, date of death. The passage is a one way ticket, the destination not in doubt. Hence time becomes central in the West. A linear time, it marks history, not as a story, but as an unrepeatable dramatic unfolding. Where is it coming from? Where is it going? And what am I doing here? These questions gain new poignancy. No wonder that with Christianity, a new sense of the personal and the subjective emerges. Never before has personal destiny taken such a threatening turn—and the possibilities of concrete reconciliation seemed so distant. No wonder the heightened need for personal salvation and its increased centrality in the thought and experience of the West.

Only Judeo-Christianity could have given birth to our modern sense of history, and to a philosophy of history as a purposeful succession of unique events, culminating in a definitive reconciliation, wherein one might see God face to face. The symbols of Christianity "are those of the drama of the divinity which unfolds throughout time" (R, 190). This is divine history, meaningful and unidirectional. Its end is a definitive resolution of death and evil. It is the salvific resolution of our finite and temporal plight. The more difficult our actual situation, the more essential the faith in its ultimate fulfillment. Before this drama of salvation, practical affairs pale. Nature, the setting for this drama, can offer nothing in the way of succor. It is the realm of suffering and death. No wonder "the hostility of historical methods of thought toward nature, which they considered as an object not for contemplation but for transformation" (R, 190). Nature was not the home of the spirit, a realm from which to seek guidance. At best it was an instrument, at worst a prison. No wonder we are overwhelmed by ecological problems. "For the Christian, as for the Marxist, nature must be subdued," while "the Greeks are of the opinion that it is better to obey it" (R, 190).

As all depends upon The End, all is judged in its light. From thinking that those who are good will be saved, it is easy to slip into thinking that those who are saved must have been good, then that what is good is what will get one saved, and finally that whatever gets one saved is good. Thus moral judgment is merged with historical success, slowly, imperceptibly, but inescapably. The ethic of worldly success tends to emerge from the bowels of the otherworldly hope for salvation. Christianity's "originality lay in introducing into the ancient world two ideas that had never before been associated: the idea of history and the idea of punishment" (R, 190). By the way it develops, history will pass judgment on individuals and movements, justly punishing those who do not live up to its demands or who deny its direction. Strip off the transcendent content of this belief system, and we see, according to Camus, "the Christian origins of all types of historic messianism, even revolutionary messianism." How else can one make sense of the *Economic and Philosophic Manuscripts* of Karl Marx, in which he speaks of Communism as the resolution of the conflict between Nature and History, Essence and Existence, and which knows itself to be such? (R, 193).

THE TRANSITION TO MODERNITY

"Metaphysical rebellion, in the real sense of the term, does not appear, in coherent form, in the history of ideas until the end of the eighteenth century —when modern times begin to the accompaniment of the crash of falling ramparts" (R, 26). The metaphysical ramparts that are falling are those that sustained the Judeo-Christian providential cosmic drama. Having introduced into history the notion of a personal god who was more than an explanatory principle or a natural force, the Jews had clearly separated the natural from the supernatural. By designating nature as God's creation, they had made the divine responsible for what happens on earth. Not surprisingly, in view of the growing emphasis on the personhood of the divinity, natural as well as supernatural events increasingly took on moral character. Or rather, the natural human tendency to evaluate natural events in the light of moral responsibility became a matter of transcendent significance.

Further, when the natural and the supernatural are separated in accord with the actions of a divine creator, it becomes possible to conceive of another who is responsible for our fate. "The only thing that gives meaning to human protest is the idea of a personal god who has created, and is therefore responsible for, everything" (R, 28). "Only a personal god can be asked by the rebel for a personal accounting" (R, 31–2). "Metaphysical rebellion presupposes a simplified view of creation—which was inconceivable to the Greeks. . . . The idea of innocence opposed to guilt, the concept of history summed up in the struggle between good and evil, was foreign to them" (R, 28). Manicheism begins to emerge with the decomposition of the ancient world, but it lacks the Judaic sense of history and the stark vision of an absolutely transcendent and personal divinity. Christianity thus breaks new ground as it incorporates Greek rationality to make sense of God's transcendent personhood from which He freely chooses to create this world—for whose fate He must then take ultimate responsibility. Here are all the ingredients of the providential drama.

For 1,500 years the West lived in terms of this drama. Its theology, philosophy, law, politics, science, cosmology, psychology, economics were Christianized. The meaning of life, the role and status of individuals, the moral rules, the hopes and fears—all were played out in accordance with this divine plan. Even rebellions were reformations of a church gone corrupt or of rulers who usurped their power. "For as long as the Western World has been Christian, the Gospels have been the interpreter between heaven and earth. Each time a solitary cry of rebellion was uttered, the answer came in the form of an even more terrible suffering. In that Christ had suffered, and had suffered voluntarily, suffering was no longer unjust and all pain was necessary. . . . Only the sacrifice of an innocent god could justify the endless and universal torture of innocence" (R, 34).

But from the moment when Christianity, emerging from its period of triumph, found itself submitted to the critical eye of reason—to the point where the divinity of Christ was denied—suffering once more became the lot of man. . . . The abyss that separates the master from the slaves opens again and the cry of revolt falls on the deaf ears of a jealous God. . . . Thus the ground will be prepared for the great offensive against a hostile heaven (R, 34–5).

The reasons are complex and obscure. The scientific revolution, the opening up of the market, technological breakthroughs, religious revivals, the rediscovery of the Ancients, the Renaissance, the discovery of the New World —all these mark a world in radical transformation. They culminate in the disintegration of the "ancien régime," which was the social and institutional base for the merging of politics and theology in the doctrine of the divine right of kings. "Theocracy was attacked in principle in 1789 and killed in its incarnation in 1793" (R, 120). "Kings were put to death long before." But previous rebels "were interested in attacking the person, not the principle." "1789 is the starting point of modern times, because the men of that period wished . . . to overthrow the principle of divine right and to introduce to the historical scene the forces of negation and rebellion which had become the essence of intellectual discussion in the previous centuries" (R, 112).

But if "1789 is explained by the struggle between divine grace and justice" (R, 112), it is preceded by centuries of struggle over the injustice of our condition. The political challenges bubbling up throughout the long period of institutional transformations leading up to the French Revolution were fought out on grounds other than metaphysical revolt. They were more matters of person, power, and legitimacy. They were often expressed in terms of competing theologies, however much they may have been instigated by the economic transformations marking the emergence of bourgeois society. During this extended period, direct theoretical challenges to the Christian order, emerging imperceptibly out of internal critiques of particular claims to legitimacy—in the Reformation, in the discussions over the State, in the developing Social Contract theories, in the attempts to make sense out of the Copernican and Newtonian theories—appear first in works of the imagination. They ultimately find explicit and historically significant expression, for Camus, in those proto-romantic French contemporaries the Marquis de Sade and Jean-Jacques Rousseau. Here, the struggle to dethrone the reigning absolute finally comes fully into the light of day.

In order to understand the logic of metaphysical revolt in the West as it develops into metaphysical revolution, we must look at its genesis and development in the imagination of these prescient theoretical forerunners. But first I must briefly specify the institutionalized form that takes hold of the West with the coming to power of the bourgeoisie. This process was no doubt furthered by the intellectual struggles that continually play themselves out in dialectical relation to the development of the bourgeois mainstream. Initially, rebellious thought is merged, and even identified, with that emerging mainstream, as both direct their attack at the ancien régime and its Christian order. Yet it is the bourgeois mainstream that increasingly becomes the subtle, even though long submerged, target of rebellious thought. Thus our metaphysical articulations in their institutional and rebellious forms are interwoven with this emerging bourgeois accession.

Bourgeois Visions

Nowhere is this relation more significant than with Marxism, perhaps the dominant challenge to the hegemony of the bourgeoisie. Camus stresses the common metaphysical roots by speaking of Marx's "bourgeois prophecy." "Marx's scientific Messianism is itself of bourgeois origin. Progress, the future of science, the cult of technology and of production, are bourgeois myths, which in the nineteenth century became dogma" (L'HR, 239; R, 193).[4]

What is crucial here is the emergence of a new faith to replace a dying one. The age of enlightenment seems to usher in a faith in progress, in which the wonders of science, industry, and technology promise to bring heaven down to earth. A brief perusal of Condorcet will suffice for one to appreciate the messianic appeal of this ideal. With one Absolute fading, only another Absolute seems able to fill the void. The Moderns win the battle with the Ancients. The triumph is complete. The Future replaces the Past as point of reference. Industry replaces the Church, and Science replaces Religion. But our providential fate is still assured. How else can one account for Adam Smith's otherwise remarkable, not to say preposterous, faith—reiterating Mandeville's fable of public virtue emerging out of unfettered private vice—in which the unseen hand will guide the market, bringing ultimate beneficence to all? Here we have the perfect "bourgeoisification" of Christian mythology. Humans are still fallen creatures. Original sin is our ineradicable self-centeredness. But through the no doubt miraculous intervention of the Holy Spirit's unseen hand, our natural selfishness, when left to its own devices, will generate industriousness, which, guided by the law of supply and demand, will bring about the "wealth of nations." No trivial myth, this.

The age of the bourgeoisie does not begin, however, with the explicit acknowledgment of the priority ultimately to be given to personal acquisition, material well-being, production, science, and industry—all subordinated to the fulfillments of an increasingly insatiable Ego. This Ego, which is supposed to think only of itself, will be well suited to a society increasingly dependent on the economic war of all against all, called "laissez-faire." But all this only reveals the hidden underside of a world that bursts forth in words as a commitment to Progress painted in moral and even religious terms. The fervor of the commitment to human rights and the declaration of the rights of man may promise a new world. It clearly is directed at the destruction of an old one.

The challenge is fundamental, while the promise is ambiguous at best. Camus singles out two key figures in this revolutionary confrontation with the ancien régime, Rousseau and St. Just. With them, the emerging rational protest begins to take shape. The metaphysics of modernity is prefigured.

Rousseau

Rousseau seeks nothing less than to replace the old faith with a new one. This is not just a revolt, but the political equivalent of Newton's revolution. "With *The Social Contract* . . . we are attending the birth of a new mystique, the general will being presented as God himself" (R, 115; L'HR, 147). "*The Social Contract* amplifies and dogmatically explains the new religion whose god is reason, confused with nature, and whose representative on earth, in place of the king, is the people considered as an expression of the general will" (R, 115).

To speak of a new religion is to highlight a profound metaphysical transformation. This inquiry "into the legitimacy of power" "assumes that traditional legitimacy, assumed to be of divine origin, is not established. Thus it proclaims another sort of legitimacy and other principles" (R, 114–5; L'HR, 146). Not only is the old world challenged, but a new one is to be put in its place. Neither the challenged nor the challenge, however, can do without absolutes upon which to rest their claims for legitimacy.

In point of fact, the values at issue for Rousseau are essentially Christian. "That is why the words that are to be found most often in *The Social Contract* are the words *absolute, sacred, inviolable*. The body politic thus defined, whose laws are sacred commandments, is only a by-product of the mystic body of temporal Christianity" (R, 115, 116).

These values, however, are to be grounded, if no less absolutely, at least with a different God. "The deification [of the people] is completed when Rousseau, separating the sovereign from his very origins, reaches the point of distinguishing between the general will and the will of all" (R, 116). By deification, Camus means that the people are here absolutized as a source of Truth. As transcendent to the flow of events, their decisions are beyond question. They are final. The same may now be said of the people as could earlier be said of the king: "Even though it is possible to appeal to the King, it is impossible to appeal against him insofar as he is the embodiment of a principle" (R, 113). Such a rule of governing is "arbitrary in principle." Claim insight into the Truth and no further challenge is possible.

Rousseau had begun with a deep desire to do justice to the nobility of humanity. He grasped the injustice of the ancien régime, which subordinated the people's needs in principle to the will of the king and in fact to a hierarchical order serving the interests of a degenerate aristocracy. Seeking to defend each person's right to dignity, he attacked the social order based on inequality and oppression at its foundations. He grasped the mystification that was the divine right of kings. Long before Proudhon, he claimed that property was theft and that, since humans are essentially social beings, only the mystification of social reality could hold people victims of this oppressive order. His was a rebellion in the service of human ennoblement, rooted in the vision of the primacy of the human order as the source of values. Thus the doctrine of the sovereignty of the people originally meant that final authority for morality and legitimacy can only reside in the will of the people. The rest is a mystification, meant to deceive in order to protect and justify exploitation. In short, he submits the king and the ancien régime, and through them God, to the challenge of Justice. He does it not simply on moral grounds, however much that may have been the source of his passion, but on metaphysical grounds.

But, to counter one absolute, another seems required. Is this a matter of logic or psychologic? Camus suggests that a way of thinking is here at stake that practically defines the West. It certainly has helped determine how rebellions have developed over the past 200 years. With Rousseau it emerges as soon as he seeks an unquestioned standpoint from which not only to challenge the ancien régime, but to point the path to a new world. In rejecting the transcendent absolute of the Christian God, he has recourse to the ultimacy and self-sufficiency of the human world. The human world is identified with the natural, which is presented not simply as what is, but as a guide to what ought to be. Here Rousseau is an heir to the tradition of natural law theory, which involves a noncritical acceptance of the natural. Whatever the importance of the role he assigns to sensibility, Rousseau remains a child of his age in identifying the natural with the moral, and both with reason. Of course, these run counter to the mainstream Christian tradition that had sustained the hierarchical order of repression. That tradition had been built on the doctrine of original sin and the untrustworthiness of nature. In a sense, these two traditions were the major alternatives in the West. To challenge the old order, Rousseau quite naturally had recourse to an alternative tradition, now being strengthened by the emerging rationalism of science and capitalism, to neither of which was he very sympathetic.

The process of deification can be seen working itself out in Rousseau through this identification of nature and virtue.

If man is naturally good, if nature as expressed in him is identified with reason, he will give expression to reason's excellence only on condition that he can express himself freely and naturally. We can no longer, therefore, go back on his decision, which henceforth hovers over him. The general will is primarily the expression of universal reason, which is categorical. The new God is born (R, 116; L'HR, 147–8).

St. Just

Rousseau is "the first man in modern times to institute the profession of civil faith." He is thus a "harbinger of contemporary forms of society which exclude not only opposition but even neutrality" (R, 116). It is, however, St. Just who "introduced Rousseau's ideas into history." Saying that "the spirit in which the King is judged will be the same as the spirit in which the Republic is established," he attacks the inviolability of the king in the name of the inviolability of the people. He thus proclaims "the transcendence of the general will." Here is the birth of "a new form of absolutism" which Camus feels "is the turning point of contemporary history." By its expectations and its consequences, "it symbolizes the desacralization of history and the disincarnation of the Christian God. Up to now, God used Kings to do his work. . . . But His historical representative has been killed. . . . There is no longer anything but a semblance of God relegated to the heaven of principles" (R, 117–20; L'HR, 149–53).

The French Revolution, brilliantly articulated and defended by St. Just, effectively destroys the ancien régime in thought as well as in deed. The rest will be commentary and consequence. The new era dawns with the definitive judgment of the king, slicing through abstract arguments with the decisiveness of the guillotine. That a French thinker would be transfixed by the French Revolution should not be surprising and may even be appropriate. Hence its importance for Camus. Here is the hinge upon which his position hangs. St. Just incorporates the dynamism of the emerging bourgeoisie, with the rationalism of modern science, and the desacralized moral vision of Rousseau. We thus glimpse the theory and practice of a world in the making. To grasp Camus's critique of modern revolutions, we would do well to attend carefully to his analysis of St. Just. We should also remember that for a brief time at the end of World War II Camus identified himself with St. Just, an identification he later regretted. This suggests that the legacy of St. Just may well be lurking under the skin of our author and his contemporaries. One might wonder, parenthetically, what happens to the sensibility and thought of a St. Just when he can no longer believe. The answer may point us in the direction of that singularly modern prophet, Jean-Baptiste Clamence, whose story Camus will tell in *The Fall*.

St. Just affirms "the divinity of the people to the extent to which its will coincides with that of nature and reason." And what happens when its will does not coincide? But that is abstract. More practically, how is one to know the will of nature and reason? And who will be the interpreter? Here we reach the center of the pathos of the intellect, the golgotha of the modern mind.

St. Just's reasoning is exemplary in its contortions. "If the general will freely expresses itself, it can only be the universal expression of reason. If the people are free," he continues, suggesting the source of a new revelation, "they are infallible. . . . They are the oracle which must be consulted in order to know what the eternal order of the world demands. *Vox populi, vox naturae*. Eternal principles govern our conduct: Truth, Justice, finally Reason" (R, 121–2; L'HR, 154).

The divinity of the people replaces the divine right of kings, nature replaces the Bible, reason replaces revelation. But there still must be morality and order. Someone must interpret nature and enforce its edicts. Fortunately, however, if evil is but the result of the oppression suffered by the people at the hands of the king, then no force will be needed to govern. The liberated people will now freely determine their destiny in accord with the law of virtue, which is that of nature. The morality of our future civic order is thus assured, and the state is free to "wither away." Only a brief transition is needed, together with a governmental order to administer the general will on a day-to-day basis.[5]

"This perfect edifice," observed Camus, "could not exist without virtue. The French Revolution, by claiming to build history on a principle of absolute purity, inaugurates modern times simultaneously with the era of formal morality." But, asks Camus,

What, in fact, is virtue? For the bourgeois philosopher of this period it is conformity with nature and, in politics, conformity with the law which expresses the general will. . . . All disobedience to the law therefore comes, not from an imperfection of the law, which is presumed to be impossible, but from a lack of virtue in the refractory citizen. . . . Each act of moral corruption is at the same time political corruption, and vice versa. Following from the doctrine itself, a principle of infinite repression thus takes hold (R, 123; L'HR, 156).

There is a tragedy here whose full effects we have yet to witness. It is a tragedy of noble souls who, in the pursuit of justice, lead us down a tortured path strewn with the victims of righteous indignation, to a promised land ringed with barbed wire over which amplifiers broadcast the truth of the revolution. Who better attests to the "implacable logic" by which "the republic of forgiveness leads . . . to the republic of the guillotine" than St. Just? How is it, wonders Camus, echoing a theme with which he is becoming increasingly preoccupied, that a man can sincerely feel that tormenting the populace is a frightful thing "and yet submit to principles that imply, in the final analysis, the torment of the people?"[6]

Camus's attempt to grasp this implacable logic in order to help break its hold on revolutionary activity is the primary inspiration for *The Rebel*. And the study of the ordeal of St. Just is crucial to the analysis that Camus works out.

If we are truly at grips with a tragedy of the Western intellect, one of its crucial forms is revealed in the struggles of St. Just to inaugurate the reign of justice. His is the bourgeois version, built around formal principles and eternal values. Camus evaluates this logic by observing, "Morality, when it is formal, devours." For St. Just, the disintegration begins almost immediately.

From the moment that the laws fail to make harmony reign, or when the unity which should be created by adherence to principles is destroyed, who is to blame? Factions. Who compose the factions? Those who deny by their very actions the necessary unity. The faction divides the sovereign. It is therefore blasphemous and criminal. It, and it alone, must be combatted. But what if there are many factions? All will be combatted, without let-up. St. Just exclaims: "Either the virtues or the Terror" (R, 124; L'HR, 157).

Observes Camus, "St. Just dreams of an ideal city where manners and customs, in final agreement with the law, will proclaim the innocence of man and the identity of his nature with reason" (R, 125). "But this is a vision of purity which is not of this world." As a dream it may invigorate and ennoble. As a guide to action it can only lead to oppression and terror. St. Just insists. He will be satisfied with nothing less. If virtue is not freely chosen, it must be imposed, consistent with Rousseau's injunction that we may have to "force them to be free."

Sade, or Debauchery in One Castle

Progress, industry, production, and the future—or the revolution, the reign of virtue, and the classless society—we are clearly in a new era. But before the temple of the new gods can be raised, that of the old gods must be destroyed. As the bourgeoisie come to power, the age of reason culminates with the ascension into the Jacobin heaven of the eternal principles in whose name St. Just seeks to bring about the republic of virtue.

If the Enlightenment is the Christian world rationalized, its vision is built upon rejection of the irrational, of the wild and daemonic, of the passions of the human soul and the call of the human heart. The faith of deism is detached and calculated. Its deity is rational and impersonal. It is oblivious to the passions and pathos of the solitary individual. The subjective, the personal, the spontaneous, have no place in the emerging era. Public repression of these dionysian forces can only lead to their private fermentation. There is a dialectic of denial that increases the force while distorting the shape of the rejected. Sade, its most dramatic expression, launches a full-scale attack on the ancien régime, on the rationalized Christianity that is the Enlightenment, and on the emerging bourgeois order (R, 37).

Sade is the repressed underside of the Enlightenment. Nature is not reason, it is instinct and power. Humans are not virtuous by nature, they are cravings for the expression of sexual passion. And society is not institutionalized civic virtue, it is an order based upon the repression of desire and the oppression of people. "Sade denies God in the name of nature . . . and he makes nature a power bent on destruction" (R, 38). "The only logic known to Sade was the logic of his feelings" (R, 36), a reality denied by the rationalists of the emerging order—though not, it should be noted, by Rousseau. His rebellion is directed against an unjust world built upon the denial of the personal, the passional, the spontaneous. "The freedom he demands is not one of principles, but of instincts" (R, 38).

But, "from rebellion Sade can only deduce an absolute negation." Rejecting a society that rejected him and a world that had no place for untamed desires, Sade's demand is for unbridled freedom. Absolute negation leads to the demand for absolute freedom. Rejection of the divinity of reason and of the view of a reasonable nature gives rise to the divinity of the passions and the view of nature as sexual instinct, power, and the will to dominate. He presciently saw the logic by which "the republic [of the revolutionaries] . . . founded on the murder of the King—who was King by divine right . . . [was] deprived . . . of the right to outlaw crime or to censure malevolent instincts" (R, 39). Hence the hypocrisy of their rule. Prisoners' "dreams have no limits and reality is no curb." Being totally rejected, he rejects totally. Being denied personal expression, he demands the right to unlimited expression. Nurtured in the bowels of a tortured soul, his rebellion is prophetic. "His desperate demand for freedom led Sade into the kingdom of servitude; his inordinate thirst for a form of life he could never attain was assuaged in the successive frenzies of a dream of universal destruction" (R, 36–7). In both the logic of his development, and the place he gives to the passions of the individual in opposition to the reigning deities, Sade points a path into our modern era for the sensitive individual.

In an age of absolutes, to reject one requires putting another in its place. Sade rejects God in the name of nature, at the same time rejecting reason in the name of the passions. Hence he rejects the established order, based as it is, at least in principle, on a reasoned and just nature. To this he counterposes a mechanical and purposeless universe of unbridled desire and the will to power. Sexual instinct becomes his god; its complete freedom of expression, the law of conduct. But such freedom knows no bounds. "Sade . . . obeys no other law than that of inexhaustible desire. But to desire without limits is the equivalent of being desired without limit. License to destroy supposes that you yourself can be destroyed. Therefore you must struggle and dominate. The law of this world is nothing but the law of force; its driving force, the will to power" (R, 41). But the law of force needs a realm in which to operate. "If they [the passions] do not reign at least over a specified territory . . . they are no longer the law. . . . The law of power . . . must fix the boundaries, without delay, of the territory where it holds sway, even if it means surrounding it with barbed wire and observation towers" (R, 42).

"The most unbridled rebellion, insistence upon complete freedom, leads," therefore, "to the total subjection of the majority. For Sade, man's emancipation is consummated in these strongholds of debauchery where a kind of bureaucracy of vice rules . . . the men and women who have committed themselves forever to the hell of their desires" (R, 42). Unbridled passion for one is the reduction of others to the status of object. It can only complete itself in the closed world of total oppression. Of course, such domination requires rational calculation. Things can't be left to chance. Thus unbridled passion dialectically defeats itself by requiring calculation. Absolute freedom requires the establishment of complete domination. Unlimited personal expression calls for the reduction of others to the status of object—which only invites others to do likewise to oneself. At the center of such a demonic universe stands the solitary individual whose passions will to dominate, but over what? A world of dead objects. Such irrational passions know no limit, not even those of the individual self. These forces of nature once absolutized and unleashed can only lead to the destruction of the human. Thus the demand for total freedom ineluctably results in total "dehumanization coldly planned by the intelligence[:] The reduction of man to an object of experiment, [and] the rule that specifies the relation between the will to power and man as an object" (R, 46–7).

But, if Sade's logic is prescient, his lesson was not widely appreciated. Rather he suggests the direction that the rebellion against rationalized Christian values was to take in the West. In one sense, passing through the Romantics it ends with the Nazis, in so far as nature as biological passion is deified in the action of the folk. More pervasively, if less obviously, the demand for personal expression of irrational and repressed sexual instincts points the way through the Romantics to a more subtle deification to which brief attention must be paid.

ROMANTICISM

Romanticism "is the cry of outraged innocence" (R, 47). Incarnating the feeling that the individual has been cheated by life, it throws back to the world its defiant challenge. Where Sade had been a solitary and rejected individual, Romanticism becomes a broad cultural movement of the disaffected. Initially rooted in an increasingly marginalized stratum of anomic artists, it gave expression to the increasing rootlessness of a population whose lives were being turned upside down by industrialization. But they initially expressed this rootlessness in terms drawn from and against a Christian world they felt had betrayed them. Their inspiration comes from an attempt to find a place for the self in a world that seems increasingly indifferent to its fate. Here Romanticism follows Sade in his demand for passionate self-expression. Facing a world that proclaims its divine justification, the Romantics respond in turn by rejecting it. Since God rules over that world, the Romantics reject God in the name of rebellion. "Lucifer-like" they challenge the ruling order. But as isolated individuals in touch more with their alienated sensibility than with any positive possibilities of collective action, a sense of impotence pervades their every effort. A rebellion without concrete possibilities of constructive expression, the positive content of their rebellion is quickly lost in the swelling tide of pent-up rage. Having been cheated by the world, they want amends. Having no specific responses to offer, they want everything changed. Condemned by their alienation from society, and from a sustaining work in process, they want adventure now. Frenzy will be the answer to boredom; apocalypse, the response to temporal dispersion and death. "The human being who is condemned to death is, at least, magnificent before he disappears, and his magnificence is his justification" (R, 51).

The Romantic has begun to confront the meaning of individualism to which the West is being increasingly condemned. More and more called upon to rely solely on personal resources—both by a capitalist ideology that prides itself on the creativity of individual initiative, to which the Romantics were not insensitive, and by the life processes of a society that was rapidly destroying traditional family and community ties—Romantics confronted the problem of death in a new light. To those who are alone in a hostile world, death is the ultimate challenge to the meaning of each life. The burden this nascent individualism places on the rootless individual challenges the West's sense of the meaning of things. Romanticism is one of the first and most poignant expressions of this developing dilemma.

The Romantic's situation is a dead end. The terms in which Romanticism struggles to express its emerging sense of isolation and purposelessness are, of historical necessity, Judeo-Christian—even as that era is being replaced by capitalism and science. Thus the burden of Romanticism's initial expression is directed at a Christian God who has betrayed them. The Romantic rejects this God as the legitimizing principle of a world to be rejected. The rebellion against death and injustice calls for a world where these principles do not reign. But it is a challenge that takes place only in the imagination. Sensing its practical impotence, it increases its fury. The passion of its rejection is totalizing. If there is no place for me in this world, then there is nothing to strive for, no values to be guided by, no goals to work for. "No longer hoping for the rule or the unity of god, determined to take up arms against an antagonistic destiny, anxious to preserve everything of which the living are still capable in a world condemned to death, romantic rebellion looks to its own attitude for a solution" (R, 51; L'HR, 72).

And what, we might ask, is possible for the uprooted and alienated? Motivated by their outrage, they might strike out in random violence, as many did. Or they might retreat into solitary dreams of revenge—certainly Sade did. Or burst forth in prodigious activity, only to burn themselves out —as did so many, perhaps retreating into the pedestrian or banal, as with Rimbaud or Lautréamont. All these are modes of impotent response; they can do nothing except oppose, challenge, or reject a world by which they feel rejected. They are challenges thrown up in the face of an insensitive deity. But they are essentially only poses, without any possibility of constructively addressing the human condition. They offer no promise of alleviating the suffering, no way out except that of the individual from this painful and unbearable world.

No wonder that the dandy personifies the Romantic's rage and impotent rebellion. Unable to envisage an objective transformation that would speak to the craving for a lost unity,

the dandy creates his unity by aesthetic means. But it is an aesthetic of singularity and negation. "To live and die before a mirror": that, according to Baudelaire, was the dandy's slogan. . . . Up to now man derived his coherence from his Creator. But from the moment that he consecrates his rupture with Him, he finds himself delivered over to the fleeting moment (R, 51–2).[7]

Here we can see the emergence of the modern concern for novelty. Presupposing a society directed toward the future, and without roots in the life of a sustaining community, increasingly isolated individuals struggle to make their lives significant in the only way that remains possible: by reflection in the eyes of their contemporaries. Not being part of a developing collective drama, they need a strategy for attracting attention to themselves. Without this attention, they are nothing—facing a death that will eternally seal their insignificance. To gain attention they must astonish with the unexpected, the novel. We are here at the center of the pathos of a civilization coming apart at the seams. The dandies live this unraveling in total impotence. The audacity of their efforts seems directly related to the loss of contact with the positive content of the rebellion, and with the natural and social roots that could suggest the direction of a more sustaining response. The dandies would like to correct creation, but can see no way out. But they do suggest the task before the West, as they give expression to its pathos. It is inevitable that others will try to develop a practical program out of this experience.

The positive side of the Romantic rebellion must not be slighted, however. It is true that "by putting emphasis on its powers of defiance and refusal," the Romantic rebellion forgot "its positive content" (R, 47). Yet Romanticism did point out the impossible position of the individual in a world in which the cosmic order was no longer sufficient. Without a pervasive sense of divine purposefulness, how can we make sense of our life? In the face of a social order undergoing rapid transformation can we still trust in God's meaning? Where are we to find a rule of life? And how can we come to terms with the uprooting and suffering all around? Both social order and cosmic order are unraveling, without apparent solution. Religion comes into question as the social order that sustained it disintegrates—and as scientific rationalism subjects religious faith to both withering critical scrutiny and the test of practical efficacy. The entire process found expression in the dramatized struggle of Ivan Karamazov, through which Dostoevsky drew out the logic of this emerging world. Nietzsche then, according to Camus, draws this vision explicitly up into his own consciousness—thus finally placing us on the metaphysical terrain of the modern era.

IVAN KARAMAZOV

When Camus writes that "Ivan Karamazov incarnates the refusal of salvation," he is calling attention to the fact that Ivan denies the relevance of any transcendent explanation. " 'If the suffering of children,' says Ivan, 'serves to complete the sum of suffering necessary for the acquisition of truth, I affirm from now onward that truth is not worth such a price'" (R, 56). The rebel affirms a limit and implicitly a human value that must be protected. The question of truth is no longer fundamental. The depth of Ivan's revolt becomes clear in the affirmation of the even-if with which Ivan incarnates the essential dimension of the rebel's no: " 'I would persist in my indignation even if I were wrong.' Which means," writes Camus, "that even if God (or Truth) existed, even if the mystery cloaked a truth . . . Ivan would not admit that truth should be paid for by evil, suffering, and the death of innocents" (R, 56).

This rebellion is metaphysical. It is directed against that which denies individuals their humanity. Here Camus sees a progression in the development of rebellion from the Romantic rebels. Their ambition was to talk to God as one equal to another. Evil was the answer to evil, pride the answer to cruelty. Vigny's ideal, for example, is to answer silence with silence (R, 55). Ivan goes farther. "He does not absolutely deny the existence of God," writes Camus, "he refutes Him in the name of a moral value." "Ivan Karamazov sides with mankind and stresses human innocence." He will accept no justification of human suffering, no explanation of the meaning of life that seeks to explain it away. "Faith presumes the acceptance of the mystery and of evil, and resignation to injustice"; thus faith is unacceptable. "Ivan will no longer have recourse to this mysterious God but to a higher principle—namely, Justice. He launches the essential undertaking of rebellion, which is that of replacing the reign of grace by the reign of justice. . . . The struggle between truth and justice is begun here for the first time" (R, 55–6).

Ivan cannot accept a truth based upon a faith that accepts, or is resigned to, unjust suffering. The authentic metaphysical foundation of revolt emerges with Ivan's rejection of the sacrifice of innocents. Any justification of the suffering of innocents is unacceptable. Without appeal to the transcendent, what then is left as a value? "Life in its most elemental form. . . . 'I live,' says Ivan, 'in spite of logic' " (R, 57). He knows that the suffering of innocents is unjustifiable, that faith and the promise of salvation cannot provide an answer; and he experiences at the center of his rebellion the irreplaceable value of life. But he cannot draw these together into a coherent pattern, a meaningful if limited rule of action. " 'I only know that suffering exists, that no one is guilty, that everything is connected, and that everything passes away and equals out.' But if there is no virtue," writes Camus, "there is no law: 'Everything is permitted,' " Ivan concludes (R, 57).

Although he rejected God and absolute justification, Ivan still seeks an absolute answer. " 'My mind is of this world,' he said; 'what good is it to try to understand what is not of this world?' But," writes Camus, "he lived only for what is not of this world, and his proud search for the absolute is precisely what removed him from the world of which he loved no part" (R, 59). He could not himself transcend the standpoint requiring the possibility of making life meaningful by bringing to it an explanation grounded elsewhere. He rebelled in the name of a concrete value and its experienced transgression; yet he was unable to maintain this standpoint in his attempt to come to grips constructively with the human condition defined by this suffering. He could not ground his meaning in that condition, but felt driven to demand transcendent support. Ivan denies God in the name of justice, but, as Camus notes, resuming the challenge Sade leveled at St. Just and his followers,

the master of the world, after his legitimacy has been contested, must be overthrown. . . . "As God and immortality do not exist, the new man is permitted to become God." But what does becoming God mean? It means, in fact, recognizing that everything is permitted and refusing to recognize any other law but one's own (R, 58–9).

As with the French Revolution, justice itself is ungrounded and Ivan's rebellion turns on its origins. Ivan's revolt has turned into metaphysical revolution with a vengeance: The order of creation is to be overthrown, as the individual becomes God. Ivan rebelled against a condition that was intolerable because it was unjust. God, if there is such a being, is impotent, indifferent, or malicious. These are the limits as revolt encounters them. But in metaphysical revolution the individual seeks to rewrite the human condition, in this case, to become God and to dictate the law—the providential design it found to be lacking.

The real problem of rebellion is found in the question, "Can one live and stand one's ground in a state of rebellion?" (R, 58). Ivan's answer is no. Beginning with the assertion of a limit, his inability to live without transcendent values and a solution to his quest for unity brought him, through an ineluctable dialectic, to the assertion that everything is permitted. And "with this . . . the history of contemporary nihilism really begins" (R, 57).[8]

NIETZSCHE

"From the moment that man submits God to moral judgment, he kills Him in his own heart. And then what is the basis of morality? God is denied in the name of justice, but can the idea of justice be understood without the idea of God?" (R, 62). For Ivan, clearly not. He went mad, thus suggesting a path for our century. Nietzsche faces this problem head on. "With him," Camus observes, "nihilism becomes conscious for the first time" (R, 65). Nietzsche begins where Ivan left off, thus constituting an advance in rebellious thought.

It was "not by choice, but by condition, and because he was too great to refuse the heritage of his time," that he saw himself becoming Europe's first complete nihilist. Camus writes:

Contrary to the opinion of certain of his Christian critics, Nietzsche did not form a project to kill God. He found Him dead in the soul of his contemporaries. He was the first to understand the immense importance of the event and to decide that this rebellion on the part of men could not lead to a renaissance unless it was controlled and directed. Any other attitude . . . must lead to the apocalypse (R, 68).

Thus if Nietzsche is a nihilist, his aim is constructive, not destructive: "to transform passive nihilism into active nihilism" (R, 68), to unmask the inability to believe in what is, which often masquerades as faith in morality and religion, in order to make possible a creative assumption of the possibilities of what can be. "Instead of methodical doubt, he practiced methodical negation, the determined destruction of everything that still hides nihilism from itself, of the idols that camouflaged God's death. 'To raise a new sanctuary, a sanctuary must be destroyed, that is the law'" (R, 66).

The sanctuary that must be destroyed is Christianity. "Christianity believes that it is fighting against nihilism because it gives the world a sense of direction, while it is really nihilism itself in so far as, by imposing an imaginary meaning on life, it prevents the discovery of its real meaning" (R, 69). "If nihilism is the inability to believe, then its most serious symptom is not found in atheism, but in the inability to believe in what is, to see what is happening, and to live life as it is offered. This infirmity is the root of all idealism. Morality has no faith in the world. For Nietzsche, real morality cannot be separated from lucidity" (R, 67). Thus traditional "morality is the ultimate aspect of God which must be destroyed before reconstruction can begin" (R, 66).

Like Dostoevsky, Nietzsche can see in socialism "only a degenerate form of Christianity" because it "preserves a belief in the finality of history which betrays life and nature, which substitutes ideal ends for real ends, and contributes to enervating both the will and the imagination" (R, 69). Both socialism and Christianity express the nihilism that Nietzsche is dedicated to annihilating, the commitment to a telos, to a purpose transcendent to life. "A nihilist is not one who believes in nothing, but one who does not believe in what exists" (R, 69). All such telic views are nihilistic, and must be ruthlessly destroyed, if creativity, the only path to the renaissance, to the *ubermensch,* is to be possible. " 'Every Church,' asserts Nietzsche, 'is a stone rolled onto the tomb of the man-god; it tries to prevent the resurrection, by force' " (R, 69). Hence "Nietzsche's supreme vocation [is] . . . to provoke a kind of crisis and a final decision about the problem of atheism" (R, 66).

But liberation from the dead weight of a nihilist tradition does not come easily. Its shock waves are everywhere—certainly throughout Nietzsche's thought and life. He recognizes,

From the moment that man believes neither in God nor in immortal life, he becomes "responsible for everything alive, for everything that, born of suffering, is condemned to suffer from life." It is he, and he alone, who must discover law and order. Then the time of exile begins, the endless search for justification, the aimless nostalgia, "the most painful, the most heartbreaking question, that of the heart which asks itself: where can I feel at home?" (R, 70).

With Nietzsche, "The 'can one live as a rebel?' becomes . . . 'can one live believing in nothing?' His reply is affirmative . . . if one accepts the final consequences of nihilism" (R, 66). And what are those consequences?

Deprived of the divine will, the world is equally deprived of unity and finality. That is why it is impossible to pass judgment on the world. . . . Judgments are based on what is, with reference to what should be—the kingdom of heaven, eternal concepts, or moral imperatives. But what should be does not exist; and this world cannot be judged in the name of nothing. "The advantages of our times: nothing is true, everything is permitted" (R, 67).

Thus it would seem that Nietzsche has been led back to the same conclusion as Ivan. With no guides to conduct, no rules by which life may find direction and at least a modicum of order, chaos is inevitable. "The essence of his discovery consists in saying that if the eternal law is not freedom, the absence of law is still less so" (R, 71). To be free may be "to abolish ends," but a world without order and values is clearly not a liberating world. "That is why he understood that the mind only found its real emancipation in the acceptance of new obligations" (R, 70–1; L'HR, 94).

Recognizing that total freedom is not liberation but a new form of servitude, Nietzsche feels the need for a source of values without transcendent purpose. " 'If we fail to find grandeur in God,' says Nietzsche, 'we find it nowhere; it must be denied or created.' To deny it was the task of the world around him, which he saw rushing to suicide. To create was the superhuman task for which he was willing to die" (R, 71–2). But if creation alone can save us, it is possible only through fidelity to this world and this life. "Nietzsche cries out to man that the only truth is the world, to which he must be faithful and in which he must live and find his salvation" (R, 72).

But—and here we enter onto perilous ground—if the world is our only home and cannot be judged on the basis of any nonexistent other, then, Nietzsche concludes, we cannot pass judgment on the world.

From the moment that it is admitted that the world pursues no end, Nietzsche proposes to concede its innocence, to affirm that it accepts no judgment since it cannot be judged on any intention, and consequently to replace all judgments based on values by absolute assent, and by a complete and exalted allegiance to this world. Thus from absolute despair will spring infinite joy, from blind servitude, unbounded freedom. To be free is, precisely, to abolish ends. The innocence of the ceaseless change of things, as soon as one consents to it, represents the maximum liberty. The free mind willingly accepts what is necessary. . . . Total acceptance of total necessity is his paradoxical definition of freedom (R, 72).

Pursuant to the logic of totality, Nietzsche moves from the rejection of transcendent belief to the affirmation of the value of immanence. From the view that one cannot take a critical standpoint toward the existence of the world in totality, he concludes that one cannot adopt a critical standpoint toward existence at all. Once again, the implicit demand for an absolute system ends in deification.[9]

Thus emerges his *amor fati* and its companion doctrine the "eternal recurrence." Nietzsche's opposition to Christianity is revealed as essentially an opposition to its dogma; the person of Christ is not condemned.[10]

With this deification of immanence, "the movement of rebellion, by which man demanded his own existence, disappears in the individual's absolute submission to the inevitable. *Amor fati* replaces what was an *odium fati*" (R, 73). "In a certain sense, rebellion, with Nietzsche, ends again in the exaltation of evil" (R, 74). The doctrine of the *ubermensch* may commence as a demand to overcome the stifling of life by a herd morality. But with the affirmation that is the meaning of the doctrine of eternal recurrence, Nietzsche relinquishes the possibility of rejecting any expression of the will to power, however perverse or degraded. "Is there nothing in his work that can be used in support of definitive murder?" asks Camus. "The answer must be yes. From the moment that the methodical aspect of Nietzschean thought is neglected (and it is not certain that he himself always observed it), his rebellious logic knows no bounds. . . . To say yes to everything supposes that one says yes to murder" (R, 76).

From the rejection of transcendence to the deification of the present, Nietzsche becomes the accomplice of servile repression against his most profound inspiration.

There is a freedom at midday when the wheel of the world stops spinning and man consents to things as they are. But *what is* becomes *what will be,* and the ceaseless change of things must be accepted. . . . Then history begins again and freedom must be sought in history. . . . The rebel whom Nietzsche set on his knees before the cosmos will, from now on, kneel before history. . . . Nietzsche, at least in his theory of superhumanity, and Marx before him, with his classless society, both replace the Beyond by the Later On. In that way Nietzsche betrayed the Greeks and the teachings of Jesus, who, according to him, replaced the Beyond by the Immediate (R, 78, 79).

By losing critical perspective through their implicit demand for an absolute, the rebellions of Marx and Nietzsche "merge into Marxism–Leninism. . . . The fundamental difference is that Nietzsche . . . proposed to assent to what exists and Marx to what is to come. For Marx, nature is to be subjugated in order to obey history; for Nietzsche, nature is to be obeyed in order to subjugate history. It is the difference between the Christian and the Greek" (R, 79). Unfortunately, however, and instructively, it comes to the same thing: the same betrayal of the origins of revolt.

Metaphysical rebellion, in its initial stages, was only a protest against the lie and the crime of existence. The Nietzschean affirmative, forgetful of the original negative, disavows the ethic that refuses to accept the world as it is. . . . Nietzsche is . . . the most acute manifestation of nihilism's conscience. . . . He compelled rebellion to . . . jump from the negation of the ideal to the secularization of the ideal. Since the salvation of man is not achieved in God, it must be achieved on earth. Since the world has no direction, man . . . must give it one (R, 77–8).

But what was required, according to Camus, was for rebellion to hold its ground within the relative space circumscribed by the yes and the no. If it attests to the impossibility of ultimately grounding its evaluations, it must seek relative guidelines for conduct within our condition. A dialectic of immersion and evaluation is called for. Nietzsche through his *amor fati* simultaneously rejects the initial form of his rebellion and affirms the values of that detested herd morality. His rebellion turns on itself. Even more, he gives ideological justification to the nihilism it was his deepest desire to transcend. Camus concludes:

Placed in the crucible of Nietzschean philosophy, rebellion, in the intoxication of freedom, ends in biological or historical Caesarism. The absolute negative had driven Stirner (and Sade) to deify crime simultaneously with the individual. But the absolute affirmative leads to universalizing murder and mankind simultaneously. Marxism–Leninism has really accepted the burden of Nietzsche's will. . . . The great rebel thus creates with his own hands, and for his own imprisonment, the implacable reign of necessity. Once he had escaped from God's prison, his first care was to construct the prison of history and of reason, thus putting the finishing touch to the camouflage and consecration of the nihilism whose conquest he claimed (R, 79–80).[11]

FROM REBELLION TO REVOLUTION

To recapitulate. The problem of *The Rebel* begins where the concerns of *The Myth* left off: with a world that lacks transcendent significance and needs a rule of conduct that can give direction to human efforts. Camus finds in revolt a reaffirmation of human dignity joined with a passionate rejection of its violation.

In assigning a limit to oppression within which begins the dignity common to all men, rebellion defined a primary value. It placed first in its frame of reference an obvious complicity among men, a common texture, the solidarity of chains, a communication of being with being which renders men similar and bound together. To the mind at grips with an absurd world, rebellion thus helped it take a first step forward (R, 281; L'HR, 347).

More than simply rebelling against oppression, however, metaphysical rebellion must bear the burden of an age that denies us the comfort of the sacred. "Decrying the human condition and its creator, [these rebels] have affirmed the solitude of man [*in the universe*] and the nonexistence of any kind of [*transcendent*] morality" (R, 100, italicized words added by me for precision). "To the 'I rebel, therefore we exist' . . . they add . . . 'And we are alone'" (R, 104).[12]

But protest is not enough. Life requires action. The metaphysical rebel must address what is to be done. Whether as an individual or as a member of a collectivity, whether in the imagination, in one's personal life, or in the public realm, the logic of rebellious negation leads directly to positive and practical affirmation. While the initial rebellion is propelled by value and outrage, it is often tempted by the extent of the suffering, the lack of practically available alternatives, or the scope of its demands, to exaggerate one side of its experience at the expense of the rest. Most clearly, for Camus, Western belief systems tend to codify and absolutize the frame of reference within which the issue of the rebellion is joined. Our particular historical danger arises in this movement from metaphysical rebellion to the demand for a complete metaphysical revolution.

An increasingly agonized sense of the injustice of the human condition precipitates an attack on the source of that injustice, which, in a Judeo-Christian world, must ultimately be the divine order of things. Since God is responsible, He must either be evil or impotent.[13]

Even more, to deny God is to leave a void. How natural then to yearn for a replacement: a new god or a new sense of the divine order or both. It is this that Camus has in mind when he observes that "the bitter end of metaphysical rebellion . . . [is] metaphysical revolution. The master of the world, after his legitimacy has been contested, must be overthrown. Man must occupy his place" (R, 58).

Metaphysical revolution as a style in art is one thing. As a practical program it is something totally different. And yet the imagination so easily suggests paths of action, especially when concerned with the effort to make sense of the human condition. Even more so in the context of the disintegrating sacred world of Judeo-Christianity. Marching forth "from appearance to action, from dandy to revolutionary," "human rebellion ends in metaphysical revolution" (R, 100, L'HR, 128).

With the throne of God being overthrown, the rebel now recognizes that it is up to him to create . . . this justice, this order, this unity . . . and, by doing so, to justify the fall of God. Then begins the desperate effort to create, at the price of crime if necessary, the empire of man (R, 25; L'HR, 41–2).

From impotence to practical action, "the spirit of metaphysical revolution openly joins forces with revolutionary movements" (R, 103).

But if the divinization of man is to replace the divinization of God, by what principle is man to rule? And to what end? Nature is the answer Sade and St. Just offer, but seen in diametrically opposed lights. For Sade liberation of the individual's biological urges is to become the new law of creation, and the passions of the self are to know no bounds. For St. Just nature is reason and virtue, not sex and power. To obey nature is to obey reason and thus bring about the eternal reign of virtue.

"St. Just is, of course, the anti-Sade. If Sade's formula were 'open the prisons or prove your virtue,' then St. Just's would be: 'Prove your virtue or go to prison.' Both, however, justify terrorism—the libertine justifies individual terrorism, the high priest of virtue State terrorism" (R, 125). Two paths by which the divinization of man is to replace the fallen deity, but one common nihilism. Metaphysical revolution, according to Camus, will continue to reveal these distinct strands, sometimes deifying the irrational, sometimes the rational, and more often than not borrowing from both, in its drive to rectify the injustice of the human condition. "Sade or dictatorship, individual terrorism or State terrorism, both justified by the same absence of justification, are, from the moment that rebellion cuts itself off from its roots and abstains from any concrete morality, one of the alternatives of the twentieth century" (R, 131–2).

In its deepest motivation Romanticism is an heir of Sade through its affirmation of single individuals and their tortured sensibility in the face of evil and death, as well as by its continual flirtation with apocalypse. This Romanticism has fed the flames of revolutionary messianism and itself been tempted by it, as for example with Breton. But, for all its yearnings, Romanticism has usually resulted in the ineffective singularities of the dandylike esthete. Others similarly motivated have not been so inconsequential.

The backdrop of the modern era is thus the disintegration of the Judeo-Christian cosmic drama, whose foreground is the struggle of metaphysical rebellion that so easily and "naturally" turns into metaphysical revolution. The drama increasingly moving to center stage in the West is not of isolated individuals, such as Sade and the Romantics, but of broad cultural and political movements of which these singular individuals may be taken as prescient and sensitive forerunners. It is to these movements and their effective spokespeople that we must now turn our attention.

10 ᕦ

Confronting Modernity

Nothing can discourage the appetite for divinity in the heart of man (R, 147).

THE BOURGEOIS ASCENDANCE

Three movements have dominated the Western stage for the last 150 years, according to Camus: bourgeois formalism and the liberal deification of progress; Marxist revolution, the myth of the classless society, and the deification of the proletariat; and fascism or Nazism and the deification of the volk in action. Each in its turn has offered itself as the instrument of human salvation, either as spiritual heir or radical alternative to the decaying Christian order. For the prophetic tradition of Marxism this deification was the "rational" product of a scientific analysis of the historical process that revealed the mission of a class and the inevitability of its ascension. For the fascists it appears as the mystical union of the pure blood of the volk in action, embodied in the nation. For the ascending bourgeoisie, on the other hand, their revolutionary messianism imperceptibly becomes the contractual rationality of daily practice as the Western world is increasingly shaped by the logic of profitability. Thus an irrational faith in progress and a commitment to personal gain have become the order of the day for much of the Western world.

All three movements seek to respond to the sense of loss of cosmic purposefulness, resulting from the eclipse of God, by turning to history as the locus of absolute values. The bourgeois response frames the project of mainstream Western civilization; the Marxian and fascist movements are seen by Camus as critical responses to the dominant bourgeois world, being directed only secondarily at Christianity. They share with their adversaries, however, the same existentio-metaphysical demand for salvation extracted from the historical process: they are messianic and eschatological.

The bourgeoisie occupy a halfway house. Deifying material progress, working through an open-ended linear history, they remain wedded to transcendent Christian values, reduced to a pure formalism, and serving to cover an unrepentant materialism and social exploitation. "They still preserve the Supreme Being. Reason, in a certain way, is still a mediator. It implies a pre-existent order. But God is at least dematerialized and reduced to the theoretical existence of a moral principle" (R, 132).

This bourgeois world is hypocritical to the core and incapable of speaking to the existential hungers of the human spirit—a point made strongly, if only by implication, in *The Stranger*. Human beings, having been robbed of their spiritual home in the drama of salvation, are offered in its place technologies and material consumption. The Faustian bargain of seduction by power and wealth has, however, not only destroyed spiritual peace, but proved to be illusory. Bourgeois ideals have rarely been realizable, except for a privileged minority at the centers of its world empire, while the spiritual and social cost of that achievement has profoundly undermined that very world. At the same time, the moral values offered to justify and guide this practice have been shown to be hypocritical formalisms, *simply used to cover the drive for power and wealth of that privileged minority*. "The entirely formal morality by which bourgeois society lives had been emptied of its substance by the gaping holes our elites have opened in it for their profit" (E, 1703).

These moral values—cut off from a spiritually sustaining community life, undermining the dignity of labor, and lacking justification other than that in divine transcendence from which they had drawn their original content—are left dangling in mid-air: to be employed by a class of exploiters to keep a lid on the people's frustrations. "The bourgeoisie succeeded in reigning during the entire nineteenth century only by referring itself to abstract principles. Less worthy than St. Just, it simply made use of this frame of reference as an alibi, while employing, on all occasions, the opposite values" (R, 132).

In short, the world of the bourgeois is one of deep spiritual malaise and an increasingly desperate sense of the meaninglessness of it all—nihilism being the subterranean offshoot—patched over in ever more unsatisfactory terms by a liberal moralism without direct bearing on the affairs of daily life, and by a panegyric to the possibilities of material well-being. The last of these is like a horizontally projected heaven offered to cover up the ever-increasing dissatisfactions felt in the present. Recognizing the emptiness and lack of justification of bourgeois values, nineteenth-century nihilists such as the Russians called for the destruction of this hypocritical shell of value in favor of commitment to material well-being and the rule of efficacy. Witness Pisarev's poignant rejection of bourgeois ideals with the assertion that a pair of shoes is worth more than all of Shakespeare, or Bazarov's commitment to material force (cf. R, 154, 254).

For Camus, two positive elements in the bourgeois position were falsified by its root hypocrisy. First was its commitment to the advancement of material well-being.[1] Second was its espousal of personal freedom. In fact, the problem of personal freedom is at the core of its world view *and* of its moral hypocrisy.

The bourgeois-liberal ideal involves free individuals working out their destiny through personal effort, guided by secularized Christian values, and supported by the "free" market allocation of resources within the confines of contracted political obligations. While the values lack reflective justification, possessing only historical momentum, their rationale is the maximization of individual freedom. Material well-being, it is argued, is the freely chosen goal of individual effort and the power that will make possible its realization.

In fact, the values by which that freedom is to be guided, having lost both their transcendent rationale and their communal content, have become a pure formalism by which the abstract search for maximization of freedom has become the practically unfettered exercise of power by those who can use it. The hypocrisy that Camus sees cutting through the bourgeois world is precisely the use of the language of a formalized transcendent value scheme to cover this exercise of power by the corporate few at the expense of the many. The demands of justice for satisfaction of the existential hunger for dignity, self-respect, and a meaningful life, including as its necessary precondition the fulfillment of essential material needs, have been submerged in the formal-ized ideology of freedom—often under the guise of unhampered free-market allocation—and idealized as historically inevitable material progress.

Karl Marx's "most profitable undertaking has been to reveal the reality that is hidden behind the formal values of which the bourgeois of his time made a great show" (R, 200). What Camus calls critical Marxism develops a theory of ideology that seeks to lay bare how bourgeois "morality prospered on the prostitution of the working classes. That the demands of honesty and intelligence were put to egoistic ends by the hypocrisy of a mediocre and grasping society was a misfortune that Marx, the incomparable eye-opener, denounced with a vehemence quite unknown before him" (R, 201). "His theory of mystification is still valid" (R, 200).

At the heart of the Marxian critique of bourgeois society, which its ide-ology seeks to cover up, lies the condition of the worker. Marxian rebellion begins, for Camus, with outrage at the assaults to human dignity that Marx details in his doctrines of exploitation and alienation. While Camus's primary concern is with the reasoning process that leads from these sources to the legitimation of oppression that is Russian communism, he wishes to remain faithful, in fact to revitalize, that initial insight. Both these matters suggest the poles of Camus's position that remain to be delineated. But I should here underscore the values underlying the critique of bourgeois soci-ety that Camus shares with critical Marxism. Camus spells it out in some detail.

The very core of [Marx's] theory was that work is profoundly dignified and unjustly despised. He rebelled against the degradation of work to the level of a commodity and of the worker to the level of an object. He reminded the privileged that their privileges were not divine and that property was not an eternal right. He gave a bad conscience to those who had no right to a clear conscience, and denounced with unparalleled profundity a class whose crime is not so much having had power as having used it to advance the ends of a mediocre society deprived of any real nobility. To him we owe the idea . . . that when work is a degradation, it is not life, even though it occupies every moment of a life. . . . By demanding for the worker real riches, which are not the riches of money but of leisure and creation, [Marx] has reclaimed, despite all appearances to the contrary, the dignity of man (R, 209).

In order to appreciate more adequately the problems and possibilities of the rebellious legacy to which Marxism has laid claim in the twentieth century, it will be helpful to give historical depth to its theoretical sources as well as brief consideration to the major countercurrent by which it has sometimes been tempted, and to which it has yet remained fundamentally opposed. Let me begin with that countercurrent.

FASCISM

Hatred of the established order and suffering from the burden of individual freedom have been pervasive underground themes of the modern world. Romanticism was nurtured in this psychic subsoil, drawing sustenance from the disintegrating cosmic order and the rootlessness of market society. Ambivalently merged here are the yearnings for a lost community, the assertion of an omnipotent ego, and the temptation of an apocalyptic consummation, in which the burdens of individuality may be relieved. When these conflicting demands seek political expression, their unifying themes tend to be a frenzy of action grounded in faith in a lost community, while the ego vicariously (and unthreateningly) realizes its aspirations for omnipotence through identification with the power of a heroic leader, the symbol of the individual's mystical ties to the people. No wonder that fascism—and, even more profoundly, variations of Nazism—have emerged as such powerful temptations in this post-Christian era.

"To those who despair of everything, not reason but only passion can provide a faith, and in this particular case it must be the same passion that lay at the root of the despair—namely, humiliation and hatred" (R, 178–9).[2] It is the self that is humiliated; it is the world that is hated. The sense of being cheated is pervasive. Not moral outrage so much as resentment fuels this movement. Revenge is demanded. The sense of being cheated by life is made into a rule of action. Hence there must be enemies. In fact, the movement defines itself by them—lacking as it does any coherent sense of value and direction. That "'hatred of form' which animated Hitler" is but the flip side of the rejection of the value of particulars, and thus of relative values. "When Mussolini extolled 'the elemental forces of the individual,' he announced the exaltation of the dark powers of blood and instinct," which constitutes a "biological justification" for "complete identification with the stream of life, on the lowest level and in defiance of all superior reality." Thus "man was nothing but an elemental force in motion." "Action alone kept him alive. For him, to exist was to act" (R, 179). But to no purpose other than action itself, by which the burden of individuality and reflection can be cut short before they begin. In fact, individuality is itself a sign of guilt. All the existential concerns threaten to become intolerable burdens that must be removed before they infect the soul or the body politic. Action must preempt the field, guilt undermine the possibility of reflective individuality or rebellion, while force shapes this headless rush into the chaotic future.

This preemptive strike at discrete and relative human values can thus be seen as one of the temptations of the modern world, given force by the psychic deadening of bureaucratic society as well as by the power of such a society to mold thought and suppress dissidence. Camus does not take fascism seriously as a theoretical response to the modern predicament, even dismissing it ultimately as an expression of rebellious thought. He does, nonetheless, take it seriously as a practical movement and a psychic temptation. It certainly has constituted one of the major responses of Western civilization to the disintegration of the prevailing order—a response steeped in resentment at betrayal and calling for revenge for the burdens that the rootless individual increasingly feels in an uncaring world.

HEGEL

If it is true that fascist revolutions "lacked the ambition of universality" and thus "do not merit the title" of metaphysical revolution (R, 177), the same cannot be said of Hegel. If ever thought aspired to totality, it was his.

"Hegel's undeniable originality lies in his definitive destruction of all vertical transcendence" (R, 142). "For the universal but abstract reason of St. Just and Rousseau," Hegel substitutes "concrete universal reason. Up to this point, reason had soared above the phenomena that were related to it. Now reason is . . . incorporated in the stream of historical events, which it explains while deriving its substance from them" (R, 133).

In seeking to bring transcendent principles into the historical process, Hegel is, according to Camus, the watershed of the modern era. "Justice, reason, truth still shone in the Jacobin heaven, performing the function of fixed stars, which could, at least, serve as guides" (R, 133).

Divine transcendence, up to 1789, served to justify the arbitrary actions of the king. After the French Revolution, the transcendence of the formal principles of reason or justice serves to justify a rule that is neither just nor reasonable. This transcendence is therefore a mask that must be torn off. God is dead, but . . . the morality of principles in which the memory of God is still preserved must also be killed. The hatred of formal virtue [which Hegel inaugurated] . . . has remained one of the principal themes of history today (R, 135).

History is no longer subject to transcendent principles. It has become autonomous. If the value question has not been resolved, it has certainly been transformed. By identifying the real with the rational and the rational with the real, Hegel gives birth to the doctrine of historical efficacy, the central target of Camus's critique. It should be noted that Hegel's doctrine is ambiguous, to say the least, and has given rise to diverse interpretations. Not only has Camus noted this fact, but he has taken pains to underscore the conservative, even quietistic interpretation by which this doctrine has often been used to justify the status quo (R, 135, 151–2).

Its primary historical significance, however, lies in its revolutionary interpretation, in which particular emphasis is given to the identification of the rational with the real. Thus revolutionaries have not only delegitimized any state of affairs that does not live up to the demands of reason, but identified reason with the essence of historical development. Here we have a continuation of the rationalized absolutism of Rousseau and the Jacobins. No longer is there any transhistorical reference point, however, by which historical events can be judged and evaluated. Reason has been thoroughly historicized while history has become self-contained and self-justifying. It is the new absolute.

With "truth, reason, and justice" now "abruptly incarnated in the progress of the world . . . these values have ceased to be guides in order to be goals. . . . From this moment dates the idea . . . that man has not been endowed with a definitive human nature, that he is not a finished creation but an experiment of which he can be partly the creator" (R, 134).

"Values are thus only to be found at the end of history. Until then there is no suitable criterion on which to base a judgment of value. One must act and live in terms of the future. All morality becomes provisional" (R, 142).[3]

If morality is provisional, the end is not. Hegel grounds the movement of history in the "desire [of consciousness] to be recognized and proclaimed as such by other consciousnesses." Thus "it is others who beget us. Only in association do we receive a human value, as distinct from an animal value" (R, 138). At this point, Hegel is but a child of Rousseau and the Enlightenment, but his conception of psychology takes him farther. "Fundamental human relations are . . . relations of pure prestige, a perpetual struggle to the death for recognition of one human being by another." Since we *are* not unless we are recognized as such, in this world without transcendent signifi-cance, the struggle to be all that one can be—by a logic that Camus does not go into and that Hegel himself may not have been fully aware of—leads "everyone . . . [to want] to be recognized by everyone." "The existence that Hegelian consciousness seeks to obtain"—no longer being obtainable from God or in an afterlife—"is born in the hard-won glory of collective approval." This results in "the entire history of mankind [being] . . . nothing but a pro-longed fight to the death for the conquest of universal prestige and absolute power. It is, in essence, imperialist" (R, 138–9).

With salvation having become the struggle for universal recognition, only the success of the endeavor can judge this process. The end of history is the goal and purpose of the struggle. We will make human beings and history in the process, recognizing that "no pre-existent value can point the way" (R, 134). Provisional morality joined to the absolutization of history yields the doctrine of historical efficacy. Hegel's gloss on this vision involves the historical transfiguration of Christian doctrine.[4]

"Nothing can discourage the appetite for divinity in the heart of man," comments Camus. Hegel has sought to give expression to this aspiration in the context of a post-Christian world in which the supernatural is no longer believable. Thus he divinized the process of history itself, assuring us of salvation at its completion. But no standards remain by which to guide historical action, save those resulting from a mystical insight into the process —a faith, perhaps, in its rationality, where rationality is itself divinized. We are no longer talking, therefore, of history as the succession of events by which the collective biography of humanity takes shape, but of an absolutized process in which fact and value are mystically merged. Insight is called for to give direction to action, the only criterion by which it can be judged being the success it achieves, retrospectively considered. This is no longer human history. It is sacred history, justified by the success of those who have won the right to interpret the process. This rationale, prepared by Hegel, nurtures the tradition of revolutionary messianism of which prophetic Marxism is both spiritual heir and material embodiment.

MARX

It is common knowledge that Marx claimed to have found Hegel on his head and to have turned him right side up. By this is meant that Hegel's doctrine is an idealism, the substance of which is geist; that is, mind or spirit. Marx rejects the idealism of history seen as the self-development of geist, while accepting the notion of the dialectical nature of historical development. To turn Hegel right side up is to see that what people think, and the consequent history of ideas or spirit, is essentially a reflection of what people do. That people's collective struggle to produce and reproduce their life determines their mode of life and thought. Put somewhat crudely, economics determines the superstructure of habits, beliefs, values, and political and legal forms.

Here is not the place for a detailed analysis of Marxism. Rather we must attend to Camus's interpretation. Further, Camus makes no claim to have offered a full analysis of Marx's thought. He does not even emphasize the textual adequacy of his analysis as it concerns the writings of Marx himself. I think it fair to say that Camus believed the aspects of Marxism he was highlighting were attributable to Marx himself. But that is not essential for his thesis. What *is* essential is that his vision of Marxism—and Marxism–Leninism and Stalinism—constitutes a fair and accurate analysis of what has passed for Marxism in Western thought for 100 years. For Camus's analysis, above all, focuses on a mode of thinking that has influenced, even directed, contemporary history. It is not primarily a scholarly study of historical texts. This point should be underscored precisely because Camus's presentation is somewhat simplistic when dealing with certain details of Marx's thought—especially as concerns his supposed economic determinism—while right on target as an exploration of the mainstream Marxian legacy. Parenthetically, Camus is quite sympathetic to the analyses Marx offered on the nature and condition of exploitation under capitalism, as previously noted. Thus, "Marxism and its successors will be examined here from the angle of prophecy," and from the perspective of "the Marxists who have made history" (R, 189).

If Marx turned Hegel on his head, emphasizing the primacy of material reality, he did not reject the structure of Hegelian thought or the centrality of the dialectic. Hegel was the linchpin of the modern era because he offered a totalized vision of history. This historicized Christianity, with its providential design, "cunning of Reason," and envisioned day of ultimate reconciliation, provided a comprehensive framework within which the struggles of the modern world could find meaning.

The absolutization of the historical process is precisely what Camus means by historicism. His critique of Marx, stripped of all the peripheral issues, comes down to claiming that Marx bought the entire structure of the Hegelian schema. He rejects both Hegelian idealism and Christian divinity, seeing both as forms of false consciousness or ideology, but his atheism is simply Hegelianized Christianity in different dress. "Marxist atheism is absolute. But nevertheless it does reinstate the supreme being on the level of humanity. . . . Socialism is therefore an enterprise for the deification of man and has assumed some of the characteristics of traditional religions" (R, 192).

Having joined Hegel in rejecting formal principles, most particularly those of morality, which he saw as ideological covers for legitimating injustice, Marx was left without any standard of judgment other than practical success. That success had to be defined in terms of the alleviation of the injustices done to working people, which had been the initial source of his outrage. But it was no longer possible to offer a moral defense of this outrage. Certainly not Christian or bourgeois morality. Thus either his outrage expresses a subjective and idealistic moralism or it must be seen as an expression of the objective process of dialectical development whose truth will be established by the consummation of history: the classless society. Hence this doctrine of the revolutionary consummation of history becomes the necessary truth of the original sense of moral outrage.

On Liberation

There is no need to recapitulate Camus's presentation of the Marxian system. What is crucial is to locate those key doctrines, adapted from Hegel, that bring about the dialectical inversion of what, in Camus's eyes, began as a liberating revolt only to end in an apologia for oppression. These are two contradictory dimensions of the absolutized historical dialectic: the deification of production and the mission of the proletariat. Together they give substance to the central Marxian myth: *the revolution,* which is supposed to put an end to exploitation and oppression, ushering in the definitive reconciliation of matter and spirit, of essence and existence, that is the classless society.

Thus the doctrine of *the revolution,* which both consummates and justifies the historically inevitable development of the dialectic, has two main dimensions. It is propelled by the development of the forces of production, which provides the material base for the ascension into posthistory. And it is assured of realization by the proletariat, whose historical mission is to bring salvation out of bondage and destitution. When put so baldly, one might ask, What could possibly give rise to such a messianic vision? What evidence could ever justify this scientific socialism? Since the answer to the second question is obviously none, we are really dealing with a religious faith, whose structure seems to replicate well Judeo-Christianity's cosmic drama. Is this Marxism conceivable outside the Christianized West? Camus doubts it. But I have already noted both the Judeo-Christian origins of prophetic Marxism as well as its similarity to bourgeois thought. Let me try to pull together the historical sources, as they converge in this historical messianism.

As a child of the industrial revolution, Marx merges his outrage at the suffering of the people, their exploitation by a relatively small class of proprietors of the means of production, with an unbounded faith in the liberating possibilities of industry. In the prophetic tradition, he rails against injustice and demands that his people, the working people, be set free. He sees history making possible for the first time the material liberation of humanity from toil and slavery to nature. But slavery to nature is being replaced by slavery to others. The present situation is all the more intolerable now that the means of liberation are at hand.

The precondition of this liberation is the fullest possible development of industry's productive forces. Only this can free humans from bondage to nature. Marx is "the prophet of production" (R, 204) because he sees it as the necessary condition of definitive human liberation. In fact, he often speaks as if it is also the sufficient condition, but then he is guilty of merging production with the historical dialectic itself. That reading leads to the narrow deterministic interpretation of Marx. Although "progress resembles 'that horrible pagan god who wished to drink nectar only from the skulls of his fallen enemies' . . . at least it is progress" (R, 205), without which liberation is not possible.

But there is a basic ambiguity in this notion. Is progress simply the growth of the productive forces, or is it the qualitative transformation of the conditions of existence? Marx intends the latter, which it is the task of the dialectic to bring about. But he often speaks as if that transformation will inevitably result from the unfettered development of the productive forces. His faith in the liberatory possibilities of production seems to blind him to its oppressive potential. He blames the division of labor for exploitation without seeing to what extent this division is furthered, and even made necessary, by the development of those forces of production.[5]

The point is that there is nothing inevitable about the liberatory role of production. The rationalization of production may lead to both an enormous increase in material goods and increasing control and subjugation of labor. "The passages by Simone Weil on the condition of the factory worker must be read in order to realize to what degree of moral exhaustion and silent despair the rationalization of labor can lead." Suggesting both the source of his own indignation and the thrust of his constructive efforts, Camus observes:

Work in which one can have an interest, creative work, even though it is badly paid, does not degrade life. Industrial socialism has done nothing essential to alleviate the condition of the workers, because it has not touched on the very principle of production and the organization of labor, which, on the contrary, it has extolled (R, 216).

In fact, as Camus notes in a footnote as confirmation of the failure of "industrial socialism," Lenin, "without any apparent bitterness," "dared to say . . . that the masses would more easily accept bureaucratic and dictatorial centralism because 'discipline and organization are assimilated more easily by the proletariat, thanks to the hard school of the factory'" (R, 217). Camus concludes that "the political form of society is no longer in question at this level, but the beliefs of a technical civilization on which capitalism and socialism are equally dependent. Any ideas that do not advance the solution of this problem hardly touch on the misfortunes of the worker" (R, 216).

The Marxist plan to abolish the degrading opposition of intellectual to manual work has come into conflict with the demands of industrial production, which elsewhere Marx exalted. . . . Division of labor and private property, he said, are identical expressions. History has demonstrated the contrary. The ideal regime based on collective property could be defined, according to Lenin, as justice plus electricity. In the final analysis it is only electricity, without justice (R, 215).

Was this a scientific mistake? To suggest this is to mistake the very essence of the thinking in question, according to Camus. What we are faced with is not simply an attempt to analyze the conditions of exploitation and to develop strategies to counter them. Rather, we are confronted with a counter mythology. Marxism at this level continues the Hegelian effort to offer a complete analysis of the human condition, and by so doing to envision the definitive resolution of the condition of human finitude and temporality.[6] Not only is its analysis presented as scientific and comprehensive, but historical development is seen as providential and necessary. Salvation is assured. We need only pursue the dialectic to its consummation.

Of course, the language of science is continually invoked. Those who are "true believers" in "scientific socialism" were deeply offended by Camus's analysis. And yet how else account not only for "the cult of production"—which, in any event, Marxism shares with bourgeois thought—but for the mystical faith in a mythologized proletariat? This proletariat, put in place by the dialectic of production, is to carry out the transformation that will usher in the classless society—that definitive resolution of historical injustice. But what qualifies the proletariat to carry out this revolution? And how can we be sure that the revolution, given its motor force by the suffering of the toiling masses, will likewise be directed by them? Out of degradation and extreme poverty, can insight and practical strategy emerge? Who could envisage that those with no experience of ruling would be able to organize themselves into a viable social order, not to say one marked by the subtle balance of freedom and justice? Camus asks:

Where is the guarantee that, in the very bosom of the revolution, estates, classes, and antagonisms will not arise? The guarantee lies in Hegel. The proletariat is . . . the universal in opposition to the particular. . . . It has nothing, neither property nor morality nor country. Therefore it clings to nothing but the species of which it is henceforth the naked and implacable representative. In affirming itself it affirms everything and everyone. . . . "Only the proletariat, totally excluded from this affirmation of their personality, are capable of realizing the complete affirmation of self" (R, 205).

But this is no longer a discussion of the conditions of working people. Nor is it a program for action. It is myth, pure and simple, however legitimated by the rationalism of Hegel's historicized Christianity. "Through its suffering and struggles" this "mission of the proletariat . . . to bring forth supreme dignity from supreme humiliation" reveals it as "Christ in human form redeeming the collective sin of alienation" (R, 205).

Practical revolutionaries have not been misled by this paean to the spontaneity of worker self-liberation. They know that such a revolution must be organized; like all holy missions, it requires a priesthood.

By failing to deal theoretically with the practical problems of strategy and organization, Marxism made certain these problems would be dealt with apart from the mythical framework, and usually in a way that belied the initial call for the self-liberation of working people. "More and more, revolution has found itself delivered into the hands of its bureaucrats and doctrinaires on the one hand, and to enfeebled and bewildered masses on the other" (R, 216). The history of Marxism is the history of the use of the myth to justify the organized opposition of elites and vanguards in the name of the revolution. It is the doctrine of the revolution, with its companion notion of the revolutionary vanguard, which stands dead center in the Marxist tradition, to which the mission of the proletariat is dedicated, and in which is encapsulated the pathology that is prophetic Marxism. Of this, Marx, of course, is only partly responsible. One would have to look elsewhere for the full development of the notion of a revolutionary vanguard, particularly in the messianic nihilism of nineteenth century Russia which leads from Bielinsky and Pisarev, through Bakunin and Nechaiev, to Lenin. Nor ought we to forget its roots in the French revolutionary radicalism of St. Just, Babeuf, and even Sade.

The Revolution

One must see the doctrine of the revolution as the central Marxian myth to which all else is subordinated. This has been the legacy and the source of the evangelical force of Marxism as a world movement. This myth is required by the historicized demand for totality which dynamized the metaphysical structure of Western beliefs. As a response to the failure of Christianity, it is nurtured by Rousseau's vision of civic faith, the Enlightenment demand for progress in accord with a reasoned nature that assured the virtues of its endeavor, and Hegel's incorporation of these themes into a historicized vision of liberation. All that was needed was to place this post-Christian drama on the solid material bases offered by the development of science and industry, while linking the development of production with the struggle of classes for liberation. The point of it all was the driving need to give absolute sense and purpose to existence in the face of a world in complete upheaval. How much masses of people would struggle for a progressive but partial amelioration of their condition may not be clear. But there is nothing like a messianic mission to galvanize them into action. Especially when they have faith that they are in the right and that their side is sure of its ultimate triumph.

Whatever the historical dynamic, and whatever the source of Marx's personal vision and determination, it is clear that the critical analysis of exploitation, when joined with faith in the power of the productive forces and the prophetic mission of the proletariat find their perfect rational union in the doctrine of the revolution. Here the historical struggle of oppressed and oppressing classes is dialectically consummated with the radical inversion that will put an end to the struggle of classes, ushering in an ideal society without class antagonisms and thus without exploitation and injustice.

And what is the promise of the revolution? "The final disappearance of political economy . . . signifies the end of all suffering. Economics, in fact, coincides with pain and suffering in history, which disappear with the disappearance of history. We arrive at last in the Garden of Eden" (R, 223). It is only as the definitive end to human suffering that the revolution can offer itself as the sole foundation of values in a world that has been denied transcendent justification. From this perspective, moral questions become matters of tactics and of efficacy. From the perspective of the Absolute what can the concerns of individuals matter? "If it is certain that the kingdom will come, what does time matter? Suffering is never provisional for the man who does not believe in the future. But one hundred years of suffering are fleeting in the eyes of the man who prophesies, for the one hundred and first year, the definitive city" (R, 207). Thus:

Utopia replaces God by the future. Then it proceeds to identify the future with ethics; the only values are those which serve this particular future. For that reason Utopias have almost always been coercive and authoritarian. . . . The golden age, postponed until the end of history and coincident . . . with an apocalypse, therefore justifies everything (R, 207–8).

Marx destroys all transcendence, then carries out . . . the transition from fact to duty. But his concept of duty has no other origin but fact. The demand for justice ends in injustice if it is not primarily based on an ethical justification of justice; without this, crime itself one day becomes a duty. When good and evil are reintegrated in time and confused with events, nothing is any longer good or bad, but only either premature or out of date. Who will decide on the opportunity, if not the opportunist? Later, say the disciples, you shall judge. But the victims will not be there to judge. For the victim, the present is the only value, rebellion the only action. . . . [Thus] the kingdom of ends is used, like the ethics of eternity and the kingdom of heaven, for purposes of social mystification (R, 209–10, 225).

We have come full circle. The inversion is complete. "How to live without grace—that is the question that dominates the nineteenth century. 'By justice,' answered all those who did not want to accept absolute nihilism. To the people who despaired of the kingdom of heaven, they promised the kingdom of men" (R, 225).

But, as with St. Just, that kingdom must be organized; justice must be interpreted and implemented. There will be disagreements. Some will claim insight into the truth. Since that truth is both absolute and our sole path to salvation, the sternest measures must be taken against those who impede its realization. In fact, since that truth offers salvation, those who oppose it must be ignorant, misled, or evil. In any case, their repression, reeducation, or elimination is more than justified. The movement from St. Just to Lenin is clear.

All that remains is to give flesh and force of arms to the mystical body of the proletariat that embodies the sacred mission of the resurrection of historical humanity.[7] Herein lies the originality of Lenin. Being totally committed to the revolution, his central concern was the seizure of power. Strategic issues are central for Lenin, because all the essential metaphysical and moral questions are resolved in advance. He is a true believer, and his is a sacred universe.

RUSSIAN MESSIANISM

Lenin's Precursors

To appreciate this sacred universe within which Leninism emerges and of which it is the evangelical doctrine—thus marking the end of one strand of historical rebellion—a brief detour back to its Russian roots is called for. We can simplify Camus's own treatment by concentrating on Bakunin and Nechaiev. Three factors must be recalled. First, Russia in the nineteenth century was a deeply Christian country in which religion and politics were never far apart. Second, its society was suffering under the burden of a decaying feudalism, coming under increasing pressure for change from the West, to which its alienated intellectuals were either looking for direction or responding with an impassioned rejection of its degenerative influence. Into this brew, Hegelian thought broke with dramatic force, shattering the intellectual world and suggesting a new world vision. In a milieu both creatively alive and culturally adrift, in which salvation and the meaning of existence pervaded most discussion, attitudes toward Hegel and the political question were hardly likely to be phrased in moderate terms.

Bakunin had buried himself in Hegel " 'to the point of madness' " only to reject Hegel's identification of the Prussian state with the realization of reason. In both commitments he attested to his demand for the absolute, for " 'the universal and authentically democratic Church of Freedom' " (R, 157). "History is governed by only two principles: the State and social revolution

. . . which are engaged in a death struggle. The State is the incarnation of crime. 'The smallest and most inoffensive State is still criminal in its dreams.' Therefore revolution is the incarnation of good" (R, 157).

By reintroducing "into rebellious action one of the themes of romantic rebellion," thus turning politics into historicized theology of the struggle of good and evil, Bakunin leaves no ground of resolution, no standard other than the triumph of good over evil by whatever means necessary. Certainly Bakunin wanted liberation, "but he hoped to realize it through total destruction." To absolutize the struggle and to see all that is established as an expression of evil is to make practical and constructive action impossible. It is to condemn in advance the values by which people live—in the very name of liberating them.

To destroy everything is to pledge oneself to building without foundations, and then to holding up the walls with one's hands. He who rejects the entire past, without keeping any part of it which could serve to breathe life into the revolution, condemns himself to finding justification only in the future and, in the meantime, to entrusting the police with the task of justifying the provisional state of affairs. . . . This is the logic by which his commitment to total liberation of humanity from the oppression of *the state,* by way of the absolute and total rejection of existing values, led to the justification of "political cynicism" and "the absolute subordination of the individual to the central committee" (R, 159).

It was Nechaiev who sought ruthlessly to put this doctrine into practice. "If history is, in fact, independent of all principles and composed only of a struggle between revolution and counterrevolution, there is no way out but to espouse wholeheartedly one of the two and either die or be resurrected" (R, 160). If you are not part of the solution, you are part of the problem. For him the revolution was all. Not friends, not morality could be allowed to stand in its way. If we follow Hegel in the destruction of transcendent values, if "the future is the only transcendence for men without God (L'HR, 207; R, 166), and if that future is defined in terms of the revolution, "in the name of what value is it possible to decide that this tactic [of systematic violence and deception] is repugnant?" (R, 163). "When revolution is the sole value, there are, in fact, no more rights, there are only duties" (R, 163). Not duties to others, but to the revolution. The absence of rights is the absence of any individual claim to respect and dignity. In the face of this sacred battle of good and evil, finite individual destiny counts for nought. Systematic political cynicism simply had to be rationally organized in order to be effective: Secret societies were organized into small cells of dedicated revolutionaries under the direction of a central committee whose rule was law, whose interpretation was reality, whose method was the use of words as an instrument of the struggle, and whose decision was final, implemented ruthlessly, and without scruples. No wonder Camus would claim that it is "the joint legacy of Nechaiev and Marx" that "will give birth to the totalitarian revolution of the twentieth century" (R, 174).

Lenin

More than anyone else, Lenin incarnated this dual legacy, giving it its modern formulation. Since for him questions of metaphysics and morals were essentially resolved in advance, being summed up in the doctrine of the revolution, the only important issues that remained were strategy and tactics. "Lenin's point of view, in order to be understood, must always be considered in terms of strategy" (R, 229). Before the task of organizing the revolution, all other matters were inconsequential. Moral scruples impede revolutionary action. Even more, the revolution is not a matter of personal expression or of collective self-determination. Spontaneous protest on its own leads nowhere. The revolution must be organized, and it must have a theory that is strategically useful and believable to the followers. You cannot rely upon the workers to develop this knowledge themselves. The proletariat may be the revolutionary class, but no dedicated revolutionary can entertain romantic myths concerning the insights generated by the degraded conditions of their existence. Lenin insists:

The workers will never elaborate an independent ideology by themselves. He denies the spontaneity of the masses. Socialist doctrine supposes a scientific basis that only the intellectuals can give it. . . . "Theory," he says, "should subordinate spontaneity." In plain language . . . revolution needs leaders and theorists. . . . The revolution, before being either economic or sentimental, is military. Until the day that the revolution breaks out, revolutionary action is identified with strategy. . . . The revolution will have its professional army as well as the masses, which can be conscripted when needed. This corps of agitators must be organized before the mass is organized. . . . From that moment the proletariat no longer has a mission. It is only one powerful means, among others, in the hands of the revolutionary ascetics (R, 227–8).

In this sacred world, human values have become matters of strategic expediency in the purview of the priestly vanguard into whose hands the mission of the proletariat has been entrusted. The revolution become dogma now promises earthly salvation. But in order to bring about complete liberation, the revolution must be organized. Democratic centralism will insure the strictest obedience to orders: "All freedom must be crushed in order to conquer the empire, and one day the empire will be the equivalent of freedom" (R, 233). Camus summarizes Lenin's thought:

From the rule of the masses and the concept of the proletarian revolution we first pass on to the idea of a revolution made and directed by professional agents. The relentless criticism of the State [as an instrument of the ruling class] is then reconciled with the . . . necessary, but provisional, dictatorship of the proletariat, embodied in its leaders. Finally, it is announced that the end of this provisional condition cannot be foreseen and that, what is more, no one has ever presumed to promise that there will be an end. After that it is logical that the autonomy of the soviets should be contested . . . and the sailors of Kronstadt crushed by the party. . . . From this moment on, the history of the interior struggles of the party, from Lenin to Stalin, is summed up in the struggle between workers' democracy and military and bureaucratic dictatorship; in other words, between justice and expediency (R, 231, 230).

The Universe of the Trial

We are no longer in limbo. The church militant is on the march. In the manichean confines of this sacred world, there is a truth into which the vanguard party is granted unique insight. There are those who have faith in the revolution and those who do not. Since the goodness of the revolutionary cause is self-evident, those who are not with us must be against us. It is not so much, even, a question of their intent—though a lack of fervor in the historic cause is grounds for suspicion—as it is a matter of "objective culpability." Failure to commit themselves to the cause, makes them objectively guilty of impeding the movement of history. Whatever their intentions, they are playing into the hands of the enemy.

We are far, it would seem, from Marxism and from Hegel, and even farther from the first rebels. Nevertheless, all purely historical thought leads to the brink of this abyss. To the extent to which Marx predicted the inevitable establishment of the classless city and to the extent to which he thus established the good will of history, every check to the advance of freedom must be imputed to the ill will of mankind. Marx reintroduced crime and punishment into the unchristian world, but only in relation to history. Marxism in one of its aspects is a doctrine of culpability on man's part and innocence on history's (R, 241).

If history is on the march to the definitive city, and if we are sure we know the way, how are we to respond to those who seek to block the path? What are we to think of their motives? Or their character? Even more, of the consequences of allowing them and their allies freedom of action? The world is the realm of the manichean struggle of classes. It is war. The forces of good must be at least as well organized as are the forces of evil. And we know that the forces of evil will stop at nothing to defend their privileges. They have tremendous resources, having controlled the state and the economy for so long. Even more, they have controlled the sphere of culture, the production and reproduction of habits and beliefs. In fact, their power and the power of entrenched habit are so great as to have infected the proletariat. Long subject to the cultural hegemony of the bourgeoisie, workers are continually tempted to go over to the enemy, out of habit and the tradition of subservience. Even they are not to be trusted, must be organized, carefully watched, and, when necessary, subjected to "iron discipline." We must exterminate not only the bourgeoisie, but the bourgeois elements lurking within the character of the proletariat. This war will continue until the last refuge of the bourgeoisie has been wiped out. Until then, eternal vigilance and the strictest discipline are demanded. Recalcitrance may be taken as a sign of resistance, of the lurking attachment to bourgeois interests. Even if that is not the case, failure to suppress such deviation gives aid and comfort to the enemy.

In this "universe of the trial," "every man is a criminal who is unaware of being so. . . . His actions he considered subjectively inoffensive, or even advantageous for the future of justice. But it is demonstrated to him that objectively his actions have been harmful to that future." But who can know for sure what will ultimately benefit human justice? Do the intentions of the individual have no bearing on innocence or guilt?

The concept of objective culpability . . . is embodied in an interminable subjectivity which is imposed on others as objectivity: and that is the philosophic definition of terror. This type of objectivity has no definable meaning, but power will give it a content by decreeing that everything of which it does not approve is guilty (R, 242).

Nothing is more successful in stamping out revolt than a sense of guilt. Individuals must be made to realize that they are nothing by themselves. No wonder the importance of making pride a sin. The unquestioning domination of a church requires the institution of such guilt, so that the citizenry will feel in advance that they deserve what they get. The church has long known that. And so does the party.

But what, it might be asked, could ever tempt the free-thinking intelligentsia to adopt such a doctrine? For it is the thought of some of the best and most humane minds in the West whose dreadful itinerary Camus has sought to chart. The movements that took shape at least in part in accord with these ideas were dedicated to the elimination of injustice and oppression. It is therefore to the character as well as the metaphysics of the West that these questions must be posed—and the disease unveiled. Camus directs himself to that task in *The Fall*, where he seeks out the bad conscience of the bourgeois intellectual. More on that subterranean world later.

The Physics of the Soul

The final point that needs to be made at this time concerns human nature. I have been exploring the logic that leads to the historical effort to carry out a metaphysical revolution. That is what Camus means by the conquest of totality. "Totality is, in effect, nothing other than the ancient dream of unity common to both believers and rebels, but projected horizontally onto an earth deprived of God" (R, 233). Totality is the effort, proceeding from a total vision of a good world, to mold historical experience in accord with the demands of that vision.

But, however noble the intentions, however brilliant the vision, nature and people are not clay that can be molded. To the extent that we are committed to totality, it is difficult not to view recalcitrance as evil. We are thus well down the path toward a holy war. Such an effort presupposes "the infinite malleability of man and the negation of human nature" (R, 237). It is committed to the transformation of the human condition—and declares war on that which resists. "From that point on, traditional human relations have been transformed. These progressive transformations characterize the world of rational terror. . . . Dialogue and personal relations have been replaced by propaganda or polemic, which are two kinds of monologue" (R, 239–40). "In the kingdom of humanity, men are bound by ties of affection; in the Empire of objects, men are united by mutual accusation" (R, 239). In short, "totality is not unity. The state of siege, even when it is extended to the very boundaries of the earth, is not reconciliation" (R, 240).

The effort to deny transcendent values has involved the rejection of limits to action other than those dictated by expediency. Concern for and respect for human nature, however uncertain our understanding of it, is no longer a limit to action. Rather, human nature becomes an object, like every other natural object, to be molded and shaped to the demands of the task. Here the NKVD pioneered in the development of "the physics of the soul." No longer a value, the soul has become a means or an impediment. Only human appetite guides actions—in the name of a future that cannot be seen, known, or revealed. But that future can become the object of a faith that will justify whatever those with the power to control both the action and the interpretation insist upon. It is only a matter of finding the enemy's weakest points.

THE DIALECTIC OF REVOLT AND REVOLUTION

If "every act of rebellion expresses a nostalgia for innocence and an appeal to being" (R, 105; L'HR, 135), how is it that it has so often given rise to murder and violence? "Is this contradiction inevitable? Does it characterize or betray the value of rebellion?"

I have sought to show how "revolution is only the logical consequence of metaphysical rebellion," revealing "the same desperate and bloody effort to affirm man in face of what denies him" (R, 105; L'HR, 135). But if "the revolutionary spirit thus undertakes the defense of that part of man which refuses to submit," trying "to assure him his reign in the realm of time," how are we to understand the relation of revolution to rebellion? Is revolution a necessary development of rebellion or the consecration of its betrayal? No other issue has been more hotly contested in commentaries on *The Rebel* than this. In a strange and perhaps revealing convergence, critics of both left and right have seen fit to counterpose revolt and revolution in Camus's thought. Critics of the left have held this opposition to be proof of Camus's reactionary turn, claiming that he thus sanctified the impotent outbursts of noble souls and the pure at heart, while condemning all effective protests to the ignominy of inevitable despotism. Most bourgeois commentators, on the other hand, especially in the English-speaking world, have commended Camus's work as a necessary and just attack on twentieth century revolutions in the name of human rights, democratic liberties, and parliamentary democracy. These commentators have praised his pacifism and welcomed his courageous attack upon revolutionary violence.

Are these critics right? If so, is any constructive action to address our collective ills left to Camus? And if the critics are wrong, how can we account for the misreading? What are we to understand as Camus's position? Finally, what is the practical upshot of these discussions? What is the path out of our present historical dead end toward that renaissance to which so much of Camus's effort was explicitly dedicated?

Camus himself is not without reponsibility for this controversy. His penchant for dramatic phrasing and symmetrically counterposed alternatives often subordinates necessary qualifications to stylistic concerns. Even more, he often fails to maintain the clarity required to keep distinct the different levels upon which his analysis moves. With respect to the present issue, for example, this is particularly significant—for he can move from a discussion of total or metaphysical revolution to a consideration of historical or political revolutions without making the transition clear. This allows for a gross misreading of his intent.[8] What then is this rebellion that is, "at first, limited in scope"?

It is only a non-coherent act of bearing witness. Revolution, on the contrary, begins with the idea. It is . . . the insertion of the idea into historical experience, while revolt is only the movement that leads from individual experience to the idea. While even the collective history of a rebellious movement is always that of an engagement without issue in deeds, of an obscure protest which involves neither systems nor reasons, a revolution is an attempt to model action in accord with an idea, to shape the world into the frame of theory (R, 106; L'HR, 136).

It must be noted here that the relation between revolt and revolution places emphasis on both the distinctive origins as well as the ongoing structure of their engagements. Further, it suggests a developmental rather than polarized relation between them.[9]

To appreciate the problem as Camus sees it we must recall the metaphysical situation that pervades modern attitudes. The disintegration of a transcendent perspective for living having provided the backdrop for contemporary struggles, Camus sees humans turning toward an absolutization of history. This "historicism," in rejecting the appeal of any values not proven by their historical efficacy, ends up as a doctrine of success at any cost, in which the ends justify the means and the winners write the moral manuals —all in the name of human salvation. Only by keeping this context in mind can the analysis Camus offers be put in perspective. "The logic of history, from the moment that it is *totally* accepted, gradually leads it, against its most passionate convictions, to mutilate man more and more and to transform itself into objective crime" (R, 246, my italics).

Nothing remains for us . . . but to be reborn or to die. If we are at this moment in which rebellion has come to the point of its most extreme contradiction by denying itself, then it must either perish with the world it has created or find a new fidelity and a new burst of energy. Before going further, it must at least make this contradiction clear. It is not well defined when one says, as do our existentialists for example (themselves subject, for the moment, to historicism and its contradictions), that there is progress in the movement from revolt to revolution and that revolt is nothing if it is not revolutionary. The contradiction is, in reality, much tighter. The revolutionary is at the same time a rebel or he is no longer a revolutionary, but a policeman or a functionary who turns against the revolution. So much so that there is no progress from one attitude to the other, but coexistence and continually increasing contradiction. Every revolutionary ends as an oppressor or a heretic. In *the purely historical universe that they have chosen,* revolt and revolution end up in the same dilemma: either the police or madness (R, 249; L'HR, 305–6, my italics).

To lose sight of the context of this analysis, namely the metaphysical world defined by historicism, is inevitably to misinterpret Camus's analysis as an all-out attack on revolutionary movements, which it most emphatically is not.

At this level, history . . . is not a source of values, but only of nihilism. . . . The thought which constitutes itself solely with history, just like that which turns itself away from history, deprives man of the means or the reason for living. The first drives him to the despair of the "why live"; the second, of the "how live." History, necessary but not sufficient, is therefore only an occasional cause. It is not an absence of value, nor value itself, nor even the material of value. It is the occasion, among others, in which man can experience the still confused existence of a value which allows him to judge history. Revolt itself makes us the promise of it (R, 249–50; L'HR, 306).

"Certainly, the rebel does not deny the history which surrounds him; it is within it that he tries to affirm himself. But he finds himself before it like an artist before reality, he rejects it without removing himself from it. But not for a second does he make of it an absolute" (R, 290; L'HR, 358). "In reality, the purely historical absolute is not even conceivable. The thought of Jaspers . . . underlines the impossibility of man's grasping the totality since he finds himself in the midst of this totality. History, as an entirety, would only be able to exist for an observer exterior to itself and to the world. In the final analysis, there is history only for God" (R, 289; L'HR, 357).

Having thus placed Camus's critique of revolution in the context of his critique of historicism, we can better appreciate the way that critique seeks to reveal the destructive dialectic of totality in order to prepare the way for the reconstitution of rebellious thought in the service of human enablement.

Absolute revolution . . . supposes the absolute malleability of human nature and its possible reduction to the condition of a historical force. But rebellion, in man, is the refusal to be treated as an object and to be reduced simply to historical terms. It is the affirmation of a nature common to all men which escapes the world of power. History, certainly, is one of the limits of man. In this sense, the revolutionary is correct. But man, in his revolt, poses in his turn a limit to history. At this limit is born the promise of a value. . . . In 1950, and provisionally, the fate of the world is not being played out as it appeared, in the struggle between bourgeois production and revolutionary production. Their ends will be the same. It is being played out between the forces of rebellion and those of caesarian revolution.

"I rebel, therefore we exist," said the slave. Metaphysical rebellion then added the "we are alone," by which we are still living today. But if we are alone under the empty sky, if therefore we must die forever, how are we really able to be? Metaphysical revolution then tried to construct being out of appearances. After which, purely historical thought came to say that being was doing. We were not, but were to be by any means necessary. Our revolution is an attempt to conquer a new being by doing, outside of all moral rules. That is why it condemns itself to live only for history, and in a reign of terror. Man is nothing, according to it, if he does not obtain in history . . . unanimous consent. At this precise point, the limit is surpassed, revolt is first betrayed, and then logically assassinated, because it never affirmed, in its purest movement, anything other than precisely the existence of a limit, and the divided being that we are. . . . When rebellion in rage or intoxication, passes to the all or nothing, to the negation of all being and of all human nature, at this point it denies itself. Only total negation justifies the project of a totality to be conquered. But the affirmation of a limit, of a dignity and of a beauty common to men . . . entails the necessity of . . . advancing toward unity without denying the origins of rebellion. . . . Rebellion's demand is for unity, historical revolution's demand is totality. . . . Revolution . . . cannot do without either a moral or metaphysical rule to balance the insanity of history. Undoubtedly, it has nothing but scorn for the formal and mystifying morality that it finds in bourgeois society. But its folly has been to extend this scorn to every moral demand. Rebellion, in fact, says . . . to revolution that it must try to act, not in order to come into being one day in the eyes of a world reduced to acquiescence, but in terms of this obscure being which is already revealed in the movement of insurrection (R, 249–52; L'HR, 305–9).

I might summarize by joining Kaliayev in noting that "though the revolution is (often, we should add) a necessary means, it is not a sufficient end" (R, 172).

The controversy surrounding the publication of *The Rebel*, and most particularly as it bears upon this point, led Camus to return with even greater clarity to this issue. In his unpublished "In Defense of *The Rebel*" he sought to make explicit the dialectical relation that binds revolt and revolution together.

Today everyone would like to take credit for the revolution without paying the price, or wear revolt in his button-hole while true revolt is without adornment. In order to avoid this temptation I have preferred to follow up the consequences of the rebellious and revolutionary attitudes. I believed that I could then say that these notions really only had reality in opposition to one another; and it was not possible to place absolute revolt in face of all historical reality in an attitude of exquisite sterility, nor, with revolutionary orthodoxy, to suppress the spirit of revolt solely for the benefit of historical efficacy. The position which I have tried to define cannot be taken, therefore, as a refutation of revolt nor as a blanket condemnation of the revolutionary attitude (E, 1706–7).

If revolt is rooted in the deeply personal demand for dignity, in the feeling that one has a right, it requires objective transformation of an oppressive condition in order to actualize that need. And such transformation—that "full circle, which passes from one government to the other after a complete transition" (R, 106; L'HR, 136)—inevitably encounters the resistance of established structures of power, calling for an institutional as well as a personal reordering. In short, practical efficacy is a necessary means to the recapturing of human dignity: Revolt must at least become radical reform, if not revolution.

If the transformation of structures of power, wealth, and status that is revolution is to be legitimized, however, revolution must answer to the deepest human needs for dignity and self-respect, thus remaining true to the original demands of revolt.

Revolt without revolution ends up logically in a delirium of destruction, and the rebel, if he does not rebel on behalf of everyone, ends by reaching an extremity of solitude where everything seems permitted. Inversely, I have tried to show that revolution, deprived of the incessant control of the spirit of revolt, ends by falling into a nihilism of efficacy, resulting in terror. The nihilism of the solitary individual like that of historical religions one day consecrates terror, on the level of the individual or of the State. This conjunction is fatal from the moment that a subversive movement —whether solitary or collective—whose principle is to place everything in question, refuses to place itself in question.

Now, only rebellion is justified in posing questions to revolution, as revolution alone is justified in questioning revolt. It is fair that Lenin give lessons in realism to the solitary terrorists. But it was, and is, indispensable that the rebels of 1905 call to order the revolutionaries who were marching toward State terrorism. Today, where this State terrorism is in place, the example of 1905 must be incessantly held up before twentieth century revolution not in order to negate it, but in order to make it once again revolutionary (E, 1707).

Here then, in this dialectical union of rebellion and revolution, lies the dramatic center of the Camusian vision around which the doctrine of *The Rebel* is sculpted. Committed to a diagnosis of the pathology of the intellect that has led rebellion down errant pathways for the last 200 years of Western history, this volume is dedicated to rescuing the rebellious outrage from its destructive furies. Not an attack upon revolution, but an attempt to salvage it from a process of betrayal that has its roots in a misguided effort to replace a failed transcendent absolute by its historical incarnation.

This is why it seemed to me good and useful to proceed with a reasoned criticism of the only instrument which claims to liberate the workers in order that this liberation might be something other than a long and disillusioning mystification. This criticism does not end up with a condemnation of revolution, but only of historical nihilism, which, by committing revolution to the denial of the spirit of rebellion, has succeeded in contaminating the hope of millions of men. The effort and success of free trade unionism, like the endurance of the libertarian and communal movements in Spain and France, are the examples to which I refer in order to show, on the contrary, the fruitfulness of a tension between revolt and revolution. . . . In order to reject organized terror and the police, revolution needs to keep intact the spirit of rebellion which has given birth to it, as rebellion needs a revolutionary development in order to find substance and truth. Each, finally, is the limit of the other (E, 1708–9).[10]

OF LIBERTY AND JUSTICE

Nevertheless, criticism, however effective, is still not a program. The major task still remains to contribute effectively to developing that renaissance in human living that is, after all, "the only task worth undertaking and persevering in" (E, 1715). The critical analysis has suggested a frame of reference. It thus has pointed us in the direction of a still uncharted terrain wherein we must, with fits and starts, endeavor to brush away a pathway to that "relative utopia" for whose achievement we may legitimately struggle and hope.

Such efforts must begin with the realization that

virtue cannot separate itself from reality without becoming a principle of evil. Nor can it identify itself completely with reality without denying itself. The moral value brought to life by rebellion, finally, is no farther above life and history than history and life are above it. In actual truth, it assumes no reality in history until man gives his life for it or dedicates himself entirely to it (R, 296).

Our engagements take place within the confines of the relative. Truths are not certain, and vision is limited by the temporal and spatial confines of our situation. "Approximate thought is the only creator of reality" (R, 295).

A revolutionary action which wishes to be coherent with respect to its origins would embody itself in an active consent to the relative. It would express fidelity to the human condition. Uncompromising as to its means, it would accept an approximation as far as its ends are concerned and, so that the approximation might be able to define itself better and better, it would allow free reign to speech. It would thus maintain that common being which justifies its insurrection. In particular, it would preserve in law the permanent possibility of self-expression (R, 290; L'HR, 358–9).

Rebellion itself only aspires to the relative and can only promise an assured dignity coupled with a relative justice. It takes its stand for a limit within which the community of men may be established. Its universe is that of the relative (R, 290; L'HR, 358).

It opened the way to a morality which, far from obeying abstract principles, discovers them only in the heat of insurrection, in the incessant movement of contestation. Nothing justifies the assertion that these principles have existed eternally; it is of no use to declare that they will one day exist. But they do exist, in the very period in which we exist. With us, and throughout all history, they deny servitude, falsehood, and terror (R, 283; L'HR, 349–50).

Having thus made clear the relative path along which we must find our way, Camus suggests some of the constraints to be placed upon our actions, as well as some of the guidelines to be followed. These issues are dealt with when considering his views on art and politics. Here it is enough to clear up a misunderstanding about Camus's supposed pacifism, thus suggesting the significant transformation in the understanding of his thought that follows from placing it clearly in its appropriate context. This will help to clear the air and set the stage for an appreciation of his constructive proposals.

While Camus is concerned with exploring and refuting the logic that leads to and justifies murder, it is wrong to think of him as a pacifist. However much he may have been repelled by killing, he never rejected the need of people to fight in their own defense, whether individually or collectively. He was an active participant in the French resistance and never suggested that it could have proceeded nonviolently. Similarly, he was a lifelong supporter of the cause of republican Spain. He always recognized that there are conditions in the world—far too many—that call for liberation struggles. All these engagements would be incomprehensible had he been a pacifist. No, his commitment and concern were different. He distinguished between the right to defend oneself and the right to condemn another person to death. It was the latter he rejected. Killing an enemy in self-defense or in the struggle for liberation is unfortunate but understandable. But capturing your opponents and then condemning them to death cannot be justified.

What is it that is unjustifiable about condemning a person to death, especially an enemy who was aiming to put you to death, and whose death would have been legitimate had it occurred on the battlefield in the heat of combat? Here we get to the core of the Camusian ethic, which he was struggling with in *Letters to a German Friend*, and which finally found expression in *The Rebel*. Values are human values. Only the human being "has a meaning . . . because he is the only creature to insist upon having one" (RRD, 22). What Camus is there struggling to say is that the source of value lies in the implicit community of men in the face of an alien or indifferent world. Revolt makes appeal to that community, seeking to give form and expression to human values. That is what sustains and justifies the rebel. Condemning another to death fundamentally violates the integrity of that community. What could justify such an act but an appeal to something higher than, or beyond, the human community? Precisely because such transcendent values are "absent or distorted in contemporary Europe," there can be no rational justification of the act by which one puts another to death. All such acts violate the implicit integrity of the human community, which is the only source for the rebel's values in an age without transcendent appeal. Having overstepped the bounds of the human community, such rebels can be absolved only by accepting their own death. This is a sort of purgation by which the community reaffirms itself and binds up the wounds that the murder had rent in its fabric.

On the level of the absurd . . . murder would only give rise to logical contradictions; on the level of rebellion it is inner laceration. For it is now a question of deciding if it is possible to kill someone whose resemblance to ourselves we have at last recognized and whose identity we have just consecrated. When we have only just conquered solitude, must we then re-establish it definitively by legitimating the act that isolates everything? (R, 281; L'HR, 347).

It should be understood that the solitude in question is metaphysical solitude in the face of a universe indifferent to human concerns. It is the human community that sustains us in that universe, thus giving a ground to human values. "If a single master should, in fact, be killed, the rebel, in a certain way, is no longer justified in using the term community of men from which he derived his justification. If this world has no higher meaning, if man is only responsible to man, it suffices for a man to remove one single human being from the society of the living in order for him to be excluded himself from it." The key is that "from the moment that he strikes, the rebel cuts the world in two. He rebelled in the name of the identity of man with man and he sacrifices this identity by consecrating the difference in blood" (R, 281; L'HR, 347–8). "On the level of history, as in individual life, murder is thus a desperate exception or it is nothing."

But all this only addresses the question of murder, the willful killing of another. *That* is not justified, as Kaliayev understood. "If he himself finally kills, he will accept death" (R, 296; L'HR, 353), torn as he is by an agonized consciousness of injustice, and an impotence to do anything constructive about it. But this dilemma faced by the isolated individual is not to be identified willy-nilly with the situation of an individual or group under attack or struggling for its rights and dignity.

Absolute non-violence is the negative basis of slavery and its acts of violence; systematic violence positively destroys the living community and the being we receive from it. To be fruitful, these two ideas must find their limits. In history, considered as an absolute, violence finds itself legitimized; as a relative risk, it is the cause of a rupture in communication. It must therefore preserve, for the rebel, its provisional character as a violation, and must always be bound, if it cannot be avoided, to a personal responsibility and to an immediate risk. . . . Just as the rebel considers murder as the limit that he must, if he is carried to it, consecrate by dying, similarly violence can only be an extreme limit which opposes itself to another violence, as for example in the case of an insurrection. If the excess of injustice renders the latter impossible to avoid, the rebel refuses in advance violence in the service of a doctrine or as a reason of state (R, 291–2; L'HR, 360).

There is, of course, a real problem in the application of such a guideline. It may be clearly applied when my life is directly threatened. But what of the situation of one who sees the lives of others being directly threatened, thus, perhaps, legitimating killing in self-defense on their part, but where "noble" rebels could themselves go off and lead lives free from such pressure, perhaps even well-off lives? We might think of the case of "the just" or of a middle-class revolutionary such as Lenin. Camus's response at this point is not completely clear, not to say convincing. The line seems, at best, quite vaguely drawn—with his leaning in the direction of "erring" on the side of caution and restraint—as is perhaps fitting for one whose personal circumstances were increasingly "comfortable" and removed from the direct heat of oppression (not to speak of the vulnerability of his family in Algiers). But this is not the strength of his position. His views here are less important for the answers they give, or fail to give, than for the concerns they insist must be expressed or the issues that must be raised. To demand that those involved in rebellious activity be highly sensitive to, and continually critical of, the justification of their efforts and the actions that such justifications invite is to contribute significantly to the legitimation of rebellion—and thus to the enhancement of human living, which, Camus clearly feels, depends in great measure on saving rebellion from its own perversion and degeneration. The greatest argument for the status quo, Camus suggests, is often the threat to human dignity posed by rebellion's perversions.

What then is the frame of that constructive position, the concrete details of which still remain to be delineated?

I will add, in conclusion, that to separate liberty from justice ends by separating culture and work, which is the social sin par excellence. The disarray of the worker movement in Europe partially derives from the fact that it has lost its true homeland —wherein it renewed its strength after every defeat—which was the faith in liberty. But the disarray of European intellectuals similarly derives from the fact that the double mystification—the bourgeois and the pseudo-revolutionary—has separated them from their only source of authenticity, namely work and the suffering of all. It has cut them off from their only natural allies, the workers. . . . I have never recognized any but two aristocracies, that of work and of intelligence. I now know that it is mad and criminal to wish to subordinate one to the other. I know that the two of them together constitute a single nobility; that in union lies their truth and especially their efficacy; and that separated they can be whittled away one by one by the forces of tyranny and barbarism, but, on the contrary, united they will constitute the law of the world (A/II, 168–9).

THE PSYCHIC SUBSOIL

With *The Rebel* the second stage in the development of Camus's thought has come to a close. Out of these two stages, a conception of revolt has begun to emerge in which it is seen initially as the reaction of reflective natural beings occasioned by their desire to live freely in the face of natural and social forces seeking to deny them that right. The force of this conception arises out of Camus's passionate attachment to the virile strength and beauty that may be the offering of the natural world, and to the shared suffering and quiet dignity that may be attested to by the human world. In short, the qualities of ordinary experience remain the touchstones of the Camusian world.

This commitment to the priority of the reflective natural being as the original and ultimate framework of constructive endeavors is what Camus is referring to when he speaks of innocence. It should be emphasized that this priority is not definitive of an end, but indicative of a policy; if it is the human being who is seeking to work out his or her destiny, reflection must not deny what is essential to that being. The all-pervasive moral dimensions of Camus's thought radiate from this initially simple and immediate demand to live, which is implicitly identical with the feeling of innocence. Revolt is simultaneously the assertion of the immediate value of living (which is the quality of active innocence in its purest state, for example, in Meursault) and the refusal to join in complicity with evil (as, for example, with Tarrou or Rieux). This latter refusal can of course take place on many levels, the two main ones being the human suffering occasioned by the physical universe (as in *The Myth*, "Caligula," and *The Plague*) and by the social universe (as in "The State of Siege," "The Just," and *The Rebel*).

The Stranger may constitute a bridge between these two worlds. As we have noted, the physical world commits the murder, thus encroaching upon and destroying the domain of the human—though it is true that Meursault has unwittingly allowed himself to become its agent as a result of his failure of lucidity. However, the social world insists on extracting from him an admission of his malevolent intentions; that is, it refuses to admit the possibility of his basic innocence and insists upon his premeditated guilt. It must, in short, find a malevolent motive behind all "evil" intrusions into the world of the human.

Innocence has become increasingly problematic, implying as it does the contingency of the social drama. The alternative seems to be the demand for a transcendent upon which to ground the values of immediate existence. Experience being felt inadequate, the socialized individual increasingly yearns to be freed from the limitations of natural existence. Free communion with other natural creatures on an immediate or direct level is made impossible by society's (and the individual's) insistence upon transcendent moral standards. From the lofty heights of such purity, the natural individual cannot help but be found guilty. We are reminded of the argument in "Caligula": "A man dies because he is guilty. A man is guilty because he is one of Caligula's subjects. Now all men are guilty and shall die. It is only a matter of time and patience" (CTOP, 29).

On this point, there is little distance from Caligula to Jean-Baptiste Cla-mence—justice has been separated from natural innocence and the individual is seen from the perspective of the truth, from which all are equally guilty; all that remains is for the guilt to be distributed so that all may feel their unworthiness and may humble themselves before some master. For the guilty only a master–slave relation is ultimately possible. To live freely would be to bear the weight of being held accountable for our actions, responsible for our choices. We would have to accept being judged by the principles we professed and said we live by. But how could we really bear on our own the weight of such judgment? We must instead find a strategy by which to disarm the potentially judging other.

The program of the judge-penitent emerges. "Is not the great thing that stands in the way of our escaping [personal judgment]," he says, "the fact that we are the first to condemn ourselves? Therefore, it is essential to begin by extending the condemnation to all, without distinction, in order to thin it out at the start" (F, 131).

The psychology of dependence removed of its transcendent master insists upon universal guilt as the means to that self-abasement that is the only possible expression of the will to dominate of a person who cannot bear the burden of freedom in a world without gods. It expresses the attitude of the judge passing judgment on life from a nonexistent perspective that he seeks to reestablish through the actualization of universal guilt. With the possibility of innocence denied, revolt too becomes impossible. Camus thinks he has unmasked with Clamence a uniquely contemporary formulation of the spirit of enslavement. The purpose of *The Fall* is thus suggested: to reveal the roots that feed the metaphysical perversion of the intellect whose logic it has been the task of *The Rebel* to lay bare. Let us now furrow through that psychic subsoil in search of more fertile ground for the nurturing of human dignity.

11 🙟

The Fall: A Study in
Metaphysical Pathology

Dialogue on a human level is less costly than the gospel preached by totalitarian religions in the form of a monologue dictated from the top of an isolated mountain. On the stage as in the city, monologue precedes death (L'HR, 350; R, 283–4).

IN THE VESTIBULE

"May I, monsieur, offer my services without running the risk of intruding?" (F, 3). Dripping with cynicism toward the establishment and with condescension toward the "worthy ape who presides over [its] fate," Jean-Baptiste Clamence thus deferentially introduces himself to his interlocutor and to us. Self-effacingly he offers to plead our case to the authorities, into whose graces he has insinuated himself, in this world without transcendent appeal where the lawyer has replaced the priest.

The Mexico City is a disreputable bar in the red-light district of Amsterdam where travelers can indulge themselves in the comforts of anonymity. Lying in wait for us there is Jean-Baptiste Clamence, a seemingly distinguished professional who pretends to be above the dissipation that surrounds us in this no-man's-land on the fringes of polite society. His presence and our interest suggest an openness to slightly shady adventures, as well as a susceptibility to feelings of guilt for past transgressions or present inclinations. All is probably not as it seems, nor are we as we would like publicly to present ourselves.

Of course, Clamence does not approach everyone. He is selective. Having "set up [his] office in a bar in the sailors' quarter," he attends to "the people of quality [who] always wind up [there] at least once . . . [lying] in wait particularly for the bourgeois, and the straying bourgeois at that" (F, 138–9; TRN, 1545). Are they not likely to feel uncomfortable there, not to say guilty? But guilty before whom, one might ask? What are these services that he is offering? And what is his motive in being so accommodating? In any case, we may certainly assume that not all those he approaches avail themselves of his generosity. Yet some are intrigued, and it is with them—or us—that he strikes up a conversation.

From Messieur to Mon Cher, slowly Jean-Baptiste insinuates himself into our confidence. Are we not made of the same stuff as he? Do we not share the same desires, anxieties, opinions, aspirations? What are we really like when we shed our cloak of respectability? Have we not dreamed "of being a complete man who managed to make himself respected . . . half Cerdan, half de Gaulle"?[1] Have we never dreamed "of being a gangster and of ruling over society by force alone"? Have we not sometimes "felt vulnerable and open to public accusation," thus hastening "to judge [others] in order not to be judged" ourselves? (F, 54, 55, 78, 80). Are we not thus imperceptibly drawn into the self-accusatory web woven by Clamence's confession turned indictment?

But Mexico City is the vestibule, a sort of limbo where this modern-day Virgil lurks, ready to lead his prey along "Amsterdam's concentric canals" spiraling deep into a "bourgeois hell . . . peopled with bad dreams" (F, 14). For the journey through Amsterdam is a spiritual voyage into the depths of our soul, where outer surroundings help set an inner moral tone.

In the most obvious sense, the monologue recapitulates Clamence's fall from the height of respectability in Parisian society, where he had made his name defending the unfortunate. What more noble calling! Yet a worm at the core of his character and lifestyle eats away at his self-confidence. Along the contrived pathways of his confession into the convoluted recesses of his mind we follow Clamence as he reawakens his memory, recapturing his past in order to construct a "portrait which is the image of all and of no one" (F, 139).

If the dramatic success of the "récit" lies in the subtle identification of reader with confidant, following upon the more explicit suggestions of identity between confidant and Clamence—who prefers to "confess to those who are like [him] and who share [his] weaknesses" (F, 83)—the full import of the monologue consists in Clamence's mirroring the essential inner dynamics of our (bourgeois) character, by whose previously hidden motives we are vitalized to succeed at the expense of others—motives that our ideology seeks to hide from us as well as from others. *The Fall* "is in fact a portrait, but not of an individual; it is the aggregate of the vices of our generation in their fullest expression" (F, v). A major step in understanding our era, according to Camus, lies in a grasp of the character of this noble Parisian lawyer.

LOST INNOCENCE

Coiled like a serpent at the heart of this modern confessional lies the person of Jean-Baptiste Clamence, a "false prophet for mediocre times" (F, 117;

TRN, 1533). The enigma of the volume is the enigma of his character and of its contrived and devious confession, in which nothing is as it seems, not even his identity. Our judge-penitent, the quintessential Parisian bourgeois, the incarnation of respectability, specialized in noble cases. He defended the victims, railing at the injustices of daily life, often sacrificing obvious personal advantages in the process. He was truly above reproach in his professional life. While "the judges punished and the defendants expiated . . . I freely held sway bathed in a light of Eden" (F, 27). Having risen "to that supreme summit where virtue is its own reward," he "enjoyed [his] own nature to the fullest" (F, 23, 20). Thus his "profession satisfied most happily that vocation for summits," cleansing him "of all bitterness toward [his] neighbor, whom [he] always obligated without ever owing him anything" (F, 25). From "well above the human ants," he "earned his living carrying on a dialogue with people [he] scorned" (F, 24, 18). Respectability and self-indulgence were two sides of the same coin with which he preyed upon his victims in the name of defending them. "It was enough for me to sniff the slightest scent of victim on a defendant," he observes, "for me to swing into action. . . . My heart was on my sleeve. You would really have thought that justice slept with me every night" (F, 17).

The prostitution of values in the name of personal advancement emerges as the core of his character. All actions are modes of self-presentation. They are strategies by which to dominate. "Buoyed up by two sincere feelings: the satisfaction of being on the right side of the bar and an instinctive scorn for judges in general," my profession "set me above the judge whom I judged in turn, above the defendant whom I forced to gratitude" (F, 18, 25). Thus able to achieve "more than the vulgar ambitious man" (F, 23), he could satisfy his need "to feel *above*," "like a king's son, or a burning bush" (F, 23, 29).[2]

But, one day, while "about to light . . . the cigarette of satisfaction . . . a laugh burst out behind" him, shattering the "vast feeling of power and . . . of completion" that he had "felt rising within" him, as he "dominated the island" in the Seine upon which he was gazing (F, 39, 38).

At first it is but a passing thought, a nagging sense that he is not what he has pretended to be, and that this "duplicity" is probably evident to "The Other." For what is conscience but The Other installed within us? And what is our sense of ourselves but a subtle and modified reflex of how we may be "for The Other"? The fall begins as a crack, ultimately widening into a fissure that rends the self in two. No more that edenic innocence by which Clamence had felt completely natural, "without intermediary between life and me" (F, 27). Realizing that his "smile was double" (F, 40), he now admires the lost simplicity of primates "who are all of a piece." It now becomes clear that "the surface of all my virtues had a less imposing reverse side" (F, 85). "Modesty helped me to shine, humility to conquer, and virtue to oppress" (F, 84). As for being concerned with others, "I was so out of pure condescension, in utter freedom, and all the credit went to me: my self-esteem would go up a degree" (F, 48).

A dramatic scenario had been orchestrated in which he was at the center of the regard of all others—and slightly above. His life was the staging of this drama. "I could live happily only on condition that all the individuals on earth, or the greatest number, were turned toward me, eternally in suspense, devoid of independent life and ready to answer my call at any moment, doomed in short to sterility until the day I should deign to favor them" (F, 68).

Incarnating an absolutized individualism, of which the Christian God is in part an idealized projection, he sought always to obligate others without himself being obligated in turn (F, 25). "Do you know why we are always more just and more generous toward the dead? The reason is simple. With them there is no obligation" (F, 33). Free and unencumbered, able to allow oneself everything, without commitments or limitations, is this not the implicit ideal of bourgeois individualism? Like the quintessential modern bourgeois figure, the salesperson, his way of being for the other is always but a strategy to gain his predetermined end. "I had principles, to be sure," observes Clamence, "such that the wife of a friend is sacred. But I simply ceased quite sincerely, a few days before, to feel any friendship for the husband" (F, 58–9). It is not true, he insists, that he had never loved. "I conceived at least one great love in my life, of which I was always the object" (F, 58). Values, even emotions, are just tools to be used in order to better dominate the surrounding world. "I kept all my affections within reach to make use of them when I wanted" (F, 68).

Before the fall he "lived consequently without any other continuity than that . . . of I, I, I . . . the refrain of [his] whole life" (F, 50, 48). He would be whatever he thought it best to be in order to get The Other to respond to him as he wished. His sense of himself was simply that of the being who he managed to be in the manipulated gaze of The Other. He was "for himself" as he was "for The Other," after having staged himself to be what The Other's idealized values dictate that he ought to be. At this point, it is no longer clear who is who, and for what reasons. We are in a hall of mirrors where contrived image molds contrived reality and nothing is what it seems, where simplicity is reduced to naïveté and sincerity is simply a more sophisticated strategy of domination.

In a sense, we are in the world so graphically dissected by Jean-Paul Sartre in *Being and Nothingness*, a Hobbesian universe of isolated egos in fundamental conflict, seeking to reduce others to objects in their world. Our gaze is a way of fixing others into their being-for-me, thus robbing them of their ability to determine themselves and their relations to me freely. Relations between people are thus conflicts oriented toward personal domination. Love between such beings is reduced to an uncertain equilibrium among contending egos. As for the sensitive opening out to another that is a prerequisite for truly sharing, that would entail letting our guard down, leaving us vulnerable to The Other's onslaught. As for joining together in a common effort out of which community might emerge—as do the main characters in *The Plague*— that can be no more than a short-term tactical maneuver. Here we are in the modern corporate world, which David Riesman so aptly defined as one of antagonistic cooperation.

All of this comes crashing down upon Clamence once he "had collapsed in public." His self-satisfaction had been predicated on his being above reproach, invulnerable to the critical scrutiny of others. Once that faith is broken, he begins to realize that his "vocation for summits" was sustained by the endless prosecution of others. How else can the self dominate if not through the subordination of others? "I learned . . . that I was on the side of the guilty, the accused, only in exactly so far as their crime caused me no harm. Their guilt made me more eloquent because I was not its victim. When I was threatened, I became not only a judge in turn but even more: an irascible master who wanted, regardless of all laws, to strike down the offender and get him on his knees" (F, 53, 55–6). How then can one maintain a sense of moral superiority, having once glimpsed its hypocritical underside? Now "I felt vulnerable and open to public accusation. . . . The circle of which I was the center broke and [my fellows] lined up in a row as on a judge's bench." One might recall Meursault's sense of the mourners at his mother's funeral, or of the audience at the trial. "The moment I grasped that there was something in me to judge, I realized that there was in them an irresistible vocation for judgment" (F, 78). That is, they are the mirror image of him. "One attributes to the rival the nasty thoughts one had oneself in the same circumstances" (F, 105).[3] Polite society functions like "those tiny fish in the rivers of Brazil that attack the unwary swimmer by thousands and with swift little nibbles clean him up in a few minutes. . . . The little teeth attack the flesh, right down to the bone. But I am unjust. I shouldn't say *their* organization. It is *ours,* after all: it's a question of which will clean up the other" (F, 7–8). "I realized this all at once the moment I had the suspicion that maybe I wasn't so admirable." "*Mon cher ami,* let's not give them any pretext, no matter how small, for judging us!! Otherwise, we'll be left in shreds" (F, 77).

But of course that is not possible. We may dream of innocence, of perfection, of freedom from the critical judgment of others. But we would have to be saints, like Tarrou. We would have to commit ourselves to the long and painful process of self-transformation, of being willing to suffer in order to bear witness to the unjust suffering of others. Is he capable of "sleeping on the floor" for another, he is asked. "Look, I'd like to be capable and I shall be. Yes, we shall all be capable of it one day, and that will be salvation" (F, 32). But that is a dream, like the Greek Isles, not a strategy or even a commitment. In reality, "we don't want to improve ourselves or be bettered, for we should first have to be judged in default. We merely wish to be pitied and encouraged in the course we have chosen. . . . We should like . . . to cease being guilty and yet not to make the effort of cleansing ourselves. . . . We lack the energy of evil as well as the energy of good" (F, 83).

Having lost his original innocence—and "God's sole usefulness would be to guarantee innocence" (F, 110)—his only concern is to protect himself from the critical scrutiny of others in order to continue to dominate them. Being slightly more insightful and perceptive than others, perhaps, or more sensitive, he is haunted by his fall from innocence and the realization of his vulnerability to their judgment. His life becomes a struggle to deflect that judgment. It is here that we must situate the strategy embodied in the new profession of judge-penitent. "The essential is being able to permit oneself everything, even if, from time to time, one has to profess vociferously one's own infamy. I permit myself everything again, and without laughter this time. I haven't changed my life; I continue to love myself and to make use of others" (F, 141–2).

But I have run ahead of my story. How does this need "from time to time" "to profess one's infamy" get rid of the laughter? How does this newfound profession serve at least as a provisional strategy? And what does he really long for? In order to address these questions we need a better understanding of the inner dynamics of his character and its historical significance.

OPPRESSIVE SPEECH

What kind of personal relations are possible for one whose life is oriented around the struggle to dominate? Mastery and servitude are the names of this game in which manipulative object relations define the power struggle over prestige. "I have no more friends; I have only accomplices," observes Clamence (F, 73; TRN, 1511). Fraternity and equality are impossible. Freedom is mine or yours; it cannot be both. Nor can it emerge from a "we" that is a concerned sharing of feelings and actions. Community is the complicity of slaves in a common humiliation. "In the kingdom of humanity, men are bound by ties of affection, in the Empire of objects, men are unified by mutual accusation" (R, 239). Such enslavement appears as a continual temptation to one whose only experience of freedom is this power struggle among egos.

The inner logic of his character, as well as the political significance of its theoretical development, is made quite clear by Clamence. "One can't get along without domineering or being served. Every man needs slaves as he needs fresh air. Commanding is breathing. . . . And even the most desperate manage to breathe. The lowest man in the social scale still has his wife or his child. If he's unmarried, a dog. The essential thing, after all, is being able to get angry with someone who has no right to talk back" (F, 44–5). One might think here of Salamano and his dog in *The Stranger*. Of course, the right to talk back is essential to the existence of the rebel. The implicit ideological conflict becomes even clearer as Clamence draws out the philosophical significance of his position.

"One doesn't talk back to one's father"—you know the expression? In one way it is very odd. To whom should one talk back in this world if not to whom one loves? In another way, it is convincing. Somebody has to have the last word. Otherwise, every reason can be answered with another one and there would never be an end to it. Power, on the other hand settles everything. . . . You must have noticed that our old Europe at last philosophizes in the right way. We no longer say as in simple times: "This is the way I think. What are your objections?" We have become lucid. For the dialogue we have substituted the communiqué: "This is the truth," we say. "You can discuss it as much as you want; we aren't interested. But in a few years there'll be the police who will show you we are right" (F, 45; TRN, 1495–6).

It is this problem of the communiqué that Camus studies in "The State of Siege," "The Just," and *The Rebel*.

And why "the communiqué? Because otherwise there would never be an end to discussion and the interchange of reasons that is the very fabric of dialogic human interaction. It is precisely this open-ended, always partial engagement of equals in a shared endeavor that Clamence finds instinctively unbearable. "Dialogue and personal relations," observed Camus in *The Rebel*, "have been replaced by propaganda or polemic, which are two kinds of monologue" (R, 239–40). The communiqué is a third.

From freedom to slavery, therefore, Clamence suggests the dialectical inversion by which the individualism of the bourgeois character nurtures the soil that breeds the will to domination and oppression. Here lies the theoretical significance of *The Fall*. For Camus was deeply concerned, even perplexed, by the ease with which liberally educated Western humanists became apologists for oppression. If *The Rebel* explores the logic by which the demand for justice may become the justification for oppression, *The Fall* seeks to portray the characterological roots of that perversion.

A HERO OF OUR TIME

To appreciate the theoretical significance of *The Fall*, therefore, we must more firmly anchor its appearance in the stormy waters of the postwar era. If this hero of our time is indeed Camus's collective portrait of "the aggregate of the vices of our whole generation in their fullest expression," this is a generation with which Camus felt "tout à fait solidaire," sharing its vices as well as its hopes. "Nothing authorizes me to judge from above an epoque with which I am in complete solidarity. I judge it from within, merging myself with it" (A/II, 83). For judge it we must, if we are to prepare the way for the renaissance in human living that was ever the center of Camus's theoretical and practical concerns. Revolt was clearly called for by all humane considerations, and yet recent history had sharply called into question its liberatory possibilities.

Confronting a world seemingly gone mad in the chaos engendered by nihilism, the response of many on the left, the traditional defenders of the rights and liberties of the oppressed, has been to embrace a new theology by which they have become apologists for a scientific despotism. Camus, himself a man of the left, is perplexed and tormented by this depressing turn of events. We must understand them if we are to find our way out of this historical dead end.

Speaking of the destroyed cities of postwar Europe, he observes:

They offer the image of this emaciated world, wasted by pride, in which phantoms wander, accompanied by an apocalyptic monotone, in search of a lost friendship with nature and other beings. The great drama of Western Man is that neither the forces of nature nor those of friendship interpose themselves any longer between him and his historical becoming (A/I, 261–2).

People in the West turned first to fascism and national socialism, then to Marxism-Leninism and Soviet communism, and most recently to religious fundamentalism in their search for this lost friendship. In a civilization whose foundations had burst asunder, with personal relations and belief systems in disarray, the tradition of revolt bequeathed by the French Revolution and its enlightenment faith in progress was increasingly succumbing to the temptation of replacing a dying Christianity with a reborn messianism, whether of the blood or of science. Whatever the conceptual forms offered, the psychic base had been well laid over centuries. So well laid, in fact, as to be felt, at least unconsciously, as absolutely essential. Without such a belief system how could anyone feel at one with life and destiny?

Out of the unbearable solitude that was the felt meaning of the death of God, revolt in the West often turned into an apocalyptic monotone in the vain hope of enforcing a solidarity that might alleviate the pangs of metaphysical solitude. Such are the metaphysical sources of the revolutionary pathology Camus seeks to define in *The Rebel*. His remarks there on the deeper significance of terror make the connection.

Terror and concentration camps are the drastic means used by man to escape solitude. The thirst for unity must be assuaged, even in the common grave. . . . The creature needs happiness, and when he is unhappy, he needs another creature. Those who reject the agony of living and dying wish to dominate. Solitude is power, said Sade. Power, today, for thousands of solitary individuals, because it signifies the suffering of others, bears witness to the need for others. Terror is the homage that the malignant recluse finally pays to the brotherhood of man (R, 247–8; L'HR, 649–50).

Germaine Brée suggests the immediate historical background of the novel.

The hero of *La Chute*, the "penitent judge," represents . . . the post-war Europe of the erstwhile humanitarians, morally shaken, guilt-ridden, and in search of a dubious justification. Contemporaneous with the penitent judge, the renegade missionary [in the collection of short stories of which *The Fall* was originally to have been a part] voices the intellectual confusion and frustrated anguish of an idealistic, Christian "left" upon which Marxism exercises a perpetual fascination (Brée, 92).

Without here dwelling on the special problems raised by "The Renegade," Mlle. Brée's observation further suggests the conflicts with which Camus found himself embroiled as European leftists strove to make sense of their recent past and find a strategy by which to bring about greater social justice. It is here that the conflict with Sartre and his *Temps Modernes* group must be situated.

Our Philosophers

"*The Fall* involved in the beginning [of the process of conception] a series of attacks—or ironic counter-attacks—directed at those appropriately called 'intellectuals of the left,' designated . . . [among others] by the formula: 'our philosophers'" (TRN, 2206).

By "our philosophers," Camus no doubt has in mind "our existentialists," of whom he wrote: "When they accuse themselves, one can be certain that it is in order to overwhelm others: judge-penitents" (TRN, 2002). Faced with almost transcendent historical evils, but shorn of transcendent solutions, they long for a communal salvation. How to come to terms with the dilemmas of our era? Existentialism, for Camus, attests to a profound cultural malaise. "Their only excuse lies in this terrible epoque. Something in them ultimately aspires toward servitude. They dreamed of arriving there by a noble pathway strewn with thoughts. But there is no royal road for servitude" (TRN, 2002).

Rather, existentialism bears witness to a profound withering of the human spirit, of its capacity for concrete values such as fraternity, loyalty, and love. Abstract brotherhood as compensation for abstract nausea has replaced the most immediate of sensuous attachments. Suggestive of their representative situation is this observation about "the men of today," which Camus offers in

"The Witness of Liberty": "At least one thing which most among them will never be able to find again . . . is the strength of love which has been taken from them. That is why they are ashamed" (A/I, 262).

Camus feels a gaping personal lacuna generating an undercurrent of guilt directed toward an undefined but salvific brotherhood. This is but a very particular version of the pervasive metaphysical malady of the modern era whose theoretical development it was the task of *The Rebel* to explore.

Existentialism is in a theoretical bind here, for Camus, because its onto-logical defense of absolute freedom has made an analysis of our historical circumstances quite difficult and a practical strategy aiming toward the in-stitutionalization of brotherhood seemingly inconceivable. Such, at least, is Camus's suggestion and challenge to Sartre in his response to the *Temps Modernes* criticism of *The Rebel*. On a more personal note, he comments: "*Temps Modernes*. They admit sin and reject grace—Thirst for Martyrdom."

Counterattack

Whatever the status of Camus's evaluation of the existentialists, a deeply personal side of his response to them clearly pervades *The Fall*. Some have even gone so far as to suggest that *The Fall* is best understood as his belated counterattack to the public debacle he suffered at the hands—or pens—of the *Temps Modernes* group. Warren Tucker counterposes passages from *The Fall* with indictments from Sartre and Jeanson. He notes the way both Cla-mence and Camus are said to manipulate style, practice guilt by association, betray a haughty superiority, present themselves as exemplary, merge serious-ness with frivolity, and claim a sincerity that their actions betray.[4] Lottman, commenting on Tucker's analysis, suggests the rationale for the volume: "No more than his hero, Camus could not accept a defeat. He chose to reply through art. He did it by exposing himself, thereby removing himself from the judgment of others. 'I am like they, of course, we're in the same soup. Nevertheless I have an advantage, that of knowing it, which gives me the right to speak'" (Lottman, 565).

Whatever be the truth of the claim, Lottman has succinctly stated the strategy of the judge-penitent. He may, at least in part, be right. Studies of Camus's life suggest many themes that find echoes in Clamence's confession. Camus's epigram makes explicit reference to this when it notes "that the author had portrayed himself and his acquaintances" (F, v). Certainly there was much in Camus's life and character of which he was far from completely proud. As early as *A Happy Death* we see signs of a Camus torn by the attraction of display—presenting a public pose other than his private self and then feeling perhaps a bit ashamed or even guilty about it. Like Patrice in the novel, he even dreamed of leaving society for the isolation and innocence of a direct relation with nature, where he might be himself. This tension-conflict seems only to have been augmented, even if different in form, by his finding himself a celebrated author in Paris. The country hick had made it; and although he did not value material wealth and possessions, he was sorely tempted by his new-found prestige and reputation. He tended to show it off—his office with a balcony at Gallimard, for example—while at the same time disliking both the pretensions of the literary establishment and his own inclinations to "play the game."

In that early novel there are also indications of his ambiguous attitude toward women, his inclination to use them for display or conquest, and his difficulty in dealing with his own jealousy. These attitudes reappear in *The Fall*. In fact, they merge with a tendency to debauchery, which itself is presented as a logical development of "egoic" individualism. Here we can see how personal traits can become generalized for Camus, taking on larger theoretical significance.

The analysis of the logical and psychological—perhaps I should say, existential—roots of this character trait serve to develop a significant cultural critique. For what is debauchery but the refusal to put limits on the ego? How different is this from Sartre's doctrine of the absolute freedom of the "For Itself"? Of course, Sartre recommends authenticity, but the moral imperative seems gratuitous. Values bind me, according to *Being and Nothingness*, only to the extent that I allow them to do so. Previous decisions have only the force that my present commitments give them. Authentic self-activity acknowledges both the nonbindingness of previous commitments and the threat posed by The Other to my freedom. It is thus that love, for Sartre, reduces to the unstable balance of masochism and sadism. In short, The Other is always threatening to rob me of my freedom, while I am not bound to keep previous commitments. Here is an ontology of the absolute or atomic individual whose relations with others are essentially power struggles for domination—efforts to reduce The Other to objects in my world before they do the same to me. How far is this from true debauchery, which "is liberating because it creates no obligations?" (F, 103). Clamence, commenting on the continuity between his debauchery and his previous respectable existence —and suggesting its deeper ontological roots—observes, "In a sense, I had always lived in debauchery, never having ceased wanting to be immortal. Wasn't this the key to my nature and also a result of the great self-love I have told you about? Yes, I was too much in love with myself not to want the precious object of my love never to disappear" (F, 102).

The link between this abstract individualism and the desire for immortality is suggested by the development of Sartre's first major theoretical work, *Being and Nothingness*, which begins with the doctrine of ontological freedom and concludes with the uselessness of man's desire to be God. Nietzsche grasped the deeper historico-religious origins of the modern bourgeois deification of the self when he observed, "The Christian doctrine of 'the salvation of the soul' [means] in plain language: 'the world revolves around me'" (PN, 619). But if the desire for immortality is the final expression of the doctrine of abstract individualism, debauchery is its ever present temptation. While Sartre's philosophy comments extensively on the social relations that such an orientation inevitably brings in its wake, bourgeois society develops a complex network of contrived and hypocritical forms with which to hide and legitimize its essentially manipulative and destructive foundation.

The point of this excursus from the consideration of Camus's use of *The Fall* as confessional is to make clear the danger of reading that work too narrowly as essentially a personal confession. Camus's secretary noted, as reported in Lottman, "that the changes he was giving her regularly [in the manuscript] went in the direction of making *La Chute* less personal and more universal" (Lottman, 564). And that was not, I am arguing, simply to camouflage its personal content. Rather he was deeply interested in the profound theoretical questions reverberating through his personal life and his social quarrels as well as in the wider cultural and political conflicts that were threatening to drown European civilization in destructive wars and oppressive social orders.

What might be as fair to say—if not more so—was that the portrait here presented is very close to the image of Camus "as he was seen by" others, by bourgeois society, and especially by the "intellectuals of the left." Perhaps, even more subtly to the point, it is the portrait of Camus as Camus comes to see them seeing him.[5] By ironically presenting himself *as they saw him*, he is subtly presenting the world and others as they appear to them. Thus the hidden dynamics of *their* world is laid open to view. The question then becomes, Why does the world—and secondarily Camus—appear thus to them? What hidden dynamics of their character undergird their perception of others? Thus the narrative by which Camus presents himself in the guise of Clamence becomes a mirror through which bourgeois professionals can finally come face to face with themselves.

A SARTREAN WORLD

Despite the French Revolution's trumpeting of liberty, equality, and fraternity, there was, in reality, no place in the market calculations of bourgeois society for an equality that would infringe on the capacity of profit-maximizing egos to take advantage of available opportunities or individuals. Similarly, fraternity has no real exchange value except as an imaginary goal to be manipulated in the pursuit of material advantage. Practical steps toward its realization, on the other hand, would clearly impede the "free" flow of capital and labor. This was also true of any concern with the achievement of specific end results. Bourgeois idealism thus tends to reduce practically to two increasingly empty formal ideals fabricated in the image of an increasingly crass materialized one. The "cash value" of bourgeois freedom becomes the demand that the "sovereign" individual be granted free reign to pursue a relatively unfettered self-interest. Even the formal virtues are swallowed up in this all-inclusive freedom. Thus equality becomes the freedom to pursue and to possess, while fraternity reduces to the freedom to associate and disassociate with whomever one chooses—subject to the obligation to respect contracts voluntarily entered into. Bourgeois individualism reduces to the free exercise of accumulated power and wealth by those who can. It is, of course, helpful, though not necessary, for such individuals to *appear* to be living by the formal rules and values that society makes such a fuss about. Duplicity is the modus operandi, and sincerity but a more clever strategy of domination.

Is this not the world depicted by Sartre in *Being and Nothingness*? A world of pervasive "bad faith," in which even the sincere man is inauthentic. Is Clamence sincere? Or is his confession but a more clever way of hiding himself? Is he truly suffering? Or does he simply want our pity? Is he agonizing about what is the right thing to do? Or does his profession of guilt serve only to undermine our faith in ourselves? Similarly with Sartre. Shall we read *Being and Nothingness* as Sartre's attempt to work out the possibilities for authenticity? Or shall we see in it but a very sophisticated strategy by which character and self-identity are undermined, and innocence is disfigured, while Sartre builds a fortress inscribed with his name from which he may lord it over others—immortalized in words? "Too many people now climb onto the cross merely to be seen from a greater distance," observes Clamence (F, 114). What are we to make of this monumental depiction of depravity, which masks as ontology and glosses itself as a search for authenticity? The ambiguity has been so pervasive that many commentators schooled in existentialism have been tempted to see in Clamence an existential hero, as did Thomas Hanna, for instance.[6] This may be taken as more than a commentary on the moral ambiguity of Sartrean existentialism. It may suggest that, lacking the necessary critical distance, we may so easily identify with Clamence that we take our unfortunate traits as models after which to aspire. The commentators may thus be making an unintentionally significant statement about a more general cultural depravity, in a sense confirming Sartre's depiction.

CLAMENCE AND MEURSAULT

Beyond the question of Sartre's own character, Clamence can be taken as a personification of Sartrean humanity. *The Fall* is true of the experiential world of the bourgeoisie, locked in the depths of their own inauthenticity. Where

Sartre concludes that for the "Pour-Soi," love reduces to sado-masochism, Camus agrees, within, that is, the confines of a certain "existence sphere," to borrow a Kierkegaardian phrase. Where Sartre talks in a footnote about the possibility of "good faith" requiring a different fundamental orientation, of "a recovery of being that has been corrupted by itself," Clamence evokes "the Greek archipelago" where he "felt as if we were scudding along . . . on the crest of the short, cool waves in a race full of spray and laughter. Since then, Greece itself drifts somewhere within me, on the edge of my memory" (F, 96), a repressed dream that Clamence is incapable of seeking or denying, not totally unlike that "desire to be God" that Sartre presents as the ontological truth of human character, which we can neither deny nor authentically affirm—in short, by which we are condemned. Neither Clamence nor the Sartrean individual seems capable of being other than the inauthentic character from which each dreams of being free. While one strives to be the impossible union of the "In-Itself-For-Itself," the other proudly announces his arrival: "I am the end and the beginning; I announce the law." Before considering the new law that Clamence announces, a few words of comparison of *The Fall* with *The Stranger* will help to better situate this volume within the frame of Camus's work.

Roger Quilliot observes that the two works, although essentially mono-logues, are stylistically opposites.

The Stranger owes its rhythm to the indirect style, the isolated expression, the desired complexities of speech. *The Fall* is nothing if not directness of style, facility of expression, fold upon fold of the word to the point of vertigo. In turn, lyrical, bawdy, insinuating, sarcastic, the judge-penitent imposes his heavy breathing and his whims upon everyone. Feigned friendship . . . hellish poetry, a fever of domination, whispers and sudden outbursts, everything there is in disorder (TRN, 2004).

With one, indirectness is a means of more directly presenting the speaker's world. With the other, the direct, and even personal accent is only a pose designed to hide the truth in question. Quilliot again: "Meursault was sim-plicity, nakedness, innocence incarnated; Clamence is duplicity, masks and dissimulation. One was reduced to a thick transparency; the other plays with mirrors, recognizing its face in the face of its interlocutor and of all its read-ers" (TRN, 2004).

Meursault is like a pane of glass through which we can observe reality, but at a distance, without personal involvement or ulterior motive. Clamence is a somewhat disfigured mirror that contrives to present itself to you in order better to gain advantage over you. The one is condemned for not playing the game; the other played the game only too well. If Mersault is "the only Christ we deserve" today, Clamence is the false pope who stole his dying comrade's water. Whereas Jesus is supposed to have taken the suffering of others upon

himself, out of love, Clamence spreads his guilt to all out of contempt—
"in order to thin . . . out" the condemnation. This modern-day John the
Baptist, having stolen "The Just Judges," proclaims the definitive separation
of justice from innocence: the reign of the new "Grand Inquisitor." Only
the sense of innocence incarnated by Meursault makes revolt possible, while
"on dead innocence the judges swarm" (F, 116). No wonder that Clamence
wanders amid the foggy waters and indistinct outlines of this modern urban
hell, whereas Meursault's world has the crisp moral contours of that Greek
archipelago where new islands constantly loomed on the horizon. "Their
treeless backbone marked the limit of the sky and their rocky shore contrasted
sharply with the sea. No confusion possible; in the sharp light everything
was a landmark" (F, 97).

Clearly, two different moral universes are at issue here. The contrast in
character could not be more extreme, nor the personal goals and emerging
social vision. I have spoken of Meursault. I must now draw out the implications of that monologue, which, as "dictated from the top of a lonely
mountain" (R, 284), seeks to "impose [its] heavy breathing . . . upon everyone." By so completing my portrait of Clamence, I will have depicted the
characterological roots of that political cynicism that constitutes the moral
climate conducive to the emergence of totalitarianism. Like the fisherman
in "The State of Siege," working people are being denied their right to live
simply and freely without a "certificate of existence." They are being en-
gulfed in a bureaucratic and ideological web of "objective culpability" which
threatens to make spontaneous and free daily living impossible. Meanwhile,
the intellectuals of the left, who traditionally speak for the disinherited, suffering a pervasive guilt whose roots are but intimated, have made common
cause with the advocates of total revolution in search of a "dubious justification." "Against this objective and collective culpability in which they are
trying to ensnare man, Camus rebels," writes Quilliot. " 'Each revolt involves
nostalgia for innocence and the call of being' " (TRN, 2000). Speaking of
those intellectuals in his introduction to *Algerian Chronicles*, he wrote, "It
seemed disgusting to me to bare our sins by castigating others, as do our
judge-penitents" (A/III, 23).

A PROVISIONAL SOLUTION

What, then, is this "provisional solution" to the problems of our time of
which Clamence is the prophet? The problem, it should be recalled, is, How
can this prototypical bourgeois dominate in a hypocritical world where, God
being dead, we no longer believe in anything but ourselves? With each of us
looking out for number one, but with each acting in accord with the rules
of the game and professing a morality we no longer believe in, how can we

deflect the criticism of others while finding a way to make them subservient to us? Obviously, a new faith of which we were the object would be ideal. Most in their heart of hearts dream of this. Lacking it, a faith of which we were the appointed disciple would certainly fill the bill. "Ah, *mon cher,* for anyone who is alone, without God and without a master, the weight of days is dreadful. Hence one must choose a master, God being out of style" (F, 133). But this awaits a vast social movement. Until then we are each of us alone and on our own. What is to be done?

Disarm the opposition, of course. Since each, like the Brazilian fish, is waiting for the least sign of vulnerability to tear us apart, we must carefully contrive our public presence to keep them at bay. But, since no one is above reproach, and all of us are thus vulnerable, it will no longer do, as Clamence had done, to take our respectability for granted. This is particularly true since there no longer is any church or value system of which we might make ourselves devotees, dominating in its name, as did the early Christians, according to Nietzsche.[7] Actually, moral values are so discredited today that protestations of belief are seen by the sophisticated as but a more clever way of selling oneself.

Lacking a church, therefore, "I had to find another means of extending judgment to everybody in order to make it weigh less heavily on my shoulders." How to get everyone involved in order to have the right to sit calmly on the outside myself" becomes his concern. "Should I climb up to the pulpit, like many of my illustrious contemporaries, and curse humanity? Very dangerous, that is! One day, or one night, laughter bursts out without a warning. The judgment you are passing on others eventually snaps back in your face, causing some damage" (F, 137). If you exercise your vocation for judgment by moralizing, you are left vulnerable to the counterattack. His strategy will be a preemptive strike.

Inasmuch as one couldn't condemn others without immediately judging oneself, one had to overwhelm oneself to have the right to judge others. Inasmuch as every judge some day ends up a penitent, one had to travel the road in the opposite direction and practice the profession of penitent to be able to end up a judge (F, 138).

Central is the induction of guilt. Those who are satisfied with their own innocence will demand respect. They may even claim the right to judge others, for outraged innocence is the root of revolt. Where then will the guilty be? Even worse, "if pimps and thieves were invariably sentenced, all decent people would get to thinking they themselves were constantly innocent, *cher monsieur,* and in my opinion . . . that's what must be avoided above all" (F, 41).

How then to induce guilt, which undermines self-respect, while not leaving oneself open to the counterattack? In our post-Christian world this problem has become more acute, original sin being out of style. There is no longer anyone to confess to without leaving oneself vulnerable. Nor is there any church through whose service our confession can become a path through absolution to domination and salvation. As for the recognition of guilt, "God is not needed to create guilt nor to punish. Our fellow men suffice, aided by ourselves. . . . [There is no need to] wait for the Last Judgment. It takes place every day" (F, 110–1). What is required is to steal a march on the others, to deflect their attack while earning the right to judge them. "Each of us insists on being innocent at all costs, even if he has to accuse the whole human race" (F, 81). If one cannot be innocent, one must spread the guilt to all. If some are able to maintain their sense of innocence, how would the rest of us be able to stand it? We must create a modern equivalent of "the little-ease," that medieval invention of genius by which "every day through the unchanging restriction that stiffened his body, the condemned man learned that he was guilty and that innocence consists in stretching joyously" (F, 109–10).

The emerging strategy reverses the procedure by which a human community is established, as communication gives way to an "interminable subjectivity which is imposed on others as objectivity." Such is "the philosophic definition of terror. This type of objectivity has no definable meaning, but power will give it a content by decreeing that everything of which it does not approve is guilty" (R, 243). While dialogue binds together, monologue isolates. "Dialogue on a human level is less costly than the gospel preached by totalitarian regimes in the form of a monologue dictated from the top of an isolated mountain" (L'HR, 350; R, 283–4). Clamence acknowledges as much when he comments, "I like all islands. It is easier to dominate them" (F, 43). Reversing the path of *The Plague*, we move away from outraged innocence to universal culpability, seeking to entrap all in the tangled web of self-recrimination.

I stand before all humanity recapitulating my shames without losing sight of the effect I am producing, and saying: "I was the lowest of the low." Then imperceptibly I pass from the "I" to the "we." When I get to "this is what we are," the trick has been played and I can tell them off. I am like them, to be sure; we are in the soup together. However, I have a superiority in that I know it and this gives me the right to speak. . . . The more I accuse myself, the more I have a right to judge you. Even better, I provoke you into judging yourself, and this relieves me of that much of the burden (F, 140).

By judging himself severely, Clamence becomes both the object condemned and the subject condemning. As object condemned he is the lowest of the low, and all can join in the universal condemnation. But as the judging subject, he is simultaneously *other* than the guilty one. As other, he is *not* guilty. Rather, he is *above* the sins by the very act of condemning them. He stands for the values by which such sins are condemned. He is *above* those who *are* guilty. By then subtly developing the condemnation of himself as other so as to implicate human nature itself, without even seeming to do so —perhaps by suggesting an ontology demonstrating that all humans are *by nature* as self-centered as he—he will have succeeded in extending his condemnation to all. Having first joined in his self-condemnation, we are now implicated. No longer can we stand outside, observing and passing judgment on his confession. Now we ourselves are called upon to confess. At the same time, attention may be turned away from the penitent one, who, now "liberated" from our critical scrutiny, is free to become our judge. In fact, to the extent that he succeeds in implicating us, we will accept his right to judge us. We will even begin to do it ourselves. Our self-confidence shaken, our unease growing, we may condemn ourselves for our egoism. Disoriented by an emerging sense of guilt, we lose confidence in our right to condemn others, Clamence included. Self-abasement is generalized, and human dignity loses its claim on individual commitment. With the spread of cynicism, the burden of guilt is lifted from the shoulders of our judge-penitent. In fact, the terrain is well-prepared for the emergence of an individual or a movement offering new directions to individuals adrift. By thus working to undermine our sense of personal dignity and self-respect, this strategy prepares us to seek out a cause or a faith to which we may feel the need to subject ourselves. The post-Christian era has found its true prophet. It now only awaits its true church.

A BOURGEOIS HELL

The rebel feels he has a right to rebel. If he can be denied that feeling—if guilt and self-abasement can be cultivated in its place—the nourishing springs of rebellious ferment will dry up, and the pathway to collective enslavement will open up before us. In fact, we will even seek it as our salvation. The judge-penitent is the dialectical fulfillment of the Christian-bourgeois project grounded in the metaphysical commitment to individualism. It responds to the anxiety that isolated individuals feel, bearing the burden of their life in the face of an impenetrable destiny, by undercutting that self-respect and promising to relieve that burden. At the extreme, it offers the promise of a collective salvation in which the burden and the freedom are no more.[8]

Here we have reached the inferno of the modern world. In these murky waters of induced self-incrimination, personal guilt has sought to assuage its lonely burden through the establishment of "objective criminality." Political cynicism spawns the "universe of the trial" (R, 240). "This philosophy of the guilty conscience has merely taught [the followers of Hegel] that every slave is enslaved only by his own consent" (R, 144). "Guided by a determinist hypothesis that calculates the weak points and the degrees of elasticity of the soul, these new techniques have . . . literally created the physics of the soul" (R, 239). It is as if Clamence dreams of

the destruction, not only of the individual, but of the universal possibilities of the individual, of reflection, solidarity, and the urge to absolute love. Propaganda and torture are the direct means of bringing about disintegration; more destructive still are systematic degradation, identification with the cynical criminal, and forced complicity. The triumph of the man who kills or tortures is marred by only one shadow: he is unable to feel that he is innocent. Thus, he must create guilt in his victim so that, in a world that has no direction, universal guilt will authorize no other course of action than the use of force and give its blessing to nothing but success. When the concept of innocence disappears from the mind of the innocent victim himself, the value of power establishes a definitive rule over a world in despair. That is why an unworthy and cruel penitence reigns over this world where only stones are innocent. The condemned are compelled to hang one another (R, 184).[9]

In short, you see, the essential is to cease being free and to obey, in repentance, a greater rogue than oneself. When we are all guilty, that will be democracy. Without counting, *cher ami,* that we must take revenge for having to die alone. Death is solitary, whereas slavery is collective, the others get theirs, too, and at the same time as we—that's what counts. All together at last, but on our knees and heads bowed (F, 136).

Is this not the definitive picture of the defeat of rebellion? Nurtured in the increasingly deranged mind of the guilt-ridden and hypocritical bourgeois, whose response to the death of God has been to assume the unbearable burden of an absolutized individualism in the context of a pervasive political cynicism glossed as morality and practical idealism, the other is reduced to either impediment or utility. Often, a confused mixture of both, suffused with a repressed nostalgia for a lost community.

"Without innocence there are no human relations and no reason," observes Camus. "Without reason, there is nothing but naked force, the master and slave waiting for reason one day to prevail. Between master and slave, even suffering is solitary, joy without foundation" (R, 144). Until then, what? And what can one do who is so brought up as to be constitutionally incapable of entering into anything but hierarchical relations of domination and subservience? The cultural roots and religious quality of this modern pathology were nicely traced by Nietzsche, to whom Camus was so deeply indebted.

One must not let oneself be led astray: "judge not," they say, but they confine to hell everything that stands in their way. By letting God judge, they themselves judge;

by glorifying God, they glorify themselves; by *demanding* the virtues of which they happen to be capable—even more, which they require in order to stay on top at all—they give themselves the magnificent appearance of a struggle for virtue. . . . One should read the Gospels as books of seduction by means of *morality*. . . . With morality it is easiest to lead mankind *by the nose* ("The Antichrist," in PN, 621).

They too proclaim their guilt in order to avoid judgment. They see clearly that for their morality to prevail others must be made to feel *their* guilt. "Only the sacrifice of an innocent god could justify the endless and universal torture of innocence" (R, 34). The doctrine of original sin rationalizes this strategy, which the appeal to God and the Christian drama of salvation legitimizes. Through the universalization of guilt, the absolved will dominate. But though the need remains, the church no longer suffices to obtain subservience. Thus "as a joke," this hero of our time volunteers for the role of new pope in the prison camp "on the sole condition that he should agree to keep alive, in himself and in others, the community of our sufferings," only to "drink the water of a dying comrade" (F, 125–6). "Thus . . . empires and churches are born under the sun of death" (F, 127).

DREAMS OF SALVATION

A mind of absolute attachments cannot do without an object of a saving faith. When one absolute fails, the psyche demands that another take its place. It may also feel deeply betrayed by the failed absolute, even violently seeking revenge against its adherents. Faith or fetish, Christ or Antichrist, at a deeper psychic level they may be one. "Nothing can discourage the appetite for divinity in the heart of man" (R, 147). From the perspective of the absolute, the finite is in principle inadequate. From the perspective of the inadequacy of the finite, only an absolute system could heal our existential wounds. There seems to be a dialectical bond uniting absolutist ideologies and self-denigration. The latter feeds the need for the former, without which it is nothing; the former gives assurance to the self that it is now worthwhile. No wonder that dominating passions can be generated on behalf of such belief systems, or that violent hatreds tend to be directed at failed absolutes. No wonder also that a failed Christianity may have nurtured a passionate search for a new and antagonistic system of ultimate belief.

The pathological depths of this commitment to absolutes is further explored by Camus in "The Renegade." While unlike *The Fall* in that its passionate hatreds are no longer sublimated—with what Nietzsche termed that "instinct directed *against* the healthy"—the Christian missionary turned renegade clearly reveals a profound need for an object of absolute attachment, as well as the violence that failed absolutes so often engender.

My confessor couldn't understand when I used to heap accusations on myself. . . .
There was nothing but sour wine in me, and that was all for the best; how can a man
become better if he's not bad, I had grasped that in everything they taught me. That's
the only thing I did grasp, a single idea, and, pig-headed bright boy, I *carried it to its
logical conclusion,* I went out of my way for punishments, I groused at the normal, in
short I too wanted to be an example in order to be noticed and so that after noticing
me people would give credit to what had made me better, through me praise my
Lord (EK, 37, my italics).

As Christianity fades away, a growing need is felt for a faith to fill the void
that is left. If not bourgeois progress, then messianic Marxism or the fascistic
volk have offered themselves as "fetishes" for the ex-believer. "Dostoevsky,
the prophet of the new religion," had declared, " 'If Aliosha had come to the
conclusion that neither God nor immortality existed, he would immediately
have become an atheist and a socialist' " (R, 60). Others, less generously
motivated, have drawn similar conclusions.

Whatever his dreams, however, our modern day judge-penitent offers
only a provisional solution. His strategy promises personal salvation on a
small scale, and only "for the duration"; so long as one is alive. After death, we
are once again reduced to the status of object for The Other, who will then be
free to dispose of us at will. The meaning of our life will be for The Other to
determine. We will be unable to speak in our own defense. Thus, the haunting
limits of this personal strategy. Death is the inevitable defeat looming on
the horizon, with others the conquerors. Tormented by the thought that he
"might not have time to accomplish [his] task"—"What task?"—"a ridiculous
fear pursued [Clamence]: . . . one could not die without having confessed all
one's lies" (F, 89–90). Incomplete or dishonest, either way he is defenseless
before the judgment of others. Thus his ambivalence. Perhaps his confidant is
really a policeman. Perhaps he will be arrested for stealing "The Just Judges,"
thus, with the establishment of a definitive law and a final judgment, putting
an end to a freedom that is becoming increasingly unbearable. Or perhaps
a new church and a new law will arrive, transforming this loneliness into
cosmic significance. Personal freedom cries out for direction and purpose.
His character longs for a redemptive master. Herein lies the ambivalence at
the core of the bourgeois absolutization of the sovereign individual.

Torn between unlimited self-centeredness and longing for an objective
meaning that will give larger direction and purpose to existence, in manic-
depressive fashion Clamence alternates between deification and destruction,
between expansive self-affirmation and constrictive self-abnegation. And,
finally, so does Sartre, according to Camus. In its most passionate apologia
for an ontological freedom, to which we are condemned and that knows
no limits other than those of self-imposed bad faith, Sartrean existentialism

seems dialectically to be preparing the way for a servitude that will remove from humanity the terrible weight of an unbearable freedom. Either absolute freedom for one who succeeds in the dehumanizing struggle to reduce the other to object-for-me; or the universal servitude that follows on the commitment to an objective historical meaning—and perhaps to the party that is its bearer and motive force—thus relieving us of the weight of personal responsibility for our life. Sartre, the foremost demystifier of bourgeois hypocrisy, burrows into the interstices of bourgeois life and character to unmask its pervasive bad faith—even when it presents itself as sincerity. Yet at the root of the Sartrean world lies the vision of an ahistorical, non-situated ego whose absolute freedom is an ontological curse from which it is condemned ever to flee in search of an impossible identity.

Whatever its pleadings for authenticity, is this being not condemned to an inescapable duplicity? Isn't its morality but a cover for a more sophisticated strategy of domination? Can its continual talk of authentic commitment be other than a clever way of camouflaging its inability to commit itself to anybody or anything?

Sartre, the quintessential bourgeois philosopher of individualism, thus represents the destructive dialectic intrinsic to the being of the bourgeois of which Jean-Baptiste Clamence may be taken as a dramatic embodiment. As for the possibility of good faith:

O young woman, throw yourself into the water again so that I may a second time have the chance of saving both of us! A second time, eh, what a risky suggestion! Just suppose, *cher maître,* that we should be taken literally? We'd have to go through with it. Brr . . . ! The water's so cold! But let's not worry! It's too late now. It will always be too late. Fortunately! (F, 147).

PART FOUR ❦

Visions and Possibilities

To give a form to the justice and liberty we need (A/II, 171).

12 ❧

The Witness of Liberty

Thanks to [revolt] the spirit begins to walk, but within the narrow confines of its condition. Toward what goal and with what possibilities depends upon freedom. . . . A comparative study of artistic creation and political action considered as the two essential manifestations of human rebellion would be able to define it with greater precision (E, 1696).

ART AND POLITICS

"The rebel does not deny the history that surrounds him. . . . But he finds himself in front of it like the artist facing reality; he rejects it without freeing himself from it" (R, 290; L'HR, 358). This identification of artistic creativity with the experience of the rebel brings us to the affective center of Camus's world. Here political revolt and artistic creativity inform each other, opening the way to a more concrete appreciation of the metaphysical significance of rebellion.

Both artist and political rebel find the given world inadequate to their demands. But this dissatisfaction becomes world-transforming. In a sense, they place themselves outside of the world—in opposition to that world that gave them birth and to which they remain inescapably bound. Their experience bears witness to the ontological demand that life have an integral ordering within which the individual may find a dignified well-being. Happiness is inseparable from personal dignity, rooted in an integrally ordered experience. As temporal beings, however, our experience moves ever onward—and death appears as the inevitable and inescapable horizon of our practical projects. Such is the ground of Camus's tragic vision.

We may respond to temporality by envisaging a transempirical unity whose achievement might well assuage that *exigence ontologique*. Upon what evidence, however, can this leap of faith be based? Is it not simply a projection of our needs? And does not the insistence upon its salvific qualities undercut the concrete possibilities that experience may offer? Such has been the concern expressed in the discussion of the absurd. As this need finds political expression, the results gain in practical consequences only by becoming the

221

source and legitimation of a more complete domination and degradation. Such has been the key to the argument in *The Rebel*.

Thus temporality constitutes the flow of our lives—with death its inevitable horizon. Both aspects make for dispersion, randomness, purposelessness, and disintegration of personality. In the discussion of art in *The Myth of Sisyphus*, Camus seems to welcome these forces of dispersion with his ethics of quantity. He argues there that if one marries them to a consciousness that, in appreciating the inevitability of a meaningless death, commits itself to drawing the utmost value from each encounter, life will offer meaning "enough to fill a man's heart." Thus his revolt finds expression in his commitment to lucidity, passion, and freedom, resulting in an ethic of quantity without any ordering principle.

He soon comes to recognize, however, the inadequacy of this position. Increasingly, he realizes that the traditional elaboration of a doctrine of absolutes is rooted in an existential demand for an integral ordering of experience that cannot be assuaged at the level of sensuous dispersal, no matter how passionately sensuous qualities may be appreciated by a consciousness heightened by the lucid awareness of an impending death. The problem of the unity of thought and action goes deeper. The concern to ground unity in the concrete affective life of the reflective animal who will die remains central. The ordering must not betray its bodily roots. Hence the centrality of the concern in *The Rebel* to define the meaning of unity against the claims of totality. "Political action and creation are the two faces of a single revolt against the disorders of the world. In both cases, the aim is to bring unity to the world" (A/I, 262). The concrete significance of art emerges in its attempt to respond to the dual dimension of human rebellions, for metaphysical insight and for historical liberation. Its answer, when successful, is a unitary expression of both needs in the achievement of an integral work that is the stylized embodiment of a concrete vision.

THE ARTWORK

Thus, the artwork can be viewed as an integral ordering of natural energies that rescues them from the dispersion at work in the flow of events. As a sensuously embodied unity of meanings it is an offering to us of a vision for which we deeply long. Ideally we confront in the work a perfect world—an embodied version of a metaphysical response in which natural experience is reconstructed so as to speak to that *exigence ontologique*. We encounter in the work a unified world in which our struggles take on the form of destiny. The consequences of actions are grasped in their inevitable flow; the balance of natural forces finds its integral expression; and our experience can appear to possess a definitive articulation. In short, the ambiguous strivings of a human soul can find definite expression in a work that offers itself as an example of what life may be.

In the world of the artwork we encounter a metaphysical revolution completed. The artist has rejected the historical world in its eternally unfinished aspect and has reorganized natural energies and qualities in terms of a vision of their ideal possibilities. We are presented with an embodied vision of our world remade in accordance with our deepest existential needs. This is accomplished in and through the style of the work. Style—the *way* the sensuous qualities and dramatic meanings are expressed in the medium—is at its best when it is least evident. Ideally, style suggests the transformation of our world in the image of a transtemporal perfection: a perfect fit between need and articulation. Even when the work embodies time, the temporal flow is recaptured in a structural unity that takes the form of a completed destiny. This is the root of the work's ontological significance, and hence the criterion by which great art can be separated from the ordinary. The reason for Camus's preference for classical drama should thus be obvious.

The artwork suggests, however, more than the image of a longed-for metaphysical revolution; it offers more than a world transformed with finality. It is an invitation to enter into that world and to experience its salvific unification of meanings; to share in that particular articulation. Beyond the unity of style that constitutes the image of a perfected world, we can share—if but for a moment—in a living dramatic unity. Deeper than the symbolic presentation of the image of a longed-for metaphysical revolution is the experiential "taste" of what such a world might mean. While there is an attraction that comes from the way art speaks to our deepest existential needs; the experience of the work is always more than the conception of it. Thus we must be acutely aware of the potential seduction involved in the likely thought that the artistic elaboration of meanings can serve as a model for the historical reconstruction of daily life.

If art offers this image of our world recaptured, and an experience of our deepest needs fulfilled, it remains but the experience of a moment. We encounter the work of art. We enter its world for but a moment in time to experience the liberation and satisfaction derived from participation in a completed drama. Whether tragic or comic, radical or reactionary, the experience of such a unity of style is felt to be profoundly significant and satisfying. We are exhilarated and relieved by the destined flow of events; this is the ontological ground of the appeal of beauty. As the perfection in expression that ennobles and enhances our experience, beauty gives us the sense at last of being at home in our world. Here lies the source of that sense of the unity of beauty with happiness. Even tragedy can be deeply satisfying, as its artistic depiction is subtly contrasted with the experienced satisfaction achieved through the integral ordering of embodied meanings that is the perfection of style.

INVITATION AND TEMPTATION

But as the artwork is offered to us, so is it taken away. Art is the experience of a moment, and that experience too is subject to dispersion. In its reconstitution of our world, the artwork offers us the sense of what our life ideally might be: a work of art. But a work of art life is not. Rather, it flows on through temporal dispersal to death. Our home in the world is temporary, our journey through time continues to its inevitable end—an end that is usually far from a consummation. The work offers us the image of a life whose style would be that integral aesthetic experience Nietzsche envisioned when he expressed the desire to so live life that he might be able when facing death to say: "Was that life? Well then, once more." As an experientially fulfilling encounter with a transformed world, the work of art is an invitation to make our life such a work. It is a visionary suggestion of that which we might aspire to. As such it is of the utmost value and promises ever to be so.

As the image of a metaphysical revolution completed, however, it may be taken to suggest the possibility of actually carrying out such a revolution in history. Here it can only be a force for the demonic. It is one thing to offer a vision to others, for them to be able to enter into its world freely for a moment, taste of its fruits, and then leave—or simply refuse the offer. It is quite another to seek to impose that world on others—and to do so definitively. While the stylistic unity of the work may be profoundly seductive and suggestive, the articulation of a transformed world involves a thesis that is always debatable and never totally realizable. Even more, the attempt to impose that world ultimately involves denying that free spontaneity that is the vitalizing source of the dramatic significance of our lives.

The experienced vitality of the work lies in the merger of its ideal offerings of a world reconstituted with the deepest sources of our freedom. The world of the work is liberatory and salvific only to the extent that it feeds the existential roots of our being; our freely projected ideals. Insofar as those ideals are empirically diverse, to that extent the significance of their aesthetic embodiment will vary. The unquenchable vitality of art lies in its ability to speak to and for these existential sources. Apart from that spontaneous marriage of offered beauty with existential need, the reorganized world of the artwork remains alien to the experiencing subject—and, if imposed upon him or her, can only be experienced as oppressive. Art lives as an imaginative offering and an invitation to realize our dreams; it dies as an attempt to constitute a definitive and unescapable world. It lives in diversity; it dies of constraint. All impositions of order from without the lived experience of the subject are oppressive. However just be the vision embodied in the artwork, its precondition is our freedom to engage it in our own way. To impose that justice on that freedom in denying the latter destroys the meaning of the former.

In short, the stylistic unity of the work as an integral ordering of experienced meanings speaks to our deepest existential needs. The aesthetic encounter is satisfying in its own right. It takes us out of the temporal stream and locates us in a longed-for world of finality and perfection. It is, in a profound sense, the experience of heaven on earth, of the eternal in the temporal. This experience of perfection is the encounter with beauty. The beauty of the artwork is but the image and suggestion of the experience it offers. No wonder we are always attracted by beauty, drawn into its orbit, seduced by its presence, often without regard for its explicit content. Beauty is the promise of a cosmic home to which first religion and then the revolution have sought to be the answer. While the formal ordering of meanings seems to speak to our deepest needs, however, the meanings presented and experienced as beautiful are in fact quite diverse. We do not all find the same works equally beautiful. In the selective diversity that is the actual experience of beauty we approach the political-historical limitations of the work of art. My experience of beauty may reflect the organization of meanings that is the dramatic root of my world, but the political attempt to impose my vision of the ideal on others will as a rule be experienced as a violation of the integrity of *their* world. The experience of beauty can be an extremely dangerous political seduction insofar as it suggests an ideal in accordance with which to mold our joint historical reality.

The uniquely rewarding experience of art is an implicit call to make life an approximation of art—and the style of the work suggests a style of life. But the specific ordering of embodied meanings is always existentially unique and politically contestable. The political relevance of the artwork must be appreciated within the limits set by a transformed reality. It can be rejected. It can be accepted in whole or in part. It can be entered into for the duration of its dramatic development. But whether the work unfolds temporally as in music or drama or dance, or is presented all at once, as in painting or sculpture, our experience always unfolds in time. Yet the experience of art is limited. It is but a phase in our lives—however satisfying or suggestive, however pregnant with significance for our future. In a sense we leave the normal flow of events and enter into the world of the work—for a time that may seem like an eternity or like no time at all. But return to the world we must. If the work is significant, no doubt we return changed in some sense pregnant with possibilities. That is an essential part of the work's meaning for us. But the consequences that follow the work are different from the experience *as had* and undergone. Accordingly, the consequences are to be judged differently. The significance of the experience of the work for the future of our lives must be considered separately from the significance of its intrinsic merits. It is here that the political-historical reality must be taken into account. The applicable criteria are not the same as those that apply to the aesthetic evaluation of the work itself. To subordinate either aspect to the other is to do violence to one of them. Aesthetic experience subordinated to political demands yields a realism as destructive of the meaningfulness of experience as is subordination of the political to the formal demands of art. This is the problem Camus is concerned with when he criticizes formalism and socialist realism. It is also the problem, in a different form, at stake in Camus's discussion of the dialectic between freedom and justice.

The significance of the formal ordering of meanings in aesthetic experience must not be confused with the partial vision of a unified world. Similarly the temporal conditions of the experience of the work must not be confused with the pervasive temporality of our lives. Further, the relation of the individual to the work as an offered world must be clearly distinguished from the political-social struggle to reorganize historical reality in accordance with a personal or group vision. The work of art is encountered essentially individually, whereas the struggle of political rebels to transform social-historical reality will, if achieved, alter the inescapable form of our daily life. Political rebels do not offer another world for our momentary experience; they seek to definitively transform this one. If they succeed, it is no longer a matter of an offering, but of a newly constituted inescapable given.

STYLISTIC EXTREMES

All great art seeks to reconcile, Camus felt. "This effort at reconciliation was deliberate," writes Germaine Brée, "the basic motivation for his writing" (Brée, 41).[1] True artists therefore have a double concern. By the nature and condition of their work, they are committed to the human spirit and the freedom that nourishes it. They are simultaneously the bearers of a vision of beauty and meaningfulness to which they strive to give articulation. By the strength of the former they are pulled toward the mass of suffering humanity with which they feel solidarity and to which they wish to communicate an ideal that offers the possibility of creative transformation; the latter drives them toward a stylization of the immediately given, a correction of creation that will give to reality the coherence, order, and significance it now lacks.

Artists may thus find themselves on the horns of a dilemma. To opt for humanity and the ideal of total communication may be to degrade art to the level of mass taste, conformity, and mediocrity of which both American television and Soviet socialist realism provide disconcertingly clear examples.

On the other hand, to opt for that perfect expression and completeness of presentation that addresses the demand for unity may be to reduce art to an esoteric pursuit of pure stylization. This reduction ends by destroying the intimate bond tying art to experience from which art draws its sustenance. The extreme example here is pure formalism.

For Camus, both temptations are dimensions of art's vital task. Art must be at once communication and stylization: reconciliative with respect to the persons involved; unifying with respect to the content and meanings expressed. Great art thrives in this tension; lesser art bends under the burden. Yet one might argue that socialist realism is stylization in the service of total communication, while formalism involves a dimension of the communicable world as well as its stylization. Camus would no doubt insist that these facts point to the impossibility of holding to either principle without the other. Pure stylization would be silence; pure communication unending repetition.

Basic to Camus's critique of socialist realism is the claim that it finds its ordering principle outside the human content it orders. The meaning of such a work lies not in the movement of the work itself, but in what it points to, as a road sign points to a city. By so doing it gives up on the ennobling of the human spirit through a stylization that is the perfection of its intrinsic artistic content. It is reduced rather to pure propaganda: the work of art as but the container, diversely fillable, into which the ideology pours its message.

Formalism, on the other hand, draws on experience for its lines and colors (cf. Mondrian) or sounds (cf. Webern), but has denuded art of its human content in the name of an order and a unity that no longer speak for human experience.

These two dimensions of art are represented by Camus as ideal types and criticized as such. They serve to delimit the scope of artistic activity, presenting in concrete shape those limits as applicable to art, of which Camus so often speaks.[2] They result from the extreme logical development of one side of a situation whose essential constitution is that of a duality in tension.[3]

One last word as to the scope of Camus's presentation. He offers what he considers to be the most basic dimensions of artistic activity. While drawing upon various works to support his position, he offers his presentation not as a scientific explanation of what in fact art has been but as a statement as to what he thinks the most vital concerns of art are. Thus conceived, we have a statement as to how he viewed his art and a suggestion as to how art may be most significantly approached and created.

UNITY IN DIVERSITY

"Art lives only on the constraints it imposes on itself," said Camus; "it dies of all others" (RRD, 208). Grounded in the spontaneity of freedom, it is one of the clearest expressions of the human need to impose order on the chaos with which experience immediately confronts us. Thus art symbolizes at a heightened intensity the tension between the need for order, justice, security, and familiarity, on the one hand, and for novelty, spontaneity, and freedom on the other.

In the work of art, as noted, the chaotic or amorphous passions with which the natural creature is endowed are given an ideal form by the creator who, by correcting the creation as it is immediately experienced, raises the experience to a new pitch of intensity, yielding a new height of spiritual fulfillment. By entering into the world of such a work the human being can, even if but momentarily, come to rest in a world in which the flow of time has been grasped in an eternal moment within which meaning is felt to be complete.

If form is the essential bearer of the meaning of art, art is destroyed by orders and forms imposed upon it from without. And if art is grounded in a free experience, any insistence that experience take a definite form prior to the encounters that constitute it can only mean the destruction of art. It is true that human experience is never amorphous: it always comes with certain shapes, forms, and lines of movement. But it comes also and always as a mass of unformulated possibilities, fringes unfocused, and ideals unexpressed, not to say unrealized. Prefabricated forms, like prefabricated thoughts, lie upon individuals like a straitjacket. Art, grounded as it is in spontaneity, speaks for the open horizon of forms into which individual experience may develop. The role of the creator is to free experience from artificially imposed, outlived, or sterile forms, thus testifying to the potential richness and diversity of human experience.

While the needs for unity and diversity clearly stand in opposition one with the other, they need not constitute unbridgeable poles but rather can offer a creative tension. Basically, they are complementary. For while experience craves an ordering that will yield a sense of fulfillment, the achievement of any final and definitive order would constitute the completion of experience as we know it—a destiny that remains but to be played out rather than lived. Thus achieved, such an ordering would incapacitate humans for experience or, at least, render the very notion of experience meaningless—simply a habit or instinct. While totality would thus constitute the destruction of experience by resolving novelty into habit and freedom into destiny, the absence of lived unities would render experience chaotic, formless; and, as the Greeks knew, this too would constitute utter meaninglessness.

Insofar as meaning can be seen on the reflective level to consist in relations perceived, so on the level of immediacy it will consist in felt dramatic continuity. In the latter, experiences are felt to lead with a modicum of fluency from one to another. Thus an experience diversely qualified at any moment or series of moments may be *felt* as a *unity* in its movement. In fact, if it is not, we would seem to have a form of psychic pathology.[4]

Reflectively considered, this same experience may be taken from diverse perspectives, in terms of which it will be seen as yielding more or less unity. From a categorical or static point of view, the unity-in-diversity that art and life so exemplify seems to pose dichotomous alternatives. Yet in the actual movement of experience they simply represent tensions, alternative directions with first the one predominating, then the other.

Within the bounds of the work of art, structure gives the shape of destiny to the passions there unfolded; but from the perspective of experience, each work of art presents itself as a potential experiential unity. Thus works of art, while taken distributively are alternative unities in conflict with one another, taken collectively they bear witness to the vitality and diversity of the human spirit. Art is thus both a commitment to the infinite qualitative diversity of human experience and a formulation and suggestion of the ideal possibilities inherent in the concrete movement of that experience.

GIVING STYLE TO ONE'S LIFE

"In every rebellion is to be found the metaphysical demand for unity, the impossibility of capturing it, and the construction of a substitute universe. Rebellion, from this point of view, is a fabricator of universes. This also defines art. The demands of rebellion are really, in part, aesthetic demands" (R, 255). Art is revolt's always provisional answer to the absurd: the construction of a limited, perfect, complete whole in a world marked by discontinuity, rupture, and partiality. Sculpture, for example,

the greatest and most ambitious of the arts, is bent on capturing, in three dimensions, the fugitive figure of man, and on restoring the unity of great style to the general disorder of gestures. . . . It erects, on the pediments of teeming cities, the model, the type, the motionless perfection that will cool, for one moment, the fevered brow of man (R, 256).

As, perhaps, the purest expression of revolt—as it had been the purest expression of absurd activity—art "is a revolt against everything fleeting and unfinished in the world. Consequently its only aim is to give another form to a reality that it is nevertheless forced to preserve as the source of its emotion" (RRD, 202).

Style—"this presence imposed on that which is always becoming"—is the crucible through which this transfiguration of time takes place. Through stylization the artist creates a world, setting it off from a daily experience not significantly different in content. All art is the product of such stylization;

and Camus's long attack against realism simply clarifies the misconceptions involved with that term: an unquestioned assumption as to the nature of the real, and a stylization consequent to that assumption.

Style is the form of the work—which, in great art, "will vary with the subjects." It is the medium through which creation is corrected. "The aim of great literature seems to be to create a closed universe or a perfect type" (R, 259).[5]

CONTRASTING MYTH AND REBEL

Stylization is an activity with metaphysical significance. "Far from being moral or even purely formal, [the novelist's] alteration [of reality] aims, primarily, at unity and thereby expresses a metaphysical need. The novel, on this level, is primarily an exercise of the intelligence in the service of nostalgic or rebellious sensibilities" (R, 264).

It is through stylization that revolt offers an answer to the absurd that time reveals. A comparison of the role of style in *The Rebel* as the instrument of a nostalgic *or rebellious* sensitivity with its suppressed role in *The Myth* as revealed in the following quote will prove instructive.

To think is first of all to create a world (or to limit one's own world, which comes to the same thing). It is starting out from the basic disagreement that separates man from his experience in order to find a common ground according to one's nostalgia, a universe hedged with reasons or lighted up with analogies but which, in any case, gives an opportunity to rescind the unbearable divorce (MS, 74).

Here again *The Rebel* reveals a continuity with, and a development from, *The Myth*. The search continues for a unifying common ground, but the lines and limits of its concrete possibility have become much clearer. With *The Rebel*, style need no longer be simply a nostalgic activity, it can be positively constructive. Within this developed perspective, the future and hope once again become viable though clearly circumscribed possibilities. The import of the above answer to the absurd carries us beyond the work of art to the experience of which it is a part. "Man . . . tries in vain," writes Camus, "to find the form that will impose certain limits between which he can be king. If only one single thing had definite form, he would be reconciled" (R, 252).

While this view is meant to cover art in all its forms—as is clear from Camus's remarks concerning painting, sculpture, and music—his major involvement was with literature and drama. In these forms the media of expression are words and actions. Literature and drama are, therefore, the most directly theoretical in import, the most able to bear explicitly and reveal philosophical intent. They are thus obvious candidates for concrete, noncategorical, philosophical expression.

From the perspective of the absurd, and within the framework it prescribes, novelists and dramatists create their worlds exactly as do philosophers. Where no ultimate explanations are possible, it makes no essential
difference whether worlds are presented in concepts or images; it comes to
the same thing. Camus writes:

The greatest novels carry with them their universe. [Each] has its logic, its reasonings,
its intuition, its postulates. It also has its requirements of clarity. . . . The philosopher,
even if he is Kant, is a creator. He has his characters, his symbols, and his secret
action. He has his plot endings (MS, 74).

Philosopher and novelist are equally presenters of worlds. Aesthetically,
the worlds may be judged on the basis of internal structure, though strictly
speaking, from the perspective of the absurd this is irrelevant. The important
factor is whether the wholes presented illustrate divorce and absurdity. Since
the absurd offers no answers, all explanations are ultimately gratuitous. The
greatest novelists, for Camus, are ones who recognize this.

Writing in images rather than in reasoned arguments, [they are] convinced of the
uselessness of any principle of explanation and sure of the educative message of
perceptual appearance. . . . The work of art . . . is the outcome of an often unexpressed
philosophy, its illustration and consummation. But it is complete only through the
implications of that philosophy (MS, 75).

"The work of art is born of the intelligence's refusal to reason the concrete" (MS, 72). It testifies to the fact that all explanation is ultimately useless,
and that

living in this case is just as much experiencing as reflecting. The work then embodies
an intellectual drama. The absurd work illustrates thought's renouncing of its prestige
and its resignation to being no more than the intelligence that works up appearances
and covers with images what has no reasons. If the world were clear, art would not
exist (MS, 73).

In the world revealed by the absurd, creation is a gratuitous effort. Lacking an ultimate scale of values, art can have no precedence over ditch-digging.
The salient question is this: Does a specific work of art assist in bringing
into awareness a lucid consciousness that—in an attitude of complete indifference to ultimate questions—can exhaust the qualities of the present? All of
Camus's heroes of the absurd were such because they were aware that their
endeavors lacked any ultimate justification. The exemplary role of the creator arises solely from the fact that new things are brought into an existence
without justification. In a task in which the temptation toward justification

is perhaps strongest, the absurd creator refuses to give in. Knowing these works are gratuitous, the artist embodies this knowledge in them.

The value of creation and of the works that flow from it resides, therefore, simply in their offering a reduplication and a diversification of an existence that can be the only value. An absurd creation can make no claim to a higher value, to a saving insight, to a final explanation. It simply presents. It offers itself as yet another experience: a quality without justification. For the absurdist, the absurd work differs from the nonabsurd simply in the degree to which a recognition of the ultimate uselessness of the endeavor of creation is embodied in the work itself. "To know that one's creation has no future . . . is the difficult wisdom that absurd thought sanctions" (MS, 84).

It is a wisdom as applicable to the world of philosophy as to that of the novel. Both worlds present an experiential content chosen as worthy of study, presuppositions that direct the study, and a logic and development that provide coherence. And both worlds have equally gratuitous conclusions. While witnessing to the *exigence ontologique,* from the perspective of the absurd, both end up as no more than expressions of the diverse and equally unjustifiable partial unities to which experience can give rise. The only priority results from lucidity, the recognition of the limits of our endeavors and the clarity that such recognition brings to the perception of the qualities of immediacy.

TO JUSTIFY EVERYTHING

If each work of art presents itself as a self-contained perfect unity, the multiplication of such unities is bound to place them in theoretical opposition with one another. But if, viewed internally, each stands in opposition to all others as ultimate perspectives, viewed externally each is but one more perspective witnessing to a diversity of vision and a potential experiential richness. What more powerful response to nihilism than human creativity? This seems to have been the view of Camus when he wrote *The Myth*; to prove this was the aim of its section on "Absurd Creation." The import of that section, and its continuity with Camus's later thought in *The Rebel*, can be adequately grasped only when placed in the perspective of the problems it sought to deal with. The general concerns of *The Myth* having been addressed in a previous chapter, it will suffice here to show that the notion of art as a witness to diversity, as developed in *The Myth*, is not in contradiction with the later emphasis on unity.

The Myth teaches that creation frees while judgment encloses. "The Artist 'is not a judge but a justifier'" (Brée, 251). From the perspective of the transcendent, experience is found wanting. Such a verdict has long since been rendered by Christianity. That is the meaning of original sin, one doctrine that Camus admits he "could never understand." It is an experience quite alien to him. Absolute judgment, however, which logically depends upon a commitment to an objective or transcendent standard of valuation, has been continually challenged by Camus: from Meursault, "the only Christ we deserve today," to Clamence, our "false prophet, crying in the wilderness." The study of St. Just, for whom the law is innocent and the people guilty, to take only one example from *The Rebel*, is yet another chapter in the exploration of this problem. *The Myth* is essentially a response to the disappearance of such standards. In opposing the nihilistic conclusion, Camus sought to offer an alternative to absolute moral standards by showing that experience could be meaningful on its own relative terms. "I want to know," he wrote in *The Myth*, "whether, accepting a life *without* appeal, one can also agree to work and create *without* appeal and what is the way leading to these liberties" (MS, 75).

Since values seemed to involve a scale, a hierarchy, and a principle that would ground that hierarchy, and since all such principles were discredited, Camus felt compelled to have recourse to an ethics of quantity, and an aesthetics of pure presentation, without explanation: an art of pure gratuity. The only possible standard of evaluation was life, more life, a heightening of life of all kinds.

The continuing importance of this point for Camus is attested to by the introduction he wrote to the French translation of Oscar Wilde's *The Ballad of Reading Gaol* entitled "The Artist in Prison." Composed in 1952, *after* publication of *The Rebel*, it maintained that "the supreme aim of art is to confound all judges, to abolish all accusations, and to justify everything, life and mankind, in a light which is the light of beauty only because it is the light of truth" (E, 1126).

The aim of art in such a context is to add experiences. As an expression of integrity it might, though it need not, assist individuals in achieving the lucid awareness that can appreciate every moment without giving way to hope in an illusory future that destroys the ability to experience the present. "For the absurd man," writes Camus, "it is not a matter of explaining and solving, but of experiencing and describing. Everything begins with lucid indifference" (M, 70). There are no ultimate metaphysical explanations in an absurd world, and recognition of this may be the first step toward overcoming the despair that had been the nihilist legacy.

Describing—that is the last ambition of an absurd thought. . . . The heart learns . . . that the emotion delighting us when we see the world's aspects comes to us not from its depths but from their diversity. Explanation is useless, but sensation remains and, with it, the constant attraction of a universe inexhaustible in quantity. . . . *In this universe* the work of art is then the sole chance of keeping . . . consciousness and *of fixing its adventures*. Creating is living doubly (MS, 69–70, my italics).[6]

In a world without transcendence, therefore, "All existence . . . is but a vast mime under the mask of the absurd. Creation is the great mime. . . . It does not offer an escape for *the intellectual ailment*. Rather . . . it marks the point from which absurd passions spring and where reasoning stops" (M, 70, 71, my italics).

Creation is a microcosm of the absurd macrocosm in which qualities are proliferated ad infinitum. Creative activity is a mirror in which individuals see an image of their futile life. This can be accomplished internally by the way in which an absurd work illustrates divorce and ultimate inexplicability; and externally by the multiplication of tentative perspectives. The intellectual ailment results from the longing for resolution. Instead, creation offers the absurd mind an indefinite number of perspectives. Instead of explanation, it offers description; instead of necessity, it is pure gratuitousness.

But if life can be found to be filled with qualities immediately experienced —with truths we can feel—then the role of absurd art becomes clear and important: It lives in the multiplication of those qualities, in the diversification of perspectives, in the way in which it offers itself for contemplation and enjoyment. Art speaks for diversity, for the proliferation of qualities ad infinitum, and against exclusiveness and finality. It thus serves to reconcile humans to a life without ultimate justification.[7]

Contrary to the opinion of many commentators,[8] Camus never repudiated this perspective, however much his center of interest may have shifted. Absurd creation speaks of the absurd artwork as the expression of a lucid consciousness seeking to augment experience through the multiplication of perspectives without ultimate resolution. It is a work self-conscious about its impotence, seeking justification in the immediate qualities of its creation and presentation. To all these values Camus holds firm, but he finds them insufficient. They are but the outlines of a position; they set the boundary conditions of the human experiment. Once these boundary conditions have been accepted, once the absurd experience has been lived through and the intellectual ailment overcome (at least insofar as the failure of ultimate explanations had incapacitated one for living), the problems of living remain: Choices must be made and consequences undergone. "Revolt. The absurd implies an absence of choice. Living is choosing. Choosing is killing. The objection to the absurd is murder" (Notebooks II, 221).

AN ETHICS OF QUANTITY

The Myth thus leaves us with but the bare bones of a perspective. "All that remains [for the creative experience] is a fate whose outcome alone is fatal. Outside of that single fatality of death, everything, joy or happiness, is liberty.

A world remains of which man is the sole master" (MS, 87). Having disposed of the question of objective transcendence, Camus suggests:

There is perhaps a living transcendence, of which beauty offers the promise, which can make this limited and mortal world preferable and more lovable than any other. Art thus leads us to the origins of revolt to the extent to which it tries to give form to a value which flees in perpetual becoming, but which the artist pursues, wishing to snatch it from the flow of history (R, 258; L'HR, 319).[9]

As the absolute diminishes as an acceptable resolution of the problems of human existence, the need for practical solutions becomes more urgent. Absurd creation sought to point us toward the qualities embodied in the present. But it was not capable of offering an answer on its own terms to that felt need for unity that demanded of experience a certain order. Yet the need had to be met. Even if total order is unattainable, may not partial orders be found? The absurd, of course, never denied this possibility, nor sought to negate its importance. What would a work of art be without order? And what else could be the role of discipline? But the concern there had been to free us from our destructive attachment to totality, to the vain and destructive hope for salvation. Thus the question of partial unities had not been broached.[10] This *The Rebel* sought to do.

"As description," wrote Thomas Hanna of *The Myth*'s theory of art, "a work of art is simply another absurd phenomenon, but the difference is that here, for the first time, this personal awareness is brought out toward others and indicates their common lot" (Hanna [I], 37). Lucid description is *The Myth*'s final injunction, never ultimate explanation or judgment, for *that* would be unjustifiable. This is the force of the ethics of quantity to which we have referred. But a problem with that notion has caused much confusion, and we would do well here to clarify its philosophical import.

From the perspective of absolutes, either you have an ultimate ground of explanation or you do not. The absolute does not admit of degrees. If you do not have absolute values, you have no justification for evaluation and choice at all. That is the situation in which individuals faced with the absurd find themselves, and that is why they so often draw the nihilistic conclusion. Camus accepted that situation as a starting point and sought to show the possibility of reaching another, equally logical, conclusion. Within this framework of the impossibility of total explanation, Camus suggests the possibility of total acceptance of the qualities of immediacy. No judgment is to be passed upon experience; all that can be said is whether there is more or less of it. Thus absurd creation, which offers no judgment and does not explain what cannot be explained. It presents its artistic unities as gratuitous offerings whose only value, if they have any, is the extent to which they increase the quantity of one's experience.

It is at this point that a significant problem arises for Camus, for he does not seem sufficiently clear as to how art can increase the quantity of one's experience, yet be simply repetition. As far as pure quantity is concerned, the only significant difference would involve the span of living, which is equivalent to a repetition of the same neutral quality. In fact, he says elsewhere in *The Myth* that there is no substitute for twenty years of life. However, the force of his point, and his ethic, seems to lie in a slightly different path from that of quantity. He may rather be taken as suggesting that by presenting *qualitatively* different experiences, between which, of course, no absolute value judgment is possible, the scope of experience is enlarged. Increasing its quantity would then be equivalent to expanding the diversity of its encounters, of the quantity of the irreplaceable immediate qualities experienced by a lucid consciousness facing an inevitable death. The repetition would not refer to a constant reduplication of the same qualities of experience, but rather to a repetition of the absurdist thematic of divorce. This interpretation is consistent with the basic line of his argument. Thus the "goal of absurd art," writes Hanna, is "that art means nothing more than itself" (Hanna [I], 37), a self that is simply the presentation of an infinite diversity of qualities.

Once the role of qualities in an ethic of quantity is understood, the continuity in theory between *The Myth* and *The Rebel* becomes less opaque. The structure of a work of art, even an absurd one, has a positive and necessary role as a response to the need for unity and coherence. The stylization, as an expression of the artist's freedom with respect to the materials, affords art its distinctiveness, by removing it from the ordinary flow of experience and giving to it a form that concentrates that experience. Art may thus increase the quantity of experience by the revelation and description of its diverse qualities.

Thus while there is some truth in the remark of Thomas Hanna—itself typical of most interpretations of Camus—that there is a break in continuity between the theory of art in *The Myth* and in *The Rebel*, to call that of the later work a "repudiation" of the earlier one is to miss the more fundamental continuity. Here is Hanna's argument:

The esthetic injunction of the absurdist experiment was to describe the world with *nothing added* to it. This of course is not the case with the esthetics of revolt. . . . The world is no longer strange and intractable, it is now capable of transformation. And, more importantly, man does not hold his nostalgia of unity in defiance of the world, but, in revolt, he now aggressively seeks to transform the world in the image of revolt's value. . . . In this earlier esthetics Camus' basic description of man and his unity, and the world and its disunity, is much the same as it is in his mature thought. The essential difference is that earlier there was no compulsion for man to create a world of unity and values in view of his own condemnation to die along with his values (Hanna [I], 187).

Hanna correctly notes the continuity of Camus's conception of human nature and the world insofar as a fundamental theoretical relationship is concerned. Then he misjudges the significance of the disparity in views by forgetting the limitations placed on the possible answers to the absurd that the posing of the ultimate questions there imposed. Remember that only three alternatives are open within the framework prescribed by *The Myth*: (1) hope for a total and transcendent meaning, beyond rational inquiry; (2) rejection of any meaning (which as the nihilist conclusion from the fact of disbelief in option one posed the immediate problem with which the essay sought to deal); and (3) commitment to the possibility of immanent meaning. The last is the only *total* alternative that remains, in view of the feeling of the absurd and the nihilist inference. In seeking to show that it is a "genuine option," Camus has not taken an explicit position for or against the possibility of relative guidelines: That would have no meaning within the framework of that inquiry. First the possibility must be shown, then the constructions may follow. That his concerns shifted is to be expected; what that involved was not a refutation of the earlier position but a clarification and theoretical development under the press of historical circumstances.

The "compulsion of man to create a world of unity" is already implicit, though not adequately spelled out, both in the presentation of the distinct worlds of philosopher and novelist, and in the notion of discipline and stylization, which is what sets the work of art off from ordinary experience. The "nothing added" that Hanna refers to does not concern the stylization and articulation of unity, but the content and answers that the absurd work presents. The absurd creation "must remain aware of its gratuitousness"; it must "illustrate divorce and revolt" (MS, 75). Only then will creation offer "the staggering evidence of man's sole dignity: the dogged revolt against his condition, perseverance in an effort considered sterile" (MS, 85). The presentation of such a work requires control, discipline, stylization—the production of an artistic unity that adds no content, offers no answers, in short, does not seek to resolve the absurd. Hanna has, in short, confused two dimensions of the problem. In Camus's later thought, the fundamental boundaries of the human condition revealed in the absurdist experiment remain intractable; but granting this, only if one has opted for meaning as a function of immanent presence—the third of the aforementioned three alternatives—can the question of the transformation of that present have meaning. Within the boundaries presented by the absurd everything still remains to be done. We must give a style to our life and art. We are free, responsible, finite beings whose future is open. The questions of revolt take their start from this point.

A THEATER WITHOUT STARS

"Every writer tries to give a form to the passions of his time. . . . Art wants to save from death a living image of our passions and sufferings" (RRD, 181–2). The work of art ideally aspires toward structural perfection or unity, thus testifying to the continual possibility of attaining concrete unities. This is ultimately accomplished by the way the work incorporates the flow of time. But experience must return ever again to its basis in flesh and movement. The work of art can offer but a temporary respite from the onrush of events. Experience can enter into the world of the work only briefly. If art is to have more than simply formal import, taking us beyond momentary fulfillment— if, in short, it is to offer a substantial glimpse of that living transcendence of which Camus spoke—then it must be drawn from, and point back toward, the experiential flow in which we are fated to live. The work of art as a self-enclosed whole may constitute an aesthete's delight, but it is gratuitous in the most precise sense of the term if it does not point beyond itself and make common cause with our struggle to shape our destiny. And this view is not a plea for a literature that is *engagé;* that would be simply propaganda.[11]

In fact, of course, the very activity of creativity points beyond itself in the sense that it already bears witness to the artist's freedom with respect to the materials. The activity of stylization is a testament to the fertility of such freedom and, as such, implicitly constitutes a challenge to all social orders seeking to restrict that freedom.

The implicit call of art to remake our lives in accord with its stylistic unity must confront therefore the dramatic variations that are the substance of political struggles. Artistic and political rebellions differ in at least two fundamental aspects: production and encounter. In the historical rebel's struggle to create an artistic politics the problem of the *subject* of the creative act, like that of the participant's experience, must be raised anew. Camus demands that political rebels strive toward the condition in which all people will be the artistic creators of their world. The idealized world that is the content of the political program, however, since it presents itself not as an offering but as a total historical transformation, must take into account the factual diversity of ideals that are vitally significant for concrete individuals. The call for partial rebellious strategies directed toward the dialogic creation of democratic communities rooted in self-management is simply the expression of the demand that historical realities place upon the attempt to make our collective life approach the conditions of art.

If the artist for Camus is the *témoin de la liberté,* it is no wonder that at the center of Camus's political vision lies the reconstitution of work. This means that workers must recapture in their daily lives the dignified self-respect that human beings demand. The artist's commitment to beauty must in the last analysis be a commitment to human ennoblement. It is and must self-consciously become a political commitment at the deepest existential levels. Beauty must be wedded to truth and to dialogue, and it must be rooted in the concrete details of daily life if a renaissance is to become possible. "By himself, [the artist] doubtless will not be able to bring about the renaissance which presupposes justice and liberty. But without him this renaissance will be without form, and hence, will be nothing" (A/II, 82).

A dialogue between beauty and truth, between artist and worker, must stand at the center of any effort aimed at the reconstitution of social living. Such a dialogue has to merge the demands of freedom and justice so as mutually to limit their claims one with the other. And it must seek to ennoble the daily life of working people, which requires the pluralistic reconstitution of that life in and through worker-managed cooperatives and communities. If a *civilisation du dialogue* is to be a concrete reality rather than a pious wish, it cannot be other than a social organization that transforms personal liberty into self-directed team efforts.

Small wonder that the central action of *The Plague* is the formation of work-teams to combat the plague, or that at the center of *The Rebel* rests the vision of a rebellion vitalized by an implicitly communitarian ideal and seeking to articulate a vision and a practice that will create those natural communities advocated by that future communard Tolain to which Camus makes reference (R, 298). Nor should it be surprising that Camus felt he learned his ethics from his participation in such team activities as sports, theater, and journalism. Or that Emmanuel Roblès, Camus's friend and co-worker in his Algerian youth, should say of Camus: "He loved to belong to a group, to integrate himself into a team. . . . He accepted its discipline, yielding to the most obscure obligations with good humor, even seeming to find apparent satisfactions in them. . . . He loved to be 'the comrade merged with the anonymous team'" (Camus, 69).[12]

Artist as worker, worker as artist—people struggling collectively to come to grips with their destiny.

The contradictions of history and of art do not resolve themselves in a purely logical synthesis, but in a living creation. When the labor of the worker like that of the artist will have obtained an opportunity for fruitfulness, only then will nihilism have been outlived and the renaissance take on meaning. It is not certain that we will arrive at this goal, but it is the only task which is worth undertaking and persevering in (A/II, 10).

TO BEAR THE PAIN AND HOPE WE SHARED

In being grounded in human freedom, as well as expressing its highest potentials, the artist carries the burden of speaking for those who cannot speak, in the name of a value they all, at least potentially, share. "We [artists] must

 never escape the common misery, and that our only justi-
there is a justification, is to speak up insofar as we can, for
do so" (RRD, 204).
e scale of the calamities of modern times, Camus's quite
with the justification of artistic activity is certainly under-
sta...

I derived comfort from the vague impression that writing was an honor today because
the act involved obligations, obligations to more than just writing. It obligated me
in particular, such as I was and according to my strengths, to bear, along with those
who were living the same history, the pain and the hope we shared (Nobel Prize
Address, E, 1072–3).

Camus felt quite strongly that the artist has a social obligation: either because in our age of totalization the artist is forced to take a stand—"Today's
tyrannies have been perfected: they no longer allow either silence or neutrality" (A/II, 174)—or because of "a sort of quasi-organic intolerance that one
either experiences or does not experience" (A/II, 180). Perhaps still more to
the point: "As artists perhaps we do not have to intervene in the affairs of the
century. But as men, we do" (A/II, 179).

The needs of freedom, the very ground of creativity, place the artist in
solidarity with those who are enslaved and suffering. The artist's task actually
reveals the basic needs of experience in concentrated form: "to finally give a
form to the justice and liberty which we need" (A/II, 171). It arises out of
experience in view of what it rejects, in order to transform it; and it returns
to that experience in view of what it accepts, in order to renew it.

Camus calls the artist the witness of liberty, who, in bearing witness to
the common suffering of humans in view of their ideal potentials, offers
to them an image of their dignity that ennobles the spirit in its common
struggles against a recalcitrant, indifferent universe. Artists must speak for
solidarity; their aim is to reconcile; and, at their best, they suggest that
human community in the experience of which life may be fulfilled. "But if
[the artist] can tell himself that finally, as a result of his long effort, he has
eased or decreased the various forms of bondage weighing upon men, then
in a sense he is justified" (RRD, 184).[13]

Thus art "cannot serve . . . anything but men's suffering or their liberty.
. . . Liberty alone draws men from their isolation; but slavery dominates a
crowd of solitudes. And art, by virtue of that free essence . . . unites, whereas
tyranny separates (RRD, 205, 206).

In his Nobel Prize acceptance speech, Camus gave a beautiful and moving
testament to his conception of the role of the artist in modern society.

Personally, I cannot live without my art. But I have never placed this art above everything else. On the contrary, if it is so necessary to me, that is because it separates me from no one and enables me, such as I am, to live on the same level as everyone else. For me, art is not a solitary enjoyment. It is a means of moving the greatest number of men by offering them a privileged image of the suffering and the joy which they have in common (E, 1071).

As an expression of the human effort to articulate an experience that will reconcile us to life, art offers the promise of that living transcendence that is found in the experiences of dialogue and love, as well as in vital participation in the activity of a concrete community. Camus suggests the importance such communal activity had for him when he observes, "On a theatrical stage . . . I am natural, that is to say that I neither think nor fail to think about being natural. I only share with my co-workers the worries and the joys of a common action. That, I believe, is what is called 'camaraderie,' which has been one of the great joys of my life. . . . For me, in any case, the theater offered to me the community which I needed. . . . Here, we are all bound to one another without each one hardly ceasing to be free: isn't that a good formula for the future society?" (TRN, 1721–2).

Here we may have the key to Camus's understanding of the only possible salvation open to humans: participation in a lived community. Creative activity, such as acting in a drama, is a valued experience of which the work of art at its height—akin to revolt in *The Rebel*—offers a promise. But art only *offers* its unity to human experience—and only occasionally and briefly. The problem facing human living is to structure experience so as to make it more sure and enduring. This is precisely the task of politics, which Camus approaches with a vague ideal that can negate but not prescribe; an integrity that insists upon facing the moral dimension of political issues; and a sensibility and an attitude (not really a methodology) rooted in the notion of dialogue. It is to a consideration of the meaning of dialogue and some of the prerequisites of its institutionalization, that we now turn.

13 ~

Searching for a Style of Life

There are two kinds of revolt—one that conceals a wish for servitude, and another that seeks desperately for a free order (R, 323).

A STRATEGIC OVERVIEW

"Conquerors on the Right or the Left do not seek unity, which is primarily the harmony of opposites," comments Camus, "but totality, which is the crushing of differences" (A/I, 263). The demand for totality springs from the human need that life be meaningful, finding reflective expression in the metaphysical demand to give a complete and definitive order to the world. Only if the cosmic drama in terms of which we live our lives can be found to have—or can be given—ultimate significance, can that hunger be satisfied. If such significance cannot be grounded beyond history, then perhaps it may be found as the meaning of the historical drama itself. This too could assuage the metaphysical hunger.

Beyond history or through history, the same demand is at stake. But if humans have an ontological need to experience their actions as meaningful and themselves as worthy of respect, it is not essential that this need be met through an absolutization of the meaning of the process. The root need is experiential, not logical. The conceptual elaboration is derivative, not primary, involving the reflective organization of experience, not its immediate constitution. Camus understood this, at least in a preliminary way, at the time of his dissertation.

The givens of nature, human and nonhuman, personal and social, must be respected if conceptualization is not to be self-destructive. The elaboration of system is an illicit development of the ontological need for a dramatic ordering of our efforts, which in its inevitably destructive consequences bears witness to an experiential pathology. By making the value of experience derivative to its formulation, the demand for totality reduces the actual community of humans facing their destiny to the level of ideological combat—thus threatening to cut off any renaissance at its existential roots.

Those who cannot find even potentially a unity integral to their immediate experience, which may well be the common root of the sense of sin and guilt, are likely to compensate by developing an apocalyptic vision of a condition in which present alienations will be overcome and concrete happiness assured. By making the meaning of life depend upon the articulation of a conceptual system—a personal utopia—we not only testify to a root personal diremption, but also commit ourselves to a type of practical action that denies to the concrete the possibility of being the source of directive insights as well as the locus of consummatory consequences. Most likely such a denial is experientially rooted in the sense of its practical impossibility. If Clamence (or Caligula, Sade, Stepan, or Lenin) reveals such a dialectic in which the experience of self-alienation roots an oppressive search for totality, Meursault (or Scipio, Cherea, Rieux, or D'Arrast) may be taken to suggest an experiential location from which unity may emerge. Totality for Camus is simply the ontological need for unity reflectively transformed into a destructive-oppressive metaphysical demand for a transexperiential salvation. By unity, on the other hand, Camus means the achievement of an integral meaningfulness, however partial, which is an essential constituent of happiness for a reflective animal.

Revolutionaries may find happiness in and through their total commitment. This ought not to be denied; even though that happiness is not likely to include appreciation of the simple joys of nature and the body. But that revolutionary commitment is likely to exact a heavy toll of hierarchical domination and oppression upon the recalcitrant many insofar as it implicitly involves an attachment to a specific brand of truth—which thus legitimates the suppression of counterrevolutionary activity. It is only when our experience is torn from within or totally impeded from without, when we cannot find a way back into that experience in terms of its integral possibilities for generating insights and practices that may prove concretely satisfying, that we are likely to give ourselves over to the ultimately vain and destructive attempt to unify the entire world in accordance with a theory. We are then embarked upon the destructive path of the logical elaboration of an ideology and the practical imposition of that ideology, no doubt personally experienced as the necessary condition of meaningfulness and sincerely believed to be legitimately imposed upon others as essential to their salvation.

This is the ontological root and the metaphysical frame for the emergence of totalitarian oppression, whether of the right or of the left. At least this seems to be Camus's claim. He has nothing positive to say about the possibility that such messianic visions may be needed to mobilize oppressed masses into action. The relation of these ideologues of totality to those who are not of their mind is thus that of an "apocalyptic monologue"; having denied in advance the possibilities of legitimate challenges to their vision, they are deaf both to natural experience and to the meaningful responses of others.

THE PATHOLOGY OF LONELINESS

Clamence has revealed only one form in which this ontological demand for unity may become the ideological demand for totality: the guilt-ridden ex-Christian bourgeois tempted by the offer of personal salvation through attachment to a new church. The experiential roots of that totalizing demand are felt by Camus to be essential to an appreciation of our historical excesses. It is not only necessary to catalogue those excesses and to reveal the ideological madness that projected them as desirable policy, thus legitimating murder; it is absolutely essential to reveal the experiential roots of that ideological frenzy before we can chart a possible pathway for a contemporary renaissance. The search for the roots of our modern pathology of the intellect is simultaneously the struggle for a practical cure. And the path to that cure begins where the pathology first found expression: in the development of the rebel's initial outrage.

Committing himself to justifying the desire for happiness against the claims of god and history, Camus grounds the rebel's confrontation with The Other in the commonality of our nature and condition that roots our felt needs. Since we are bound together in fact, what is called for is a strategy that transforms this factual commonality into a mutually sustaining recognition of value. This is the promise to which revolt bears witness—and the source of the value to which it makes claim. Both nature and others are essential to me; they are constituents of my experience and of the possibility of a dignified happiness. I cannot live, I cannot even conceive of myself, without them. But as they are essential to me and share the same conditions of existence as I do, so I am essential to them. We are both constituents of the being and the possibility of The Other, as well as being limits to The Other's activity.

When, in *The Plague*, Rieux suggests that Rambert is right in struggling to be happy, Rambert responds that one cannot be happy alone. Camus suggests not simply that we have a moral responsibility not to buy our happiness at the expense of others; but that the very constitution of happiness itself involves the happiness of others. The self that I am is a particular expression of the quality of social experience. Abstract morality ultimately must be grounded in the metaphysics and ontology of community. The quality of my community is an essential ingredient of the quality of my experience. Our shared condition and our shared destiny—joined to the fact of our felt need for dignity—not only set the practical boundaries of possible meaningfulness but, in and through the experience of revolt, offer the promise of a value. The value suggested by revolt is the transformation of this prereflective community of fact into a program for the concrete and always partial realization of a reflectively constituted and consciously appreciated developing communal experience. Here the ontological hunger (which roots the metaphysical demand) can find actual satisfaction by bringing individuals out of their solitary confrontation with destiny to a communal sharing that is the concrete experience of unity. The quality of the experience is transformed, the sense of impotence at least partially assuaged, by the realized social power to create within limits our own future. The range of our sensibility and the quality of our satisfaction are thus expanded and enriched. While the experience of community cannot answer to any absolutistic demands, it may thus mitigate and even remove the reflective demands by healing the experiential wounds rooted in a deep-seated existential isolation. This is the ground of the implied metaphysic of *The Myth*.

In sum, the experience of the absurd is the experience of isolation and impotence. Its theoretical source for us may lie in the breakdown of absolutistic belief systems—ultimately the death of the Christian God and the end of His cosmic drama. But, as the example of Clamence is meant to suggest, its deeper personal roots lie in the experience of isolated individuals who, in feeling cut off from others, even when surrounded by them, are forced to face their destiny alone, and bear the burden of their freedom without communal or cosmic support. For such people, for whom others are at best indifferent, and at worst continually threatening, it is probably true that "Hell is other people." Clearly the weight of such "freedom" is unbearable. If suicide does not draw them, or offers only a temptation—as if to prove that they scorn their destiny and are above the judgment of others—then the dialectical alternative of mastery and servitude is the likely experiential ground wherein to take their stand against an implacable fate. The universal servitude of Clamence or the mass graves and total destruction of the Nazis become the appropriate final consequences of this pathological expression of the existential need for a unity betrayed.

WAGING A MORE EFFECTIVE BATTLE

All this is not to say that the encounter with the absurd has failed to reveal its profound truths. But the encounter is impotent to provide a practical and viable program. To build a program upon the absurd is impossible. At this level, Caligula and Clamence are as legitimate as Cherea or Meursault. The struggle for unity at the level of the absurd is blind and directionless. Camus implicitly recognized this when he said of the "Letters to a German Friend" that their purpose "was to throw some light on the blind battle we were waging and thereby to make our battle more effective" (RRD, ix).

The light to be shed was in terms of those concrete values to which revolt could lay claim—or at least offered a promise—even in the face of the truth of the absurd. There the struggle was to point a direction and articulate some essential preconditions for the renaissance in human living that Camus considered both the promise of revolt and the only kingdom open to humans in this post-Christian era. Humans must reject the vain lure of absolute utopias for the relative utopias that are not assured and can never be final. "The dawn of truth has not been promised to us. . . . But truth remains to be constituted, like love, like intelligence. In effect, nothing is given or promised; but everything is possible for those who are willing to struggle and to risk. We must grasp this wager at this time, in which we are being smothered by lies" (A/II, 30).

The wager of our generation is for the relative values that revolt promises and experience may offer. Truth is not given to us. Nor is it a matter of transcendent insight to be imposed upon experience from without. Life is not simply plastic to the demands of Reason. Truth is relative, emerging out of experience in which we risk ourselves in a struggle. Truths emerge as experience takes a shape and its movement a direction that responds—at best momentarily, never once and for all—to the demands of an integral and aesthetic ordering of natural energies.

Truth, love, intelligence can thus be won in the relative, for the moment, only through a concrete risking in which humans, recognizing their common destiny, commit themselves to the construction of an experiential sharing. Only the construction of community can draw us out of the metaphysical isolation to which the experience of the absurd bears witness. Only here can the *exigence ontologique* find concrete satisfaction.

It is toward the possibility of community that Camus's thought incessantly turns. And it is the preconditions of such a kingdom that he is so concerned to elaborate and defend. This is the meaning of his call for *une civilisation du dialogue*. If the concern for community is not to be but another ideological cover for an oppressive praxis; if it is to have any chance of giving birth to that renaissance without which we are condemned to wander through life in a desert of desiccated souls and desecrated nature, then it must be a mode of social living that places dialogue at the center. It is not *what* people will talk about that is at issue here. That is for them to decide within the developing processes of communal life. The concern rather is for means, which, however, constitute qualitatively and methodologically an essential ingredient in the end to be achieved. The notion of dialogue suggested here is the notion of a democratically developing, open-ended, communal process in which the means are inextricably wedded to an end that is always a partial and relative achievement of experienced values.

The search for absolutes being forsworn as a major source of oppressive violations of daily living, a relative and open-ended means of dialogue in part constitutes the end, namely the concrete development of democratically self-defining communities that are the experienceable unities possible for human beings. Democratic community becomes for Camus an ontological concern, and dialogue the essential means. "The democrat, after all, is he who admits that our adversary may be right, who, therefore, lets him express himself, and who is prepared to reflect upon his arguments" (A/I, 125). What then is this dialogue at the center of Camus's vision?

To engage in dialogue is to join with another in mutual respect. For I cannot speak to one whom I do not respect. I can only speak at; I cannot *talk with*. Dialogue, in being dialogic, recognizes the transaction between two "logoi"—two modes of speaking, two ways of being-in-the-world. In such a transaction both parties remain open to learning, to growing, and, to the extent an issue is at stake, to the mutual modification of their initial positions in response to the speech of the other. As an open-ended transaction it bears witness to respect for the possible contributions of The Other and thus to the lack of finality of one's own position. It involves implicit recognition that one's own position is only a partial articulation of a more encompassing experience in which The Other has a legitimate—nay, an essential—place. It is not simply a discussion about an issue. It is an active listening to the speech of The Other, an entering into The Other's world. It thus involves, at a deeper level, a respect for the person of The Other as one who may have a contribution to make, but in any case has a right to take a stand and have a say. It further involves recognition that there is no privileged access to the truth, no path of insight that is in principle inaccessible to The Other. It thus undercuts any claim of a right to suppress the views and oppress the person of The Other. In short, there can be no transcendent legitimation of power in a dialogical encounter. "When parties or men find themselves sufficiently persuaded by their reasons in order to accept the closing of the mouths of their contradictors violently, then democracy no longer exists" (A/I, 225).

Dialogue as a method and a process is thus also at least implicitly a metaphysic of persons that grounds an ethic. It is a commitment to a world of partial truths, multiple angles of vision, and encompassing and open-ended social experiences. To insist upon an absolute truth would be to short-circuit the dialogic process, to lay claim to an insight that transcends the experiential encounter and thus in principle cannot be modified by the speech of The Other. This would necessarily undercut democratic equality and seem to prepare the way for the legitimation of domination.

To reject dialogue is to turn human relations into a struggle for power and prestige.[1] Relations between people become competitions between objective powers. Human communities collectively seeking to work out their destinies in a partial and groping manner are replaced by the totalizing demand for absolute vision and a "metaphysical revolution." The result can only be the destruction of freedom in the name of justice through the imposition of a totalitarian order. Camus observes, "Tolain, the future Communard, wrote: 'Human beings emancipate themselves only on the basis of natural groups.'" And he goes on later to note that "the first preoccupation of the historical and natural state has been . . . to crush forever the personal nucleus and communal autonomy" (R, 298). This is the root of Camus's critique of metaphysical revolutions in the arena of history. "It is a matter . . . of defining the conditions of a modest political thinking . . . delivered of all messianism, and freed from the nostalgia for a terrestrial paradise" (A/II, 259).

INTERWEAVING ART AND POLITICS

It is not an insignificant fact of Camus's career that he often felt personally moved and practically obligated to take stands on pressing political issues. A brief consideration of the attitudes and perspectives thus revealed can help us understand the philosophical significance of his work. In politics as in art, Camus always spoke for metaphysical concerns.[2]

If art and politics are the two major prongs in the constructive offensive of *l'homme révolté*, they stand in an interesting relationship with one another. From one angle, art may be seen as an end of living, an activity in which meaning is complete and experience fulfilled, whereas politics is always a means, never an end in itself—the engagement of individuals in the manipulation of objective and intersubjective relations toward the end of achieving human well-being. In the experience of art, meaning is complete; in the experience of politics, it is never so. As poetics was the ideal perfection of history for Aristotle, so art may be seen as the ideal perfection of politics for Camus. In fact, it might even be said that politics is the means that makes possible the experience of art—or, better, of aesthetic experience. Camus certainly suggests as much in his reaction to the reverse view of orthodox Marxists.

Yet the experience of art remains brief and temporary. Most human beings seem to be in need of art, but to have time for it only momentarily or tangentially; it is only a limited minority who are able to devote extensive periods of time to it. While art is for most people, therefore, but an occasional and temporary respite from the toils of living, politics bears witness to the continuing struggles with power that theme daily existence. Few of us are ever free of involvement with others and with conflicts of power. Even Thoreau left the society of his compatriots for only a couple of years—and at that, he took books with him. The meanings and values of other times and societies were his companions, not to speak of his regular walks to town. He too lived off the fruits of society. Thus the *means,* politics, is the continuing reality of our lives, while the *end,* art, is but the momentary respite from daily toils.

Furthermore, the artist is usually an individual or a small group, and likewise the respondent. Yet the message of art is unity and reconciliation. Art offers us an image of our potentials; but it can do nothing more toward their actual realization in the only world and the only life we have. This task of constructing concrete and enduring unities, of institutionalizing an artistic style of life is precisely the goal of politics. Here art is the means and politics the end. In a different sense, however. For whereas art is a function of individual stylization seeking to give expression to isolated ideal styles of life, politics is the conjoint activity of humans coming together in the hope of giving style to their shared life. Thus while each work of art is a unique whole presented to experience in finalized form, the experience itself is an ongoing reality in need of its own unique form, which ideally is the political art work. Thus the quality of the ongoing experience stands as a constant check on the formulations that seek to give it expression, while the formulations themselves stand in need of mutual reevaluation in view of their constantly conflicting ideals.

If art therefore speaks ideally for a certain quality of human experience, its goal is an abstraction apart from the practical steps required for its realization; and these steps constitute the core of politics. Ideally, art and politics, ends and means, ought to come together in a coherent whole; but this remains a vague vision whose use is the manner in which it may aid in giving direction to the movement of the present. In this practical movement toward the achievement of reconciliation art can only *offer* its insights; it remains for politics to strive intersubjectively to give it form and substance. As the later experiences of artists provide a constant critique of their earlier expressions, so the conflicting perspectives offered by the members of society are the continual sources of an ongoing collective reevaluation that constitutes the dialogic movement of community experience.

THE CENTURY OF FEAR

"Of course, the twentieth century has not invented hatred," noted Camus in 1951. "But it cultivates a particular variety, dispassionate hatred, wedded to mathematics and large numbers. The difference between the massacre of innocents and our settling of accounts is a difference in scale. Do you know that in 25 years, from 1922 to 1947, 70 million Europeans, men, women, and children, have been uprooted, deported, or killed? That is what has become of the land of humanism which, despite all protests, we must continue to call ignoble Europe" (A/II, 33).

It was this "ignoble Europe" in which he lived, against which he struggled, and to which he referred in his Nobel Prize speech of 1957 when he suggested that, while other generations had thought their task was to build a new world, this generation is more modest: It sees its task as simply to save the world it has.

Camus was not always so pessimistic. Yet he felt it incumbent upon contemporary thinkers to take cognizance of the "blood-stained face which history has taken on today" (RRD, 53). This, to say the least, they have not always done.

In "The Century of Fear" he zeroes in on the particular tragedy of the modern world. "Something in us has been destroyed by the spectacle of the years through which we have just passed. And this something is man's eternal confidence which has always led him to believe that human responses could be drawn from another man by speaking to him the language of humanity" (A/I, 142).

The historical question aside, the import is clear. A certain bond that, at least implicitly, unites us—sharing as we do a common condition, a common destiny, and a naïve confidence in the humanity of others that dialectically tends to confirm our own humanity—this bond has been broken and our sense of humanity thrown into question by the events of the past twenty-five years. Something new has entered into the relation of person to person, and our priorities have been changed. Camus continues: "We have seen lying, degrading, killing, deporting, torturing, and on each occasion it was not possible to persuade those who did it not to do it, *because* they were *sure of themselves, and because one does not persuade an abstraction, that is to say, the representative of an ideology*" (A/I, 142–3, my italics).

Persuasion and all it entails have been negated. In its place has come Truth in the person of the representative of an ideology. A claim to the possession of Truth is certainly not unique in history. But Camus's analysis of the implications of such claims, specifically with respect to public policy formation and the nature of dialogue and persuasion, has revealed a new dimension in political discussion. With directness and simplicity, he comments that "the long dialogue of man has come to a stop. And, of course, a man that one cannot persuade is a man to be feared" (A/I, 143).

The problem is twofold and gathers together a basic line of my argument: First, what is involved in the destruction of dialogue? Second, how may dialogue be reconstituted and developed? After treating these two questions, I shall conclude with a reconsideration of the importance of dialogue to the metaphysical concerns that have been the themes of Camus's life and thought.

A Brief Review

To recapitulate, in studying the development of Camus's thought I have traced the emergence of human awareness first with respect to the natural and individual conditions of existence, and then with respect to our common situation and ultimate destiny. My theme has been a conception of revolt in which individuals strive to reflectively construct a meaningful life out of the givens and possibilities available to them, while refusing to go beyond such experience for justification. In a sense, the attempt has been to show that experience can be self-justifying, and to suggest what is involved in such a position.

In this context, revolt was faced with an internal contradiction that had to be met. The experience of a meaning and dignity ingredient in the human situation had given rise to theories that justified the suppression of a portion of humanity. Born out of communality, revolt seems to have justified oppression. It was this problem that Camus addressed in *The Rebel*. In the search for guides to conduct, he had to make clear the difference between the experience of revolt and the dialectical inversions often involved in its expression. But if, in treating this problem, I revealed the nature of the ideological perversion, I have not yet given detailed consideration to its practical implications. These are, however, precisely the problems that political thought must face.

The limited nature of this problem must also be kept in mind. Camus's concern is always directed toward the reconstitution of social life in order to make a renaissance possible. The political question must be seen as focusing upon the form and context of collective engagements with respect to the formulation and execution of public policy. Hence the remarks concerning dialogue and persuasion are not presented as a complete analysis of these experiences, but rather only to suggest their essential political role. For example, dialogue is not to be taken as identical with persuasion. Two may share a world in terms of which they speak with one another, without addressing any questions of policy.

Persuasion

Persuasion is an intersubjective act with both personal and social consequences for policy. To undertake to persuade someone is implicitly to affirm the value of that person's opinion and, tactical considerations aside, of his or her person. It is almost to say: "You are a human being with a certain interest in this area; I therefore respect your right to be considered. Now, I believe my views are correct, and I would like you to consider them in full. If you do, I am sure you will agree as to their correctness." The attempt to persuade is, therefore, apart from purely tactical considerations, more an offering of a position for consideration than an insistence upon its finality for policy. It is a dialogic act, bearing witness to:

1. Respect for the person of the other.
2. Concern for the opinion of the other.
3. Belief in the correctness of one's own opinion.
4. Faith in the availability of that correct opinion to the other.
5. Commitment to the intersubjective nonultimacy of any belief concerning public policy.

While the individuals concerned, as representatives of divergent positions, are explicitly at odds on the issue at stake, implicit in their commitment to persuasion is the bond of unity arising out of their common universe of discourse that alone makes dialogue possible. Implicit is a mutual commitment to the world of the other out of which that universe partially arises. It is to the importance of such a common world that Camus refers when he speaks of the attempt to make dialogue possible.

A commitment to persuasion is therefore a commitment to the value of another's world as at least equal, if not prior, to that of the prevailing of one's own truths. It is important to note here, in qualification, that the intersubjective commitment need not involve the surrender of one's own truths or even a willingness to consider them as possibly dubitable, even though that would be the expected psychological accompaniment. Rather, we might continue to hold privately to our truths as indubitable, certain, and ultimate, while not *insisting* that others do likewise, and even permitting other views, however "erroneous", to hold sway in the "objective" or "intersubjective" world of public policy formation.

There can clearly be two distinct kinds of commitment to persuasion: political and metaphysical. The commitment may be to the most desirable way of forming public policy; or it may be to the very evolving nature of truth itself. Furthermore, equally strong and competing authoritarian views as to the nature of truth have on occasion given rise to practical conceptions of the virtues of democratic procedures in policy formation; witness John Locke's position on toleration. It is only when the commitment to the value of the individual becomes more than simply a practical consideration dictated by the exigencies of power, however, that such discussion becomes dialogue and the commitment to democracy gains existential depth. Thus the existential commitment to dialogue in the realm of the political bespeaks a totally different metaphysical conception of the nature of truth and value. Short of that metaphysic, political toleration is a holding action dictated by a balance of power. The fruitfulness of the doctrine of toleration lies in its potential for opening up the deeper and more fecund existential region given expression in dialogue. It is to the political essentials of that world that my remarks are here directed.

The metaphysical commitment to persuasion includes (1) the right of individuals to their own world and (2) the belief that individual worlds are united by common meanings, values, or interests. Language is but one quite significant way of objectively expressing these implicit common interests. And democracy, while in one sense but the practical instrument of toleration between competing worlds in transformed guise, becomes the essential means by which this metaphysical commitment finds political expression.

Similar to the decision of the Roman Catholic Church at the Second Vatican Council, this political commitment means that, while error may have no rights, the erring individual does. And while the Catholic Church clearly believes there is a transcendent Truth and it is in possession of the unique source of that Truth—revelation—it has taken the political position that this Truth cannot be imposed upon others. In other words, the priority of the individual conscience has been asserted in regards to the coming to a preexistent Truth.

Here is a clear example of the distinction between a metaphysical commitment and a political position. Whether ultimately these become incompatible would seem to depend upon the exact nature of the metaphysical commitment. To the extent that its theoretical formulation is exclusive and final, the political position can only be a holding action, a tactical decision resulting from a recognition that one is unlikely to make one's final Truth prevail now. To the extent that the Truth is not exclusive—for example, that erring individuals apart from their beliefs may be likewise an ultimate value—these commitments may not be ultimately incompatible. The *may not* here concerns the rigidity of one's attachment to, the finality attributed to, and the essential nature of, the ultimate Truth in question. The two may be maintained simultaneously. If pushed to their logical extremes, however, they might be forced into exclusiveness and contradiction.

The dilemma of the Church is, therefore, quite instructive for this discussion of dialogue. It places in clear relief the contrasting positions that Camus seems to have had in mind when, in his speech to the Dominican monks in 1946, he asserted that "between the forces of terror and the forces of dialogue, a great unequal battle has begun" (RRD, 55). The equation seems to be between the forces of terror and a political commitment to a definitive metaphysical Truth. Ideology, as we have seen, involves just such a commitment. And Camus sees the question quite directly: If we claim possession of an absolute, indubitable Truth; and if we cannot persuade the erring other of our Truth; then we must insist that we have some special and privileged insight into that Truth (such as revelation, intuition, or scriptures); and that this source yields special privileges. If we insist upon the right of that Truth to prevail politically, we are then compelled to deny the value of any "erring," contrary opinion insofar as it seeks to assert itself. Ultimately we are led to the denial of the value of the bearer of such an opinion. The destruction of dialogue becomes complete in the destruction of the person.

In sum, the claim to the possession of Truth, accompanied *as it must be* whenever Truth alone matters by the claim of a special or privileged insight or access, *in the political, public, or intersubjective situation* is ultimately the claim to special rights and privileges. It is the claim to superiority and, if necessary, the right of suppression. It involves the destruction of any prior commitment to the ultimacy of the person of the other. Through the transformation of priorities, it leads to the destruction of the possibility of dialogue. When pushed to its logical extreme, without regard to the specific content of the theoretical position at issue, such a claim must result, at least implicitly, in the transformation of others into impediments, objects of manipulation, and thus in the reduction of human relations to a state of incipient war, the final arbiter of decision being nothing other than force, implied or exerted.

Those who, as Camus noted, were sure of themselves because they represented an ideology were in fact abstractions, individuals who identified people not as that specific complex of qualities and tendencies concretely encountered, but simply as the bearers of this or that view on the important questions. The encounter with others therefore cannot take place as between particular persons but only as between those for or against. Since only our theoretical positions matter, those with whom we disagree clearly have lost their value.[3]

The claim is the following. The possibility of dialogue is destroyed as soon as a claim to the Truth, and to the privileged insight upon which it must ultimately be based, insists upon public recognition. Any metaphysical claim that Truth is the only basis for public policy would seem to be implicitly just such a tyrannical act. The abstract conclusion having replaced the concrete inquirer as the ultimate value, the latter is logically (and eventually, no doubt, concretely) reduced to an appendage whose opinion *per se* is of no value: It is transitional and purely instrumental, at best; dispensable, at worst. A human situation—the encounter of persons in search of an ever corrigible way of living together—is thus replaced by confrontation in which one attempts to make Truth, privately arrived at, hold public sway by brute force. The dialectally inevitable result of such an insistence should be clear. The concept of constructive opposition has here been outlived. No wonder that an individual so possessed is to be feared.

It would be difficult to make this point more forcefully than does Camus:

There is no life without dialogue. And over the largest part of the world dialogue today has been replaced by polemic. . . . But what is the mechanism of polemic? It involves considering the adversary as an enemy, consequently in simplifying him and in refusing to see him. I am no longer aware of the character or the appearance of the man whom I insult, nor whether he happens to smile, and in what manner. Having become three-fourths blind thanks to polemic, we no longer live among men, but in a world of silhouettes.

There is no life without persuasion. And contemporary history only knows intimidation. Men exist and only can exist on the idea that they have something in common in terms of which they can always renew themselves. But we have discovered this: there are men that one does not persuade. It was and it remains impossible for a victim of a concentration camp to explain to those who degrade him that they should not do it. The fact is that these latter no longer represent men, but rather an idea carried to the extreme limits by the most inflexible of wills. He who wishes to dominate is deaf. Faced with him, one must fight or die. That is why men today live in terror (A/I, 252–9).

RECONSTITUTING DIALOGUE

Faced with this analysis of the implicit terror of the contemporary situation, a result of the increasing breakdown of dialogue, the question inevitably arises: How may dialogue be reconstituted as a modus vivendi of sociopolitical life, "in order at least to make the future possible"? (A/I, 175). Camus addressed this question in the most trying of circumstances: the Algerian civil war. Neither the actual failure of his appeals nor the criticism leveled at aspects of his specific political stance need diminish the theoretical significance of his approach to what might be called the transcendental preconditions for the reconstruction of a dialogic community. These failures might be taken, rather, as suggesting that the situation was out of control—or at least beyond the possibility of a dialogic resolution. Certainly nothing in Camus's thought suggests he believed that cannot happen. That it has in fact happened quite often in the twentieth century is precisely the problem of terror to which Camus so often refers. The practical failure of his approach may be taken as evidence for one of two things:

1. His failure to recognize that the situation had proceeded well beyond the range of discussion: that there was no available common ground.
2. His lack of a political strategy to deal with structural conflicts between opposed groups. This strategic weakness points toward Camus's deeper failure to appreciate adequately the role of historically developed institutional structures in ordering political realities. This failure accounts in large part for the abstractness with which his treatment of political problems is often plagued.

A consideration of this situation in which dialogue has broken down may enable us to see more clearly those preliminary steps that Camus saw as basic to its reinstitution. However necessary they may be as preconditions, though, Camus never assumed that their achievement was ever more than problematic. That would require courage and chance.[4]

Letter to an Algerian Militant

In the Algerian situation, according to Camus, each side was convinced of the rightness of its cause and the evil of the other's. They were "pitted against each other, condemned to inflicting the greatest possible pain on each other, inexpiably" (RRD, 94). Inflexible positions at grips with each other constituted a vicious dialectic. Hegel could not have expressed it more powerfully: "Forced to live together and incapable of uniting, they decide at least to die together. And because each of them by his excesses strengthens the motives and excesses of the other, the storm of death that has struck our country can only increase to the point of general destruction" (RRD, 95).

In this extreme situation, reminiscent of the cry of Sisyphus and suggesting the nature of the transition from the individual to the social, the French Camus writes to the Algerian Kessous:

If anyone dares to put his whole heart and all his suffering into such a cry, he will hear nothing but laughter and a louder clash of arms. And yet we must cry it aloud, and, since you plan to do so, I cannot let you do such a mad and necessary thing without telling you that I stand beside you like a brother (RRD, 95).

Whenever a relationship between individuals is reduced to a combat between exclusive Truths, dialogue is replaced by force. With the destruction of the felt bonds that unite us, we exist in isolation or in incipient antagonism. The human concern must be to limit the scope of the ideological, to circumscribe the claim to Truth by the claim to the rights of humans in that which we share as humans. Of course, to circumscribe truth is to make its meaning relative to particular contexts, purposes, and limits of applicability.[5] "The essential thing is to leave room, however limited it may be, for the exchange of views [la place du dialogue] which is still possible" (RRD, 95).

The détente involves easing the grip of an exclusive ideology upon the individuals concerned, establishing a common ground of meaning that would make dialogue possible and constitute the initial step toward the construction of community.

To Save the Bodies

In his "Appeal" some months later Camus returns to this problem and develops the projected steps. Briefly, they are:

1. The definition of a common ground of meaning.
2. The willingness of each to reflect upon the views of the other, thus the implicit recognition that their own positions are not necessarily final and that the other's views might make a constructive contribution—or, at any rate, deserve to be heard.
3. The willingness to turn toward a primary consideration of future possibilities and the consequences of action rather than dwelling upon past responsibilities, guilts and punishments, and the causes of problems.

4. The explicit recognition of the possibility and importance of difference.

Granted the situation in which ideological warfare is total and dialogue nil (as in Algeria in 1956), Camus suggested these four steps. The assumptions are human freedom, however circumscribed by events, and the factual commonness of a joint situation, however limited by contrary objectives. Let us follow the development of these points in detail.

1. Ideologies are positions closed to external criticism. Camus proposes to go beyond the destructive combat of such closed positions by appeal to concrete instances in which the competing parties might realize common objectives: "a purely humanitarian appeal that might, at least on one point, silence the fury and unite most Algerians, both French and Arab, without their having to give up any of their convictions" (RRD, 98). Founded upon the belief that "no cause justifies the death of the innocent" (RRD, 100), the call is for a truce with regard to the civilian population.

The attempt, if successful, would slightly open these positions to one another in order that some contact could be made, so that a certain intercourse, however limited, might begin. From the point of view of content, on the other hand, the procedure that Camus adopts is revealing of his orientation from *Two Sides of the Coin* onward: He turns toward the implicit communality of human beings with respect to death. In this connection one story from *Exile* is especially revealing. In "The Silent Ones," the relation between employer and employees had been reduced to that of power implicit in the employer's take-it-or-leave-it. After that, no dialogue was possible. The revolt crushed, the workers were reduced to the sullen silence of the humiliated. In their relation to their employer, the sense of common dignity —which alone could support a revolt, a strike—was suppressed, and they were reduced to the relation of master and servant. Yet in the face of death, which the illness of the boss's child brought to the fore, resentment gave way to an almost embarassed sympathy—and to the experience of the complicity of humans in the face of a condition common to them all. Here the take-it-or-leave-it was implicitly overcome; the encounter with death called forth the conjoint human response somewhat similar to the response of the Oranais in the face of the plague.

In "To Save the Bodies," in the series of essays entitled "Neither Victims Nor Executioners," Camus suggests the point in question in a more general way as a first article of political faith. In opposition to ideologies of total salvation, he writes, "My conviction is that we can no longer reasonably entertain the hope of saving everything, but that we can at least propose to ourselves *to save the bodies in order that the future may remain possible*" (A/I, 149, my italics).

Noteworthy here is his attitude toward the limits of commitment as well as the suggestion, in the italicized phrase, of the basic direction of his political thought. By grounding the possibility of human community in the natural conditions of existence, he seeks to build a community into and through these conditions. Since certain conditions are *in fact* common to humans, *recognition* of them can yield the ground of essential common interests upon which the community of dialogue may be constructed.

We can now better understand the significance of Camus's evaluation of anarcho-syndicalism as expressing the need to construct community upon natural relations.[6] It is quite wrong to view these remarks in *The Rebel* as added on simply in order to give a positive dimension to his position. To say that is to miss both the fundamental nature of his argument in the book, and to fail to see the metaphysical position and program that he offers.

In his "Appeal" Camus takes exactly this point in a slightly more urgent context: "Without recalling again the mistakes of the past, anxious solely for the future, it is possible . . . to agree first and then to save human lives. In this way we may prepare a climate more favorable to a discussion that will at last be reasonable" (RRD, 100).

2. What would be required to create a "climate more favorable to a discussion that will at last be reasonable"? "If each individual, Arab or French, made an effort to think over his adversary's motives, at least the basis of a fruitful discussion would be clear" (RRD, 100).

Dialogue is not possible, sharing of experience and a felt unity are clearly unattainable, so long as at least one side of the combat believes it is in possession of a Truth that leaves nothing more to be said. If one side holds to its Truth absolutely, the other side will be forced into an equivalent stance. As soon as the opposition is discounted as a possible source of insight, there is clearly no need to waste time in listening to it. Thus the attempt to break open an encrusted orientation, to reveal the possibilities of novelty inherent in the encounter, is a prerequisite of the movement toward dialogue. "'No further discussion is possible'—that is the slogan that sterilizes any future and any possibility of life" (RRD, 101–2).

3. With common interests recognized and the parties opening up to the possibilities inherent in an encounter with others, the concern must shift, if the experience is to prove fruitful, toward joint policy and control of consequences, rather than remaining fixated upon past guilt and the legalistic attitude that leads only to recrimination. "I believe in a policy of reparation in Algeria rather than in a policy of expiation. *Problems must be seen in relation to the future* [C'est en fonction de l'avenir qu'il faut poser les problèmes], without endlessly going back over the errors of the past" (RRD, 89, my italics).

While the actual situation in Algeria gives poignant meaning to the view that we must learn to live together or we will die together, these words clearly have a deeper metaphysical significance. The destructive dialectic of closed positions reveals more clearly than anything else the need to pose the problem in the relative and with respect to the future.[7] Nothing was more repugnant to Camus and more destructive of dialogue than the dialectic of recrimination and expiation. "The frightful aspect of that solidarity is apparent in the infernal dialectic that whatever kills one side kills the other too, each blaming the other and justifying his violences by the opponent's violence. The eternal question as to who was first responsible then loses all meaning" (RRD, 101).

4. Finally, with respect to the construction of community, Camus approaches the issue of difference. Any attitude that insists upon uniformity of views and actions cannot, of course, expect to achieve this through dialogue. Any bearer of Truth will find it unreasonable to permit expression of contrary positions, which are *a fortiori* false—unless, that is, the attitude toward Truth is not final or not ultimate, or unless the person is willing to grant to the opposition regardless of the content of their opinion, value in their own right.

This point bears repeating. Insistence upon uniformity is bound to sterilize human encounters. If the constructions are taking precedence over the people by or for whom the theories or values are developed, then dialogue has preconditions that render the encounter impossible as a free exchange on the questions at hand. If, however, one points away from a fixation upon a specific theoretical product, and moves toward the view that theory is an aid to the expansion and fulfillment of experience rather than its end and justification, then the encounter with difference takes on a new dimension. No longer need it be viewed as a threat; instead, it is the very key to liberation and development. Perhaps only at this point is creation possible. "Our differences ought to help us instead of dividing us. As for me, *here as in every domain,* I believe only in differences and not in uniformity. . . . Differences are the roots without which the tree of liberty, the sap of creation and of civilization, dries up" (RRD, 101).

HISTORICAL TASKS

The power of Camus's political ethics is rooted in recognition of the value and right of difference. The right to differ is a formulation of the commitment to the unique individual person as the source of values, prior to consideration of the person's opinion. The one limit is that this right not involve an exclusion, thus leading to the denial of The Other's freedom of speech. To differ is one thing, to exclude is another. It is the moment of exclusion that closes off time and polarizes discussion, reducing the dialogue between individuals to ideological warfare and a struggle for power.

To exclude is to leap out of the relative as far as truth is concerned and to claim a source of insight that transcends the human community. It is only within the limits of that community, however, that ethics is a living matter. The entire discussion of politics takes place from this perspective. Ideology means for Camus an absolute commitment to fixed categories. Attachment to such categories involves a leap out of the present and the meaning it continually offers. The denial of freedom and novelty is implicit in such an attachment because Truth, in transcending the present, transcends the movement and continual novelty that time offers. Thus it implicitly affirms that no present and no future can yield any meaning that would significantly modify the Truth to which the ideology makes claim. Time, the meaning it embodies, and the evaluative standpoint it implies are thus transcended as the fount and source of values. Ideologists are thus freed to do with others as they wish in view of their insight.

In this context, the so-called historical truth of Hegel or Marx is no different from the ahistorical truth of St. Thomas. In the last analysis, the movement of time is no more fundamental in the one than in the other. What *is* fundamental is the form of time. Whether dialectical or not, it is closed, and thus experientally tyrannical. Perhaps the key difference between Hegel, Lenin, and possibly Marx, on the one hand, and Dewey and the pragmatists, on the other—and the reason why Camus in many ways is more American and closely allied to the pragmatists than to classical European thought— resides in their relations to time. For Hegel, Lenin, and Marx time seems closed, the laws of movement fixed, the available resources limited; while for Dewey and the pragmatists the reverse holds, novelty being an ever present possibility. Thus categories are loosened and relativized, possibility is taken seriously, and dialogue can replace polemic on a metaphysical level.

With respect to historical tasks Chiaromonte reports Camus as saying, "If the problem of mankind boils down to a historical task, whatever that task may be, man is no longer anything but the raw material of history, and one can do with him what one wishes" (quoted in Parker, 104).[8]

The question of unity and totality, to which Camus often makes reference, is but another way of posing this problem. Unity, for Camus—"before every-thing the harmony of contraries" (A/I, 263)—is the experience of shared meanings achieved through the conjoint endeavors of individual centers of value. A social structure that can facilitate such experience is the aim of his politics. On the other hand, totality, which is "the obliteration of differ-ences" (A/I, 263), refers to any attempt to impose homogeneity of values or goals on individuals in view of a unique source of value that transcends those individuals. Such a source is usually the product of a special or original insight or revelation formulated in an abstract conception and logicized into an ideology.

OF LIBERTY AND JUSTICE

"When one wishes to unify the world in the name of a theory, there is no other way . . . than to cut the very roots which attach man to life and to nature" (A/I, 269).[9] "In simplest terms," observes Parker in discussing Camus's conception of politics, he "thought that the chief aim of political and governmental organization was 'to render freedom and justice compatible'" (Parker, 90).[10] If Camus did not often define these terms, his meaning was usually clear.[11] Meursault, in jail, complains to the jailer about his sexual privation. The jailer responds, "It's precisely for this reason that you were put in prison." "What do you mean?" asks Meursault. "Well, your freedom is being taken away, that's all" (STR, 63).

However admirably direct, of course, this is but one formulation, with a clearly defined and limited purpose. Furthermore, Camus usually formulated the problem on the social rather than the individual level suggested by these remarks. He is never primarily a motivational psychologist. Liberty or freedom and justice or necessity—all are matters of the individual and his social and natural world, not problems of psychology.

The dialectical relation between liberty and justice and its bearing on ideology is broached in *The Rebel*:

Absolute freedom is the right of the strongest to dominate. Therefore it prolongs the conflicts that profit by injustice. Absolute justice is achieved by the suppression of all contradiction; therefore it destroys freedom. The revolution to achieve justice, through freedom, ends by aligning them against each other (R, 287–8).

An important footnote clarifies this issue. In referring to his teacher and master, Jean Grenier, Camus writes, "In his *Entretiens Sur le Bon Usage de la Liberté (Conversations on the Correct Use of Freedom)* . . . [he] lays the foundation for an argument that can be summed up thus: Absolute freedom is the destruction of all value; absolute value suppresses all freedom" (R, 288).[12] A further note: "Likewise Palente: 'If there is a single and universal truth, freedom has no reason for existing.'" Camus continually insists upon the necessity of relativizing the terms of the discussion. In so doing, he reaffirms his view that rebellion and revolution are opposed only when they are absolutized. "There is, it would seem, an irreducible opposition between the

...it of revolt and the achievements of revolution. But these antinomies exist only in the absolute. They presuppose a world and a mode of thought without mediations" (R, 288; L'HR, 356).

Since absolutized, each excludes the other, they must only be defined concretely and in relation to one another. "Absolute freedom mocks at justice. Absolute justice negates freedom. To be fruitful, the two ideas must find their limit in each other" (R, 291; L'HR, 359).

A brief definition of liberty and justice was offered by Camus in *Combat*:

We shall call . . . justice a social state in which each individual receives every *opportunity* at the start and in which the country's majority is not held in abject conditions by a privileged minority. And we shall call liberty a political climate in which the human being is respected for what he is as well as for what he expresses (*Combat*, 10/1/44, my italics; TRN, 1527–8).[13]

This is clearly not an exhaustive definition, nor was it so intended—Camus would probably not have even tried to offer one—and it could probably be shown to have been influenced by certain political conditions then obtaining. Yet it is a revealing statement. With respect to justice two points bear special emphasis: (1) Justice is defined not in terms of fact but of opportunity. (2) It is contrasted with a structure based on privilege, which is the social equivalent of the epistemological claim to a unique source of, or privileged insight into, Truth. Camus is not, of course, speaking for a simple egalitarianism; all our remarks on unity and the value of difference should counteract such an interpretation. He rather speaks of "two aristocracies, that of work and that of intelligence" (A/II, 168–9). These, however, are *open* aristocracies, based upon the creative ability to assume and develop the roles required. The only privileges are those that accrue as a result of the appropriate activity. Justice is thus defined in terms of opportunity, that is, fundamentally in terms of freedom; and "Freedom [*la liberté*] is nothing else but a chance to be better" (RRD, 76).

Liberty, on the other hand, is defined in terms of the being of individuals, not primarily in terms of any specific thing they have said or done. Individuals can give value to a social system; and we are always more than any particular expression of ours. We are the possibility of growth and development, of responding in a novel way to novelty, and of endowing life with new meaning. Such is our nature, as Camus sees us; and it is this that must be protected. "When one knows of what man is capable, for better or for worse, one also knows that it is not the human being himself who must be protected but the possibilities he has within him—in other words, his freedom" (RRD, 75).

While justice is defined ultimately in terms of opportunity and liberty,

liberty must finally be so defined in terms of individuals that it is self-defining in terms of others, that is, in terms of justice. But such definitions can never be adequately given before the fact. Camus had written less than two months prior to the previous remark (*Combat*, 8/21/44), "We wish to realize without delay a true people's and worker's democracy . . . a constitution under which freedom and justice recover all their guarantees, *profound structural reforms without which a policy of freedom is a mockery*" (quoted in Parker, p. 74, my italics). He was interested only in the concrete reconciliation of freedom and justice, which depended upon the achievement of a jointly accepted *policy* that would progressively institutionalize the steps required. To define these concepts and then (deductively) achieve their union through an analysis of the meaning of the terms did not interest him.

It might be said, on the contrary, that the important question for Camus —in the spirit of William James—is what these concepts are experienced *as*. Logical categories or Platonic forms remain to be incarnated. And the act of incarnation is not akin to the metaphor of the wax and the ring. Only with a static conception of time could such an image be tenable. Dynamically considered, the *a priori* formal determinations mean little without the dialectic of concrete articulation. In response to the orthodox Marxist view of the classless society as the end of history for which present liberties must be sacrificed, Camus writes, "There is no ideal liberty which one day will be suddenly given to us as we receive our pension at the end of our life. There are liberties to be conquered, one by one, painfully; and those that we already have are steps, insufficient to be sure, but steps nevertheless along the road of a concrete liberation" (A/II, 10).

More fundamentally, "We do not believe here in definitive revolutions. All human effort is relative. The unjust law of history is that immense sacrifices are required of man often for ludicrous results. But as slight as the progress of man towards his own truth may be, we believe that it always justifies his sacrifices. We believe exactly in relative revolutions" (*Combat*, 9/19/44; TRN, 1527).

ENDS-IN-VIEW

The framework for a political program in accordance with the position we have sought to outline was offered by Camus in 1946:

The peace movement of which I have spoken would have to be able to gain expression within nations in working communities, and beyond national frontiers in reflective communities. The first, as a result of co-operative contracts determined in accordance with individual wishes, would relieve the greatest possible number of individuals;

the second would try to define the values on which this international order will live, while . . . pleading for this order on every occasion.

More precisely, the task of the latter group would be to oppose with clear words the confusions of terror, and . . . to define the values indispensable to a pacified world. An international code of justice whose first article would be general abolition of the death penalty, *a making explicit of those principles necessary for any dialogic civilization,* these would be able to be its first objectives. This work would speak to the needs of an age which cannot find in any philosophy the necessary justification of the thirst for friendship for which the western spirit today yearns. *But it is clear that it would not be a matter of constructing a new ideology. It would only be a question of searching for a style of life* (A/I, 172–4, my italics).[14]

Claims to absolute justice or absolute freedom are but extrapolations based upon concrete experiences of justice and freedom. These extrapolations can be maintained as absolute only by being removed from the actual contexts that provide their constant critiques. The problem of ideology, which I have been considering as the negation of the dialogic civilization, is but another way of posing the question of ends and means. Perhaps the fundamental question of political ethics for Camus, that of the legitimation of murder, is precisely this question of justifying the means by the ends. The claim of ideology being that of an absolute insight that transcends time, the only practical question concerns the certainty and speed with which the assured values are instituted. The question of efficacy alone remains. Camus concludes:

Terror is only legitimate if one admits the principle: "the end justifies the means." And this principle can be admitted only if the efficacy of an action is posed as an absolute end, as is the case with nihilistic ideologies (everything is permitted, all that matters is success), or with the philosophers who make an absolute of history (Hegel, then Marx: the end being the classless society, everything is good which leads to it) (A/I, 150).

Lenin explicitly drew this conclusion. Camus summarizes this point in *The Rebel* and levels the essential critique.

When the end is absolute, that is to say, historically speaking, when it is believed certain of realization, one can go as far as sacrificing others. When it is not, one can only sacrifice oneself in the engagement of a struggle for common dignity. The end justifies the means? That is possible. But what will justify the end? To this question which historical thought leaves hanging, revolt answers: the means (R, 292; L'HR, 361).

Ends, which are only ideas conceived by individuals within the context of their experience, become hypostatized, taken out of, and isolated from, that concrete flux. An experienced idea—certainly in its psychological basis —gains content from empirical situations, is limited by perspectives, and is subject to transformation resulting from the flow of events, needs, and purposes. Such an idea is of an end or goal—in John Dewey's words, an end-in-view. It is a hoped-for goal, a projection of the ideal possibilities inherent in the present situation in view of our purposes and needs. In short, an end-in-view can never be an ultimate; it is always part of present experience, having claim over that experience only in light of its purposeful nature and its grasp of present tendencies. It is not so much a revelation of transcendent Truth as a means to meaningful and effective present action. It therefore remains always revisable in the light of novel experiences. It opens out to the future rather than closing us off from it. It is ultimately always relative to that future—which is nothing more than the permanent possibility of novel presents.

The problem with ideology is that involved with any absolute commitment to a proposed end as the justification of present action. The only justification for the commitment to such an end would be a transempirical leap, an insight that does not receive its justification in experience, whatever may have been its origin. Not receiving its justification *in* experience, it is not capable of refutation *by* experience. As a source of values transcending experience it reduces the latter as a point of validation to irrelevance. It thus constitutes a permanent and irreparable breach in temporal experience considered as a permanent possibility of meaning.

An end as a final entity to which all is to be subordinated, as in an ideology, is therefore but a hypostatization of such a limited idea. When the idea is taken out of the context of discussion and correction, it is made sacred. This is the root of ideology. This reification turns historical products into universal Truths. The fixation on an abstraction from experience has the result when pushed of depriving experience of its vitality in favor of the life of the idea, which life becomes its *logic*—that is, an ideo-logy. This process of reification, which Marx called thingafication, is the essence of the notion of alienation. It constitutes the end of dialogue. Ideology, says Camus, "reigns over a universe of things, not of men" (R, 292; L'HR, 360).

Camus claims that the absolutization of knowledge involves the destruction of our vital tie to experience. Experience can be meaningful and fruitful only to the extent that knowledge is relativized and opened to the flow of time. "In history, considered as an absolute, violence finds itself legitimized; as a relative risk, it is . . . a rupture of communication" (R, 291–2; L'HR, 360).

"The truth is that no one, neither individual nor party, has a right to absolute power or to lasting privileges in a history that is itself changing."

A DIALOGIC CIVILIZATION

If there is an absolute for Camus, it is an absolute of evidence grounded in human possibilities. It is an absolute given; its significance remains hypothetical and nonexclusive with respect to others, but it defines the range of our commitment. If experience is to prove fruitful, thought must be relativized and corrigible. "Persuasion demands leisure," observes Camus, "and friendship a structure that will never be completed" (R, 247). We are recalled once again to the definition of dialogue: an open inquiry among persons. The persons are the basic unit; the inquiry seeks to achieve and to maintain guidelines for interaction; while the openness refers to the recognition and acceptance of the permanent possibility of novelty entering into human experience.

The political problem therefore becomes that of seeking to institutionalize, first, the method of inquiry; and second, its always provisional and pragmatically considered results. The freedom, dignity, and growth of the person and the collectivity are the reference points and limits of action. To pose the problems outside these limits is to remove the discussion from the ethical dimension.

The institutionalization of the method of dialogue just referred to is what Camus means by democracy. He has written: "Justice implies rights. Rights imply the liberty to defend them. In order to act, man has to speak. We know what we are defending. . . . I am speaking for a society which does not impose silence" (A/I, 229).

Such an act requires a commitment to values that transcend the purely political. The commitment to democracy is at bottom just such a politically transcending commitment to the human community. "The democrat, after all, is the one who admits that the adversary may be right, who permits him to express himself, and who agrees to reflect upon his arguments" (A/I, 125).[15]

What is fundamental is not any specific political society or set of laws by which it may be given constitutional embodiment. These structures are no more fundamental than the concepts we use to regulate our lives. The actual basis of such arrangements is to be found in the experience of community, which is essentially the experience of unity—that is, the felt communality of actions ground in common practices and common perceptions of meaning. Here we have the core notion of community: shared meaningful activity through time. Its method of communication through reciprocal approximations and mutual development of meanings in response to novel experiences is what is meant by dialogue. "What must be fought today is fear and silence, and with them, the separation of minds and souls which accompanies them. What must be defended is dialogue and universal communication among men. Servitude, injustice, lies are the curses [les fléaux] which break this communication and prevent dialogue" (A/I, 177).

Speaking of the principles revealed by revolt, which provide the basis for dialogue, Camus sums up much of our thesis in these words:

Nothing justifies the assertion that these principles have existed eternally: it is of no use to declare that they will one day exist. But they do exist, in the very period in which we exist. With us, and throughout history, they deny servitude, falsehood, and terror.

There is, in fact, nothing in common between a master and a slave; it is impossible to speak and communicate with a person who has been reduced to servitude. Instead of the implicit and untrammeled dialogue through which we come to recognize our similarity and consecrate our destiny, servitude gives sway to the most terrible of silences. If injustice is bad for the rebel, it is not because it contradicts an eternal idea of justice, but because it perpetuates the silent hostility that separates the oppressor from the oppressed. It kills the small part of existence that can be realized on this earth through the mutual understanding of men. . . . The mutual understanding and communication discovered by rebellion can survive only in free exchange of conversation. Every ambiguity, every misunderstanding, leads to death; clear language and simple words are the only salvation from this death. The climax of every tragedy lies in the deafness of its heroes. Plato is right and not Moses and Nietzsche. Dialogue on the level of mankind is less costly than the gospel preached by totalitarian regimes in the form of a monologue dictated from the top of a lonely mountain. On the stage as in reality, the monologue precedes death (R, 283–4).

Dialogue grounded in truth and integrity is all that can protect us from the despair of nihilism in a world that offers no meaning beyond what we can conjointly construct. "We have a right to think," Camus wrote a year or two before he died, "that truth with a capital letter is relative. But facts are facts. And whoever says that the sky is blue when it is grey is prostituting words and preparing the way for tyranny" (quoted in Carruth, 180).

This is not so much an implied theory of knowledge as a statement of the moral role of intelligence. The question of Truth becomes derivative; the importance of truths for experience, fundamental. Intelligence must bear witness to the facts of existence. It must disintoxicate politics, as an essential condition for maintaining dialogue.

By democracy is meant the attempt to institutionalize the principles of dialogue in order to contribute to dialogue's continual possibility. Democracy therefore involves recognition of the limited scope to be given to any human construction with respect to its role of facilitating meaningful interactions. Ultimately, of course, dialogue cannot be institutionalized; and the experience of community is beyond any framework. It serves rather as the point of critical reference for all frameworks.

Democracy thus finds its limit and its method in the expression of others. "It is a form of society in which the law is above the governors, this law being the expression of the will of all as represented by a legislative body"

164). This law that the joint will of all has given rise to is self-con-
~~~ly intersubjective in nature, not objectively founded. It is above the
governors but not above the people. It is not a mechanism of judgment and
retribution, but of organization and direction; never an end, but a means of
constructing a unified experience. As an expression of the will of all it must
find its limit in the will of each; and it must ultimately be based on, and grow
out of, the concrete exigencies of the felt human situation.

This emphasis upon theory and structures as emergents from the natural
conditions of existence, which Camus so often insisted on, explains his support of *le syndicalisme revolutionnaire*. It was truly revolutionary, not simply
efficacious, because it

began from the concrete base, the occupation, which is to the economic order
what the commune is to the political, namely the living cell upon which the
organism develops itself, while caesarian revolution begins with doctrine and seeks
its realization by force. . . . It cannot, by its very way of operating, avoid terror and
doing violence to the real. In spite of its pretensions, it begins with the absolute
in order to reshape reality. Rebellion, inversely, relies on the real in order to wend
its way in a perpetual struggle toward the truth. The first tries to realize itself by
working from top to bottom, the second from bottom to top. . . . If [rebellion] wants
a revolution, it wants it on behalf of life, not against it. That is why it primarily relies
on the most concrete realities, the occupation, the village, in which the being, the
living heart of things and of men, can be found (R, 298; L'HR, 367–8).

An important footnote continues this reasoning: "The first concern of the
historical and rational state has been . . . to crush forever the occupational
cell and communal autonomy."

Finally, and most simply, "human beings only emancipate themselves in
the midst of natural groups" (R, 298; L'HR, 368). It is on this basis alone
that the individual can achieve the felt intersubjective meaning by opening
out to others in the conjoint endeavors that constitute the moment of community. Dialogue, the social formulation of the doctrine of open inquiry, is
the movement toward and continuing support of the community that Camus
sees as our only possible salvation. It would be realized in a developing experience in which, at least for the moment, meaning is felt as sufficient. Totality,
demanding unity in the name of a preconceived and definitive theory, can
coerce external agreement; but actual community depends for its achievement on a word whose meaning will develop in the interaction of the speaker
with those to whom it is offered. "If revolutions can succeed by violence,
they can only maintain themselves through dialogue" (A/I, 267).

Only in dialogue and the felt community it establishes can the passionate
human quest for a unity of experience be at least partially assuaged.

14 🆂

Concluding in a Dialogic Mode

The kingdom which is in question . . . coincides with a certain free and open life that must be found in order for us finally to be reborn. Exile, in its manner, will show us the path to that kingdom only if we know how to refuse both servitude and possessiveness (E, 2031).

THESIS: IN THE SPIRIT OF CAMUS

In Camus's last completed original work, *Exile and the Kingdom*, Daru, the main character in the short story "The Guest," reflecting on his life, offers a symbolic commentary on human destiny:

He had requested a post in the little town at the base of the foothills separating the upper plateaus from the desert. There, rocky walls, green and black to the north, pink and lavender to the south, marked the frontier of eternal summer. He had been named to a post farther north, on the plateau itself. In the beginning, the solitude and the silence had been hard for him on these wastelands peopled only by stones. Occasionally, furrows suggested cultivation, but they had been dug to uncover a certain kind of stone good for building. The only plowing here was to harvest rocks. Elsewhere a thin layer of soil accumulated in the hollows would be scraped out to enrich paltry village gardens. This was the way it was: bare rock covered three quarters of the region. Towns sprang up, flourished, then disappeared; men came by, loved one another or fought bitterly, then died. No one in this desert, neither he nor his guest, mattered. And yet, outside this desert neither of them, Daru knew, could have really lived (EK, 97–8).

Here are the essentials of the Camusian world. Individuals, dreaming of an "eternal summer," find themselves in a "wasteland," with only "a thin layer of soil . . . to enrich paltry village gardens." The experience of solitude and silence, the fact that ultimately "no one in this desert, neither he nor his guest, mattered," this "metaphysical isolation" is the source of the absurd, reflection upon the consequences of which themed Camus's thought. The absurd testified to the need for a unity in which experience would be felt as complete at the same time that it revealed the essential incompleteness of that experience. This constitutes the root problematic in Camus's thought. The terms of the confrontation are a natural world opaque to human meanings and a person who cannot exist without such meanings. Without denying these terms, and thus remaining true to the fundamental exigencies of his— and, I would suggest, our—experience, Camus seeks a concrete way in which this human need for unity can be assuaged.

In this struggle, Camus is echoing the most profound need of a culture that has lost its roots in the eternal and not yet found them in the finite. Taking seriously both the individual's need—as expressed by the whole of Western culture—for a unity in which life would find its raison d'être, and the experience of recent history, which, to say the least, has made any transcendent justification of life seem implausible, Camus has sought to re-pose the fundamental question. In facing the absurdity of this situation he has insisted only that integrity is the precondition of the possibility of any viable "solution." That integrity of human beings to their condition is what he means by lucidity, the insistence on squarely facing the consequences of the absurd confrontation that is our lives.

From a lucid encounter with the absurd Camus finds revealed certain boundary conditions that delimit the scope of the humanly possible. He also concludes that nihilism is not a necessary logical consequence of the experience of absurdity but of the dead end to which certain metaphysical presuppositions of Western thought have led. As long as the meaningfulness of life depends upon its being seen as having transcendent significance, nihilism is the inevitable result with respect to the value of concrete experience. But the transformation of our need for unity from transcendent theory to the practical struggles to achieve lived unities within the flow of temporal experience offers, according to Camus, real possibilities for the rejuvenation of that experience. The struggle to achieve such meaning is precisely what Camus finds at the origin of revolt. And it is revolt that is the crucial constructive force in Camus's world.

Revolt gives expression to the need for unity in experience. It is a manifestation of our determination to give to life a style and a movement that, at a minimum, will preserve human dignity in the face of indifference, repression, or destruction. Even more, revolt may open to us a realm of concrete possibilities in which that experience can achieve a fulfillment consonant with its richest insights. The development of such revolts in the service of community is the key to Camus's vision.

In this experience of community the existential isolation that is the legacy of the absurd and the revolt that opens out a positive alternative to despair find their culmination. Only in communal experience can isolated individuals at grips with an inescapable destiny come together in common activities in view of shared meanings and goals by which to overcome the anguish and loneliness, which is the legacy of an impenetrable eternity. Perhaps it is only in such joint activity that our experience can be enriched and partially fulfilled.

The basic pattern for such a unified experience Camus finds in the work of art. There the individual's passion for a unified whole has found objective expression in a completed vision that can be presented to others as a suggestion of what may be a permanent ideal possibility for their own lives.

The offering of the ideal that is the work of art remains, however, from the point of view of experience, but a suggestion still awaiting concrete articulation in a style of life that might be called artistic. Apart from such a response, the promise of the work is illusory, the experience abortive. It falls to politics, therefore, conceived as the conjoint effort of individuals seeking to structure and institutionalize their concerns, to turn ongoing community experience into the closest possible approximation of an aesthetic whole.

While it is in the movement toward community that Camus locates the most positive responses to the absurd, obviously there are other possibilities. Nihilism and suicide are possible responses on the individual level, as is the life of a mystic withdrawing from society to seek union with the natural world. Totalization and concentration camps are alternatives to existential isolation on the social level. "Terror and concentration camps are the drastic means used by man to escape solitude," writes Camus. "The thirst for unity must be assuaged, even in the common grave" (R, 247).

Suicide and concentration camps are responses to the absurd, however, only to the extent that they destroy one of its basic terms, those inquiring creative centers of experience who demand unity. As extreme alternatives they constitute less pervasive challenges to human experience than those that grow out of daily encounters. It is usually failure to resolve satisfactorily conflicts growing out of such encounters that lays the groundwork for resort to the extreme solutions. Crucial contemporary social and political problems arise out of the conflicting and often mutually exclusive demands that individuals and groups—in expressing their needs to be important and to relate meaningfully to others—tend to make as the precondition of the establishment of community.[1] Not being able to live without others, and yet not knowing how to live with them, we formulate theories that, in seeking to define a program for joint experience, close us off from the criticism that is the precondition of the mutual accommodation upon which alone unity can be established. To "live with" others—in community—means to value their lives and perspectives as essential constituents of any living unity. Unity can only arise from within the encounter of those inquiring creative centers of experience and can only go as far as those centers individually and collectively deem desirable. That each perspective be both a contribution to, and a constant critique of, any achieved structure is essential to the maintenance of any community.

The nature of ideology and its challenge to community thus becomes clear. Community rests upon the give-and-take of dialogue, that open inquiry among persons, in which each perspective offers a world in terms of which the common world must be continually revised. But ideology challenges this process, and in its place seeks to substitute the Truth: the "logicized idea" beyond whose scope there can be no appeal. If in *une civilisation du dialogue* there is no final formulation, no Truth, but only a constantly revisable theory whose justification is the facilitation of the experience of the human centers concerned, then ideology constitutes an inversion of the "proper" role of thought, the hypostatization of ideas and their removal from the ongoing experiential drama that constitutes their permanent critique.

In sum, if the question of Truth is not posed as a function of an ongoing experience that constitutes its permanent critique, the Truth eventually becomes tyrannical. This results from the fact that it can only find its justification in a claim of access to a beyond that has evaluative priority over the movement of experience. Whether that beyond was literally seen as beyond, as transcendent, or as original and grounding, would not seem to make any difference. It is the *form* of the attachment that is crucial, and the resultant logical impossibility that experience in its movement out to others and on to the future might provide a critique thereof. If the Truth is grasped, its evaluative priority is assured, and the inquiry and the inquirer become secondary. On the other hand, if it is only *a* truth that is in question, no matter how solidly founded, its context, its relevance, its meaning, become relative to the purposes of the inquirers; their direction and experience become the priorities that control its use.

The construction of community thus has certain clear preconditions, not the least of which is the non-ultimacy of any specific formulation of its path. Once claims to ultimacy are abandoned, at least insofar as the intersubjective formulation of common policy is concerned, the encounter of conflicting theories can turn from incipient hostility to potentially fruitful dialogue. But the limits to any specific formulation and its ultimate subservience to the nonexclusive needs of the inquirers remain the ever present frameworks within which alone dialogue can proceed.

In addressing the Dominican monks at the Latour-Mauberg Monastery in 1946 Camus faced the problem of entering into dialogue with those of a fundamentally different metaphysical persuasion. He began, and in a sense concluded, with the following observation on the nature of this effort:

Not feeling that I possess any absolute truth or any message, I shall never start from the supposition that . . . [your] truth is illusory, but merely from the fact that I could not accept it. . . . I shall not try to change anything that I think or anything that you think (insofar as I can judge of it) in order to reach a reconciliation that would be agreeable to all. On the contrary, what I feel like telling you today is that the world needs real dialogue, that falsehood is just as much the opposite of dialogue as is silence, and that the only possible dialogue is the kind between people who remain what they are and speak their minds (RRD, 52–3).

ANTITHESIS: CRITICAL REFLECTIONS

I have tried to show how Camus's thought places before us in the most emphatic terms the root metaphors of the cosmic drama by which the European world has been vitalized for more than two thousand years. Being situated affectively on the margin of that civilization by the chance of birth and upbringing, Camus was able to bring a distinct critical sensibility to bear on his analysis of the Western world whose drama became the horizon of his vision. He was drawn into a reflection on the cultural roots of that world: Appreciation of its Greco-Roman and Judeo-Christian origins, climatically at one with the world of his birth, permeated his thinking more deeply than is likely to be appreciated by a totally acculturated European or North American. From the very first moments of his reflective life, Camus sensed the possibilities for rejuvenation of the West offered by this marginal sensibility.

Not only did the genesis of his sensibility prefigure the possibilities of a historical rejuvenation, but the social rooting of this sensibility in a poor working class district on the margin of European power centers gave Camus a degree of critical distance with respect to those very mainstream value and belief systems that became his philosophical horizon. They were not matters of a taken-for-granted way of being-in-the-world, as much as they were vital offerings to be inspected prior to adoption. But adopt them he did, however much those cultural robes did not always fit that pagan body. The Western world became his world, but never was it taken for granted. His relation to its drama was never simply that of a subject who lived comfortably within the confines of its conceptual horizon, viewing objects and goals from its angle of vision. What is so remarkable about Camus's thought is that while that European horizon became his, he continued to maintain, to nurture, and to share that pagan sensibility, offering to us a unique critical perspective from within the horizons of our cultural drama. In fact, he lived that tension self-consciously as a sustained tragic vision, his pagan sensibilities offering us the echo of those experiential roots from which we have become increasingly detached. It is here in part that his unique strength and significance for us lie. He situated himself at the center of the Western drama with a sufficiently intimate yet self-conscious and critical relationship to that world so as to have incorporated its essential contradictions into his very being. And he revealed them in his writing in starkly abstract yet deeply personal terms. In Camus's life and work the West confronts an existential mirror wherein the meaning of our world is laid bare. The weaknesses of our strengths and the strengths of our weaknesses are dialectically revealed. We come face to face with ourselves.

It is only as this unique combination of abstract structure and personal experience that the mythic force of Camus's titles can be adequately appreciated. As the articulation of the controlling root metaphors of the drama of our civilization, they lay bare the essential structure of the existential being of the West. The horizon stretches out before us; the tensions in our landscape find their appropriate tragic shadings. We might draw the image of the assertive, perhaps masculine, Prometheus–Faust rising up to confront the receptive, perhaps feminine, Sisyphus–Meursault: Fire out of sea; destiny's child confronts its motherly origins. Here is the mythic root of that most misunderstood confrontation between the north of Europe and the *pensée du midi* that Camus tries to sketch at the conclusion of *The Rebel*. This tension between humanity's aspiring historical-spiritual ideals and its rooting in an earthly body born to die is for Camus the locus of those central philosophical-religious problematics that have long plagued the Western mind: mind-body, fact-value, and theory-practice. In short, Western philosophical dualisms have an existential rooting in the way in which the living of our cosmic drama has involved the denial of its earthly moorings.

If the strength of Camus—his significance and continuing appeal—is thus clear, and if this work has helped to reveal the essentials of that dramatic vision with its reconstitutive as well as existentially descriptive force, the inadequacies of that Camusian vision are nonetheless palpable and significant, emerging tragically as the underside of his very strengths. The point, it must be noted however, is not simply to evaluate critically his vision. To the extent that I am right in claiming that Camus lived, and his thought reveals in a unique manner, the essentials of the Western drama, to that extent the limitations of his work bear searing import for the future possibilities of the West. In fact, it is part of my essential thesis that Camus's weaknesses as much as his strengths go to the core of the being of the West. Where Camus failed, so likewise has the West. And the renaissance he so passionately desired will remain a vain hope unless we in the West take stock of our "ownmost" inadequacies and find a means to transcend them. Let us in conclusion briefly consider these limitations.

It is appropriate here to return to the roots of the Camusian vision, for in truly tragic fashion his weaknesses emerge as the dialectical pole of his strengths. And if his vision of the fundamentals of our cosmic drama was in part a function of the marginality of his personal sources, so too were his theoretical inadequacies. His North African roots generated a bodily sensibility that preserved the genuineness of his encounter with Western ideas, constantly requiring that the articulation and development of that drama respect the existential needs of that earthly body. But the passionate individualism of that bodily immersion in the natural world tended to suggest a contrast between the worlds of Algeria and of Europe that slowly, prereflectively, and at the level of image rather than of explicit thought, tended to merge into a vision of a conflict between nature and history. In addition, and at a different level, since the Algeria of his youth was French colonial Algeria, the working class ethic that provided the existential locus for his reflective identification with that Western drama was a white colonial implantation in an alien cultural setting. Thus subtly but perhaps not surprisingly the surrounding Arab world finds itself situated beyond the horizons of his vision. I am speaking here, of course, not of the reflective focus of his thought, but of the qualitative fringe of associations in which that thought is bathed and by which its articulations seem to be guided at a prereflective level. There are here personal lessons as well as those with wider cultural import.

First, the matter of nature and history. As Algeria was the bodily source while Europe was the mental horizon, so the Algerian youth was able to look toward Europe with a mixture of attraction and repulsion. Attracted by the grandeur of the European drama, by the scope of its technological and artistic achievements, its historic resonances and its untapped potentials, its urban life and its majestic philosophy, Camus was repelled by the hypocrisy of its cultural scene, the misery of its exploited populations, and the depersonalization of its refined speculations. As Algeria offered the experience of the body immersed in the waters of nature, so Europe was the locus of the historical drama of hopes and humiliations. Europe was where the action was, but at times it was also a grotesque scene from which he had to maintain a critical detachment if he was to preserve his vitality and emotional balance. The Europe of cities is the Europe of evil and history, while the Algeria of the body is the source of the individual's solitary encounter with nature and with death.

Thus at a prereflective level the attitude of the Algerian youth confronting Europe with a mixture of rapt amazement and horror subtly yielded a thinking torn between the drama of history and the demands of nature. As the Algerian youth could imagine the possibility of entering Europe, maintaining his distance and sometimes withdrawing to refresh himself in the more earthly world of his origins, so the reflective observer of the historical scene could study, critically analyze from a distance, then choose to become involved in that unfolding drama—while entertaining the option of withdrawal at any time into nature-body-self for rejuvenation. What I am suggesting here is not an explicit position held by Camus, but rather a prereflective fringe by which his thought seems bathed and sometimes guided, as it were, behind his back.

As the world of Algeria was drawn into the historical processes that were the developing European drama—owing in part at least to capitalist expansion, imperialism, and colonialism—making the refuge of Algeria increasingly a matter of historical nostalgia, so the nature nurtured at the roots of Camus's vision is itself being molded and shaped by the forces of history. In short it is becoming a culturally historicized nature. Collective human effort is working a transformation not only of society, but of the natural world that was its prehistorical source. This historicization of nature calls for a vision capable of going beyond the tragic-tension-dualism that counterposes nature against history. And while Camus struggled at a reflective level to grasp the outlines of such a movement that alone would make a renaissance in the West possible, the qualitative feel of those controlling root metaphors that structured the horizon of his thought worked strongly against the possibility of such a breakthrough.

Beyond the personal level of this tragedy of vision lies a wider cultural lesson. For the image of nature confronting history is also the vision of the individualized body confronting a manipulative social world with its manifold illusions by which it seeks to hide the questionableness of its social drama. This angle of vision does offer to Camus an often fruitful perspective from which to lay bare the hypocrisies, the mystifications, and the oppressions by which people dominate one another in the service of cultural lies—by which organized society can deny to individuals their most vital possibilities. The residual sense, however, of the individual person demanding meaning and dignity, while confronting a society that employs its hypocrisies to deny that person, tends to become at times—and, at a deeper level, perhaps throughout—a metaphysical perspective that sees the individual against the society. All too often it seems as if this sense becomes the qualitative ground through which Camus assimilates the drama of the West into the interstices of his personal world. The Algerian youth immersed in nature develops an essentially liberal sense of the individual, counterposing him to the unfolding historical drama that is the essence of the Western social event. The liberal world of the West becomes so easily and "naturally" the horizon of his thought because it offers a set of readily available root metaphors with which to articulate the existential sense of the individual's confrontation with others, nature, society, history, and death. Thus the deeply personal, and in some sense irreducible, quality of the individual's encounter with destiny and death—which plays such an important role in Camus's life and through which he continues to speak to us in the West—so easily and subtly becomes the articulation of a liberal vision of the individual confronted by society and history.

But as the personal encounter becomes the individual's reflective articulation of the conditions of self-esteem and dignity, wherein lies the possibility of grasping the self itself as the product of a socially historicized natural process?

The answer is obvious. No wonder that when Camus comes to write about Marx, while appreciating the incisiveness of the Marxian critical analysis as well as the dangers inherent in the Marxian prophetic tradition, he totally misses (as Sartre suggested) the center of Marx's vision: humanity's collective self-creation through time—in short, Marx's philosophical anthropology.

As nature must increasingly be seen as historicized nature, so humans must increasingly be understood as the product of their own natural, historical, collective self-creation. To counterpose the personal self against the institutional world is to generalize to the point of irrelevance a series of practical struggles. It is to make the historical genesis of social evil fundamentally unintelligible, to legitimate the separation of theory and practice, and to reduce any praxis directed toward the reconstitution of human living to a moralism calling for an attitude it cannot historically instantiate.

It is in this context that we can see the deeper significance, as well as the root weakness, of Camus's conception of history as "only an open opportunity that remains to be rendered productive through vigilant revolt" (R, 290). The attitude toward history expressed here is similar to the liberal conception of nature and technology: a simplified instrumentalism in which individuals encounter a generally plastic medium that awaits shaping by intelligent and dedicated artist-rebel-technicians. The materials of historical-technical existence are grasped as essentially separate from the individual. They confront the individual and can be used either constructively or destructively. They can ennoble the environment or destroy it. But they do not constitute its inner being. They are not the stuff of its character and destiny. In short, implicit here is an almost atomistic, transcendent individualism that believes it can view history, technology, and institutions from without, free to choose its attitude and practice with respect to them. But such a perspective can never adequately grasp the extent to which the self I am is itself an integral result of the historical process of natural and institutional transformations. It cannot see the extent to which personal character, consciousness, and behavior emerge from within the historical drama—or that evil and suffering, as well as the possibilities of a practice directed toward a sociocultural renaissance, must be rooted *within* an engulfing history. Transcendence makes practical sense only as an emerging moment dialectically grounded *in* such a concretized history. Moral demands must emerge from within such a historically concretized concatenation of forces and must be bound to realizable possibilities. Otherwise such demands are bound to degenerate into moralisms of attitude by which the historical creator is reduced to the critical judge who takes a stand above it all. Ironically, the imposition of order from without upon an alien material is Camus's own definition of revolutionary oppression.

In short the personal strength of Camus's vision, generated by a marginal sensibility that incessantly returns us to the earthly moorings of our cultural drama whose essential myths it so starkly reveals, falls prey to the illusion of its very strengths. It fails to grasp the extent to which that individualized bodily sensitivity is itself a cultural emergent from within an increasingly historicized nature. Camus's profound sense of the body does save him from the body–mind dualism that has plagued modern Western thought. It offers him the prereflective sense of the nature and possibilities of a transformed cultural life. His community is to be an earthly union of living persons, not of imagined souls. Yet the conditions of the emergence of that community remain abstract, offering at best but the dialogical preconditions of any such community. Camus's thought, suffering from what I should call "sociological myopia," fails to grasp adequately the institutional-cultural constitution of the personal self and its "ownmost" possibilities. Is it surprising, therefore, that his practical proposals often tend to be little more than moralisms? On the basis of such a metaphysics, theory and practice fall apart. The mind's ideals remain awkwardly situated in a body itself only accidentally located in the historical process, while the values to which individual revolt gives promise must remain at best articulations of moral preconditions. At worst, they degenerate into appeals to the attitudes of others, always at odds with the concrete possibilities that the facts of history alone can reveal.

It is perhaps relevant to note here that the Marxian insights on this matter that might have proved so fruitful for Camus were denied to him by historical and cultural experiences. His encounters with communist authoritarian manipulations of the worker–peasant struggles in Algeria in the 1930s, as well as in immediate post–World War II France and in the emerging cold war, led him to associate Marxism with the Stalinist perversions. It seems to have framed the horizon through which he studied the thought of Marx, thus blinding him to the Marxian philosophical anthropology.

Ultimately this sociological myopia is rooted in a transcendent sense of the individual as a natural being confronting, in a Sisyphean mold, an eternally recurrent destiny. Rooted in the earth, the dignity of humanity is under continual attack from history, society, and ideology. An eternally vigilant and lucid revolt is necessary to preserve human beings from these onslaughts. This metaphysical perspective grounds an individualism that strives in vain to articulate a concrete vision and a practical communalism commensurate with its deepest existential needs. Thus, tragically, the metaphysical roots work strongly against his "ownmost" needs.

The sociological myopia is thus grounded in a bourgeois individualism that it often feels obliged to defend in terms of an ill-defined and sometimes substantialized conception of human nature. As that conception becomes detached from the historical processes in which it is immersed and out of which it has dialectically emerged, so the fierce defense of our dignity tends to become unreflectively identified with the conditions for the achievement of dignity historically appropriate for its emergence—namely, those of the classical West. Camus's conception of dignity is essentially Western, but he has no self-critical sense of its limited historical rooting. He thus tends to become a captive of his own unexamined assumptions, and the sociologically myopic individualism easily slides into a "cultural myopia."

The contrasts between nature and history, between the individual and society, so easily and subtly become the contrast between we and they, between the West and the non-West—most particularly between a liberal West and the totalitarian communist and Arab worlds. Here his North African origins can hide more than they reveal if one fails to appreciate the profound metaphysical significance of the colonial experience. Camus came to self-consciousness as a European in an Arab world. Identification with Christian European civilization came easily to him, while the world of Islam was always "Other." Only thus can one fathom the otherwise appalling fact that Arabs are never the *subjects* of his fiction—only at times its objects. As Conor Cruise O'Brien shows so well, in *The Stranger* the Arab is simply the other. In *The Plague*, set in the Arab city of Oran, all the characters are European, and Arabs are mentioned only once, in passing. In *Letters to a German Friend* Camus speaks of "we, free Europeans." And at the height of the Algerian war his friend Jean Daniel reports being surprised and shocked by Camus's casual references to *we* and *they* when speaking of the Arabs of Algeria.

In short, in addition to being the source of a bodily sensibility and a metaphysical vision, Camus's North African origin was the source of his European horizon with profound political, social, and cultural implications, whose full significance neither he nor most of his Western literary and political admirers have adequately appreciated. No doubt this is because his myopia so easily merges with theirs—that is, ours. This cultural myopia, like its sociological variant, emerges out of the most profound existential roots of his being, which grounded his metaphysical vision. Thus the theoretical as well as personal anguish he felt when confronted by the Algerian war. He was deeply moved by the suffering of the Arabs under French rule, and he championed their cause long before it became fashionable in left-wing European circles to do so. Yet he could never sanction *their* demands for self-determination or for independence. Their outrage generated a revolt that defined the felt conditions of their dignity, which he was not able to appreciate. Western dignity he understood, but not Arab dignity as defined by and for Arabs. Hemmed in by a vision whose horizon was framed by its cultural moorings, he is all too often reduced, in spite of himself, to benign paternalism in the service of Western colonialism. While speaking a left-wing and often radical idiom, he found himself at times supporting right-wing positions and being a bit uncomfortable with his bedfellows.

Not only does his politics reach a dead end here—and this was a matter of the deepest personal anguish for him as well as a profound challenge to the very source of his creativity—but at a deeper level, so does his imagination and its sustaining metaphysic. And it is at the point of confronting this tragic metaphysical–political field of vision that my study of Camus's work must close. Incapable of adequately and creatively grasping the Western vision that offers the opportunity of transcending its "ownmost" metaphysical limitations—that is, the Hegelian-Marxian conception of humanity's collective self-creation by labor through time—Camus is left with a tragic vision at a practical dead end. Western dualisms remain his limiting horizon, even though his experience of the body offers the promise of a way beyond. Nature and history, individual and society, fact and value, European and barbarian, ends and means. He sensed the inadequacy of these dualisms, and he found in theater, sports, and journalism experiences that pointed toward a concrete, embodied, dialogic community that offered the promise of that earthly kingdom. But he was unable to envisage a way beyond their tragic confrontation. These competing forces are balanced, they are weighed, they remain in tragic tension—but they offer no creative future. His radicalism ends in a political–personal dead end, incapable of concretely pointing the way toward the renaissance that was his deepest wish. Here we encounter the limits of the bourgeois imagination in the shipwreck of the "conscience of the West": offering a propaedeutic to any radical politics that may propose itself as a just response to human suffering, but incapable of historically instantiating any creative praxis. We are left with Nemesis, in the name of Sisyphus, challenging Prometheus not to become Caesar, but incapable of concretely determining how dialogically to produce that communally rooted "first man" that would ground the renaissance for which he so deeply longed.

Notes

Bibliography

Index

NOTES ✑

1. All citations are referenced in the body of the text. The key to the abbreviations is in the bibliography, which includes only works actually used in researching this study. In the interest of space, references to and commentaries on other works about Albert Camus have been kept to a minimum. For an extensive consideration of the literature on his thought, see my unpublished dissertation, *Revolt, Dialogue and Community*, Penn State University, 1968.

2. Cf. his essay "On the Future of Tragedy," in LCE, 295–310. In that essay, in which he sets forth his belief that ours may be an age ripe for tragic drama, his description of the contours of the modern world echoes *The Rebel*'s presentation of the conditions that nurture rebellion.

3. "But one must regret the tragic *after* having looked at it, not before" (AJ, 43).

4. Throughout this work, two titles have been retranslated in order to clarify their meaning. *The Rightside and the Wrongside (L'Envers et L'Endroit)* is retranslated as *Two Sides of the Coin*, and "The Just Assassins" ("Les Justes") is retranslated as "The Just."

5. In the late 1930s he had already set forth the frame of his work. A series on the absurd, a second on revolt, each to include a philosophical essay, a play, and a novel. The design for the following series is less clear, though in 1946 he is envisioning two more on we-are and on love. Cf. Lottman, 194, 393–4. At other times, community and judgment appear as possible themes.

6. Roger Quilliot reports a revealing conversation with Camus in 1954 in which Camus envisaged an essay that would "begin with the values established by revolt, and, after having brought forth their logical consequences, confront them with concrete experience, merging them with the sensual richness of daily life" (TRN, 2029–30).

Beyond this projected development of the theme of revolt, his continuing concerns can be gauged by his political involvements, pursuant to the publication of *The Rebel*. Philip Thody observes that these "can be divided into four main sections: his support for Pierre Mendès-France in 1955, his protests against the repression of the Hungarian revolt in 1956, his attack on the death penalty in 1957, and his numerous articles on Algeria. The guiding theme in everything he did and wrote is his intense concern for human suffering" (Thody, 198).

More generally, his activities in the 1950s might be seen as efforts to contribute to a cultural rebirth—what might be called strides toward concrete reconciliation —in two directions. Artistically he was engaged in, and writing for, the theater, where he found that living community "which had been one of the joys of my life." (Throughout this period he tried to obtain his own theater where he could produce the kind of works he felt were appropriate. At the time of his death he was on the verge of achieving his objective, thanks to De Gaulle's Minister of Culture, André Malraux.)

Theoretically, he developed the themes to which this essay has been primarily devoted. Occasional pieces on art, politics, and the events of the day addressed these concerns practically. They appeared in journals or newspapers or as letters or public speeches, some of which were collected in *Actuelles II*, *Chroniques Algeriennes*, and *Resistance, Rebellion, and Death*.

CHAPTER 1

1. On occasion, I have retranslated passages in order to better capture the original meaning. Whenever this occurs, I cite both the popular English translation and the French original.

2. In his *American Journals* Camus wrote: "Remake and recreate Greek thought as a revolt against the sacred. But not the revolt against the sacred of the romantic—which is in itself a form of the sacred—but revolt as putting the sacred in its place" (AJ, 49).

3. While overstated, the point is clear. Parker continues, "The Algerian Man, like all barbarians, possessed a kind of wild innocence. This innocence, as Jean Bloch-Michel points out . . . 'reigns over happy bodies that are pre-occupied only with themselves. It is situated outside of history, since it suspends the passage of time and restores to the world the freshness of its first moorings.' . . . The bronzed youths on the Algerian beaches [concludes Parker] had grasped a fundamental truth of human existence, and Camus would not, like the jury that condemns Meursault, judge them guilty. But he did recognize that this truth was only a point of departure, not an end in itself. If one did not go beyond that truth, one ran the risk of annihilation by one of the many manifestations of the absurd" (Parker, 41–2).

4. This is precisely the conclusion Camus comes to in his unfinished first novel, *A Happy Death*, which he was working on at about the same time.

5. Drawing upon Camus's remarks in his preface to the essays of Jean Grenier, Philip Thody outlines the stages in Camus's development to this point.

The first, which goes up to the age of twenty and rather curiously includes both his first attack of tuberculosis and his recovery from it, is one of instinctive, animal enjoyment of the life of the senses. . . . Then comes the shock of discovery when he read Grenier's *Les Isles*, understood the reason for his "sudden melancholies" and ceased to live "in sensation, on the surface of the world, among colors, waves and the fine scent of the earth." This awakening produced *L'Envers et L'Endroit*, with its reaction in favor of an insistence upon the darker side of experience and on the value of intellectual awareness. Then . . . comes the triumphant reaffirmation of the life of the body in *Noces*, the song of the nuptials between man and the earth which contrasts so sharply with the detached irony of the mood of the first essay (Thody, 20).

While the import of these texts is somewhat more nuanced than Thody suggests, and insufficient attention may have been paid to his earlier experiences as well as to his reading of *La Douleur*, these remarks do offer a fair outline of the movement of Camus's thought.

CHAPTER 2

1. A. J. Ayer is perhaps the best-known philosopher who was guilty of that error. Cf. "Albert Camus," *Horizon*, March 1946, pp. 155–68.

2. Critics of the left and of the right tended to agree in this mistaken portrait. On the left, for example, were Jeanson, Barth, and the representatives of the Communist party. On the right were Hanna, Parker, and Brée, among others. These issues are treated at greater length in the chapters on *The Rebel*, *The Fall*, and the analysis of political thought. Concerning the Marxist misreading, of special interest are Camus's responses to Jeanson and Hervé in A/II, 69–76, 85–124. These misreadings were systematic and possibly willful. Camus is presenting a logical analysis of modes of thought, not primarily a historical analysis of specific events. The extent to which such reasonings are themselves historical causes certainly concerned Camus. But the logical analyses must not be confused with an explanation of historical causation, as all too often they were.

CHAPTER 3

1. All references to the English edition of *The Stranger* are to the excellent translation by Kate Griffith, published by the University Press of America in 1982. This version is far better than the more popular one by Stuart Gilbert.

2. Recall the discussion of Vincent in Chapter 1.

3. Quoting from Camus's essay "Between Yes and No," Barrier comments perceptively, "A philosophical Meursault: 'yes, everything is simple. It is men who complicate things. Let no one tell us stories. Let no one say to us of a man condemned to death: "He is going to pay his debt to Society" but "He is going to have his neck cut."'" Barrier goes on to say, "What the author refuses are the abstract ideas with which one discreetly covers the concrete, palpable horror of the existent fact" (Barrier, 77).

4. We might consider the similar situation confronted by Kaliayev in "The Just," which is dealt with further on. The explicit effort of the police chief, Skouratov, and the Grand Duchess to extract Kaliayev's complicity in their values is an effort to undermine the base of his opposition and thus to destroy his rebellion. The rebel must feel the rightness of his cause. He must experience both indignation and justification. The most effective counter by which society can incapacitate rebellion involves its delegitimation. With respect to an individual insurgent, a potent strategy consists in reducing social protest to the status of a personality disorder, thus inducing guilt. This counterrevolutionary effort is explicitly presented in the dialogue between Nada and The Fisherman in "The State of Siege," while its logic is explored more fully in *The Fall*. That work probes the existential foundation of the personal effort to destroy rebellion's roots in autonomous self-expression by inducing pervasive guilt.

5. "In the last chapter of the book," writes Barrier, "before the arrival of the chaplain, it clearly seems as if the narrator is struggling to reconcile two incompatible attitudes in the face of death, and everything takes place as if he were repeating to

himself: 'In a sense it is too horrible to think about. But in another sense, since it must be thought about, let's be reasonable'" (Barrier, 76).

6. While a bit unclear about the meaning of "l'absurde," Mlle. Germaine Brée goes to the heart of the matter when she observes: "The very essence of *l'absurde* in his case is that out of indifference he linked forces with violence and death, not with love and life. . . . He fails to ask any questions and thereby gravely errs. In *L'Etranger* Camus thus suggests that in the face of the absurd no man can afford passively just to exist. To fail to question the meaning of the spectacle of life is to condemn both ourselves, as individuals, and the whole world to nothingness" (Brée, 117). There is reason to question the use of the word "indifference" here. Furthermore, it is an overstatement to suggest that human beings *must* question the spectacle of life, lest life be rendered meaningless. Many people lead rather normal and not unrewarding lives without engaging in a great deal of philosophical reflection, while objective circumstances seem to have much to say about when and to what extent inquiry is initiated. We are not dealing with an all or nothing here, nor with an intellectualist bias about the importance of reflection. More to the point is the consideration that the significance of an individual life and the degree to which it can be given meaning depend in large part upon one's ability to break through the tedium of encrusted habit. The call for lucidity in the face of death is only an invitation to make the most of that which is given to us.

7. Actually, the initial complicity of Oran's citizens with the rule of plague is not at all unlike the collaboration of the people of Cadiz with The Plague in "The State of Siege." In both of these encounters with the plague, however, there are significant differences from the situation of Meursault, and the resolutions differ accordingly. In response to the natural evil in *The Plague* the citizens establish community action teams that take us beyond the essentially individual level of response to the absurd studied in *The Stranger*. In the play, on the other hand, the evil has become social, and the response thus takes us to a more complicated political level in considering the nature of revolt.

8. We might think of *The Stranger* as Camus's literary portrayal in cameo of Hegel's *Phenomenology of the Spirit*.

9. Camus's review of "The Wall" appeared in "Alger Republicain" on March 12, 1939. It criticized Sartre precisely for taking the absurd as a conclusion, not as a starting point (cf. LCE, 203–6).

10. *The Stranger* depicts the process by which an individual may come to consciousness of his condition; *Nuptials* explores this perspective as an attitude. While the world may be the home within whose bosom we are born, *Nuptials* poignantly expresses our emerging realization of the tenuousness of our occupancy. The power of nature, the inexorable flow of time, the experiential distance that inevitably separates human lives from each other, these shatter illusions as to the permanence of our residence. "There are two convictions about which the prose of *Nuptials* winds all of its themes," writes Thomas Hanna.

The first is that nature or the world is distinct from and foreign to the understanding and desires of man, but is at the same time his home where he is fascinated, surpassed, and finally conquered. This conviction is developed in the Tipasa and Djémila sections. The second conviction is that death is the final and inescapable destiny of all men, and that man must adjust his life and actions to this inescapable destiny. The second conviction is the core of the last two sections entitled "Summer in Algiers" and "The Desert" (Hanna [I], 8).

By dwelling upon these "inescapable facts" of which Meursault had become conscious, *Nuptials* takes in hand "the geography of a certain desert" (*Noces*, 99; LCE, 105), outlining the boundaries of human action. It seems like the stranger reflecting upon his life and finding it good, when Camus writes:

There is a feeling actors have when they know . . . they have made their own gestures coincide with those of the ideal character they embody. . . . That was exactly what I felt: I had played my part well. I had performed my task as a man, and the fact that I had known joy for one entire day seemed to me . . . the intense fulfillment of a condition which, in certain circumstances, makes it our duty to be happy. Then we are alone again, but satisfied (LCE, 71).

In responding to the priest, Meursault had said that he had no use for, nor could he conceive of, another life unless it was filled with the qualities of this one. In this he was echoing an attitude already expressed in *Two Sides of the Coin* (cf. LCE, 50).

Nuptials depicts the terrain within which the stranger is condemned to live, inviting us to take up residence in the only home that can be truly ours.

"This clearly involves undertaking the survey of a certain desert . . . accessible only to those who can live there in the full anguish of their thirst. . . . Only then is it peopled with the living waters of happiness" (*Noces*, 99–100; LCE, 105, slightly modified).

CHAPTER 4

1. Italicized part was deleted from final manuscript.

2. The personal quality of *The Myth* is subtly evident throughout. For example, Camus's involvement with his characters is suggested, in earlier versions by his initial identification with the conqueror. He had written, "There is but one luxury for us— that of human relations": only to replace *us* with *them* in the published version (MS, 88; E, 167, 1446).

3. Quilliot comments that "the attitude of mind evoked here is not without relation to that of Meursault in his prison" (E, 1440).

4. It is equally foolish to insist that Camus is or is not a philosopher, or that he is primarily an artist. These academic classifications presuppose a compartmentalization of experience that Camus rejects. Of course, on occasion he too fell prey to these misleading simplifications, as when he denied being a philosopher. But there he was seeking to distinguish himself from the kind of academic philosophy of which he wanted no part. The more deliberate judgment is revealed by his discussion of Kant and the novel in *The Myth*.

5. Cf. his discussion of Kafka as the "adventure of a soul in quest of its grace" (MS, 129).

6. " 'For three years,' says Kirlov, 'I sought the attribute of my divinity and I have found it. The attribute of my divinity is independence.' Now can be seen the meaning of Kirlov's premise: 'If God does not exist, I am god.' To become god is merely to be free on this earth, not to serve an immortal being. Above all, of course, it is drawing all the inferences from that painful independence" (MS, 107–8).

7. "I have been nought, I shall be all," said Marx's proletariat. Totality will fill the void left by God's disappearance. From nihilism to absolutism, the psychodynamic path is clear. Tempted by this need to fill the void, Camus had written in *The Myth* that the conqueror wants "all or nothing" (MS, 86). Claiming that "a revolution is always accomplished against the gods . . . the demands of the poor are but a pretext" (MS, 87), Camus suggests, in another context, that "the way matters little; the will to arrive suffices" (MS, 47). In this passionate will to recapture a lost absolute lies the ground of that historicism to which *The Rebel* seeks to offer the diagnosis. Sartre's complicity in what Camus later came to see as a pathology of the intellect has thus been sensed early on. "Caligula" dramatizes this will to arrive, while the successive rewritings of that play testify to the maturation of Camus's appreciation of its significance.

8. "Mechanical" might have been better expressed as "habitual."

9. For the ancient Hebrews, existence was ordered by Yahweh, but there was no apparent concern for personal immortality.

10. "Happiness" in an earlier manuscript had been "sadness," which gives a more sensitive touch to the vision.

11. The images that flower upon this liberation from metaphysical illusion might remind one of flowers at Djémila or Tipasa; or, more generally, of the experience of nuptials with the earth.

12. Problems of community, dialogue, and society in general are implicit throughout but separable from the issues considered here. "The social question . . . cannot be avoided by absurd thought (even though that thought may put forward several solutions, very different from one another). One must, however, limit oneself" (MS, 104n).

CHAPTER 5

1. Roger Quilliot explores this relation in his brilliant early work on Camus, *La Mer et Les Prisons*. So does James Arnold, among others, in his more recent efforts to reconstruct in detail the initial history of *Caligula*.

2. The English version leaves out the phrase about changing the order of things. A more detailed version appears in a November 1939 entry in his *Notebooks*. Cf. TRN, 1735.

3. In later versions, Camus even removes passages discussing where and how one might catch the moon. Cf. TRN, 1765.

4. In the 1944 edition, this passage ends with "it's absurd, but normal" (TRN, 1762).

5. Camus's growing cynicism about public realities is further attested to by his addition, in the 1958 edition, of a passage in which he favorably contrasts Caligula's

honest appropriation of his subjects' inheritance with the "slipping in of indirect taxes on those basic commodities without which people cannot exist. To govern is to steal," observes Caligula. At least, "I will steal openly" (TRN, 22).

6. Earlier editions offer variants of this passage in which "to judge" replaced "to condemn," "without justice" replaced "without a judge," and "everything is condemnable" is first replaced with "all are accused" before yielding to "no one is innocent" (TRN, 1769).

7. The reduction of human concern to an object of ridicule is nowhere more evident than in Caligula's treatment of the poets. Here, in what may be viewed as the original "Gong Show," they are paraded before the emperor to be mocked, told to shut up, and dispensed with (cf. TRN, 86–100).

8. But not, of course, as Martha in "The Misunderstanding." Dora, in "The Just," bridges the gap between these types, giving expression to the longing to live in the here and now without a programmatic future, while giving up her life to a future in which such love will "at last" be possible.

9. Scipio now goes so far as to claim, "My suffering is to understand everything" (TRN, 83; CTOP, 56), thus expressing a youthful pretentiousness not yet matured sufficiently to appreciate the limits of its own insights. Many accused Camus of sharing such an attitude. Somewhat upsetting is Cherea's claim, in this same dialogue, that only Scipio and his reasons are pure. This supposed motivational innocence in matters of political action raises questions about the sophistication of the perspective here being suggested. It does smell of that moralistic attitude for which many took Camus so severely to task. Was this the author's orientation when the play was initially conceived and developed? If so, why does he leave it in? Unless he still believes it or thinks it rings true to the characters he is portraying. The issue remains in doubt.

10. In having Scipio leave Rome, in the 1958 edition, rather than join in the assassination of Caligula, Camus suggests an increasing, though clearly nuanced, discomfort with aspects of postwar political action. This finds forceful expression not only in the works we are explicitly considering, but in most of his occasional pieces, including "Reflections on the Guillotine."

11. In an earlier version he had "had a novel to finish" (TRN, 1747).

12. The "Letters" can be taken as a more sustained effort to give expression to the position being defended by Cherea. Camus is there struggling quite explicitly for the first time with the challenge to conduct posed by the absurd. Speaking to a hypothetical German friend, he writes:

For a long time we both thought that this world had no ultimate meaning and that consequently we were cheated. I still think so *in a way*. But I came to different conclusions from the ones you used to talk about. . . . I tell myself now that if I had really followed *your reasoning*, I ought to approve what you are doing. And this is so serious that I must stop and consider it. . . .

You never believed in the meaning of this world, and you therefore *deduced the idea that everything was equivalent* and that good and evil could be defined according to one's wishes. You supposed that in the absence of any human or divine code the only values were those of the animal world—in other words, violence and cunning. Hence you concluded that man was negligible. . . . And, to tell the truth, I, believing I thought as you did, saw no valid argument to answer you except a fierce love of justice (RRD, 20–1, my italics).

But that "fierce love of justice" begs the question of the rational justification of values. Camus recognizes this as he struggles to distinguish the efforts of the resistance from those of the Nazis. "Where lay the difference?" he asks. "Simply that you saw the injustice of our condition to the point of being willing to add to it, whereas it seemed to me that man must exalt justice in order to fight against injustice. . . . I merely wanted men to discover their solidarity in order to wage war against their revolting fate." But this response is no better. It is simply one set of preferences against another. On what basis does he claim justice for his positions? Camus then makes appeal to the force of "human evidence."

What is truth, you used to ask? To be sure, but at least we know what falsehood is; that is just what you have taught us. What is spirit? We know its contrary, which is murder. What is man? There I stop you, for we know. *Man is that force which ultimately cancels all tyrants and gods. He is the force of evidence. Human evidence is what we must preserve.* . . . If nothing had any meaning, you would be right. But there is something that still has a meaning (RRD, 10).

Here an almost instinctive revolt gives expression to a faith that human life can generate its own meanings. Reflecting upon this emerging perspective, Camus takes a major, though tentative, step in the direction of the position that ultimately finds expression in *The Rebel* when he observes:

I continue to believe that this world has no ultimate meaning. But I know that something in it has a meaning and that is man, *because he is the only creature to insist on having one.* This world has at least the truth of man, and our task is to provide its justification against fate itself (RRD, 22, my italics).

With this "because" Camus has transformed the problem, opening up the possibility of developing a dialectical defense of justice and rebellion. He has also suggested the theoretical task to which he was to devote himself during the following years.

13. Cherea makes clear when he joins the Patricians in their revolt against Caligula that he does not do so for the same reasons. "If I am with you, I am not for you. . . . You credit him with trivial motives, when he has only the most grand. . . . I will thus not serve any of your interests, wishing only to regain peace in a world which once again obtains its coherence" (TRN, 34–5; CTOP, 20–2).

14. No one better incarnates this hypostatization of the traditional than the Old Patrician, who mouths one cliché after another: Nature is a great healer (l'age efface tout); there's no smoke without fire (il n'y a pas de fumée sans feu) (TRN, 8; CTOP, 4–6).

15. It is one of the aims of *The Fall* to dramatize this attitude.

16. Camus had written in 1937, "Men of action must also be men of ideals and industrial poets. We must live our dreams—and act on them" (TRN, 1734).

CHAPTER 6

1. Suggesting the perspective that underlies this work, Camus writes in *The Rebel*, "Every equivocation, every misunderstanding, leads to death. Only clear language and direct speech can save us from this death" (E, 350; R, 283).

2. In addition, the image of prison plays an important role in any concern with politics, as Tarrou's discussion makes clear. This concern reverberates through all the works that follow *The Plague*: "The State of Siege," "The Just," *The Rebel, The Fall*, even *Exile and the Kingdom*.

3. Paneloux: "pan" = whole; "loux" = praise; that is, Father Praise-the-Whole.

4. Tarrou summarizes Paneloux's dilemma as an all or nothing that puts the foundation of his faith in question; cf. P, 207.

5. See Camus's 1946 essay "Neither Victims nor Executioners" for his presentation of a political position motivated by these moral concerns. The issue is discussed at length in Chapter 13.

6. See Camus's remark in *Combat* on the death sentence meted out to the collaborationist Pierre Pucheu, for example.

CHAPTER 7

1. For the classical statement of the nihilist's attitude toward the natural, see Bazarov in *Fathers and Sons*.

2. Camus's public argument with Gabriel Marcel on the role of the Catholic Church during the Spanish Civil War resulted from this paragraph. Cf. "Why Spain" in RRD.

CHAPTER 8

1. The emergence of fascism served only to underscore its historical significance. Camus's *Letters to a German Friend* testifies to the personal bearing of this philosophical problem, which found dramatic expression in *The Plague*, "The State of Siege," and "The Just." Throughout these works is woven, like Ariadne's thread, Camus's effort to find a way out of the dead end of nihilism which does not itself lead to the legitimation of murder. In part at least, the continual reworking of "Caligula" can also be attributed to this need to make clear why Caligula's path was not the right one.

2. For the most part, the opening section of *The Rebel* appeared as a separate article published in 1945 under the title *Notes on Revolt*. While the order of exposition undergoes transformation, the basic ideas that explain the transition from absurd to revolt are the same. Cf. "Remarque sur la Revolte," E, 1682–97.

3. For a more detailed discussion of the nature of mindscapes and cultural drama see my *The Drama of Thought*.

4. "Everything that separates, horrifies me," wrote Camus in 1956 (in Lottman, 572). In a 1946 interview with the *New York Post* he had spoken of four series of his work: absurd, revolt, we are, and love. Cf. Lottman, 393–4.

5. With the development of the feminist movement, itself a form of rebellion, we hear far less of that far less satisfying response to oppression, bitchiness.

6. By "origins" Camus means nothing from which anything can be deduced. If time is taken seriously, origins are never definitive of a problem, but simply initiative, originating. They can give rise to a mode of thinking, and thus set the conditions

of, and hint at, the problem's solution. They function in Camus's thought like an impulse, called forth by, and erupting into, a habitual pattern. An investigation is bound up with its origins, then, as the intelligent search for means is bound up with the impulse that initiates it: One neither *denies* an impulse, nor deduces from it the end that may serve as its fulfillment. One seeks, rather, to direct the impetus toward a course of action that may transform both impulse and situation. The aim should be to correct creation in such a way as to do justice to the original yet inarticulate demand. And so with origins.

Camus never says that one cannot deny the origins of one's thought. In fact, if they are definitive as to conclusions only in deductive schemes, then certainly one *may* deny the force of their suggestions elsewhere. Camus seeks only to show that these origins have almost always been denied—with results that are the direct consequences of that denial.

If the importance of origins is seen in this light, one can draw the thematic of the inquiry from an understanding of the boundary conditions that the origins of revolt imply, as well as of the direction toward which the original movement has pointed; but one cannot reasonably return to the origins as grounds upon which to rest one's case. Origins justify nothing, though they may rule out certain modes of action as inappropriate, inadequate, or irrelevant. When, on the other hand, the products of thought are investigated and studied simply on their own terms, and then used to determine a line of conduct, we become the victims of ideology.

7. Thody reports a January 1946 comment by Camus expressing an opinion of Hegel's philosophy that sheds light on the position he eventually develops in *The Rebel*: "When one believes, like Hegel and the whole of modern philosophy, that man is made for history and not history for man, one cannot believe in dialogue: one believes in efficacy and in the will to power. Ultimately, one believes in murder" (Thody, 105).

8. Cf. note 2 to Chapter 2.

9. "The idea of messianism [is] at the base of all fanaticisms" (AJ, 49).

CHAPTER 9

1. Cf. note 2 to the Preface. The contrast between Greek and Judeo-Christian sensibility is also relevant here.

2. I refer to the Christian cosmic drama when emphasizing the modern world and to the Judeo-Christian when speaking of the origin and sources of our history.

3. See the writings of Mircea Eliade, for example.

4. "If we add . . . that Marx owes to the bourgeois economists the idea which he made his own of the exclusive part played by industrial production in the development of humanity, and that he took the essentials of his theory of labor value from Ricardo . . . our right to say that his prophecy is bourgeois in content will doubtless be recognized" (L'HR, 242–3; R, 196–7).

5. For the discussion of St. Just's project in which "the religion of reason quite naturally establishes the Republic of law and order," cf. R, 122–3.

6. Note this emerging theme also in "The Just," *The Fall*, and "The Renegade."

7. "Profligate, like all people without a rule of life, he is coherent as an actor. But an actor implies a public; the dandy can only play a part by setting himself in opposition. He can only be sure of his own existence by finding it in the expression of other's faces. Other people are his mirror. A mirror that quickly becomes clouded, it is true, since human capacity for attention is limited. It must be ceaselessly stimulated, spurred on by provocation. The dandy, therefore, is always compelled to astonish. . . . Perpetually incomplete, . . . he compels others to create him, while denying their values. He plays at life because he is unable to live it. . . . More than a century of rebellion came to fulfillment in these audacities of 'eccentricity'" (L'HR, 72–3).

8. Commenting upon St. Just, Camus had noted, "His principles are not in accord with what is. Things are not what they should be. The principles are thus silent, isolated, and rigid. To abandon oneself to them is, in truth, to die, and to die of an impossible love which is the opposite of love" (R, 129; L'HR, 164). St. Just dies a self-defeating death, that of absolute commitments to the transcendent.

If major principles have no foundation, if the law expresses nothing but a provisional inclination, it is only made in order to be broken or to be imposed. Sade or dictatorship, individual terrorism or state terrorism, both justified by the same absence of justification, are, from the moment that rebellion cuts itself off from its roots and deprives itself of any concrete morality, one of the alternatives of the twentieth century (R, 131–2; L'HR, 165).

9. "The rebel, who at first denies God, finally aspires to replace Him. . . . Nietzsche's message is that the rebel can only become God by renouncing every form of rebellion. . . . 'If there is a God, how can one tolerate not being god oneself?' There is, in fact, a god—namely, the world. To participate in its divinity, all that is necessary is to consent. . . . To say yes to the world, to reproduce it, is simultaneously to recreate the world and oneself. . . . Nietzsche's message is summed up in the word *creation* . . . replacing critical values by creative values; by respect and admiration for what exists. . . . Nietzsche thought that to accept this earth and Dionysos was to accept his own suffering. And to accept everything was to be king of all creation" (R, 73–4).

10. "What is the profoundly corrupt addition made by Christianity to the message of its Master? The idea of judgment, completely foreign to the teachings of Christ, and the correlative notions of punishment and reward" (R, 69). "If he attacks Christianity in particular, it is so only so far as it represents morality. . . . 'Basically,' he writes, 'only the God of morality is rejected.' Christ, for Nietzsche as for Tolstoy, is not a rebel. The essence of His doctrine is summed up in total consent and in non-resistance to evil. Thou shalt not kill, even to prevent killing. The world must be accepted as it is; nothing must be added to its unhappiness, but you must consent to suffer personally from the evil it contains" (R, 68). This is where Father Paneloux arrives at the time of his second sermon, having moved from the bastardized Christianity of judgment and reward and punishment to the person of Christ for whom "only an inner inclination . . . allows us to make our actions coincide with these principles and . . . can give us immediate salvation" (R, 68).

11. The limits of Camus's consideration of Nietzsche should be noted. He is

concerned in *The Rebel* only with the doctrine that is to be found in *The Will to Power*. It is now known, as it was not in Camus's time, that this book is not a work of Nietzsche's, but rather a selection from, and ordering of, his notes by his sister, a noted German nationalist and rabid anti-semite, both of which "diseases" Nietzsche detested. One must therefore take analyses drawn from this work with a great deal of caution. That need not, of course, affect an analysis of the historical significance of his work, since, for the period in question, all readers of Nietzsche were ignorant of the source of this volume. I should also note here the tension in Nietzsche's work between the doctrine of the *ubermensch* and that of the eternal recurrence. Camus senses this. Much of Camus's analysis hinges upon a contradiction related to this tension. But he, like most students of Nietzsche, fails to grasp the dramatically developing tension by which these doctrines struggle with one another, with the latter doctrine, in the image of the snake slowly dominating that of the eagle. An appreciation of this development would have strengthened Camus's own interpretation. I am much indebted to my friend and colleague Professor James Edwards of Nassau Community College for his analyses of these issues. Professor Edwards incisively suggests that Nietzsche's failure resides in his inability to break out of his loneliness and to establish solidarity, thus suggesting the linking in Nietzsche's own life of two of Camus's themes: the experience of exile and the longing for the earthly kingdom.

12. "Human insurrection, in its exalted and tragic forms, is only, and can only be, a prolonged protest against death, a violent accusation against the universal death penalty. . . . The [metaphysical] rebel does not ask for life but for reasons for living. . . . In the eyes of the rebel, what is missing from the misery of the world, as well as from its moments of happiness, is some principle by which they can be explained. The insurrection against evil is, above all, a demand for unity. . . . He is seeking, without knowing it, a morality or a sacred" (R, 100–1; L'HR, 128–9).

13. Often, notes Camus, the effort is made to save the person of Christ from these attacks by treating Him as a simpleton. Consider the efforts of Dostoevsky in *The Idiot*, for example.

CHAPTER 10

1. "It is worth specifying that productivity is only injurious when it is considered as an end, not as a means, in which case it could have a liberating effect" (R, 218).

2. Here is the dynamic behind Camus's story of "The Renegade" in *Exile and the Kingdom*.

3. Kojève, spiritual godfather to French Hegelianism, situates the source of this legacy: "What then is the morality of Hegel? . . . What exists is good inasmuch as it exists. All action, being a negation of the existing given, is therefore bad, or sinful. But sin may be forgiven. How? By its success. Success absolves the crime because success is a new reality that *exists*. But how can success be estimated? Before this can be done, History must have come to an end" (Kojève, 95).

4. "The City of God will coincide with the city of humanity and universal history,

sitting in judgment on the world, will pass its sentence by which good and evil will be justified. The State will play the part of Destiny and will proclaim its approval of every aspect of reality on 'the sacred day of the Presence'" (R, 142).

5. "From the moment that productivity is developed to enormous proportions, the division of labor, which Marx thought could have been avoided, became inevitable. Every worker has been brought to the point of performing a particular function without knowing the over-all plan into which his work will fit. Those who coordinate the individual work have formed, by their very function, a class whose social importance is decisive" (R, 214–5).

6. For Camus's evaluation of the Marxian inversion of Hegel, cf., for example, R, 197–8.

7. "What remains true in [Marx's] vision of the economic world is the establishment of a society more and more defined by the rhythms of production. But he shared this concept . . . with bourgeois ideology. The bourgeois illusions concerning science and technical progress, shared by the authoritarian socialists, gave birth to the civilization of machine-tamers, which can, through the stresses of competition and the desire for domination, be separated into enemy blocs, but which on the economic plane is subject to identical laws: the accumulation of capital and rationalized and continually increasing production. The political difference, which concerns the degree of omnipotence of the State, is appreciable, but can be reduced by economic evolution. Only the difference in ethical concepts—formal virtue as opposed to historical cynicism—seems substantial. But the imperatives of production dominate both universes and make them, on the economic plane, one world" (R, 218).

8. To give but one example. In one sentence on page 107 he claims, "Total revolution ends by demanding . . . the control of the world." In the following paragraph he observes, "All revolutionaries finally aspire to world unity and act as though they believed that history was concluded." As a complete analysis of all historical revolutions, the latter would not only be false, but worse, it would clearly lead, in accord with Camus's own argument, to a total condemnation of the revolutionary attitude and the project of revolution. But in the context of the argument in the text and pursuant to its logic, all that is being said is a development of the argument in the previous paragraph. For the English-speaking world the problem is made infinitely worse by the poor and biased Bower translation. One example should suffice. Where Camus, underlining the always relative and temporally open nature of rebellious activity, speaks of rebellion as being "without issue," Bower's translation refers to it as a "fruitless struggle" (R, 106; L'HR, 126). But a struggle that may be without definitive result as far as the ultimate is concerned, that might even be termed "fruitless" *from that perspective,* clearly has a different meaning both for Camus and for the engaged rebels when we attend to its concrete significance. To call it "fruitless" caters to an interpretation of Camus's work that would have it taking pride in the impotence of rebellion. That, I hold, is quite far from the truth.

9. The English translation botches this subtle distinction by, for example, translating *a l'origine* as "by nature" instead of "at first" or "in the beginning."

10. "An affirmation which appears to me, moreover, remarkably faithful to the dialectical reasoning which today all quite vocally demand" (E, 1708–9).

CHAPTER 11

1. Marcel Cerdan was middleweight champion of the world and a French celebrity in the late 1940s.

2. We must not confuse this portrait of the professional, the lawyer, the intellectual, the member of "society," the professional humanist, with that of all members of bourgeois society, for Camus has a very different sense of the character of the average working person. While many on the left, and Sartre above all, taxed him with having an inadequate appreciation of class conflict (in *The Rebel* and in *The Plague*, for instance), it was they, not he, who could easily include practically all members of bourgeois society in their critiques of a decadent capitalism. Camus, on the other hand, has a more precise sense of the differences of character and motivation between the true bourgeoisie, and petit-bourgeois compatriots, on the one hand, and working people on the other. His portrait of the latter may be somewhat idealized, as in "The Silent Ones," "Summer in Algiers," or "The State of Siege," but he never simply identifies them with the middle or upper classes. In fact, his analyses of contemporary European society always place in the forefront the need to recapture for the workingman his appropriate dignity and self-respect: to dignify labor, which, along with intelligence, is one of the only two aristocracies he recognizes. His references to Simone Weil in *The Rebel* and his agreement with her portrait of the character of decadent bourgeois and pseudo-revolutionary societies have no other significance.

3. This comment, like much else in *The Fall*, may be read as Camus's evaluation of Sartre and company's perception of him.

4. Warren Tucker, "La Chute: voie du salut terrestre," *French Review*, April 1970, 737–44.

5. I have long been of the opinion that Sartre's critique of Camus is really an attack on the being that Sartre had been, which he now projects onto Camus. A careful reading of Sartre's critique of Camus in *Les Temps Modernes* shows that he did not pay careful attention at all to *what* Camus actually said. He rather imputes to Camus precisely those positions that he, Sartre, once held but has since come to repudiate.

6. Cf. Thomas Hanna, *The Thought and Art of Albert Camus*, 213–37.

7. Relevant here is Nietzsche's analysis of the character and strategy of the priest who must create sin and guilt in order to obtain the subservience of others, which is essential if he is to lord it over them. Cf. *The Antichrist* in PN, for example.

8. The malady by which guilt is transformed into the defense of a saving brotherhood was nowhere more clearly revealed than in Sartre's diatribe on behalf of the Communist party as the legitimate defender of the objective interests of an idealized working class in *Communists and the Peace*. Appropriately, the first installment appeared in the July issue of *Temps Modernes*, between the May issue in which Jeanson's critique of *The Rebel* appeared and the August issue containing the replies of Camus, Sartre, and Jeanson.

9. For an excellent brief analysis of the procedure of modern totalitarianism in using self-criticism and self-recrimination to stifle any stirrings of revolt, see M. Natanson's essay on the Moscow trials in his collected essays. Those observations might be compared with the comments of Diego, The Plague, and The Secretary in "The State of Siege."

CHAPTER 12

1. The dramatist Copeau, whom Camus called the only master, maintained, according to Camus, that "a dramatic work has to bring the audience together in a single emotion or laugh, and not divide them" (TRN, 1697).

2. We have said nothing of an art that gave up all concern for unity and was simply the pure play of the moment—a happening, for instance. Camus would be unlikely to consider that art.

3. The similarities with his political discussions of the dialectic of freedom-justice should not be missed.

4. Even a break in experience may be meaningful here—often tragically so—but only insofar as it is experienced as a "break-from." Consider William James's discussion in *The Principles of Psychology* (PP, 240): "What we hear when thunder crashes is not thunder *pure,* but thunder-breaking-in-on-silence-and-contrasting-with-it. . . . The *feeling* of thunder is the feeling of the silence just gone."

5. Cf. Camus's discussion of Piero della Francesca, whose "subjects give the impression that, by some miracle of art, they continue to live, while ceasing to be mortal" (R, 257).

6. The italics are used to suggest: (1) The limited scope of the analysis and (2) the role of style and the exigence toward unity, still underplayed and to be developed, which are seen by the absurd mind.

7. In order to counter nihilism, Camus quotes Dostoevsky as saying, "One must love life before loving its meaning. Yes, and when the love of life disappears, no meaning consoles us for it" (Notebooks/II, 218).

8. Consider Thomas Hanna's work for a typical expression of this point of view.

9. Check Bower's translation for a particularly egregious rendering of this passage.

10. Cf. especially "The Desert" in *Nuptials.* The continuity of Camus's thought is evident in his notion of art as an ordering within a disunited world. At the same time, these early essays reveal an almost religious attachment to the concrete and sensual. In *Nuptials* he writes that painters, "the novelists of the body, . . . work in that magnificent and trivial matter called the present. And the present always shows itself in a gesture" (LCE, 94).

11. For an ironic statement on the *engagé* artist, cf. "Jonas" in EK.

12. Roblès continues: "At the time of his first theatrical efforts, he recommended . . . 'A theater without stars, where the actors do not take bows, where the performers are also machinists, painters, electricians, stage hands, costume makers.'"

13. "Art," Germaine Brée observes, "is the contrary of silence; it is rooted in reality, therefore it is communicable to all men; it is an invitation to dialogue and therefore freedom. Because it requires the artist to create his own order, it is in itself a manifestation of freedom and cannot submit to any other order; in fact it is a challenge to any other order" (Brée, 250).

CHAPTER 13

1. Hegel is the classical exponent of this conception of human relations, for Camus. Cf. R, 133–48.

2. As Camus was not a "philosopher," so he was not a "politician." He seemed ill at ease in the give-and-take of politics, feeling more at home with the clarity of moral judgment. His aim was "by a simple objective criticism to introduce the language of morals into the exercise of politics" (A/I, 51). This caused him to be criticized, sometimes rightly, theoretically as too manichean, practically as too naïve. Yet these critics almost invariably missed the point. For Camus was actually seeking to introduce a new language and a new approach into the sociopolitical world. Often he was ill at ease in politics because competing intellectuals insisted upon seeing that sociopolitical world in essentially manichean terms—of which the dominant European ideology of Marxism, primarily in its Marxist-Leninist version was but one clear expression. And when he was too naïve, it was often the result of a judgment upon his activities passed by those whose thought was essentially ideological.

His understanding of the human condition took him directly into the realm of political discussion as that of Marx had taken him into economics. Being a European intellectual of the World War II period, Camus had to come to terms with Marxist thought; and, from one point of view, the major burden of his attack on ideology, explicitly in *The Rebel* and implicitly elsewhere, was directed at Marxism, in what he called its prophetic dimension. Critical Marxism remained for him a positive and liberating critique whose usefulness in furthering precisely that concrete freedom that Marx sought was greatly hampered by being attached to the ideology and dogmatism involved in the prophetic Marxism of one such as Lenin. The difference between the critical and the prophetic is generalized into that between the "ideologue of the absolute" who seeks totality and the artist working with resistant materials who seeks unity. Camus's thought, like that of Marx, was motivated by the desire for freedom and reconciliation, but was essentially general and directional rather than specific and programmatic. Unlike Marx, however, he never attempted to develop a systematic methodology or claimed definitive understanding of the political world. His aim was to suggest the attitudes and values that must be maintained if the political world is to become truly liberating.

3. Parker suggests that the attitudes criticized here are similar to ones Camus held during the resistance, but then began to reconsider. He had even signed some editorials "St. Just," and had written that the country " 'does not need a Talleyrand. . . . It needs a St. Just' " (Parker, 67). Also, in speaking of dealing with the collaborators after the war, he said, " 'It is not a question of purging much, but of purging well' " (Parker, 182).

4. The key articles here are "Letter to an Algerian Militant" and "Appeal for a Civilian Truce in Algeria"; both are to be found in Camus's *Algerian Chronicles*.

5. This analysis suggests that treating ethical issues in terms of prescriptions and commands tends to reduce decisions to matters of power.

6. Consider, for example, his comparison of revolutionary syndicalism with caesarian revolution in *The Rebel*, or his continued support of the cause of republican Spain, as well as his long-time close relationship with the exiled Spanish anarchists.

7. For illustrations of this destructive dialectic, which Camus calls *des methodes de pensée perimée*, cf. A/I, 168, 188–9.

8. Parker goes on to say of this speech, "Camus was axiomatically opposed to any form of human action dependent upon terror, whatever its final aim, since it posed

the unavoidable choice of 'kill or be killed,' and rendered communication impossible. 'That is why [Camus is reported as continuing] we refuse any ideology that claims any jurisdiction over human lives.'"

9. On the quest for totality, cf. A/I, 195, 260, 263; A/II, 61, 95–6; A/III, 176; RRD, 176. The quest for totality is a quest for the sacred. Camus chronicles this quest for the sacred and for its totalization after the fall of Western religion not only in *The Fall*, but throughout *The Rebel*, as well as briefly in "Reflections on the Guillotine." Cf. RRD, 170 ff.

10. From an article in *Combat*, October 1, 1944, p. 1.

11. Parker observes, "Camus seldom bothered to define such terms as liberty and justice. He usually used these terms in their traditionally accepted meanings, which derive fundamentally from centuries of philosophical speculation concerning the problems of achieving a balance between freedom and necessity" (Parker, 90).

12. I have changed "Good" to "Correct" in the translation of the title.

13. Commenting on this statement, Parker writes that Camus "insisted once again that the definition of principles was rudimentary, while the detailed work of incorporating the principles in a workable social-political-economic structure was endlessly complex" (Parker, 91).

14. This observation proceeds: "To speak more concretely, let us say that the men who in all circumstances would decide to oppose example to power, preaching to domination, dialogue to insult, and simple honor to cunning; who would refuse all the advantages of the existing society and *would only accept the duties and obligations which bound them to other men* . . . such men would not act in a utopian manner . . . but in *accordance with the most honest realism*."

15. His criticism of capital punishment follows directly. He wrote in *The Rebel*, "He who cannot know everything cannot kill everything" (R, 289). In "Reflections on the Guillotine" he observed that "forbidding a man's execution would amount to proclaiming publicly that society and the State are not absolute values, and that nothing authorizes them to legislate definitively or to bring about the irreparable" (RRD, 175).

CHAPTER 14

1. Nothing is here said about the possible institutional sources of these conflicting positions, of which more later.

BIBLIOGRAPHY ⌒

WORKS BY CAMUS
(in order of initial publication)

Révolt dans les Asturies: Essai de création collective. Alger: Charlot, 1936.

L'Envers et l'endroit. Alger: Charlot, 1937; Paris: Gallimard, 1958. [*L'Envers* in LCE]

Noces. Alger: Charlot, 1938. [*Noces* in LCE]

L'Etranger. Paris: Gallimard, 1942. *The Stranger*, tr. Kate Griffith. Washington, D.C.: University Press of America, 1982; tr. Stuart Gilbert. New York: Alfred A. Knopf, 1946. [STR]

Le Mythe de Sisyphe. Paris: Gallimard, 1942. *The Myth of Sisyphus and Other Essays*, tr. Justin O'Brien. New York: Alfred A. Knopf, 1955. [MS]

Le Malentendu. Paris: Gallimard, 1944. "The Misunderstanding," in *"Caligula" and Three Other Plays*, tr. Stuart Gilbert; preface by Camus, tr. Justin O'Brien. New York: Alfred A. Knopf, 1958. [CTOP]

Caligula. Paris: Gallimard, 1944. "Caligula." [in CTOP]

Lettres à un ami allemand. Paris: Gallimard, 1945. "Letters to a German Friend." [in RRD]

"Remarque sur la révolte." In *L'Existence*. Paris: Gallimard, 1945.

La Peste. Paris: Gallimard, 1947. *The Plague*, tr. Stuart Gilbert. New York: Alfred A. Knopf, 1948. [P]

L'Etat de siège. Paris: Gallimard, 1948. "The State of Siege." [In CTOP]

Les Justes. Paris: Gallimard, 1950. "The Just Assassins." [In CTOP]

Actuelles I, chroniques 1944–1948. Paris: Gallimard, 1950. [A/I]

L'Homme révolté. Paris: Gallimard, 1951. *The Rebel*, tr. Anthony Bower. New York: Alfred A. Knopf, 1954. [L'HR; R]

Actuelles II, chroniques 1948–1953. Paris: Gallimard, 1953. [A/II]

L'Eté. Paris: Gallimard, 1954. "Summer." [*L'Eté* in LCE]

La Chute. Paris: Gallimard, 1956. *The Fall*, tr. Justin O'Brien. New York: Alfred A. Knopf, 1957. [F]

L'Exile et le royaume. Paris: Gallimard, 1957. *Exile and the Kingdom*, tr. Justin O'Brien. New York: Alfred A. Knopf, 1957. [EK]

Réflections sur la peine capitale: Introduction et étude de Jean Bloch-Michel, par Arthur Koestler et Albert Camus et al. Paris: Calmann-Levy, 1957. "Reflections on the Guillotine." [In RRD]

Adaptation of *Requiem pour une nonne*. Paris: Gallimard, 1957.

"Discourse de Suède" and "L'Artiste et son temps." Paris: Gallimard, 1958. "Speech of Acceptance upon the Award of the Nobel Prize for Literature," tr. Justin O'Brien. New York: Alfred A. Knopf, 1958. Also as "Camus in Stockholm" in *The Atlantic Monthly* (May 1958). [Nobel Prize Address]

Actuelles III, chroniques algériennes 1939–1958. Paris: Gallimard, 1958. [A/III]

Adaptation of *Les Possédés*. Paris: Gallimard, 1959. *The Possessed*, tr. Justin O'Brien. New York: Alfred A. Knopf, 1960.

Resistance, Rebellion, and Death, tr. Justin O'Brien. New York: Alfred A. Knopf, 1960. [RRD]

Carnets I, mai 1935–fev. 1942. Paris: Gallimard, 1962. *Notebooks 1935–1942*, tr. Philip Thody. New York: Alfred A. Knopf, 1963. [Notebooks/I]

Oeuvres Complètes. Paris: Bibliothèque de la Pléiade, Gallimard). I: Théâtre, récits, nouvelles, ed. Roger Quilliot, 1962. [TRN]. II: Essais, ed. R. Quilliot and L. Faucon, 1965. [E]

Carnets II, jan. 1942–mars 1951. Paris: Gallimard, 1964. *Notebooks 1942–1951*, tr. Justin O'Brien. New York: Alfred A. Knopf, 1965. [Notebooks/II]

Lyrical and Critical Essays, tr. Ellen Conroy Kennedy. Ed. and notes by Philip Thody. New York: Alfred A. Knopf, 1968. [LCE]

La Mort heureuse. Paris: Gallimard, 1971. (Cahiers Albert Camus I). *A Happy Death*, tr. Richard Howard. Afterword and notes by Jean Sarocchi. New York: Alfred A. Knopf, 1972.

Le premier Camus, par Paul Viallaneix, suivi des Ecrits de jeunesse d'Albert Camus. Paris: Gallimard, 1973. (Cahiers Albert Camus II). *Youthful Writings*, tr. Ellen Conroy Kennedy. New York: Alfred A. Knopf, 1961.

Journaux de voyage, ed. R. Quilliot. Paris: Gallimard, 1978. *American Journals*, tr. Hugh Levick. New York: Paragon House Publishers, 1987. [AJ]

WORKS ON ALBERT CAMUS

Albérès, Boisdeffre, Daniel, Gascar, Lebesque, Parinaud, Roblès, Roy, Simon. *Camus*. Paris: Librairie Hachette, 1964. [Camus]

Barrett, William. *Irrational Man: A Study in Existential Philosophy*. New York: Doubleday & Co., 1958.

Barrett, William. *Time of Need: Forms of Imagination in the Twentieth Century*. New York: Harper & Row, Publishers, 1972.

Barrier, M. G. *L'Art du récit dans L'Etranger d'Albert Camus*. Paris: Nizet, 1962. [Barrier]

Brée, Germaine. *Camus*. New York: Harcourt, Brace, and World, 1964. [Brée]

Brée, Germaine. *Camus and Sartre*. New York: Dell Publishing Co., 1972.

Brée, Germaine, ed. *Camus: A Collection of Critical Essays*. Englewood Cliffs, N.J.: Prentice-Hall, 1962. [Brée 2]

Brisville, Jean-Claude. *Camus*. Paris: Gallimard, 1959.

Carruth, Hayden. *After* The Stranger: *Imaginery Dialogues with Camus*. New York: Macmillan Co., 1965. [Carruth]

Champigny, Robert. *Pagan Hero: An Interpretation of Meursault in Camus'* The Stranger, tr. Rowe Portis. Philadelphia: University of Pennsylvania Press, 1970.

Collins, John. *The Existentialists: A Critical Study*. Chicago: Regnery, 1952.

Cruickshank, John. *Albert Camus and the Literature of Revolt*. New York: Oxford University Press, 1960.

Denton, David E. *The Philosophy of Albert Camus: A Critical Analysis*. Boston: Prime, 1967.

Gay-Crosier, Raymond, ed. *Albert Camus 9: La Pensée de Camus*. Paris: Minard, 1979.

Gay-Crosier, Raymond, ed. *Albert Camus 1980*. Gainesville: University Presses of Florida, 1980.

Hanna, Thomas. *The Thought and Art of Albert Camus*. Chicago: Regnery, 1958; Gateway edition. [Hanna (1)]

Hanna, Thomas. *The Lyrical Existentialists*. New York: Atheneum Publishers, 1962. [Hanna (2)]

Hermet, Joseph. *Albert Camus et le Christianisme*. Paris: Editions Beauchesne, 1976.

Lazere, Donald. *The Unique Creation of Albert Camus*. New Haven: Yale University Press, 1973.

Lebesque, Morvan. *Portrait of Camus*, tr. T. C. Sharman. New York: Herder & Herder, 1971.

Lottman, Herbert R. *Albert Camus: A Biography*. Garden City, N.Y.: Doubleday & Co., 1979. [Lottman]

Luppé, Robert de. *Albert Camus*, tr. John Cumming and J. Hargreaves. London: Merlin, 1966.

McCarthy, Patrick. *Camus*. New York: Random House, 1982.

Maquet, Albert. *Albert Camus: The Invincible Summer*, tr. Herma Briffault. New York: George Braziller, 1958.

Masters, Brian. *Camus: A Study*. Totowa, N.J.: Rowman and Littlefield, 1974.

Meagher, Robert E. *Albert Camus: The Essential Writings*, with a preface by Germaine Brée. New York: Harper & Row, Publishers, 1979.

O'Brien, Conor Cruise. *Albert Camus of Europe and North Africa*. New York: Viking Press, 1970.

Parker, Emmett. *Albert Camus: The Artist in the Arena*. Madison: University of Wisconsin Press, 1965. [Parker]

Petersen, Carol. *Albert Camus*, tr. Alexander Gode. New York: Frederick Ungar, 1969.

Quilliot, Roger. *La Mer et les prisons: Essai sur Albert Camus*. Paris: Gallimard, 1956.

Rizzuto, Anthony. *Camus' Imperial Vision*. Carbondale and Edwardsville: Southern Illinois University Press, 1981.

Roeming, Robert F. *Camus: A Bibliography*. Madison: University of Wisconsin Press, 1968.

Thody, Philip. *Albert Camus: 1913–1960*. London: Hamish Hamilton, 1961. Revision of *Albert Camus: A Study of His Work*. New York: Macmillan Co., 1957. [Thody]

ADDITIONAL WORKS DIRECTLY CITED

Becker, Ernest. *The Denial of Death*. New York: Free Press, 1973.

Becker, Ernest. *The Structure of Evil: An Essay on the Unification of the Science of Man*. New York: George Braziller, 1968.

Dewey, John. *Art as Experience*. New York: G. P. Putnam's Sons, 1958.

Dewey, John. *Experience and Nature*. New York: Dover, 1958.

Dewey, John. *Human Nature and Conduct*. New York: Henry Holt & Co., 1922.

Dewey, John. *The Quest for Certainty*. New York: G. P. Putnam's Sons, 1960.

Dewey, John. *The Theory of Valuation*. International Encyclopedia of Unified Science, vol. II, no. 4. Chicago: Chicago University Press, 1962.

James, William. *The Principles of Psychology*, vol. I. New York: Dover, 1950. [PP]

Kojève, Alexandre. *Introduction to the Reading of Hegel*, ed. Allan Bloom, tr. James H. Nichols, Jr. New York: Basic Books, 1969. [Kojève]

Nathanson, Maurice. *Literature, Philosophy and the Social Sciences*. The Hague: Martinus Nijhoff, 1962.

Nietzsche, Friedrich. *The Portable Nietzsche*, ed. Walter Kaufmann. New York: Viking Press, 1954. [PN]

Sartre, Jean-Paul. *Being and Nothingness: An Essay on Phenomenological Ontology*, tr. Hazel Barnes. New York: Philosophical Library, 1956.

Sartre, Jean-Paul. *The Communists and the Peace: With a reply to Claude Lefort*, tr. Martha H. Fletcher; reply, tr. Philip R. Berk. New York: George Braziller, 1968.

Sartre, Jean-Paul. *Nausea*, tr. Robert Baldrick. London: Penguin Books, 1965.

Sartre, Jean-Paul. *The Wall (Intimacy) and Other Stories*, tr. Lloyd Alexander. New York: New Directions, 1969.

Sartre, Jean-Paul. *The Words*, tr. Bernard Frechtman. New York: George Braziller, 1964.

Sartre, Jean-Paul, Director. *Les Temps Modernes*, vol. 7, no. 79, Paris, May 1952; and vol. 8, no. 82, Paris, August 1952.

INDEX